WORSHIP RESOURCES

FOR THE CHRISTIAN YEAR

Worship Resources

for the

Christian Year

>>>>>>>>>>>>>>>>>>>>>><<<<<<<<<<<<<<<<<<<<

EDITED BY

CHARLES L. WALLIS

Such are the fixed festivals of the
Eternal, which you must proclaim as
sacred gatherings. LEVITICUS 23:37 *(Moffatt)*

HARPER & BROTHERS NEW YORK

Special acknowledgment is made to the following who have granted permission for the reprinting of copyrighted material from the books listed below:

ABINGDON PRESS for extracts from sermons by Samuel L. Joekel, Water Pope Binns, John M. Versteeg, Stephen J. Corey, Edward Hughes Pruden from *American Pulpit Series,* copyright 1945 by Whitmore & Stone; extracts from sermons by John S. Stamm, John L. Hill, Hobart D. McKeehan from *American Pulpit Series,* copyright 1946 by Stone & Pierce; prayer from *A Book of Pastoral Prayer* by Ernest Fremont Tittle, copright 1951 by Pierce & Smith; litany from *Challenge and Power,* edited and copyrighted 1936 by Wade Crawford Barclay, reprinted by permission of Abingdon Press; extracts from sermons by F. Gerald Ensley, Henry Hitt Crane, John S. Stamm from *Communion Meditations,* edited by Gaston Foote, copyright 1951 by Pierce & Smith; selection from *Everyday Religion* by Joseph Fort Newton, copyright 1950 by Pierce & Smith; "Prayer on Good Friday" from *The Glory of God* by Georgia Harkness, copyright 1943 by Whitmore & Stone; extract from *Here's a Faith for You* by Roy M. Pearson, copyright 1953 by Pierce & Washabaugh; "Oblivion" from *Hilltop Verses and Prayers* by Ralph S. Cushman, copyright 1945 by Whitmore & Stone; extracts from *How to be a Transformed Person* by E. Stanley Jones, copyright 1951 by Pierce & Smith; extract from *Invitation to Worship* by A. C. Reid, copyright 1942 by Whitmore & Stone; prayer from *The Lectern* by Carl A. Glover, copyright 1946 by Stone & Pierce; "Bread" and "Son of Man" from *The Life of Jesus in Poetry and Pictures* by Leslie Savage Clark, copyright 1953 by Pierce & Washabaugh; extract from *Making Prayer Real* by Lynn J. Radcliffe, copyright 1952 by Pierce & Smith; selections from *Meditations for Men* by Daniel Russell, copyright 1945 by Whitmore & Stone; extract from *New Light from Old Lamps* by Roy L. Smith, copyright 1953 by Pierce & Washabaugh; extract from *Not a Sparrow Falls* by Paul Quillian, copyright 1952 by Pierce & Smith; extract from *A Protestant Manifesto* by Wilfred E. Garrison, copyright 1952 by Pierce & Smith; prayer from *The Resurrection and the Life* by Leslie D. Weatherhead, copyright 1948 by Pierce & Smith; extracts from *Sermons for Special Days* by Charles M. Crowe, copyright 1951 by Pierce & Smith; selections by William Everett Roberts and J. Richard Sneed from *Strength for Service,* edited by Norman E. Nygaard, copyright 1950 by Pierce & Smith; prayers by Fitzgerald S. Parker, Frank J. Scribner, W. A. Smart, Frank G. Smith, Wilbur F. Tillet from *Talking with God,* edited by Alfred Franklin Smith, copyright 1929 by Lamar & Whitmore; extracts from *The Way* by E. Stanley Jones, copyright 1941 by Stone & Pierce.

AMERICAN BAPTIST PUBLICATION SOCIETY for extracts from *Cowards or Conquerors* by Herschel H. Hobbs, copyright 1951 by the Judson Press; extract from *Interpreters Needed* by Edward Hughes Pruden, copyright 1951 by the Judson Press; extract from *The Newton Chapel* by George E. Horr, copyright 1920 by the Judson Press; selection by Everett C. Herrick from

LIBRARY OF CONGRESS CATALOG CARD NUMBER: 54-8999

The Secret Place, copyright 1940 by the Judson Press; selection by Herbert W. Hansen from *The Secret Place,* copyright 1939 by the Judson Press; extracts from *Sermons for Everyday Living* by Albert W. Beaven, copyright 1933 by the Judson Press.

ANDERSON HOUSE for extract from *Eleven Verse Plays* by Maxwell Anderson, copyright 1936 by Maxwell Anderson, published by Harcourt, Brace & Co.

CHARLES ANGOFF and THE NEW YORK TIMES for "Home" by Charles Angoff, copyright 1953 by *The New York Times.*

ASSOCIATION PRESS for extracts from *Laymen Speaking,* edited by Wallace C. Speers, copyright 1947 by the International Committee of the YMCA; "Who Is So Low" and prayers from *Prayers for Times Like These* by S. Ralph Harlow, copyright 1942 by the International Committee of the YMCA; extract from *Religion for Today* by A. J. William Myers, copyright 1941 by the International Committee of the YMCA; extract from *Religious Living* by Georgia Harkness, copyright 1937 by the Edward W. Hazen Foundation, Inc.; selections by Rufus M. Jones, George Wharton Pepper, G. A. Studdert-Kennedy from *Worship Resources for Youth,* edited by David R. Porter, copyright 1948 by the International Committee of the YMCA.

SAMUEL BLAIR for prayer by Albert W. Beaven and extract from sermon by Merton S. Rice from *The Master's Memorial,* edited by Samuel Blair, published and copyrighted 1929 by Abingdon Press.

BOBBS-MERRILL Co. for extract from *I Am a Protestant* by Ray Freeman Jenney, copyright 1951 by Bobbs-Merrill Co.

WALTER RUSSELL BOWIE for extract from *Remembering Christ* by Walter Russell Bowie, published and copyrighted in 1940 by Abingdon Press, reprinted by permission of the author.

BRANDT & BRANDT for prayer from *We Stand United and Other Radio Scripts* by Stephen Vincent Benét, copyright 1942 by Stephen Vincent Benét and published by Rinehart & Co., Inc.

BROADMAN PRESS for extract from *Kept by the Power of God* by John W. Phillips, copyright 1941 by the Sunday School Board of the Southern Baptist Convention.

CAMP FIRE GIRLS, INC., for "Fire Maker's Desire" by John Collier from *Book of the Camp Fire Girls,* copyright 1948 by Camp Fire Girls, Inc.

JONATHAN CAPE LTD. and LAURENCE HOUSMAN for "And the Word Was Made Flesh" from *Little Plays of St. Francis* by Laurence Housman, copyright 1932 by Jonathan Cape Ltd., published by Sidgwick & Jackson Ltd.

CHRISTIAN BOARD OF PUBLICATIONS for selection by P. Henry Lotz from *Worship Services for the Church Year,* edited by P. Henry Lotz, copyright 1944 by Christian Board of Publications.

CHRISTIAN CENTURY FOUNDATION for "Drink Ye All of It" by E. Dent Lackey.

CHRISTY & MOORE, LTD. for extract from "The Gate of the Year" by M. Louise Haskins.

THOMAS CURTIS CLARK for "The Call," "The Dream Abides," "He Shall Speak Peace," "The Kingdom," extract from "My America" from *God's Dreams,* copyright 1943 by Thomas Curtis Clark, published by Harper & Brothers.

GEORGE ARTHUR CLARKE for extract from *The Pathway to the Cross* by George Arthur Clarke, copyright 1942, published by Association Press, reprinted by permission of the author.

JAMES CLARKE & CO., LTD. for extracts from sermons by Charles Brown and James Reid from *Harvest Home,* copyright 1939 by James Clarke & Co., Ltd.

CONGREGATIONAL CHRISTIAN CHURCHES OF THE UNITED STATES OF AMERICA for prayers by Boynton Merrill from *A Book of Worship for Free Churches,* copyright 1948 by the Congregational Christian Churches of the United States of America, published by Oxford University Press.

CROWN PUBLISHERS, INC. for "The First Christmas" from *Top o' the Column* by Keith Preston, copyright 1925 by Covici, Friede.

DODD, MEAD & Co. for extract from *The Brother and the Brotherhood,* copyright 1908 by Dodd, Mead & Co.

DOUBLEDAY & Co., INC. for selections from *One Moment Please!* by James Keller, copyright 1950 by Doubleday & Co., Inc.; extract from "Love's Lantern" from *Poems, Essays and Letters* by Joyce Kilmer, copyright 1914, 1917, 1918 by Doubleday & Co., Inc.; extract from *Adventures in Contentment* by David Grayson, copyright 1907 by Hurst & Co.

E. P. DUTTON & Co., INC. for litany and prayers from *A Book of Common Worship,* edited by Wilbur P. Thirkield and Oliver Huckel, copyright 1932 by E. P. Dutton & Co., Inc.; extract from *Chronicles of the Pilgrims* by John Masefield, copyright 1910 by E. P. Dutton & Co., Inc.; extract from *How You Can Find Happiness* by Samuel H. Shoemaker, copyright 1947 by

maker and John R. Mott from *Upper Room,* copyright 1947 by General Commission on Evangelism of the Methodist Church; "Association with the Lord" by Grace Noll Crowell from *Upper Room,* copyright 1948 by General Commission on Evangelism of the Methodist Church.

VIKING PRESS, INC. for extract from *Men Are Brothers* by Eva Taylor, copyright 1937 by Viking Press, Inc.

A. P. WATT & SON LTD., DOUBLEDAY & CO., INC., MRS. GEORGE BAMBRIDGE and MACMILLAN CO. OF CANADA for extract from "The Explorer" and *The Five Nations,* copyright 1903, 1931 by Rudyard Kipling, reprinted by permission of Doubleday & Co., Inc.

ESTATE OF H. G. WELLS for extract from *The Outline of History* by H. G. Wells, copyright 1920, 1921 by Macmillan & Co., and 1947 by G. P. Wells.

WESTMINSTER PRESS for prayers from *The Book of Common Worship,* copyright 1946 by the Board of Christian Education of the Presbyterian Church in the U. S. A.; extracts from *Design for Christian Living,* edited by Donald C. Kerr, copyright 1953 by W. L. Jenkins; extracts from *This Year of Our Lord* by Andrew W. Blackwood, copyright 1943 by Westminster Press.

WHITESIDE, INC. for prayers by Stephen Hole Fritchman and Vivian Pomeroy from *Prayers of the Free Spirit,* edited by Stephen Hole Fritchman, copyright 1945 by Whiteside, Inc., published by Woman's Press.

WILLIAMS & NORGATE LTD. for extract from *From the Human End* by L. P. Jacks, copyright by Williams & Norgate Ltd.

LELAND FOSTER WOOD for "The Main Aims" from *Beatitudes for the Family and Other Verses* by Leland Foster Wood, copyright 1952 by Round Table Press, reprinted by permission of the author.

YALE UNIVERSITY PRESS for "Pronouns" from *Burning Bush* by Karle Wilson Baker, copyright 1922, 1950 by Yale University Press.

YOUNG WOMEN'S CHRISTIAN ASSOCIATION (NATIONAL BOARD) for litany from *A Book of Services for Group Worship,* copyright 1929 by the National Board; prayers by Richard Roberts from *Fellowship Prayers,* edited by Sarah Dickinson, copyright 1928 by the National Board; extract from *The Untried Door* by Richard Roberts, copyright 1921 by the National Board.

LIN YUTANG for extract from *Between Tears and Laughter* by Lin Yutang, copyright 1943 by John Day Co.

Special acknowledgment is also made to the following persons and organizations for permission to reprint the materials indicated:

AMERICAN BIBLE SOCIETY for extracts from sermons by Elmer George Homrighausen, Paul B. Kern, James I. Vance; FRANCIS H. BANGS for "Blind" by John Kendrick Bangs; ESTATE OF WILLIAM HENRY BODDY for selection "My Church" by William Henry Boddy; JOHN SUTHERLAND BONNELL for extract from sermon broadcast on *National Vespers,* November 21, 1948; ROY A. BURKHART for "The Tried and the Untried"; FRED S. BUSCHMEYER for "The Rock That Is Higher"; LESLIE SAVAGE CLARK for "Christmas Candle"; BERNARD C. CLAUSEN for extract from sermon; W. W. COBLENTZ for "Boundaries" and "The Housewife" by Catherine Cate Coblentz; GRACE NOLL CROWELL for "The Church School" published in *The Secret Place,* 1946; RALPH S. CUSHMAN for "Principles of Stewardship"; ESTATE OF LLOYD C. DOUGLAS for prayer published in *The American Magazine,* 1934; CHESTER BURGE EMERSON for selection "The Old and the New"; JOHN ERSKINE for "Childhood"; FRANK B. FAGERBURG for extracts from sermons; DOROTHY CANFIELD FISHER for prayer; FORWARD MOVEMENT PUBLICATIONS OF THE EPISCOPAL CHURCH for "Litany of the Disciple's Way"; HARRY EMERSON FOSDICK for litany and prayers published in *The Church Monthly,* extracts from sermons from *National Vespers*; MRS. ROBERT FREEMAN for extract from "The Heathen" and "The Men of Earth Said" by Robert Freeman; ELMER A. FRIDELL for prayer; WINFRED ERNEST GARRISON for "The Book"; CHARLES K. HARTMAN for "The Bible, a Rural Book"; PERCY R. HAYWARD for "Credo" and "The Person in a Different Skin"; WILLIAM ERNEST HOCKING for extract from article in *The Saturday Review,* 1946; GEORGE EDWARD HOFFMAN for "December 26"; RAYMOND KRESENSKY for "I Looked for Christ"; QUENTIN T. LIGHTNER for selection "Our Home"; ADELAIDE LOVE for "Alchemy"; HALFORD E. LUCCOCK for extracts from *The Haunted House;* SARAH C. MACGREGOR for "This Is My Church" by Charles P. MacGregor; MARTHA B. MORELAND for "Faith" and "His Hands" by John Richard Moreland; RICHARD K. MORTON for litanies; IDA NORTON MUNSON for "Easter Light"; JAMES MYERS for prayers from *Prayers for Self and Society,* published by Association

Press, 1934; NATIONAL COUNCIL OF THE CHURCHES OF CHRIST IN THE UNITED STATES OF AMERICA for prayer and litanies of unknown authorship, prayers by George T. Kerr and C. R. McBride and "Ten Commandments for Modern Parents"; G. ASHTON OLDHAM for extract from sermon; ARMIN C. OLDSEN for prayer; BONARO W. OVERSTREET for "To One Who Doubts the Worth of Doing Anything If You Can't Do Everything"; ANGELO PATRI for "A Parent's Prayer"; LADY NEYSA PERKS for "Overheard in an Orchard" by Elizabeth Cheney; PULPIT DIGEST for "His Jerusalem and Ours" by Edgar DeWitt Jones, "On the Meaning of the Lord's Supper" by David E. Roberts and "Jesus and Young Men" by Leslie D. Weatherhead; PULPIT PREACHING for "The Difference Christ's Coming Has Made" by Binney Simpson Black, "The Joy of Christmas" and "My Home" by Robert W. Burns, "Enlightened by Easter" by Teunis E. Gouwens, "The Conqueror of Death" by Ralph W. Sockman; HARRIS FRANKLIN RALL for "My Money Creed"; RAND MCNALLY & CO. for "Emphasis," "Gethsemane" and "The Goal" by Ella Wheeler Wilcox; JOHN D. ROCKEFELLER, JR., for "An Industrial Creed"; ORA SEARLE for "An Easter Canticle" and "Thanksgiving" by Charles Hanson Towne; FREDERICK F. SHANNON for extract from *Sermons for Days We Observe*; ABBA HILLEL SILVER for "America's Making"; JOHN R. SLATER for prayer from *Living for the Future*; HILDA W. SMITH for "The Carpenter of Galilee"; WILLARD L. SPERRY for litany; INA B. STIDGER for "The Cross and the Tree" and "I Saw God Bare His Soul" by William L. Stidger; ELEANOR B. STOCK for "A Teacher's Prayer"; HOWARD THURMAN for "A Christmas Affirmation" and "Gifts That Are Mine"; THOMAS WEARING for "New Year"; CLARE WHITAKER for "My Country" by Robert Whitaker; MARSHALL WINGFIELD for extract from sermon; GEORGE W. WISEMAN for "Easter Must Be Reclaimed," selection from "The Repentance of Peter," "A Youth's Prayer"; ZIONS HERALD for "A Mother's Creed" by Ozora Davis.

To my mother
Caroline Langworthy Wallis
and the mother of my wife
Lucille Watson Maslyn

CONTENTS

PREFACE

The Christian Year dates back to the early church and is a great spiritual heritage of all Christians. This source volume includes worship and homiletic materials for the special days, occasions, and concerns generally included in the calendar of present-day evangelical Protestantism. Attention has been rather arbitrarily focused on those days and seasons which represent a balanced program for the non-liturgical or "free" churches.

The book incorporates those civil days in which the church and Sunday school have a vested interest or testimony. A number of the times and seasons designated on the traditional church calendar are not featured.

The book is divided according to four major emphases:

> Part I—The Christian Heritage
> Part II—The Christian Mission
> Part III—The Christian Home
> Part IV—The Christian Nation

The materials selected for each of the thirty-one subdivisions have been separated into six categories: (1) calls to worship and other opening Scriptural sentences, (2) invocations and prayers appropriate for the beginning of worship, (3) litanies and responsive prayers, (4) prayers for pulpit use and group worship, (5) brief, suggestive, and quotable poems suitable for particular days and seasons, and (6) topics, texts, and other homiletic suggestions.

When possible, the materials have been verified with original sources. All Scriptures are from the Authorized Version except those otherwise indicated.

The abbreviations used for Bible books are:

Old Testament	*New Testament*
Ge.—Genesis	Mat.—Matthew
Ex.—Exodus	Mk.—Mark
Le.—Leviticus	Lu.—Luke
De.—Deuteronomy	Jn.—John
Jos.—Joshua	Ac.—Acts
Ju.—Judges	Ro.—Romans
Ru.—Ruth	1 Co.—1 Corinthians
1 S.—1 Samuel	2 Co.—2 Corinthians
2 S.—2 Samuel	Ga.—Galatians
1 K.—1 Kings	Ep.—Ephesians

Old Testament	*New Testament*
2 K.—2 Kings	Ph.—Philippians
1 Ch.—1 Chronicles	Col.—Colossians
2 Ch.—2 Chronicles	1 Th.—1 Thessalonians
Ezr.—Ezra	2 Th.—2 Thessalonians
Ne.—Nehemiah	1 Ti.—1 Timothy
Es.—Esther	2 Ti.—2 Timothy
Jb.—Job	Tit.—Titus
Ps.—Psalms	Phm.—Philemon
Pr.—Proverbs	He.—Hebrews
Ec.—Ecclesiastes	Ja.—James
S. of S.—Song of Solomon	1 Pe.—1 Peter
Is.—Isaiah	2 Pe.—2 Peter
Je.—Jeremiah	1 Jn.—1 John
La.—Lamentations	2 Jn.—2 John
Eze.—Ezekiel	3 Jn.—3 John
Da.—Daniel	Jude—Jude
Ho.—Hosea	Re.—Revelation
Jo.—Joel	
Am.—Amos	
Ob.—Obadiah	
Jon.—Jonah	
Mi.—Micah	
Na.—Nahum	
Hab.—Habakkuk	
Zph.—Zephaniah	
Hag.—Haggai	
Zch.—Zechariah	
Mal.—Malachi	

Other abbreviations are: *Book of Common Worship* (CC) for *Book of Common Worship,* Church of Christ, 1932; *Book of Common Worship* (P) for *Book of Common Worship,* Presbyterian Church, U. S. A., 1946; *Book of Worship* (ER) for *Book of Worship,* Evangelical and Reformed Church, 1940; and *National Council* for materials prepared by the National Council of the Churches of Christ in the United States of America. An asterisk (*) indicates the use of a shortened or adapted form.

There are five indexes. The first lists contributors and sources. Titles of books and periodicals from which quotations have been taken are given so that the extracts may be located in their complete context. The Textual Index lists texts which accompany prose materials. The Poetry Index lists titles, first lines, and poets. The Cross-Index of Special Days and Occasions is a master list of more than 100 days and concerns taken from the yearbooks of the national denominational groups. The Subject Index lists topically all prose materials.

Work on this volume began seven years ago when the editor was assisting James Dalton Morrison in the compilation of his *Masterpieces of Religious Verse*. Dr. Morrison, a professor of preaching and worship specialist, discerned the need of a volume of this kind and suggested a number of features to be included. His untimely death made impossible the preparation of this volume as a co-operative effort.

The editor wishes to acknowledge the generous assistance of Mrs. Frances V. Wilkens, librarian, Keuka College, Keuka Park, N. Y., and Theodore Trost, librarian, Colgate-Rochester Divinity School, Rochester, N. Y. Source materials were also secured through the co-operation of librarians in the New York Public Library and the Union Theological Seminary Library, New York, N. Y.; the New York State Library, Albany; the Rochester Public Library and the University of Rochester Libraries; and the Library of Congress.

The Christian year sets up the great human life. The building of the perfect man is the noblest work that can go on in the world. The seasons come and go, the harvests ripen and are gathered in, the mountains are built up and decay; but all these are sights that cannot match in dignity and interest the spectacle of a full, strong man's life. First God prepares for him the place where he is to live. Then his life comes and takes place, a strong and settled fact. Then it puts forth its power and influences other men. Then suffering comes to it and matures it, but finally it issues out of suffering, refined and triumphant. And at last, when it has passed away out of the world into new regions of activity and growth, it leaves its power behind it to bless men after it is dead. There is nothing so round and perfect as such a life in all the world. It is the very crown of God's creation.

Such a complete life is pictured in the church's year. It has its Advent, Nativity, Epiphany, Lent, Easter, Whitsunday, Trinity Sunday. It fills the years with its increasing, slowly maturing beauty. This is the true meaning of the year, with all its sacred seasons. Let us be true churchmen and give it all its richness. Only, dear friends, we do not really honor the venerable beauty of the church's calendar when we make it a badge of our denominational distinction, or deck its seasons out with all the trickery of colored altar-cloths, purple and white and green, but when we see in it the story of a human life slowly ripened from God's first purpose to the full-grown, glorified manhood standing before God's presence and sending forth God's power to its fellowmen.

PHILLIPS BROOKS

I. The Christian Heritage

A. ADVENT

Advent, the season of preparation, penitence, and expectancy, begins on the Sunday nearest to St. Andrew's Day (November 30) and continues through the four subsequent Sundays. The period recognizes the spiritual and psychological need for the readying of the believer's mind and soul not only for the anniversary of Christ's coming as the Babe of Bethlehem but also for his coming into the hearts of those who love him and his second coming both to judge the world and to reign supreme. The first day of Advent marks the beginning of the church year and the commencing of what is sometimes called "the winter Lent." Preaching emphases for Advent are the proclamations of Christ's coming in the Creation, in the Law and the Prophets, and in the mission of John the Baptist.

Calls to Worship

(Boldface type indicates responses.)

1 Prepare ye the way of the Lord, make straight in the desert a highway for our God. . . . And the glory of the Lord shall be revealed, and all flesh shall see it together: for the mouth of the Lord hath spoken it.

Blessed be the King that cometh in the name of the Lord: peace in heaven, and glory in the highest.

Is. 40:3, 5; Lu. 19:38

2 Arise, shine; for thy light is come, and the glory of the Lord is risen upon thee. . . . Lift up thine eyes round about, and see.

From the rising of the sun even unto the going down of the same my name shall be great among the Gentiles . . . saith the Lord of hosts.

Is. 60:1, 4; Mal. 1:11

3 Sing and rejoice . . . for, lo, I come, and I will dwell in the midst of thee, saith the Lord. It is high time to awake out of sleep: for now is our salvation nearer than when we believed. The night is far spent, the day is at hand: let us therefore cast off the works of darkness, and let us put on the armour of light.

Zch. 2:10; Ro. 13:11–12

4   And it shall be said in that day, Lo, this is our God; we have waited for him, and he will save us; this is the Lord; we have waited for him, we will be glad and rejoice in his salvation. Watch therefore, for ye know neither the day nor the hour wherein the Son of man cometh.

Is. 25:9; Mat. 25:13

Invocations

5   O Almighty Father, source of all being, fountain of light and salvation: we adore thy infinite goodness in sending thy only begotten Son into the world, that, being in him, we may not perish, but have everlasting life; and we pray thee that, through the power and grace of his first advent to save the world, we may be ready to meet him at his second advent to judge the world; through the same Jesus Christ our Lord. Amen.*

William Walsham How

6   Our Father, in whose grace all our light is born, and in whose love is the font of our festivity: mercifully lead us into the holy mysteries of the Christmas-tide. Grant us to know true and searching, inward preparation for the coming of the King. In the open-heartedness of our needy lives, bring us into the eternal things of this blessed season; in Jesus' name. Amen.

Herman Paul Guhsé

7   O God, who didst prepare of old the minds and hearts of men for the coming of thy Son, and whose Spirit ever worketh to illumine our darkened lives with the light of his Gospel: prepare now our minds and hearts, we beseech thee, that Christ may dwell within us, and ever reign in our thoughts and affections as the King of love, and the very Prince of peace. Grant this, we pray thee, for his sake. Amen.

Author Unknown

8   Prepare our hearts, O God, for the coming of Jesus Christ thy Son. By the memory of the world's great need of a Saviour, deepen our joy in making ready for the anniversary of his lowly birth at Bethlehem. By true faith in him as the divine Redeemer, strengthen our loyalty and our hope, that at his appearing in glory, we may welcome him as our risen Lord, our royal Master, the Saviour of our souls. Amen.

Book of Common Worship (CC)

9   O Lord Jesus Christ, in all the fulness of thy power most gentle, in thine exceeding greatness most humble, bestow thy mind and spirit upon us, who have nothing whereof to boast; that clothed in true humility, we may be exalted to true greatness. Grant this, O Lord, who livest and reignest with the Father and the Spirit, one God for evermore. Amen.

Primer of 1559

Litanies

(Boldface type indicates responses.)

10   O Lord, who hast set before us the great hope that thy Kingdom shall come on earth, and hast taught us to pray for its coming, make us ever ready to thank thee for the signs of its dawning, and to pray and work for that perfect day when thy will shall be done on earth as it is in heaven. For the work of thy Spirit within and beyond the bounds of thy visible church:
We thank thee, O Lord.
For the work of thy Spirit in the history of the world, through peaceful advance, and through pain and tumult:
We thank thee, O Lord.
For the work of thy Spirit in the history of our own country, through its heroes and leaders, in statecraft, law and industry:
We thank thee, O Lord.
For the work of thy Spirit in science and commerce, in literature and art:
We thank thee, O Lord.
For the work of thy Spirit in the slow triumph of truth over error:
We thank thee, O Lord.
For the work of thy Spirit in the growing desire for true brotherhood, between men of every class and nation:
We thank thee, O Lord.
For the work of thy Spirit in the spread of education, and in the development of a fuller life for individuals, with healthier surroundings and better conditions:
We thank thee, O Lord.
For the work of thy Spirit in the deepening sense of human worth in all nations and classes, and in the growing reverence for womanhood and childhood:
We thank thee, O Lord.
For the work of thy Spirit in the church, which will not cease until it joins

all nations and kindreds and tongues and peoples into one great family, to thy praise and glory:

We thank thee, O Lord. Amen.

The Kingdom, the Power and the Glory

11   That we may prepare the way for the Eternal in our lives, and that we may grow in the vitality of our faith and the power of our service unto all men:

Incarnate the spirit of Jesus in us, O God.

That we may perpetuate the heritage of the ages fulfilled in him, and that we may bring to fruition the work of disciples of old:

Incarnate the spirit of Jesus in us, O God.

That we may develop the same consciousness of thee, the same self-sacrificing way of life, and the same love of man:

Incarnate the spirit of Jesus in us, O God.

That there may be the proper foundation for an approach to the study of man and the solution of the problems of society:

Incarnate the spirit of Jesus in us, O God.

From failure to gladden the heart of childhood in these days, and from blindness to the beauty of simple things and the blessings of kinships and fellowships:

Guard and keep us, we pray.

From arrogant self-reliance, shallow faithlessness, lack of appreciation of the influence of Jesus upon the world:

Guard and keep us, we pray.

From timidity and slowness in attacking the problems of peace, health, unemployment, and proper social regulations which threaten to destroy the influence of Jesus upon men:

Guard and keep us, we pray.

From worldly power, allurement of selfishness and power, and every interest that does not build a better world:

Guard and keep us, we pray.

From failure to enable men in these days to interpret the principles of Jesus in their own way and to meet with his spirit the situation in their own environment:

Guard and keep us, we pray.

From light dismissal of the way of Jesus, the power of religion, the moral obligations of man, or the necessity for brotherhood and justice and love in the world to which he came:

Guard and keep us, we pray.

Richard K. Morton

Prayers

12   O God, most merciful, thou hast set in our hearts a haunting hope, tremulous yet unconquerable, of a desired, delayed, inevitable day when love and joy shall rule the life of man. Yea, thou hast given us a token and pledge of thy high purpose for our humanity, in him whose sonship to thee is the ground and prophecy that our dream, though delayed, will not be defeated.

Renew within us the high prophetic anticipation of our faith, the sense of a beauty ever about to be realized, of a victory ever about to be won; the hope, ever coming true, of the advent of Christ. Recall thy church to its old expectant joy, that it may go forth to meet him who comes glorious in blessing, and does not wait, when he seems to delay, for our coming to him. Rebuke our dismay, and give us eyes to see that thou art coming into thy world to its final satisfying peace; coming swiftly, gently, with the tread of the dawn.

Even so come quickly, O God; come thou in us, overcoming our evil by thy abundant goodness, casting out our fear by thy love. Reign thou in us, where fear and care and sin have ruled to our shame and undoing. Attune our life and labor to the rhythm of a great hope, assured that thou wilt yet have thy way with us and with our tangled world; by the grace of Jesus Christ. Amen.

Joseph Fort Newton

13   O God of hope, who waitest through the centuries for a people prepared to receive the gift of thy Spirit: we beseech thee to draw us to thyself, and to fit us for thy service. By thy mighty power, free us from the sins which deaden conscience and keep us low. By thy providence guide us towards paths of usefulness and lead us in thy way. By the quickening of thy Spirit, lift our thoughts towards things true and lovely and of good report, and grant us visions of thy Kingdom of good will upon the earth. By the gracious face of Jesus, teach us the beauty of holiness and satisfy us with the life which is life indeed.

O God, for whose Spirit our world hungers and thirsts, bless us with peace and righteousness the world over as the season of good will comes upon us. Let thy Spirit rule among the nations, that concord and mutual service may be established, and the mind of Christ bind people with people, and race with race in brotherhood. Support all those at this season who think and plan to give happiness to others, and give them the deepest happiness in their tasks. Sustain all those who must bear added burdens to provide cheer for others. Help us all to be mindful of them, and to add no unnecessary task to their portion. Bring the light of thy Spirit into every home, that affections may be rekindled and loyalties be renewed in the gladness of the time. Send new life into thy church, that there may be a new spirit of devotion to Christ and his Kingdom. Free us from all concerns for the things that matter little, and keep us true to all the things that matter much—justice and mercy and faith.

Most merciful God, abundantly bless those in whose hearts there is little room for joy because sorrow has come close to them. May the Christ who has been the sharer of their joys and their comrade in toil now come to them as the Great Comforter, and in the knowledge of his sympathy and love may they find the peace that knows no end. Amen.

Morgan Phelps Noyes

14 Eternal Spirit, the light of the knowledge of whose glory we have seen in the face of Jesus Christ: we worship thee. In the order and symmetry of the universe, its unity, beauty, and law-abiding nature, we trace thy mind and will, and wherever goodness and truth are we see the overflow of thine eternal fountain, the light from thine everlasting sun. But thanks be to thee for that fuller witness of thy presence among us, thy care for us, thy purpose concerning us, which thou hast unveiled in Christ our Lord.

Make real to us today his living presence, and give us humble hearts that shall find room for him in our inns.

We seek the penitence that his coming inspires. We are not worthy of his visitation. There are ill tempers in us, uncleanness, passions and prejudices alien to his spirit that soil our hearts. We must choose between them and him. Create in us a clean heart, O God, and renew a right spirit within us.

We seek the hope that his coming brings. For the world is very dark, and as of old, when he first came, Herod the king sought to slay him, so the murderous passions of men lie in wait for him still. Yet he is our hope. We have seen his light. Once seen, we never can forget it. He is our salvation. He is the first-born among many brethren. We would believe in him afresh today and follow him with more loyal hearts. Thanks be to thee for him whom thou didst send, full of grace and truth! Amen.*

Harry Emerson Fosdick

15 O God, our heavenly Father, who in thine infinite love hast given thy Son to be our Saviour: we confess that so often when he has come to us we have been blind to his presence and deaf to his call. Through our ingratitude, our disobedience, and our hardness of heart we have been unready to welcome him. We have forgotten thy promises, and questioned thy love. We have been unfaithful to the trust thou hast laid upon us, and have wasted the precious gifts committed to our charge. Grant us truly to repent of all our sins, to forsake that which is evil, and to hold fast to that which is good. Bestow upon us, we beseech thee, the gift of pardon; and enable us to rejoice in thy salvation; through Jesus Christ our Lord. Amen.

Prayers and Services for Christian Festivals

Poems

16 THY KINGDOM COME

"Thy Kingdom come," on bended knee
The passing ages pray;
And faithful souls have yearned to see
On earth that Kingdom's day.

The day in whose clear-shining light
All wrong shall stand revealed,
When justice shall be clothed with might,
And every hurt be healed.

Frederick Lucian Hosmer

17 THE CHRIST

The good intent of God became the Christ.
And lived on earth—the Living Love of God,
That men might draw to closer touch with heaven,
Since Christ in all the ways of man hath trod.

John Oxenham

18 HE COMES

Go, preach, the Kingdom is at hand,
The King is at the gate,
Go, sound the news in every land,
He comes for whom I wait.

He comes with lightning and in wrath,
He follows down the sea,
He sweeps the briars from his path,
To set the captives free.

He comes with laughter in his eyes
  Soft as the yellow dews,
And hungry children hush their cries
  To shout the glad, good news.

He comes, he comes with healing balm
  For all the hurts of men
He comes, he comes with peace and calm
  Where all the wars have been.

Sound bugles, sound in golden flood,
  His reign that shall not cease.
He comes to make of all one blood,
  Triumphant Prince of Peace.

Author Unknown

19   *ASSOCIATION WITH THE LORD*

Association with the Lord can bring
To any life a dignity and grace,
And ever looking up to him will give
The high, white look of Christ to any face.

Grace Noll Crowell

20   *THAT HOLY THING*

They all were looking for a king
  To slay their foes and lift them high:
Thou cam'st a little baby thing
  That made a woman cry.

O Son of man, to right my lot
  Nought but thy presence can avail;
Yet on the road thy wheels are not,
  Nor on the sea thy sail!

My fancied ways why shouldst thou heed?
  Thou com'st down thine own secret stair;
Com'st down to answer all my need,
  Yea, every bygone prayer!

George Macdonald

21   *NONE OTHER LAMB*

None other Lamb, none other Name,
   None other Hope in heaven or earth or sea,
None other Hiding-place from guilt and shame,
   None beside thee.

                         ❋

Lord, thou art Life tho' I be dead,
   Love's Fire thou art, however cold I be:
Nor heaven have I, nor place to lay my head,
   Nor home, but thee.
                                    Christina G. Rossetti

22   *O LEST WE STARVE*

O lest we starve, and lest we die
   In our stupidity,
Come, Holy Child, within and share
   Our hospitality.
                                    Ralph S. Cushman

23   *From SAINT GREGORY'S GUEST*

Unheard, because our ears are dull,
   Unseen, because our eyes are dim,
He walks the earth, the Wonderful,
   And all good deeds are done to him.
                                    John Greenleaf Whittier

24   *From* THE WINGLESS VICTORY (Act III, Sc. ii)

The earth rolls toward the dark,
and men begin to sleep. God of the children,
God of the lesser children of the earth,
the black, the unclean, the vengeful, you are mine
now as when I was a child. He came too soon,
this Christ of peace. Men are not ready yet.
Another hundred thousand years they must drink
your potion of tears and blood.
                                    Maxwell Anderson

Topics, Texts and Themes

25 THE COMING OF THE LORD

Jn. 1:1–14

My Lord came as *word*. He came as the expression of the mind of the eternal God. Ordinary words could not have carried the "good news." Ordinary language was an altogether inadequate vessel for this new wine. And so the mighty news was spoken in the incarnation of the Lord.

My Lord came as *life*. "In him was life." But not a mere cupful of life, or even a cup running over. He came as "the fountain of life." Nay, if I had the requisite word I must get even behind and beyond this. For he was the Creator of fountains. "The water that I shall give him shall be in him a well." Yes, he was the fountain of fountains!

The Lord came as *light*. "The life was the light." True light is always the child of life. Our clearest light comes not from speech or doctrine, still less does it emerge from controversy. It is the fine, subtle issue of fine living. And my light is to "shine before men" by reason of the indwelling life of the Christ.

And my Lord came as *power*. "To them gave he power." All the power I need for a full, holy, healthy life I can find in him. Every obligation has its corresponding inspiration, and I am competent to do his will.

John Henry Jowett

26 CHRIST HAS COME

Christ has come, the Light of the world. Long ages may yet elapse before his beams have reduced the world to order and beauty, and clothed a purified humanity with light as with a garment. But he has come: the Revealer of the snares and chasms that lurk in darkness, the Rebuker of every evil thing that prowls by night, the Stiller of the storm-winds of passion, the Quickener of all that is wholesome, the Adorner of all that is beautiful, the Reconciler of contradictions, the Harmonizer of discords, the Healer of diseases, the Saviour from sin.

He has come: the Torch of truth, the Anchor of hope, the Pillar of faith, the Rock for strength, the Refuge for security, the Fountain for refreshment, the Vine for gladness, the Rose for beauty, the Lamb for tenderness, the Friend for counsel, the Brother for love. Jesus Christ has trod the world. The trace of the divine footsteps will never be obliterated.

Peter Bayne

27   *THE DAY OF GOD'S VISITATION*

In this advent of the Redeemer there was nothing outwardly remarkable to the men of that day. It was almost nothing. Of all the historians of that period few, indeed, are found to mention it. This is a thing which we at this day can scarcely understand; for to us the blessed advent of our Lord is the brightest page in the world's history; but to them it was far otherwise. Remember, for one moment, what the advent of our Lord was to all outward appearance. He seemed, let it be said reverently, to the rulers of those days, a fanatical free-thinker. They heard of his miracles, but they appeared nothing remarkable to them; there was nothing there on which to fasten their attention. They heard that some of the populace had been led away, and now and then, it may be, some of his words reached their ears, but to them they were hard to be under-stood—full of mystery, or else they roused every evil passion in their hearts, so stern and uncompromising was the morality they taught. They put aside these words in that brief period, and the day of grace passed.

And just such as this is God's visitation to us today. Generally, the day of God's visitation is not a day very remarkable outwardly. Bereavements, sorrows —no doubt, in these God speaks—but there are other occasions far more quiet and unobtrusive, but which are yet days of grace. A scruple which others do not see, a doubt coming into the mind respecting some views held sacred by the popular creed, a sense of heart loneliness and solitariness, a feeling of awful misgiving when the future lies open before us, the dread feeling of an eternal godlessness for men who are living godless lives now—these silent moments unmarked, these are the moments in which the Eternal is speaking to our souls.   *Frederick W. Robertson*

28   *LIGHT MASTERS DARKNESS*

The light shineth in darkness; and the darkness comprehendeth it not.
JN. 1:5

Goodspeed translates the above text as follows: "The light is still shining in the darkness, for the darkness has never put it out." . . . Most of us have thought that the latter part of the text meant simply that the darkness did not understand the light. But the word "comprehend" has other meanings. Kent says, "did not overcome it"; Weymouth, "has not overpowered it"; Moffatt, "did not master it." The essential meaning is: Light is the master of darkness; although we may pass through times of distress, we may be comforted, because he is the Light of the world, and his Light cannot be put out.
                                    Clare Purcell

29   *THE ETERNALNESS OF THE CHRIST*

And the light shineth in darkness; and the darkness apprehended it not.
JN. 1:5 (ARV)
The Light shines on in the darkness, and the darkness has never over-
powered it. (Weymouth)

There is no story of the nativity in John's Gospel. When Christmas comes
we shall have our pageants and programs celebrating the birth of the Saviour.
If we portray the story of the angels and the shepherds, we shall go to Matthew.
But John brings no description of Bethlehem's story. And this is most logical.
According to John, Jesus was never born! "In the beginning was the Word.
. . . The same was in the beginning with God. . . . And the Word was made
flesh, and dwelt among us." The event in Bethlehem was merely the bringing
of the eternal Word, the eternal Light, into the world in the flesh. When he
was accused by the Jews of making himself greater than Abraham, he answered
simply, "Before Abraham was [born], *I am*."

                                                            Samuel L. Joekel

30   *THE UNVEILING OF GOD*

Lo, the star . . . went before them, till it came and stood over where the
young child was. MAT. 2:9

The advent of Jesus is more than a date—it is an event; not simply an incident, but an era: it is the unveiling of God and humanity. The long periods—
B.C. and A.D.—are the "folding doors of history," when prophecy was fulfilled.
The time and place and persons involved in this story are all of deep significance to us, and the question that the wise men came asking, "Where is he?"
is the deepest question of the ages.

                                                            S. Stephen McKenney

31   *THE DIFFERENCE CHRIST'S COMING HAS MADE*

In him was life; and the life was the light of men. JN. 1:5

Why is Jesus the greatest of all the sons of men? It is because of what he
was, because of what he said, and because of what he did. His incomparable
greatness in these respects is seen in the fact that Jesus has changed the world
—its current. This becomes increasingly clear as the generations pass, and as
Christians find Paul's doctrine of the living Christ verified in their own

experience of Christ's presence and power in their lives each day. Yes, Jesus Christ has changed the world. What would be the difference if he had not come?

Binney Simpson Black

32   *LEARNING WHO HE IS*

He comes to us as one unknown, without a name, as of old by the lakeside he came to those men who knew him not. He speaks to us the same word, "Follow thou me," and sets us to the tasks which he has to fulfill for our time. He commands. And to those who obey, whether they be wise or simple, he will reveal himself in the toils, the conflicts, the suffering which they shall pass through in his fellowship, and as an ineffable mystery, they shall learn in their own experience who he is.

Albert Schweitzer

33   *NONE GREATER THAN JESUS*

Mankind in its totality offers an assemblage of low beings, selfish and superior to the animal only in that its selfishness is more reflective. From the midst of this uniform mediocrity, there are pillars that rise towards the sky, and bear witness to a nobler destiny. Jesus is the highest of these pillars which shew to man whence he comes, and whither he ought to tend. In him was condensed all that is good and elevated in our nature. . . . Will great originality be born again, or will the world content itself by following the ways opened by the bold creators of the ancient ages? We know not. But whatever may be the unexpected phenomena of the future, Jesus will not be surpassed. His worship will constantly renew its youth, the tale of his life will cause ceaseless tears, his sufferings will soften the best hearts; all the ages will proclaim that, among the sons of men, there is none born who is greater than Jesus.

Ernest Renan

B. CHRISTMAS

The celebration of December 25 as Christmas began in Rome about A.D. 325. The popularity of the day dates from the twelfth century. Most of the customs and traditions associated with the annual observance of Christ's birth have sprung from the folk of many lands. The lighting of candles, for instance, suggests symbolically that Jesus is the Light of the world and the exchange of gifts is a recognition of Christ as the gift of God's love and of the presents offered by shepherds and magi. Although Christians must guard against the domination of pagan customs and a commercialization which omits Christ on the anniversary of his birth, this day for Christians is one of good cheer, joy, and generosity. Many churches hold services of music and meditation at a late hour on Christmas Eve, and sometimes a worship service, often community-wide in nature, is scheduled for the morning of Christmas Day.

Calls to Worship

(Boldface type indicates responses.)

34 In this was manifested the love of God toward us, because that God sent his only begotten Son into the world, that we might live through him. For God, who commanded the light to shine out of darkness, hath shined in our hearts, to give the light of the knowledge of the glory of God in the face of Christ Jesus. *1 Jn. 4:9; 2 Co. 4:6*

35 Unto us a child is born, and unto us a son is given: and the government shall be upon his shoulder: and his name shall be called Wonderful, Counsellor, the mighty God, the everlasting Father, the Prince of Peace.
Let us now go even unto Bethlehem, and see this thing which is come to pass, which the Lord hath made known unto us.
Is. 9:6; Lu. 2:15

36 Behold, I bring you good tidings of great joy, which shall be to all people. For unto you is born this day in the city of David a Saviour, which is Christ the Lord.
Glory to God in the highest, and on earth peace, good will toward men. *Lu. 2:10–11, 14*

37　How beautiful upon the mountains are the feet of him that bringeth good tidings . . . that saith unto Zion, thy God reigneth! Break forth into joy, sing together, ye waste places of Jerusalem: for the Lord hath comforted his people, he hath redeemed Jerusalem.

Is. 52:7, 9

Invocations

38　Eternal Spirit, breathe into the hearts of living men the expectation of the Christmas host, the hope of comradeship for all earth's children, the quickened impulse for a world at peace. Make our feet messengers of succor and relief. Bring to our eager souls all the glory born in Bethlehem, the confidence of man in man, the love of God cradled in a human heart. Amen.

Stephen Hole Fritchman

39　O Almighty God, who by the birth of thy holy child Jesus hast given us a great light to dawn upon our darkness: grant, we pray thee, that in his light we may see light to the end of our days; and bestow upon us, we beseech thee, that most excellent Christmas gift of charity to all men, that so the likeness of thy Son may be formed in us, and that we may have the ever-brightening hope of everlasting life; through Jesus Christ our Lord. Amen.

William Angus Knight

40　Merciful and most loving God, by whose will and bountiful gift Jesus Christ our Lord humbled himself that he might exalt mankind; and became flesh that he might restore in us the lost celestial image; and was born of the virgin that he might uplift the lowly: grant unto us the inheritance of the meek, perfect us in thy likeness, and bring us at last to rejoice in beholding thy beauty, and, with all thy saints, to glorify thy grace, who hast given thine only-begotten Son to be the Saviour of the world. Amen.*

Ancient Collects

41　O Loving Father, who has brought us again to the glad season when we commemorate the birth of thy Son, Jesus of Nazareth: grant that his spirit may be born anew in our hearts this day and that we may joyfully welcome him to reign over us. Open our ears that we may hear again the angelic chorus of old; open our lips that we too may sing with uplifted hearts, Glory to God in the highest, and on earth peace, good will toward men. Amen.

Henry W. Foote

42   Grant us, O God, such love and wonder that with humble shepherds, wise men, and pilgrims unknown, we may come and adore the holy Babe, the heavenly King; and with our gifts, worship and serve him as our Lord and Saviour Jesus Christ. Amen.

James Ferguson

43   Almighty and everlasting God, the brightness of faithful souls, who didst bring the Gentiles to thy light, and made known unto them him who is the true light and the bright and morning star: fill, we beseech thee, the world with thy glory, and show thyself by the radiance of thy light unto all nations; through Jesus Christ our Lord. Amen.

Gregorian Sacramentary

Litanies

(Boldface type indicates responses.)

44   We thank thee for the birth of Jesus, that thy Spirit was upon him, that he was anointed to preach good tidings to the poor, to proclaim release to the captive, the recovering of sight to the blind, to set at liberty them that are bruised:

Help us to make our present world the acceptable year of the Lord.

O God, enable us, as we worship thee, to kindle with the joy of simple shepherds long ago at the thought of all that came to the world in the birth of the child Jesus:

Cast out our sin and enter in; be born in us today.

Help us, O God, in the light of the shining star to realize the wastes and desolations of the world, to feel the weight of the world's sorrow and need, to be made aware of the power of evil, to see that spiritual loss is caused by man's hatreds and sins:

Help us with Jesus' spirit to build the old wastes and to raise up the former generations.

Forgive us, O God, for our weariness of heart after great conflict and exertion. Suffer us not to become creatures and nations of selfishness, of narrow foolish pride, marred with hardness of heart and weakened by fear and suspicion:

Grant unto us that we being delivered out of the hand of our enemies may serve thee without fear.

Help us to build America in love rather than in provincial selfishness; help us to keep America a land of hope for all mankind; help us to find in our patriotism the cross of humanity's desires:

May the dayspring from on high visit us, to shine upon us when in darkness we lose our faith in thee. Amen.

Modern Worship

45   O Lord God, who art in the midst of us, mighty to save, who dost rejoice over us with joy: we praise thee that thou art shown unto us in love and mercy, in holiness and devotion everywhere, so that thou art never without witness among thy people. Especially do we praise thee for those members of thy family who so serve thy will that having seen them, we behold thee. May the star of their lives burn before us until we too have made thy will our own and know that thou art with us always.

Open our eyes, O Lord, that we may see thy glory round about us.

Make us quick to know each one of whom thou dost say, "Hear ye him," that we may follow the voices of the shepherds of mankind. Let no accent of thy Holy Spirit be lost in us, that we also may wonder at the words of grace which proceed out of the mouths of thy holy prophets. We would sit at the feet of Jesus on the mount and be taught of blessedness and love.

Open our ears, O Lord, that we may hear the multitude of the heavenly host.

Father, thou alone knowest the cares that press upon us and the burdens that weigh us down. When we are beset by fears, when we are disheartened, lonely or sorrowful, freshen our faith in thee and in thy kindly providence, that we may praise thee for the hand that bears us up. In hours of victory and joy as well, save us from ingratitude and from forgetfulness of thee.

Open our mouths, O Lord, that we may sing, Glory to thee in the highest.

Make us humble of heart, that we may be a fit abiding place for thee, even as the manger for the holy Child. Purify our minds, that we may move only to thy purposes; and kindle our affections, that our love may be broad as thy redeeming love. We would that the spirit that was in Jesus should be born in us, that we, as thy beloved children, may call thee Father.

Quicken us, O Lord, that we may receive these things and ponder them in our hearts. Amen.

Author Unknown

Prayers

46   O Christ of Bethlehem, let us not forget thee on thy birthday. In our busy preparations and our joyous festivities may we not crowd thee out of our thoughts as thou wast crowded out of the inn on that first Christmas long ago.

Forbid that we should spend all for transient pleasures and fail to find the deeper, richer joys that pass not away at eventide. Draw us back to thy manger cradle, rekindle our sense of wonder and worship, and grant that, finding thee in the likeness of a little child, we may feel a new reverence for childhood and a more earnest devotion to those qualities of heart which childhood incarnates. Forgive our cynicism and our pride, banish our doubts, and restore our faith in the things we cannot see or hear: the star that shines in the souls of men, and the song of peace that lingers on in a troubled world. Like the shepherds may we return to our humble tasks feeling that heaven is not so far away, and praising God that he is to be found not only in temples but also among the common things of life. Amen.

James Dalton Morrison

47   O God, our heavenly Father, who through Jesus Christ did teach us to pray: grant that this, our prayer, may be to thy glory, fervent in spirit and full of true wisdom for thy name's sake.

We pray to thee for peace on earth. We pray not because we have been men of goodwill, but because we have come at last in our bewilderment to long for thee that we might become men of goodwill. Forgive us if lightly we have read the Christmas story through the years and have heard the angel song through ears that have been dulled by the din of our discordant wills. Today we pray for little children, hungry and helpless and longing for life. We pray for those in every land who hide amid the ruins of their hopes and suffer from the cruelties of sin. We bow our heads in shame for any part that we have had in visiting thy lovely world with ghastly terror and with tears of human pain.

Today we pray for messengers of peace: boys and girls who claim the love of Christ; youths and maidens who approach thee with a faith that fain would grow; men and women sharing of their store to spread the message of the world's redemption. We thank thee for these faithful folk in every land, who name thy name yet do not fully recognize that they are truly builders for the glad new day of peace.

Grant us, we pray, the calm that comes when thou dost enter in. Grant us the faith that dares to risk its all on love. Grant us the will to make our own amid the blackness of the night the angel song of peace on earth. Strengthen the wise in every land to the end that love may be transmuted into deeds decisive for the ends of peace. May we live close enough to thee to know that only holy methods will produce thy heavenly ends; that love alone survives defeat and ushers in the resurrection morn.

O God, our heavenly Father, whose word is from everlasting to everlasting and whose promises cannot fail, unto thee do we come in this our prayer. And even as we come, the fevered frenzy of our earthly souls is turned to confidence anew; our hearts are calmed; our souls are comforted; and music from the heavenly hosts is heard above the tumult of our fears. By faith we sing again our gladsome song of brotherhood in thee. Amen.

Elmer A. Fridell

48 Our heavenly Father, who didst give an assurance of thy love by coming to us in Jesus Christ: accept our gratitude as we celebrate his birthday. Grant unto us grace of spirit to behold the glory of the Incarnation, even though our sinful eyes can see but dimly. Once again we join the wise men and the shepherds as we place our gifts and our devotion before the Bethlehem manger.

We pause, O God, to consider for a moment what our life would be without Jesus. And when we imagine the unchecked cruelty and lust, the spiritual barrenness, and the drab despair of lost men, we draw back from the abyss in fear and horror. Then there surges over us the faith in him which saves us, the hope in him which lifts up our hearts, and the love of him which is shed abroad in our land and in our homes. We know that we cannot live without him and our hearts overflow with our gratitude to thee for this most precious of all thy gifts to us.

Let this Christmas season be a renewing of the mind of Christ in our thinking, and a cleansing of our lives by his pure presence. Give us new courage to preach his word to this generation and help us bear witness to his saving grace before all our brethren. Let his joy come to our weary world through us.

And grant, O God our Father, the assurance that each day the Lord Jesus may be born again in us, and that every new morning may find us conscious that we live in him. We pray in the name of him who is our Redeemer and our Lord, even Jesus Christ. Amen.   *Gerald Kennedy*

49 O great and eternal Father, thou who hast revealed thy wondrous love in the holy Child of Bethlehem: our hearts are gladdened in the glorious presence of thine only-begotten Son. When the morning stars sang together and all the angels of heaven proclaimed the Saviour's birth, there came the everlasting song, in which we would humbly and earnestly join this hour, "Glory to God in the highest, and on earth peace, good will toward men." The good tidings of great joy find an echo in our hearts as we rejoice in the one who gives us light even amid darkness, and who guides our feet into the way of peace.

Like the shepherds of old, may we climb the holy hill of Bethlehem to behold thy Son, our blessed Lord. May his great love so fill our souls that we will go forth in his service, bringing to our fellowmen cheer and hope, understanding and affection. May we so reflect his spirit that we will be a blessing unto the sad and lonely, the wretched and forlorn.

We pray for the happiness and well-being of all thy children of every race and color, of every clime and coast. We beseech thee, O God, to bless those who are linked to us by the sweet bonds of family and friendship. Enable us by the witness of thy spirit to know that love will never lose its own, and thou dost keep thy children ever near to thee both in this world and in the world to come; through Jesus Christ, the holy Child of Bethlehem. Amen.

Paul Lambourne Higgins

Poems

50   *AND THE WORD WAS MADE FLESH*

Light looked down and beheld Darkness.
    "Thither will I go," said Light.
Peace looked down and beheld War.
    "Thither will I go," said Peace.
Love looked down and beheld Hatred.
    "Thither will I go," said Love.
So came Light and shone.
So came Peace and gave rest.
So came Love and brought Life.

Laurence Housman

51   *ETERNAL CHRISTMAS*

In the pure soul, although it sing or pray,
The Christ is born anew from day to day;
The life that knoweth him shall bide apart
And keep eternal Christmas in the heart.

Elizabeth Stuart Phelps

52   *FAR TRUMPETS BLOWING*

A king might miss the guiding star,
A wise man's foot might stumble;
For Bethlehem is very far
From all except the humble.

But he who gets to Bethlehem
Shall hear the oxen lowing;
And, if he humbly kneel with them,
May catch far trumpets blowing.

Louis F. Benson

53   *AH, PEACEFUL SHEPHERDS*

Ah, peaceful shepherds of the plains,
    You saw, and so you knew;
But, shepherds, we who have not seen
    Went down to Bethlehem too.
We did not take the road you trod,
But still we found him, Son of God.

Will Allen Dromgoole

54   *From BEFORE THE PALING OF THE STARS*

Born in a stable,
    Cradled in a manger,
In the world his hands had made,
    Born a stranger.

Christina G. Rossetti

55   *I SAW A STABLE*

I saw a stable, low and very bare—
A little child in the manger.
The oxen knew him, had him in care;
To men he was a stranger.
The safety of the world was lying there,
And the world's danger.

Mary Elizabeth Coleridge

56   *From CHRISTMAS*

The shepherds sing; and shall I silent be?
    My God, no hymne for thee?
My soul's a shepherd too; a flock it feeds
    Of thoughts, and words, and deeds.

The pasture is thy word; the streams thy grace
   Enriching all the place.
Shepherd and flock shall sing, and all my powers
   Out-sing the day-light houres.

George Herbert

57   *A CHRISTMAS CRADLE*

   Let my heart the cradle be
   Of thy bleak Nativity!
   Tossed by wintry tempests wild,
   If it rock thee, Holy Child.
   Then, as grows the outer din,
   Greater peace shall reign within.

John Banister Tabb

58   *CHILDHOOD*

   To be himself a star most bright
   To bring the wise men to his sight,
   To be himself a voice most sweet
   To call the shepherds to his feet,
   To be a child—it was his will,
   That folk like us might find him still.

John Erskine

59   *From A CHRISTMAS CAROL*

   What can I give him
   Poor as I am?
   If I were a shepherd,
   I would give him a lamb,
   If I were a wise man,
   I would do my part,—
   But what I can I give him,
   Give my heart.

Christina G. Rossetti

60 *GIFTS THAT ARE MINE*

Place these gifts on my altar this Christmas;
  Gifts that are mine, as the years are mine:
The quiet hopes that flood the earnest cargo of my dreams:
  The best of all good things for those I love,
  A fresh new trust for all whose faith is dim.
The love of life, God's precious gift in reach of all:
  Seeing in each day the seeds of the morrow,
  Finding in each struggle the strength of renewal,
  Seeking in each person the face of my brother.
I place these gifts on my altar this Christmas;
Gifts that are mine, as the years are mine.

Howard Thurman

61 *ALCHEMY*

The whole, wide world, turned selfless for a day,
Lays down its gift beneath the Christmas fir,
And, strangely, touched by memory of a star,
Each gift is gold and frankincense and myrrh.

Adelaide Love

62 *CHRISTMAS CANDLE*

Perhaps he walks your streets tonight,
The Child of Bethlehem,
Beneath the blazing lights which form
The city's diadem.
Perhaps he finds the inn is full
And seeks a lodging where
Your candle glows upon the sill
To bid him welcome there.

Leslie Savage Clark

63 *WHEN CHRISTMAS COMES*

Have you any old grudge you would like to pay,
Any wrong laid up from a bygone day?
Gather them now and lay them away
  When Christmas comes.

Hard thoughts are heavy to carry, my friend,
And life is short from beginning to end;
Be kind to yourself, leave nothing to mend
    When Christmas comes.

William Lytle

64   *DECEMBER 26*

Chants, incense, and the glory pass and die:
    The festive lights diminish; solemn prayer
Gives way to ribald song and pageantry,
    And market cries again confuse the square.

And he whose spirit held us for one day,
    Seeing love consumed again by doubt and fear,
Sorrowing, returns the long and thorny way
    Until we make him welcome through the year.

George Edward Hoffman

65   *THE FIRST CHRISTMAS*

Peter was a fisher boy helping with the haul;
Pilate was a shavetail leading troops in Gaul;
Judas was as innocent as little child can be;
The wood that made the crucifix was still a growing tree;
Unminted was the silver that made the traitor's pay;
And none had yet commercialized the spirit of the day.

Keith Preston

Topics, Texts and Themes

66   *THE JOY OF CHRISTMAS*

Behold, I bring you good tidings of great joy. LU. 2:10

    Christmas is a happy season. It has been so from the first observance when the
angel said, "Behold, I bring you good tidings of great joy." Ever since then we
have been singing at Christmas. Our overflowing hearts cannot be still. Our
exultation must find some expression. It often has been observed that atheism
and infidelity have no songs. There is nothing in them which stirs people so
deeply that music is produced. Part of the glory of our faith is that on the lips
of humanity has been formed a song.

What are the elements of this Christian Christmas joy? The laughter of a little child, the smile of a baby, are part of the joy we celebrate at Christmas. . . . The pleasure of giving was part of the joy of that first Christmas. . . . The joy of the future was part of the thrill of the first Christmas.

Robert W. Burns

67 *CHRISTMAS HASTE*

They came with haste, and found both Mary, and Joseph, and the babe lying in a manger. LU. 2:16

Modern life is fine in many of its aspects; it is diligent in its labors, honest in its investigations, courageous in its enterprises. But it lacks one thing needful. It is too reasoned, and not sufficiently spiced with the recklessness of men whose idealism is a controlling force that sends them to the Bethlehem manger with the racing feet of Christmas haste.

Charles H. Brent

68 *STAR OVER BETHLEHEM*

When they saw the star, they rejoiced with exceeding great joy. MAT. 2:10

There is a significant fact about the magi and the star. They had seen it in the east, and had come to Jerusalem to find the King whose birth it announced. But they made the journey without its light. Only when they came to Bethlehem did they see it again. No wonder they rejoiced. They were on the right road, and the promise of the star was about to be fulfilled. How many doubts they must have had on their long journey! How foolish it must have seemed to go so far on such an uncertain mission. But when the star appeared again, they knew that they were right at last. They would see the new-born King, and their gifts might bring the message of their hope and trust in him.

It is no wonder that the star over Bethlehem has been the symbol of rejoicing ever since. The world had hoped so long for release from its bondage. The night had seemed so dark, and the dawn so far away. To some, there was no hope. The Greeks looked backward to their golden age, and expected nothing better than the present. So many of us now sigh for vanished peace, and vainly strive to capture the mood of a day that is gone. But wise men now, as then, look for a star, and when they see it in the coming of a Saviour, they rejoice. The song of joy is the song of Christmas. Pain there is, and was, in plenty. Suffering and cruelty and injustice and misfortune are all about us. But when the star shines for us, when our hopes are confirmed in Christ, then no matter

how dark the path has been and no matter what dangers lie before us, we are
sure that God is with us and that he will never forsake his own.

Walter Dale Langtry

69   *A TIMELY BIRTH*

Now when Jesus was born . . . in the days of Herod the king. MAT. 2:1

A heart of love was born in the days of cruelty.

The good became incarnate in the days when evil walked the earth in the
rotting flesh of a tyrant. Josephus tells us that this reference to rotting flesh is
not a figure of speech.

A star shone in the sky when the earth was covered with darkness.

The light began to shine in the days of darkness and the darkness could not
put it out.

The consolation of Israel came in the days when the hearts of old men needed
comfort.

The grace of God came in the days when men were burdened by the law.

The wisdom of God came in the days when the wisdom of Greece had failed.

The inner rule of love in men's hearts came in the days when Rome wielded
an outer authority of force.

A true High Priest came in the days when the temple priests had sold their
office for gold.

A shepherd came in the days when the sheep were astray upon the mountain.

A physician came in the days when lepers cried "Unclean! Unclean!" beyond
the city walls.

A creative teacher came in the days when men knew only to repeat by rote
the joy and tittle of ancient parchments.

A Savior came when men were lost in sin.

A Redeemer came when men were afraid of death.

A God came when the gods were dead.

M. K. W. Heicher

70   *KEEPING CHRISTMAS*

He that regardeth the day, regardeth it unto the Lord. RO. 14:6

There is a better thing than the observance of Christmas day, and that is,
keeping Christmas.

Are you willing to forget what you have done for other people, and to remember what other people have done for you; to ignore what the world owes you,

and to think what you owe the world; to put your rights in the background, and your duties in the middle distance, and your chances to do a little more than your duty in the foreground; to see that your fellow-men are just as real as you are, and try to look behind their faces to their hearts, hungry for joy; to own that probably the only good reason for your existence is not what you are going to get out of life, but what you are going to give to life; to close your book of complaints against the management of the universe, and look around you for a place where you can sow a few seeds of happiness—are you willing to do these things even for a day? Then you can keep Christmas.

Are you willing to stoop down and consider the needs and the desires of little children; to remember the weakness and loneliness of people who are growing old; to stop asking how much your friends love you, and ask yourself whether you love them enough; to bear in mind the things that other people have to bear in their hearts; to try to understand what those who live in the same house with you really want, without waiting for them to tell you; to trim your lamp so that it will give more light and less smoke, and to carry it in front so that your shadow will fall behind you; to make a grave for your ugly thoughts, and a garden for your good thoughts, with the gate open—are you willing to do these things even for a day? Then you can keep Christmas.

Are you willing to believe that love is the strongest thing in the world—) stronger than hate, stronger than evil, stronger than death—and that the blessed life which began in Bethlehem nineteen hundred years ago is the image and brightness of the Eternal Love? Then you can keep Christmas.

And if you keep it for a day, why not always?

But you can never keep it alone.

Henry van Dyke

71 *THE CHRISTIAN CHRISTMAS*

The light of the glorious gospel of Christ, who is the image of God. . . .
For God, who commanded the light to shine out of darkness, hath shined
in our hearts, to give the light of the knowledge of the glory of God in the
face of Jesus Christ. 2 co. 4:4, 6

All the world keeps Christmas. The real problem of the Christmastide is that so many people keep the festival in the wrong way. We would never dream of writing the play of *Hamlet* with Hamlet left out, yet thousands keep Christmas with both syllables of the very word itself forgotten: the Christ in whose honor the day is fixed, and the service of the Christ-mass, or Holy Communion, in which he is remembered.

A goodly proportion in America commercialize the day. Alert men in business manage somehow to cast a glamour over their unromantic shops; clerks are "dead to the world" before the holiday time is over, even though we try to do our shopping early; mail-carriers stagger under a load of badly tied parcels and incongruous greeting cards.

Of course, there is something fine about it, even if it is done to help business. To have one day in the year with an out-flowing generosity as the expression of its spirit is something not to be sneered at or jested away. It does show human nature at its best, in its kindliest mood, and it is good to have Christmas kept, even if it is commercialized. . . .

All the world keeps Christmas; some commercialize it, some sentimentalize it; but "whether in pretense or in truth," we can rejoice that Christmas is kept. Only, I wish we could have a better Christmas. To me it is pathetic beyond words to have Christmas with the Christ left out. To busy oneself with planning Christmas gifts and mailing many Christmas cards, and yet to have so little faith in the reality of the Greatest Gift the world has ever received and so little understanding of the greatness of the day's message—that is, indeed, a matter of serious concern, even though we know that many are carrying to others much of the spirit of the Christ whom they seem to have forgotten.

Charles Fiske

72   *BETHLEHEM CONTRASTS*

Little wonder that Christmas has been largely confined in stories, poetry, pictures, and song. These are the popular methods of expressing the beautiful but unreal. Certainly there is much about the Christmas story that seems unreal because it conflicts with our normal manner of thinking and living. May not Christmas be God's way of reminding us over and over again as if he were saying to man: "Take care! We cannot both be right. Look once more at my way of appraising values. No, we cannot both be right. It is either you or I. Beware! Now choose again."

At most the first Christmas was the incarnation of God in a human life. At least it was the birth of the greatest personality in history. I choose the former definition, but in either event it was the most important thing that has ever happened. But how it happens! Such contrasts with man's traditional ways of thinking and judging! Indeed for me one of the marks of validity about the Christmas story is this very thing. It is so amazing in its simplicity and its utter differentness from anything man could have imagined that man could not have invented it.

Frank B. Fagerburg

73   THE DECISIVE BABIES OF THE WORLD

From our youth up we have heard about the decisive battles of history. But now Christmas comes again, engaging the thought and warming the heart of multitudes around the globe, and it concerns not a decisive battle but a decisive baby. "Unto us a child is born, unto us a son is given."

Even today, when all the world is obsessed with the fear and clash of arms, Christmas suggests how much more decisive a baby can be than a battle. When Jesus was born in Bethlehem, what were the decisive elements in the world's life? Surely, Tiberius upon his throne, the Roman Empire's vast extent and power, and Caesar's legions tramping every road—any realistic mind would have pointed to such potent factors as the determining elements in mankind's life. As for a baby, born of a lowly mother in obscure Bethlehem upon the far fringes of the Empire, it would have been madness then to have supposed that two millennia afterwards millions of us would be singing of that event,

> Yet in thy dark streets shineth
> The everlasting Light;
> The hopes and fears of all the years
> Are met in thee tonight.

That is the miracle of Christmas—that a baby can be so decisive.

Harry Emerson Fosdick

74   THE LUMINOUS CHRIST

The light of the knowledge of the glory of God in the face of Jesus Christ.
2 co. 4:6

The real Christmas experience for any one is the turning on of the light within, which comes from the spirit of the indwelling Christ. It is still his incoming that makes the difference between a darkened inn and a glorified stable. Before we go on with our Christmas preparation, let us ask ourselves whether the real Christmas has come to us; whether what we are going through is just a form, a bartering of gifts, a forced holiday, or whether we have the real experience that makes Christmas a joy and not a bore. Christ taken in and then given out, that makes it a genuine Christmas for us and for others; for "God shined in our hearts" that the light might be passed on. All about us are those who wait for our coming: lonely people, discouraged people, heart-sick people living starved lives, with so little of love and joy. Christmas opens our eyes and challenges us to let our light shine outside our own little circle and give cheer where it is needed most, to the cheerless, the lonely, the destitute.

Albert W. Beaven

75   *IF EVERY DAY WERE CHRISTMAS*

If the spirit of Christ were with us every day . . . some revolutionary events would occur:
Selfishness would die a death of starvation.
Avarice would be hung higher than Haman.
Foolish pride would go down in crushing defeat.
Senseless strife and silly bickerings would shame each other to death.
The prayer of Jesus for the unity of his followers would be answered.
Racial animosities would be drowned in a sea of brotherhood.
War, with all its horrors, its brutality, its devilishness, would be an utter impossibility.
"Peace on earth" would become a glorious reality.

Edgar DeWitt Jones

76   *EVERY DAY IS CHRISTMAS*

Christmas is not a day or a season, but a condition of heart and mind. If we love our neighbors as ourselves; if in our riches we are poor in spirit and in our poverty we are rich in grace; if our charity vaunteth not itself, but suffereth long and is kind; if when our brother asks for a loaf we give ourselves instead; if each day dawns in opportunity and sets in achievement, however small; then every day is Christ's day and Christmas is always near.

James Wallingford

77   *LOST IN THE CROWD*

The man who had been cured did not know who it was; for Jesus had gone out unnoticed, there being a crowd in the place. JN. 5:13 (Weymouth)

This is a parable for modern life, and we might call it the fate of true religion in the overcrowded life. It is especially relevant as we approach the Christmas holidays. Holiday comes from holy day, but there is precious little of the holy left in it. It is a time for shopping, for gaiety, for parties, for the interchange of trinkets, and in the haste and fatigue of celebrating Christmas the most forgotten man is the man Christ Jesus. He goes out of our lives unnoticed, there being a crowd in the place. But the Christmas season is only a striking example of a condition that prevails throughout the year.

Harold Elliott Nicely

78   *THE DAY AFTER CHRISTMAS*

When the angels went away. LU. 2:15 (RSV)

There is Christmas Eve; there is Christmas Day; and there is the day after
Christmas. . . . Where now the glad expectation of Christmas Eve, and the
strange joy of Christmas Morning? Christmas, when it is past, may seem as a
dream, a beautiful dream from which, alas, we must waken to the hard realities
of the world and life. We may well believe, however, that the spiritual letdown
of the day after Christmas is not inevitable. True, the pure exaltation of Christmas Eve cannot always be maintained, nor the sheer joy of Christmas Morning.
Perhaps it is not necessary, nor even desirable, that we should be always at a
high pitch of emotion. But the Christmas vision can be kept after Christmas
Day is past. . . .

The Christmas vision has to do with the final reality and power of the world.
Hunger, cold, desperation, and chaos, greed, cruelty, tyranny, and intrenched
injustice, these are among the realities of today's world. But they are not the
final reality. The final reality with which we have to deal is God—the God of
Jesus Christ. . . . The supreme reality with which we have to deal is the power
that keeps the stars in their courses and, taking the form of servants, stoops to
minister unto the children of men. This is what we see on Christmas Eve when
candles are lighted and carols sung and the world is strangely still and our
hearts are stilled and lifted up. And we somehow know on Christmas Eve that
what we see is not illusion but is eternal truth.

This vision of the love of God can be maintained on the day after Christmas
and every day after that. It can be maintained on the condition that we do not
neglect the heavenly vision but undertake to live by it. . . . What would it mean
to live by the vision which comes on Christmas Eve? It would mean to trust
God and not give way to worry and faithless fears. It would mean to act on the
faith that the supreme power in the universe is not military force but is the love
of God seeking good for all men everywhere. It would mean to practice love in
daily life, at home and in every human relationship.

Ernest Fremont Tittle

79   *A CHRISTMAS AFFIRMATION*

Christmas is the season of affirmation.
I affirm my faith in the little graces of life:
    The urgency of growth, the strength of laughter, the vitality of friendship.
I affirm my confidence in the dignity of man:

His fortitude in despair, his strength in weakness, his love in hatred.
I affirm my joy in the experience of living:

> The fragrance of nostalgia, the scattered moments of delight, the exhilaration of danger.

I affirm my need of my fellows:

> The offerings of faith, the gifts of variety, the quality of difference.

I affirm my hunger for God:

> The desire for fulfillment, the ache for understanding, the sense of peace.

Christmas is my season of affirmation.

Howard Thurman

C. LENT

Lent, a derivative of the Anglo-Saxon word *lencten* meaning spring, is a period of soul-refreshment. Since the fourth century this season has been devoted to Christian nurture through discipline and penitence. Lent begins on Ash Wednesday, the fortieth weekday before Easter, and concludes at noon on the Saturday of Holy Week. The forty days are variously identified with the forty days during which Jesus fasted in the wilderness, the forty days spent by Moses on Sinai, the forty hours of Christ's entombment, and the forty days between the resurrection and the ascension. Objections to what may become a mechanical or spiritually blind observance of certain physical disciplines ought not to lessen the possibility of making this period one of genuine spiritual restoration, commitment, and re-creation. The negative overtones of gloom and grief occasionally associated with Lent seem inconsistent with the joy and victory of the Easter message.

There are six Sundays in Lent. The fifth is designated as Passion Sunday and the sixth is Palm Sunday.

Lenten preaching and worship which are not centered in the life, teaching, and sacrificial death of Christ seem inappropriate. The significance of Lent is emphasized by special noonday services, prayer meetings on Ash Wednesday and subsequent weekdays, and study and training sessions.

Calls to Worship

(Boldface type indicates response.)

80   Seeing that we have a great high priest, that is passed into the heavens, Jesus the Son of God . . . let us therefore come boldly unto the throne of grace, that we may obtain mercy, and find grace to help in time of need.

He. 4:14, 16

81   O send out thy light and thy truth: let them lead me; let them bring me unto thy holy hill, and to thy tabernacles. Then will I go unto the altar of God, unto God my exceeding joy.

Hope in God: for I shall yet praise him, who is the health of my countenance, and my God.

Ps. 43:3-5

82   Jesus saith, I am the way, the truth, and the life: no man cometh unto the Father, but by me. As ye have therefore received Christ Jesus the Lord, so walk ye in him: rooted and built up in him, and stablished in the faith, as ye have been taught, abounding therein with thanksgiving.

Jn. 14:6; Col. 2:6–7

83   Man shall not live by bread alone, but by every word that proceedeth out of the mouth of God [Jesus saith]. If any man will come after me, let him deny himself, and take up his cross, and follow me.

Mat. 4:4; 16:24

84   [Jesus saith], Behold I stand at the door, and knock: if any man hear my voice, and open the door, I will come in to him, and will sup with him, and he with me.

Re. 3:20

Invocations

85   O thou living God, our Father, who art ever more ready to give than we to ask, thou to whom the things are possible that are impossible to us: grant us today, we beseech thee, a new vision of thyself, that seeing thee as thou art, in thy majesty, in thy holiness, in thy compassionate and understanding love, we may desire thee, and, desiring thee, may surrender to thee, and, surrendering to thee, body, soul and spirit, without reserve, may find our lives transformed by thy creative Spirit into the likeness of Jesus Christ. For thy name's sake we ask it. Amen.

William Adams Brown

86   Almighty God, who dost summon us to be born again and forever reborn into the world of the spirit: grant that through the indwelling of Christ in both our hearts and our minds we may be changed into his likeness. Amen.

Willard L. Sperry

87   Eternal God, we pray that thou wilt direct our minds to thy Son, Jesus Christ our Saviour. Help us to capture his vision of goodness, and truth, and love. Enable us to take that spirit of his into our daily round of affairs. Through him, may we live life in a new dimension; and through lives transformed by him, may this broken world find its way to truth and peace; in the Master's name. Amen.

Raymond J. Pontier

88   O God, whose blessed Son did suffer for all mankind: grant unto us that, rightly observing this holy season, we may learn to know thee better, to love thee more, and to serve thee with a more perfect will through the same Jesus Christ our Lord. Amen.

Book of English Collects

89   Almighty God, who hast shown us in the life and teaching of thy Son the true way of blessedness, thou hast also showed us in his suffering and death that the path of love may lead to the Cross, and the reward of faithfulness may be a crown of thorns. Give us grace to learn these hard lessons. May we take up our cross and follow Christ, in the strength of patience and the constancy of faith; and may we have such fellowship with him in his sorrow, that we may know the secret of his strength and peace, and see, even in our darkest hour of trial and anguish, the shining of the eternal light. Amen.

The Kingdom, the Power and the Glory

Litany

(Boldface type indicates responses.)

90   O God the Father, who didst create all things and made man in thine own image:

Have mercy upon us, for forgetting and neglecting the divine image within us.

From deadly sins of the soul; from pride and wrath; from envy and avarice; from gluttony, lust and sloth:

Good Lord, deliver us.

From lying and slander; from dishonesty and unfaithfulness; from cruelty and injustice; from harsh judgments and unwillingness to forgive:

Good Lord, deliver us.

From unconcern at the wrongs and evils of the world; from lack of sympathy with suffering, and from want of care for the souls of men; from all denial of brotherhood and withholding of love to others:

Good Lord, deliver us.

From selfishness and meanness; from treachery and contempt; from false ambitions and unholy desires; from cowardice and the fear of truth:

Good Lord, deliver us.

From impenitence, and rebellion against thy will; from indifference to spiritual things and disobedience to the heavenly vision; from quenching of the Spirit:

Good Lord, deliver us.

We beseech thee to grant us grace, O Lord, that we may grow in love, joy, and peace; in long suffering, kindness, and goodness; in faithfulness, meekness, and self-control:

Grant us thy grace, good Lord.

That we may deal justly, love mercy, and walk humbly with our God; that we may care for the fatherless and the widow, and keep ourselves unspotted from the world:

Grant us thy grace, good Lord.

That we may deny ourselves, take up our cross and follow thee; that we may witness a good confession, fight the good fight of faith, and lay hold of eternal life:

Grant us thy grace, good Lord.

Almighty God, who hast promised to hear the petitions of them that come to thee in true penitence, we beseech thee mercifully to incline thine ear to us that have now made our prayers and supplications unto thee; and grant, that those things which we have faithfully asked according to thy will, may effectually be obtained, to the relief of our necessity, and to the setting forth of thy glory; through Jesus Christ our Lord. Amen.

Book of Common Worship (CC)

Prayers

91   Our divine Redeemer and our Father, in humility we express our thanks for thy love, thy providence, and thy redemption given freely through the death and resurrection of thine only begotten Son, our Saviour and Lord.

In penitence we meditate upon the Cross and contemplate thy dynamic love offering to each salvation and redemption. Every word of Christ speaks a living message of hope and peace and pardon to our hearts. In praise and adoration we pray

> Were the whole realm of nature mine
> That were an offering far too small
> Love so amazing, so divine
> Demands my life, my soul, my all.

We present our bodies a living sacrifice, which is our reasonable service for all that thou hast wrought in our hearts and in the world.

Help us to make the meaning of the Cross a greater inspiration for deeper consecration and nobler living and fuller service. When we come to thee, under the shadow of the Cross, we pray that we may become "an hiding place from the wind, a covert from the tempest, rivers of water in a dry place and the shadow of a great rock in a weary land" to the people with whom we come in contact.

Blessed Holy Spirit, make this Lenten season a vital period of spiritual and moral development. May we know Christ and the power of his resurrection, the fellowship of his suffering, and may we become conformable to his death.

We pray that the hearts and minds of multitudes may in these weeks experience the blessing of true penitence, confession, restitution and the joy of salvation in Christ who came to give us life abundant. Through Jesus Christ we ask these things. Amen.

Gordon Palmer

92   O Christ the Life: awaken us; that we, confronted by the majesty of God, the nearness of thy Kingdom, and the power of thine immortality, may rise, ashamed, from dreams of self, and enter into life, and serve the sovereign Will.

O Christ the Light: shine in our minds; that shadowed places may entice us not, and that, secure in thine interior radiance, we may walk through darkness undefiled.

O Christ the Bright and Morning Star: grace the horizon of our world with promise of a new and holier day; that all the peoples of the earth may take fresh courage, and that the terrors of darkness may be put to flight.

O Christ the Bread: enhearten us; that, fainting not nor wearying, we may be strong to bear our neighbor's burden and swift to ease our brother's hurt.

O Christ the Truth: garrison our souls with wisdom for our earthly conflict; that no device or power of falsehood may prevail against us, and that, in all things, we may be more than conquerors.

O Christ the Way: make bold our feet; that we may follow whithersoever thou dost lead, until faith shall issue in certitude that underneath us is abiding rock.

O Christ the Door: open unto us; that we may see the Father's face, and know the joy of sins forgiven, and the health of wounds assuaged.

O Christ the Shepherd of the Sheep: be watchful lest we stray beyond thy voice, or wander from the strong protection of thy staff. Recall, admonish, chasten us, as seemeth to thee good. Provide us with all needful mercies, and carry the helpless in thine arms, until the eventide. Then do thou gather us together, safe and warm, within thy fold; who livest and reignest with the Father and the Holy Spirit, one God, world without end. Amen.

John Underwood Stephens

93   May the wisdom of God instruct me, the eye of God watch over me, the
ear of God hear me, the word of God give me sweet talk, the hand of God
defend me, the way of God guide me.

> Christ be with me.
> Christ before me.
> Christ after me.
> Christ in me.
> Christ under me.
> Christ over me.
> Christ on my right hand.
> Christ on my left hand.
> Christ on this side.
> Christ on that side.
> Christ at my back.
> Christ in the head of everyone to whom I speak.
> Christ in the mouth of every person who speaks to me.
> Christ in the eye of every person who looks upon me.
> Christ in the ear of everyone who hears me today. Amen.

St. Patrick

94   Eternal Spirit in whose light thou hast promised that we should see light:
we turn to thee in the courts of thy sanctuary. We who, through another week,
have viewed our lives in the shadows of this deceiving world would carry them
up into thy radiance. Thou hast lighted every man coming into the world. Deep
within our souls there is the flame which came from thee. Forgive us that often
we have let it die into embers and cinders, too seldom rekindled at thine altar.

O God, today help us to see our lives illumined by thee. Shine upon our sins.
Too easily we deceive ourselves concerning them and with vain excuses cover
them. Help us to see clearly what our tempers and selfishness, our cherished
grudges and vindictiveness, our mean ambitions and our smallness, signify to
other lives than ours. Set us against the white background of thy Cross that we
may be ashamed of the things that are shameful and may love the things that
are lovely.

Light up our joys, we beseech thee. Forgive us that often they fall into the
shadow and we forget. Illumine the beauties of our lives, our friendships and
families, the glory of great books, the stimulus of music, the heritage of a great
tradition bought by other sacrifice and other tears than ours. Shine upon us, we
beseech thee, and rekindle gratitude.

Light up our labor, we beseech thee. Forgive us that daily work becomes
drudgery and sinks from high dignity to trivial meaning. Open to us the doors

of insight that we may see how richly around us, in our daily, familiar, friendly contacts, lie the opportunities for usefulness.

Light up the world to which we go from here. Make plain to us the nobilities that are latent there. Help us never to forget the deep and silent heroism with which multitudes of ordinary folk live out their days. Save us from cynical disbelief in the possibilities of human nature. O Christ, who didst die for man because thou didst believe man worth dying for, illumine our world.

Shine, too, upon the ugliness of life. Help us not to deceive ourselves, for thou art not mocked. Send us out with an insight into the miseries which men suffer and the burdens which they bear, until we hate the things that dispossess thy children of their heritage and shut the doors of opportunity upon thy human family. O God, when wilt thou save the people? So illumine the world, we beseech thee, that we with a new faith and courage may go forth to help build thy Kingdom here. We ask it in the spirit of thy Son. Amen.

Harry Emerson Fosdick

95   O Rock of Ages, we who are storm-tossed and buffeted by the tempest of circumstances, come to thee for refuge.

O Sun Forever Shining, we who walk amid the shadows and the chill of time, come to thee for light and warmth.

O Great Physician, we who are sick with disappointment and wounded by adversity, come to thee for the healing of our wounds and the cure of our ills.

O Infinite Wisdom, we who are so beset by ignorance about matters great and small, come to thee to learn the way of righteousness and truth.

O Loving Heart, we who need compassion and understanding more than anything else, seek that fellowship with thee who alone can answer the hunger of our hearts.

O Infinite Patience, we who have so often sinned against thee, come once more asking for forgiveness.

O Limitless Strength, we who are so weak and inadequate, so often broken by our heavy burdens and snared by our temptations, come to thee for victory. Through Jesus Christ our Lord. Amen.

Albert E. Day

Poems

96   *From LENT*

It's true, we cannot reach Christs forti'th day;
Yet to go part of that religious way,

Is better then to rest:
We cannot reach our Saviours puritie;
Yet we are bid, *Be holy e'en as he.*
In both let's do our best.

Who goeth in the way which Christ hath gone,
Is much more sure to meet with him, than one
That travelleth by-wayes:
Perhaps my God, though he be farre before,
May turn, and take me by the hand, and more
May strengthen my decayes.

George Herbert

97   *TO KEEP A TRUE LENT*

Is this a Fast, to keep
The larder lean,
And clean
From fat of veals and sheep?

Is it to quit the dish
Of flesh, yet still
To fill
The platter high with fish?

Is it to fast an hour,
Or ragg'd to go,
Or show
A downcast look and sour?

No: 'tis a Fast to dole
Thy sheaf of wheat
And meat,
Unto the hungry soul.

It is to fast from strife,
From old debate
And hate;
To circumcise thy life.

To show a heart grief-rent;
  To starve thy sin,
    Not bin:
And that's to keep thy Lent.

Robert Herrick

98   *LENT*

To search our souls,
To meditate,
Will not suffice
For Lent.

To share the Cross,
To sacrifice,
These are the things
God meant.

Jane McKay Lanning

99   *I BIND UNTO MYSELF TODAY*

I bind unto myself today
  The power of God to hold and lead,
His eye to watch, his might to stay,
  His ear to hearken to my need;
The wisdom of my God to teach,
  His hand to guide, his shield to ward;
The word of God to give me speech,
  His heavenly host to be my guard.

Christ be with me, Christ within me,
  Christ behind me, Christ before me,
Christ beside me, Christ to win me,
  Christ to comfort and restore me,
Christ beneath me, Christ above me,
  Christ in quiet, Christ in danger,
Christ in hearts of all that love me,
  Christ in mouth of friend and stranger.

Walter Russell Bowie

100   *From CHRISTS VICTORIE IN HEAVEN*

He is a path, if any be misled,
He is a robe, if any naked bee,
If any chaunce to hunger, he is bread,
If any be a bondman, he is free,
If any be but weake, howe strong is hee?
To dead men life he is, to sicke men health,
To blind men sight, and to the needie wealth,
A pleasure without losse, a treasure without stealth.

Giles Fletcher

101   *I SAW GOD BARE HIS SOUL*

I saw God bare his soul one day
    Where all the earth might see
The stark and naked heart of him
    On lonely Calvary.

There was a crimson sky of blood
    And overhead a storm;
When lightning slit the clouds
    And light engulfed his form.

Beyond the storm a rainbow lent
    A light to every clod,
And on that cross mine eyes beheld
    The naked soul of God.

William L. Stidger

102   *MY MASTER'S FACE*

No pictured likeness of my Lord have I;
He carved no record of his ministry
    On wood or stone.
He left no sculptured tomb nor parchment dim,
But trusted for all memory of him
    Men's hearts alone.

Who sees the face but sees in part; who reads
The spirit which it hides, sees all; he needs
   No more. Thy grace—
Thy life in my life, Lord, give thou to me;
And then, in truth, I may forever see
   My Master's face!

William Hurd Hillyer

103   *From THE MAN, CHRIST*

He built no temple, yet the farthest sea
Can yield no shore that's barren of his place
   For bended knee.

He wrote no book, and yet his words and prayer
Are intimate on many myriad tongues
   And counsel everywhere.

He left no wealth, yet year by year there came
Accumulated beauty of the world
   To bear his name.

❉

What artless witness in this world—to be
Content to reckon every rising sun
   From his nativity!

Therese Lindsey

104   *MASTER OF THE MULTITUDE*

O Master of the multitude,
   Toilworn, dust-stained, and tanned,
The rich and poor, refined and rude,
   Of every time and land—
Come, walk with us and talk with us,
   And share our grief and woe;
O Master of the multitude,
   Teach us thy love to know.

O Master of the multitude,
   The millions wander still
Without a guide, without a light,
   Without an aim or will—
Come, walk with us and talk with us
   Among our people move;
O Master of the multitude,
   Redeem us by thy love.

Chauncey R. Piety

105   *EASTER MUST BE RECLAIMED*

Easter must be redeemed
From revelry that marks the end of Lent,
And worshippers who yearly are content
To journey to God's house, and then forget
That Christ still lives when Easter's sun has set.
The vision fades, the power soon is lost
If Easter does not lead to Pentecost.

Easter must be reclaimed.
Too long the world has missed the Easter glow,
Claimed by the glitter of a fashion show;
A dress parade; a gala holiday,
With church-bound manikins upon display.
The faith of Easter never will be caught
By making Christ a fleeting afterthought.

George W. Wiseman

Topics, Texts and Themes

106   *ASH WEDNESDAY*

Another Ash Wednesday opens for us today another Lent. If we have really
swept aside our ordinary occupations and thoughts in any real way, it is that
we may look in upon our own lives and souls, which our ordinary thoughts
and occupations hide from us at other times, and see them as they really are.
The abandonment of any thoughts or occupations is not something that is
good in itself, unless the things which we give up are intrinsically bad, and
then we ought to have nothing to do with them any time, in Lent or out of it.
It is the sight of ourselves which our simplified life in these weeks will give

us that makes them valuable. It ought to be as when the clouds over a landscape part, and one who has been standing above, seeing only the clouds which the hot ground had flung up from its bosom, sees suddenly the landscape through the clouds—fields, wood, and hills lying quietly down below. So it is when a man for a few moments or a few days breaks through the cloud of crowded businesses that hide his soul from his own eyes and really see himself.

Phillips Brooks

107   *THE MEANING OF LENT*

> Brethren, we are debtors, not to the flesh, to live after the flesh. For if ye live after the flesh, ye shall die: but if ye through the Spirit do mortify the deeds of the body, ye shall live. ro. 8:12–13

What do Christian people mean by their Lenten discipline, assuming that they are honest in entering upon it? It springs from a fact which any man can know, and which every "religious" man does know, to be true. That is that each man's inner and essential self is solicited in opposite directions by two rival attractions. They are the "flesh" and the "spirit." Of course, these words are not terms of scientific precision. But people know sufficiently well what they mean. The "flesh" is a comprehensive word for all those facts and forces which the senses take account of. The "spirit" may stand for those higher and deeper but less insistent facts and forces with which the soul deals directly. These two sides of life clamor constantly for the right to dominate the ego. But everybody knows that the solicitations of the flesh draw more powerfully than those of the spirit. Pleasure is pleasant right now; while goodness only promises to become pleasant by and by. The flesh pays cash; the spirit waits upon time. It is about impossible for many to believe that business or professional success, bringing with it leisure, luxury, power, and self-satisfaction, is not really the best thing possible for the ordinary man. It is a good thing; but it may come too high. Not a few men have paid for it all with their souls. They have no souls now. They have assassinated them because they disturbed their owners' peace. They "lived to the flesh" and have died. They still live, to be sure—that is, they have not yet learned that they are dead.

S. D. McConnell

108   *ON FASTING*

As I fasted and sat upon a certain mountain and was thanking the Lord for all the things he had wrought with me, I saw the shepherd sitting by me and saying, "Why art thou come hither thus early?" "Because, sir," quoth I, "I am keeping a station."

"What," quoth he, "is a station?" "I am fasting, sir," quoth I. "What fast," quoth he, "is this that ye fast?" "As I was wont, sir," quoth I, "thus I fast."

"Ye know not," quoth he, "how to fast unto the Lord, neither is this your unprofitable fasting unto him a fast." "Wherefore, sir," quoth I, "sayest thou this?" "I tell thee," quoth he, "this is not a fast which ye think ye fast; but I will teach thee what is a full fast and one acceptable unto the Lord. Hearken," quoth he, "God desireth not such vain fasting; for by fasting thus unto God thou shalt do nothing for righteousness. But fast thou such a fast as this unto God. Do no wickedness in thy life, and serve the Lord with a pure heart. Keep his precepts and walk in his ordinances, and let no evil lust arise in thy heart; but believe in God. If thou do these things and fear him, and contain thyself from every evil deed, thou shalt live unto God; and these things if thou do, thou shalt accomplish a great fast and one acceptable to God."

From *The Shepherd of Hermas*

109 *THE SHADOWED CHURCH OR THE RADIANT CHRIST*

These things have I spoken unto you, that my joy might remain in you, and that your joy might be full. JN. 15:11

Traditionally the church has gone into this period with the shadow of that ancient tragedy hanging heavily about it. It has put on the garments of grief, and the ashes of mourning as it has recalled how, with cruel ruthlessness, the world flung his young life away and trampled it down. The mood of Lent has, therefore, been the mood of mourning and of penitence; of mourning that one so loved and so altogether lovely should have moved so soon into the concealing shadows of a too sudden evening; of penitence because our race, which he came to bless with light and love and joy, so grievously misunderstood him and so cruelly cast him out. Over these weeks has fallen the long, dark shadow of the Cross. . . .

If we are to have a set period of penitence and of official grieving for this ghastly error and for our personal shortcomings, too, then this is probably as good a period as the church could find. But when we have confessed and admitted all this, and when we have given the traditional observance of Lent its full measure of praise, and have set about cleansing our own hearts of those things whereof we do by conscience stand accused, and when we have done it all with sincerity, there remains yet something more to be said. Lent is not to be surrendered entirely to gloom. Shadows did lie thick across this period. We need to remember, however, that those shadows were shot through and through with splendor!

Boynton Merrill

110   *FINDING JESUS*

We have found him. JN. 1:45

Finding Jesus is the greatest experience in life. Indeed, one never knows life at its highest and best until he feels the thrill of this wonderful discovery which Philip announced to Nathanael. Acquaintance with Jesus is not a mere acquisition to one's life, rather it is the very secret of life itself. "I came that they may have life, and may have it abundantly." "And this is life eternal, that they should know thee the only true God, and him whom thou didst send, even Jesus Christ." . . .

The glory of Jesus is not that he was a certain character in history nineteen hundred years ago but that he can enter into our loves today and demonstrate his power in our experience. The glorious fact is that our experience says "Amen" to the experience of the early disciples. What they found in him, we find. His radiant humanity sheds its light upon us. His sinlessness is our perfect ideal. He is God's prophet, our authoritative teacher. He is our high priest, our sin-offering; he bore our sins upon the tree. In our hearts we crown him king. He is our Lord and our God.

It is a longing, weary, waiting world to which Jesus came. Philip gave a startling message when he announced to Nathanael, "We have found him." Human nature and human needs have not radically changed. All about us are men who live in a restless, struggling, weary, sinning world. It is ours to gladden their hearts with the triumphant message which we can deliver from our own experience: "We have found him."

Walter Pope Binns

111   *THE CROSS CONFRONTS OUR EASY-GOING*
                         CHRISTIANITY

This sermon springs from the conviction that our popular Christianity is very easy-going. Indeed, the history of the church could be written in terms of the ingenious ways in which Christians have tried to make their Christianity easy. They have done it by ritual and sacrament, whose observance costs but little. They have done it by making consent to formal creeds the test of orthodoxy, whereas Calvary suggests another test of orthodoxy altogether: "If any man would come after me, let him deny himself, and take up his cross daily, and follow me." It is said of Lord Haldane that even though he did not know one note from another he used to go to Beethoven concerts all the same, out of deference to fashion. One knows well that in the churches, especially on Palm Sunday and Easter, that kind of procedure is reduplicated. Even when it is not so bad as that, who does not know the kindly, happy-go-lucky, complacent Christianity into which all of us are tempted to fall? It does not cost us much. We are very easy-going and whatever else the Cross stands for it does not stand for that.

Harry Emerson Fosdick

112   *THINKING IN TERMS OF THE CROSS*

Any one who does not take up his cross and follow where I lead is not worthy of me. MAT. 10:38 (Weymouth)

Thomas à Kempis tells us, getting very near the heart of things, that if you and I wish the Cross of Christ to come home and grow real to us, we also shall effect that best, not by arguing about its meaning, not even by long brooding on it in a hush of spirit, but by carrying it after him—we too. And how? Each of us must of course particularize that for himself. There are sins, our individual sins, that each of us must crucify in Jesus' strength; and sacrifices, our personal sacrifices, that each of us must make for Jesus' sake. But, for complete success, we need something less spasmodic and occasional, broader and more general, than that. The spirit of the Cross must, as it were, be soaked into the very stuff and fibre of our mind. It must become the standard by which we judge everything, the background before which our whole life is enacted, so that that solemn shadow falls across it all, and tells on every incident.

Arthur John Gossip

113   *TRANSLATING THE CROSS*

And it was written in Hebrew, and Greek, and Latin. JN. 19:20

Over the Cross of Jesus on Calvary there was written an inscription in three languages, Hebrew, Latin and Greek. For multitudes of people that inscription has never been translated into English. It is still Greek to them. The real meaning of the Cross is still locked up in a dead language.

Halford E. Luccock

114   *THE PERIL OF A CROSS-LESS LIFE*

He that findeth his life shall lose it: and he that loseth his life for my sake shall find it. MAT. 10:39

This is one of those startling paradoxes so often spoken by Jesus. In it he exposes the fallacy of much modern thinking which assumes that the Cross is an elective course in life's curriculum, and that we are now clever enough to eliminate what we do not like in life and choose only its cross-less experiences. . . . A life obsessed with saving itself from a cross will lose itself in nothingness. A life that will lose itself in the Master's cause may find a cross, but it will find also a rich and eternal significance in all that is done, and will realize the truth of what the beloved disciple meant when he said, "The world passeth away but he that doeth the will of God abideth forever."

Albert W. Beaven

115   *ONLY FOLLOW HIM*

Does he keep you from sin? Call him Saviour.
Does he free you from the slavery of your passions? Call him Redeemer.
Does he teach you as no one else has taught you? Call him Teacher.
Does he mold and master your life? Call him Master.
Does he shine upon the pathway that is dark for you? Call him Guide.
Does he reveal God to you? Call him the Son of God.
Does he reveal man? Call him the Son of Man.
Or in following him are your lips silent in your incapacity to depict him and his influence upon you? Call him by no name, but follow him.

Carl Hopkins Elmore

116   *THE HOLY SEPULCHRE*

The tomb of Jesus is evermore the symbol of the buried and discarded past. Into that sepulchre there went the superstitions and cruelties that marked the first experience of the race. There were left the crude and impossible conceptions of God and of religion. Out from that grave came the world's new light and joy. And through the ages it is ever the same. Each new generation brings to the grave of Jesus its unprofitable and discarded forms and dogmas, and waits expectant for the new and better faith to rise with him from the mystery of death. May this be no less true of our own lives. With him alone can we rise from our dead selves to higher things.

The Daily Altar

117   *WHY ARE WE HERE?*

Jesus knowing . . . that he was come from God, and went to God . . . took a towel, and girdeth himself. JN. 13:3–4

What a sequence it is!—such knowledge followed by such a ministry! With such knowledge what would you do? "Took a towel and girded himself and began to wash the disciples' feet." The next time you are inclined to ask what it's all about, just try supposing that it's all about *us,* and the tender mercy we can show to weary lives, dusty from the road, and with the stain of travel on them. It would be a high mission, would it not? Men who have served in it have had greatness thrust upon them. Do you suppose the day will ever come when the world shall find in that Spirit the solution of all its difficulties and the way out of all its anguish? It is so utterly clear, so simple a remedy for the troubled wrongs of living. Here we are in the midst of a life that is sick for love, where everything that's awry is awry because there isn't enough love; in an order where love is the only discoverable way of salvation, as God knows it's the only hope of our own. Well, what if that were the answer? Love willing to gird itself in the service of humanity; Love willing to stoop because it comes from a Throne to its task, and when the task is done goes to a Throne again; Love that can afford to be lowly because it's great; Love that a soul can grow by, and it doth not yet appear what it shall be? I say, what if that were the answer? And Christ were real? And Eternity itself nothing but an adventure with God in Love, which is the only thing that can make even Eternity worth while!

Paul Scherer

118   *IN A WORLD OF TANGENTS*

In whom all things hold together. COL. 1:17 (Moffatt)

St. Paul's conception of Christ as the one "in whom all things hold together" is a timely gospel for a world which is splitting apart. It is an arresting interpretation of the significance of Christ. The words "hold together" are a marginal reading, one of those searchlights set in the margin of the Bible which throw a flood of white light over a page. The reading, "In him all things consist," is more familiar, but the word "consist" has lost most of its picturesque, primary meaning. The large conception which Paul had of Christ strikes the imagination with greater force when more literally rendered, as by Moffatt, "In whom all things cohere," or "Through him the universe is a harmonious whole."

Halford E. Luccock

119   *TOO GREAT FOR OUR SMALL HEARTS*

He was too great for his disciples. And in view of what he plainly said, is it any wonder that all who were rich and prosperous felt a horror of strange things, a swimming of their world at his teaching? Perhaps the priests and the rulers and the rich men understood him better than his followers. He was dragging out all the little private reservations they had made from social service into the light of a universal religious life. He was like some terrible moral huntsman digging mankind out of the snug burrows in which they had lived hitherto. In the white blaze of this kingdom of his there was to be no property, no privilege, no pride and precedence; no motive indeed and no reward but love. Is it any wonder that men were dazzled and blinded and cried out against him? Even his disciples cried out when he would not spare them the light. Is it any wonder that the priests realized that between this man and themselves there was no choice but that he or priestcraft should perish? Is it any wonder that the Roman soldiers, confronted and amazed by something soaring over their comprehension and threatening all their disciplines, should take refuge in wild laughter, and crown him with thorns and robe him in purple and make a mock Caesar of him? For to take him seriously was to enter upon a strange and alarming life, to abandon habits, to control instincts and impulses, to essay an incredible happiness. . . .

Is it any wonder that to this day this Galilean is too much for our small hearts?

H. G. Wells

120   *THE WONDER OF JESUS*

The New Testament proclaims the wonder inspired by Jesus in the early Christians. And Jesus, after nineteen centuries, remains an object of wonder. There is something wonderful in the very fact that he has escaped oblivion. What chance, on any human reckoning, did he have to be remembered? A Jew, living in a small and remote province of the Roman Empire; an obscure Jew belonging to the peasant class; a man of whom the vast majority of his contemporaries never heard, and who moreover left no written record of anything that he had said or done or dreamed; a man rejected and repudiated by the leaders of his nation, and deserted at the last even by his disciples. Out of obscurity he came; and when, an object of hatred and derision, he was put to death on a gallows, it might well have been supposed that into oblivion he would go. But upon the contrary, the name of Jesus, in Emerson's phrase, is "not so much written as ploughed into the history of the world."

You cannot tell the story of music or letters or art, and leave Jesus out. No one else has made so marvelous a contribution to the cultural heritage of the race. And what of his influence in the realm of character? Once, in a discussion of the world's great religious leaders, a Chinese scholar, who himself was not a Christian, said concerning Jesus: "He seems to me to have the power to create a more sensitive conscience." Well, when it comes to that, all you need do is to trace to its source any unusual manifestation of human concern for the poor, the suffering, the downtrodden and oppressed. Whence the compassion that moves Father Damien to go to the leper colony on the island of Molokai and there remain as a devoted priest and friend until he dies? Whence the concern that drives Lord Shaftesbury to spend a lifetime in unwearied effort on behalf of exploited women and children in English mills and mines? Whence the magnanimity that leads Abraham Lincoln to say: "With malice toward none, with charity for all"?

Nineteen centuries after his birth we cannot forget that there once lived in this world a man of the name of Jesus. There is the Christian Church to remind us. There is the art of Michelangelo and the music of Bach. There is an "apostolic succession" that is truly apostolic—a succession of saintly lives down the ages, a magnificent tradition of unselfish devotion and service. There is a civilization influenced to some extent by Christian beliefs and principles. There is our own individual conscience, which to a far greater extent than we realize reflects the teaching and example of Jesus; and the conviction, now widely held, that the things which Jesus Christ stands for, these and these alone, are the things that make for peace.

The wonder expressed in the New Testament appears fully justified in view of the historical result of the coming of Jesus. And how will you account for so amazing a result, if not in terms of the Christian Faith that in Jesus of Nazareth the almighty and everlasting God entered into human life with saving power?

Ernest Fremont Tittle

121 *THE GREAT NAME IN HISTORY*

Jesus Christ is the great name in history. There are others for whom men have died; he alone is adored by all people, in all nations, and in all times.

He who bears this name is known throughout the world. Even among the savage and degenerate tribes of the human race, his apostles preach without ceasing that he died upon the Cross; and the off-scourings of mankind may be saved by loving him. Those who are neutral, in the modern world, recognize that none is better for the weak and miserable.

The greatest intellects of the past would be forgotten if memorials, as palaces, obelisks or tombs, if written testimonies, as papyrus or parchments, bricks, columns, or medals, had not preserved their memory. Jesus survives in the conscience of the faithful: there is his witness and indestructible monument. The church founded by him fills time and space with his name. She knows him, she loves him, she adores him.

Henri Didon

122   *SPOKEN TRUTHS AND SPIRIT INCARNATE*

[Jesus] originated no series of well-concerted plans; he neither contrived nor put in motion any extended machinery; he entered into no correspondence with parties in his own country and in other regions of the world, in order to spread his influence and obtain cooperation.

Even the few who were his constant companions, and were warmly attached to his person, were not, in his lifetime, imbued with his sentiments, and were not prepared to take up his work in his spirit after he was gone.

He constituted no society with its name, design, and laws all definitely fixed and formally established.

He had no time to construct and to organize—his life was too short—and almost all he did was to speak.

He spoke in familiar conversation with his friends, or at the wayside to passersby, or to those who chose to consult him, or to large assemblies as opportunity offered.

He left behind him a few spoken truths—not a line or word of writing—and a certain spirit incarnated in his principles and breathed out from his life; and then he died.

John Young

123   *KNOWING CHRIST*

Do you know Christ as a man knows his friend, or do you know him as you know about Julius Caesar? Do you know Christ because you live with him and he with you, or do you know about him in that fashion in which a man in a great city knows about his neighbor across the street, that has lived beside him for five and twenty years and never spoken to him once all that time? Is that your knowledge of Christ? If so, it is no knowledge at all. "I have heard of him by the hearing of the ear," describes all the acquaintance which a great many of my friends here have of him! Oh, my brother! the very fact that he has been so long with you is the reason why you know so little about him. People that live close to something, which men come from the ends of the earth to see, have often never seen it. A man may have lived all his life within the sound of Niagara, and perhaps never have gone to look at the rush of the waters. Is that what you do with Jesus Christ? Are you so accustomed to hear about him that you do not know him? Have you so long heard of him that you never come to see him? "Have I been so long with you, and yet hast thou not known me?"

Alexander Maclaren

124   *WHAT JESUS DOES FOR ME*

He comes to me as a Living Spirit today as well as a historic person who lived 1900 years ago. He gives me assurance that if I accept him as Saviour and Guide and follow him, I shall be saved from sin and wrong and helped to live as God would have me live. He gives me an ideal to live by—a pattern for life, and helps me as I try to live up to that ideal. He assures me of forgiveness when I fail and helps me to try again and do better. His teachings give me guidance and counsel, truth and ideals, in a world of doubt and fear, and in the midst of changing standards and ways of life. He is a living presence in my daily life—there is a spirit and purpose in me that would not be there but for him. He helps me in the choices of life to know right from wrong and to choose the best of the many good things life offers. He gives me courage and hope in the testing hours of life and in the face of the problems of my generation. He gives me the joy of introducing others to him and to the happiness of the Christian life. He calls me to work with him in his Kingdom and makes me dissatisfied with anything in the life about me that is not in accord with his principles and spirit. He introduces me to a fellowship that transcends all human barriers of race and creed, of space and time. He gives me in his church a place of worship and training, of fellowship and service. He shows me that, with all my shortcomings, I can be of use to him and to the world mission in which he calls his followers to serve. He helps me day by day to live in love and confidence and inner peace. He assures me of life eternal beyond the grave and calls me to live for eternity now.

Theodore F. Adams

125   *THE ADEQUATE CHRIST*

Lord, to whom shall we go? thou hast the words of eternal life. JN. 6:68

Adequate is the only word that properly describes Christ. There is no situation or condition to which he is not adequate. A simple blackboard equation would properly illustrate this truth. On one side of the sign of equality would be enumerated man's sins, weaknesses, needs, temptations, ambitions, disappointments, sorrows, burdens, failures and so on; on the other side would be the name of Christ. The equation would read: Christ equals all the needs that man can have.

John L. Hill

126   THE CHARACTER OF JESUS

The life and character of Jesus are the sufficient attestation of his profession when he says, "I am from above." Unfolding as a flower from the germ of perfect youth, growing up to enter into great scenes and have part in great trials, harmonious in all with himself, he is a Lamb of innocence, a God in dignity. He advances the most extravagant pretensions without show of conceit or fault of modesty. He suffers, giving an example of gentleness and patience. He undertakes a plan, universal in extent, perpetual in time, to unite all nations in a kingdom of righteousness, laying his foundations in the hearts of the poor, as no teacher had ever done before. In his teaching he is perfectly original, distinct from his age and from all ages; never warped by the expectation of his friends; always in a balance of truth, running to no extremes, clear of superstition, and equally of liberalism; presenting high doctrines in low and simple forms, establishing a pure, universal morality, never before established; with intense devotion to truth, never anxious, perceptibly, for the success of his doctrine; finally, he grows more great, and wise, and sacred, the more he is known. This is Jesus, the Christ.

Horace Bushnell

D. PALM SUNDAY

Palm Sunday commemorates the triumphal entry of Jesus into Jerusalem when, according to Jn. 12:13, the common people showed their welcome by holding aloft leaves of the regal Palestinian palm tree. The use of palm leaves on the anniversary of this occasion dates back to an early period in the history of the Jerusalem church and continues to be an appropriate symbol for the day which marks Christ's popular though temporary triumph and anticipates by a week the day of Christ's everlasting victory.

Calls to Worship

(Boldface type indicates responses.)

127   Open to me the gates of righteousness: I will go into them, and I will praise the Lord.

This is the day which the Lord hath made; we will rejoice and be glad in it.

Blessed be he that cometh in the name of the Lord: we have blessed you out of the house of the Lord.

O give thanks unto the Lord: for he is good: for his mercy endureth for ever.   *Ps. 118:19, 24, 26, 29*

128   Rejoice greatly, O daughter of Zion; shout, O daughter of Jerusalem: behold, thy King cometh unto thee: he is just, and having salvation; lowly, and riding on an ass. Now is the Son of man glorified, and God is glorified in him.

Zch. 9:9; Jn. 13:31

129   God hath highly exalted him, and given him a name which is above every name: that at the name of Jesus every knee should bow, of things in heaven, and things in earth, and things under the earth; and that every tongue should confess that Jesus Christ is Lord, to the glory of God the Father.

Ph. 2:9–11

130   *INVOCATIONS*

As on this day we keep the special memory of our Redeemer's entry into the city, so grant, O Lord, that now and ever he may triumph in our hearts. Let the King of grace and glory enter in, and let us lay ourselves and all we are in full and joyful homage before him; through the same Jesus Christ our Lord. Amen.

Handley C. G. Moule

131   O God, whose dearly beloved Son was greeted by the crowd on Olivet with halleluiahs, but who in that same week was mocked as he went lonely to the Cross: forbid that our welcome to him should be in words alone. Help us, we beseech thee, to keep the road open for him into our hearts; and let him find there not another crucifixion, but love and loyalty in which his Kingdom may be established evermore. Amen.

Walter Russell Bowie

132   Almighty and everlasting God, who, of thy tender love towards mankind, hast sent thy Son, our Saviour Jesus Christ, to take upon him our flesh, and to suffer death upon the Cross, that all mankind should follow the example of his great humility: mercifully grant, that we may both follow the example of his patience, and also be made partakers of his resurrection; through the same Jesus Christ our Lord. Amen.*

Book of Common Prayer (1549)

133   Our Father, we have taken our place among the glad multitude who hail the King of kings. Stir us, and our complacent city and land anew, because of his coming. Give us grace to cut from life the vital branches of sacrifice; and may our garments of plentiful things be cast upon the highway of his coming. Grant us depth of faith, honesty of purpose to raise ever new standards of welcome to Christ our Lord. Amen.

Herman Paul Guhsé

Litany

(Boldface type indicates responses.)

134   Rejoice greatly, O daughter of Zion, behold thy king cometh unto thee:
Blessed is he that cometh in the name of the Lord.
    In his days shall the righteous flourish; and abundance of peace so long as the moon endureth:
Hosanna to the son of David.
    He shall have dominion, also from sea to sea, and from the river unto the ends of the earth:
Blessed is he that cometh in the name of the Lord.

The voice of rejoicing and salvation is in the tabernacles of the righteous:
Hosanna to the son of David.

God has highly exalted him, and given him a name which is above every name:
Blessed is he that cometh in the name of the Lord.

Behold my servant, whom I uphold; mine elect, in whom my soul delighteth; I have put my spirit on him:
Enter into his gates with thanksgiving, and into his courts with praise.

Prayers

135   O God of Love, whose most gracious Son rode into a city which hailed him and then rejected him, we look to thee, a company of men and women who would give themselves to be his followers. We give thee thanks that his spirit is forever seeking entrance into our world's life—coming as the impulse to sympathy between man and man, as the will to brotherhood eager to banish all suspicion and hatred, as the self-giving spirit which bears the burdens of others even to a Cross. Give us responsive spirits, that as he meets us in the life of our time, we may know him for the revelation of thy truth, and receive him as our Lord and King. Forbid that we should hail him as Master when all men speak well of him, and then deny him in the lonely hour of his rejection. Increase our faith in him as thine own Word to us, that we may deny ourselves and take up what cross thou givest us, and follow him.

Father of mankind, who bearest on thine own heart the sufferings and the sins of thy sons and daughters, we beseech thee to pardon us that we so often close the gates against the entrance of his spirit. Forgive us for the love of self, which will not suffer him to lead us to a larger life. Deliver us from the rivalries and ambitions which hold him from his rightful leadership of the nations. Free us from the deluded pride which forbids his spirit to create friendliness among the races. Pardon us for our unwillingness to let him fill industry and commerce with friendliness and common service. As our world this day echoes with the ancient story of the meek King who came into his own, grant that we may break down every barrier which we have built against his entrance, and say from our hearts, Blessed be he that cometh in the name of the Lord.

Most compassionate Father, who longest to lead all thy children out of darkness into thy marvellous light, send the spirit of thy Son this day to all who sit in darkness within the walled cities of their own sorrows or perplexities. May they hear the song of rejoicing of those who have found him their Saviour and

Helper, and fling wide the gates of their spirits that he may bring them peace. Amen.

Morgan Phelps Noyes

136   Ride on, thou mighty Lord of love, Leader of all the powers of goodness against the brute forces of evil; Captain of an unarmed army of peace, marching amid the shout of peasant hosts and the song of little children. Caesar has fallen into dust and his glittering armor rusts; but thou, O Christ, makest thy triumphal entry into every age, holding in thy broken hand a palm of peace.

Ride on in majesty, O gentle divine Invader; enter our cities, take captive our homes, and purify our hard hearts; cleanse thy temple of all ugliness and unreality; drive out those who traffic in human souls. Reign thou, O merciful Master, till all injustice, all uncleanness, all unkindness is defeated; until every evil that defiles the life of man is dethroned and destroyed.

Ride on, thou invincible and inevitable Christ, ever-living and all-loving, Revealer of life and Conqueror of death; take command of thy world to the confounding of all tyrannies that oppress and all terrors that affright; order our life by thy law of love; make ready the earth for the City of God; lift the agonies of man into an anthem of praise to the glory of God, the Father. Amen.

Joseph Fort Newton

137   Almighty God, our heavenly Father, we recall the precious memory of our Saviour's triumphal entry into Jerusalem. When we think of his life among men, we marvel in our hearts, and thank thee. When we ponder how he came into the holy city as a messiah to save his people, we rejoice in thy great goodness, and cry out, Blessed be the King that cometh in the name of the Lord! But when we remember the high calling that is ours and how we have failed to serve thee and thy Kingdom, we are filled with remorse and implore thy mercy and forgiveness.

We beseech thee, O God, that the living Christ might enter and possess our souls today. May the evil in our lives be overcome by his goodness, and may every dark thought be cast out of us. May we reflect his spirit in all our ways, becoming instruments of peace and envoys of reconciliation. We ask that thou wilt quicken men's hearts everywhere with a zeal for truth and good will, hastening the consummation of that great day when brotherhood will be a reality and love the only law.

Grant us the courage to stand for the right, the grace to live nobly and well, and the wisdom to seek first thy Kingdom. We pray that we may so experience and know the eternal Christ in our souls that we will live unafraid, fulfilling

the calling that is ours in this life and rejoicing in the life to come. Unto thee
be all the glory, O holy Father, holy Son, and holy Ghost. Amen.

Paul Lambourne Higgins

Poems

138   *LIFT UP YOUR HEADS*

Lift up your heads, ye mighty gates!
Behold the King in glory waits,
The Prince of Peace is drawing near,
The hope of longing hearts is here;
The end of all our woe he brings,
Wherefore the earth is glad and sings.

Fling wide the portals of your heart!
Make it a temple, set apart
From earthly use for heaven's employ,
Adorned with prayer and love and joy;
So shall your Sovereign enter in,
And new and nobler life begin.

George Weissel
Tr. by Catherine Winkworth

139   *FLING WIDE THE GATES*

Love Divine, love lowly-hearted,
Our city's gates stand widely open to thy welcome.
Without thee the people are uncrowned,
Tumult and rebellion break forth,
Truth is perished in the street,
And justice fallen at our gates.
Come and establish thy Kingdom in our midst,
Sending peace on the earth,
Peace in the hearts of men.
Apart from thee all temples stand desolate,
Unblessed by sacrifice,
Unsanctioned by altar fires,
Unhallowed by thankful song.

Hear us as we cry:
Hosanna in the highest;
Blessed is he that cometh in the name of the Lord.

Author Unknown

140   *From THE SONG OF THE PSALMS*

He is coming! He is coming!
We hear triumphal shoutings from the eager marching throng;
We catch the thrilling music of the children's lifted song;
The very stones are throbbing to break into acclaim,
And all the hills exultant to reecho back His name.
Break all our fronded branches and strew them in His way,
Our strength and all our beauty belong to Him to-day!

John T. McFarland

141   *CONSENT*

"Hosanna in the highest!
Hail the King!"
The people cried.
"Thou art the Son of God!"
They spread a festal way with palms,
"And we are in thy train!"

"Crucify!" the people cried,
"This fool, the king
Of all the Jews!
If thou art king, come down!"
He died on Calvary with the thieves.
"Come, save thyself, come down."

Thy mercy, Lord, forgive;
I scattered palm,
I wove the thorns
Consenting to the Cross.

Nathaniel B. Dexter

142   *HE—THEY—WE*

They hailed him King as he passed by,
They strewed their garments in the road,
But they were set on earthly things,
And he on God.

They sang his praise for that he did,
But gave his message little thought;
They could not see that their souls' good
Was all he sought.

They could not understand why he,
With powers so vast at his command,
Should hesitate to claim their rights
And free the land.

Their own concerns and this world's hopes
Shut out the wonder of his news;
And we, with larger knowledge, still
His Way refuse.

He walks among us still, unseen,
And still points out the only way,
But we still follow other gods
And him betray.   *John Oxenham*

143   *AYE, DOWN THE YEARS*

Aye, down the years, behold, he rides,
    The lowly Christ, upon an ass;
But conquering. Ten shall heed the call,
    While a thousand idly watch him pass.

They watch him pass, or lightly hold
    In mock lip-loyalty his name:
A thousand—were they his to lead!
    As meek, without a sword, he came.
                                    Allan Knight Chalmers

144   *PALM SUNDAY AND MONDAY*

They pluck their palm branches and hail Him as King,
    Early on Sunday;
They spread out their garments; hosannas they sing,
    Early on Sunday.

But where is the noise of their hurrying feet,
    The crown they would offer, the sceptre, the seat?
Their King wanders hungry, forgot in the street,
    Early on Monday.

                              Edwin McNeill Poteat

Topics, Texts and Themes

145   *A LOOK OF EXPECTANCY*

And the Lord turned, and looked upon Peter. LU. 22:61

Palm Sunday commemorates Christ's entry into Jerusalem. To ask what there is noteworthy about that action is to confess ignorance of the circumstances in which the significance of the action is concealed. To enter Jerusalem as the avowed Messiah of the nation might have been a safe thing for some to do, but for him it was fatal, as he very well knew. He would be called an impostor and put to death. But there is something more in the action than courage to run that risk. To know that God meant him to be the Messiah, to know that he would be despised and rejected by the rulers of the nation, and still to journey steadfastly to Jerusalem, with its waiting trial and rejection and death, is to set a standard of fidelity before all his followers for all the years to come. Christ has looked at us many times during the year, and in many ways; sometimes with affection; sometimes with reproach; sometimes with compassion; sometimes—more often than we think—with amusement. Beginning on Palm Sunday he looks at us with expectation. We may wince and turn away, change the subject, put him out of our minds. It is of no avail. The look never changes. It is fixed and patient. It seems to hover between hope and disappointment. It is haunting, almost unbearable. Every new Palm Sunday renews it, and will renew it, until we answer it by our fidelity to the Voice that speaks in our hearts.

                              Charles E. Park

146   *THE ASCENDING WAY*

He went before, ascending up to Jerusalem. LU. 19:28

It is uphill all the way from Jericho to Jerusalem; a weary road for sandled feet—with a Cross at the top. That was the seen ascent. The unseen ascent was in the clear vision of consequence and the complete consecration to his Father's will with which Jesus went to his passion.

The great ways of life are always ascending ways. Duty is an ascent from aimless irresponsibility; knowledge an ascent from ignorance; goodness an ascent from evil deeds and imaginations; love an ascent from self and selfishness. Faith is an ascent from the seen to the unseen. The spiritual is always on the higher-up side of life.

Gaius Glenn Atkins

147   *THE MEEK KING*

Behold, a sower went forth to sow. MAT. 13:3.

Jesus of Nazareth began his ministry by the Sea of Galilee, a small inland body of water set in the midst of the fertile crescent between Africa the unknown, Asia the inscrutable, and Europe, the womb of western civilization!

Jesus of Nazareth gathered to himself disciples, untutored fishermen, laborers and tax-gatherers.

Jesus of Nazareth resisted the temptation to be diverted from his self-imposed task of purifying the religious and moral life of his people.

Jesus of Nazareth preached and practiced a gospel of a friendly universe, a companion God, a universal helpfulness that counted all men as sons of God whose obligation it became to observe the spirit of God's moral law, that in the fullness of time that spirit should become the ruling spirit on earth as it is in heaven.

Behold now his triumphant entry into Jerusalem, where the populace misunderstanding his mission to be the leader of a revolt against the Roman occupation, hailed him with shouts of "Hosanna!" and the strewing of palm branches in his path, a symbol of victory and devotion to the victor.

Behold Jesus of Nazareth crucified upon a Cross between two thieves, a symbol of degrading rejection and failure.

Behold a sower! . . . and the fruits of his sowing.

In Christian tradition there are few more cherished memories than that of the triumphal entry into Jerusalem. Many Christian churches celebrate Palm Sunday with a pomp and circumstance second only to their celebration of Easter. For, to many Christians, Christ the King entering into the city while the multitude shouted their hosannas, waving palm branches and strewing flowers in his path, is a much more congenial picture than Jesus the meek, walking the dusty roads of Galilee from humble village to humble village, preaching his Gospel.

Richard M. Steiner

148   *KING FOR A DAY*

Tell ye the daughter of Sion, Behold, thy King cometh unto thee, meek, and sitting upon an ass, and a colt the foal of an ass. MAT. 21:5

King for a day! That is the tragedy of the triumphal entry, but it need not be. He still rides through the world conquering and to conquer. He can come into our hearts and into our homes, and into our national and international life and when he comes, he will satisfy all our dreams and hopes, causing us to consecrate to him all that we are and have and setting our lives to the music that is the gladness of the world.

Hugh Thomson Kerr

149   *HE RODE IN TRIUMPH*

And Jesus entered into Jerusalem. MK. 11:11

In the days of ancient Rome the highest military honor that could be obtained by a general was the triumph by which he celebrated the victory he had won and the power he had achieved over his enemies. He entered the city in a chariot drawn by four horses, preceded by his captives and spoils and followed by his army. With this escort he passed through the streets leading to the Capitol, where he sacrificed a beast to the god of victory.

The pathos of Jesus' triumphal ride into the city of Jerusalem lies in its one vivid contrast to the Roman scene. There were many contrasts, it is true: Jesus was celebrating no victory past, but a victory to come; he was preceded by no slaves or spoils, followed by no army; he rode not on a horse-drawn chariot, but on the humblest burden-bearing animal of the farm. But the one overwhelming tragic contrast was that whereas the Roman general knew he was entering a career of high privileges, the Jewish carpenter knew he was riding to his death. . . . It was no dumb beast that was to be sacrificed. Jesus knew that the death that was in store was for himself and no other. Here was a new way to face an evil day—to ride in truimph toward it!

Douglas Horton

150   *THE PALMS AND THE CROSS*

On Palm Sunday one is given the picture of a man riding into a great city, hailed by the multitudes. There, bobbing along on the surface of a sea of faces, is the man himself, who is terribly alone and knows he is alone. The multitudes are happy and excited, eager in an exultant and hysterical anticipation. He has no illusions since he knows indisputably that tragedy is coming. He can see that these cheering throngs will turn against him to cry for his death just as intensely as now they hail his leadership. He knows that his intimates will lose their courage and play the coward. So the picture is one of utter tragedy. In a sense it is more bitter than that which will surround his death. Here they are hailing him; then they will sullenly condemn him. Here they are excited with false anticipation; then they will be bitter as they watch a man go down to defeat. Here they are roused in their passion; then they will be still, as the flame of their emotion has died low.

There is, therefore, a remarkable contrast between the symbols of the Palms and the Cross. . . . Yet what is even more amazing is that, when the new religion creeps from the catacombs to take possession of the world, its symbol is not the Palms but the Cross. . . . For the paradoxical fact is that, when men do look at life bravely and unafraid, they understand how much sorrow and defeat there is in it, and therefore any religion with power must enable them to face life as it is.

John C. Schroeder

151   *THE CHRIST IN OUR CITY TODAY*

When he was come near, he beheld the city, and wept over it. LU. 19:41

Twice our Saviour is said to have wept. Once he shed tears of sorrow over the tomb of a friend whom he loved as a brother. Again our Lord wept tears of shame over a city that he loved more than any other place on earth. Such was the bleak background of the first Palm Sunday. Today it has to do with the coming of King Jesus into our city. If we could stand near the Dome of the Rock in old Jerusalem we might almost see Christ and his little band as they wend their way down from the Mount of Olives. Even from afar we may now behold him as he weeps over the city that should receive him as Saviour and Lord.

Let us, therefore, think about the welcome to Christ in our own city. At other times throughout these days before Easter, every one should listen for the knocking of his dear hand, since the Lord Christ waits to pass through the portals of the hearts where he longs to rule. Likewise should we all acclaim him as King of our nation, as well as of our world, for he alone can reign as Prince of Peace. At present we should look up to him as the Ideal Ruler of our city. From this point of view let us inquire whether or not our spirit resembles that of Jerusalem on the first Palm Sunday.

Andrew W. Blackwood

152   *HIS JERUSALEM AND OURS*

And it came to pass, when the time was come that he should be received up, he stedfastly set his face to go to Jerusalem. LU. 9:51

Life holds for us all the Jerusalem road, over which our unwilling feet must go. We cannot hope to match the heroic, selfless, dauntless spirit with which Jesus took that road. But we can, if we will, approximate it.

A disciple is not above his Master; but he can, if he so purposes, follow where the Master leads.

We cannot hope to escape the Jerusalems of life, nor should we deceive ourselves in the conceit that we can evade or escape the long, hard road without betraying the finer instincts of our souls.

Edgar DeWitt Jones

153   *A DISTURBER OF THE PEACE*

I wonder how many good orthodox Christians, when they wave palms on Palm Sunday, know what sort of a man it is whom they celebrate. I wonder if they realize that he was a disturber of the peace whom they laud and exalt. I wonder how many of them go from the celebration to be like their master, disturbers of the peace. Always the routine needs to be upset. Always the conventions of action, morals, thought, need to be exposed. Always the establishments of today need to be condemned in the interests of the judgment and the new world. I can think of a few departments of our present life that are in such need, and you can think of many more. Hosanna, to the disturbers of the peace in the church! Hosanna, to the disturbers in the field of education! Hosanna, to the disturbers of our political peace! . . .

Life tends to stagnate for the awakeners, and everyone who truly prays "Thy kingdom come" pledges himself to the company of the awakeners. Discipleship is a claim often lightly made, but it is difficult to understand how anyone can profess and call himself a follower of the prophet of Nazareth who is not very much alive. To wave the palm implies a vision of the world "nearer to the heart's desire," a faith that it shall be, and a readiness to pay the price of being a disturber of the peace.   *John Howland Lathrop*

E. MAUNDY THURSDAY

Maundy Thursday offers an opportunity for the celebration of the Lord's Supper at an hour when, perhaps, the associations are most fraught with meaning and responsive feeling. The name by which the day is identified is a corruption of the Latin word *mandatum,* meaning mandate, and refers to Christ's new commandment "that ye love one another" found in Jn. 13:34. The washing of feet, not now generally practiced, does, however, suggest the humility and service which the spirit of the day typifies. On this day many pastors offer communion in the homes of shut-in members. Most of the materials included in this section are appropriate for the observance of the Lord's Supper at other times in the church year.

Calls to Worship

(Boldface type indicates responses.)

154   I am the living bread which came down from heaven [saith Jesus]: if any man eat of this bread, he shall live for ever: and the bread that I will give is my flesh, which I will give for the life of the world.

Jn. 6:5

155   What shall I render unto the Lord for all his benefits toward me? **I will take the cup of salvation, and call upon the name of the Lord.** Christ our passover is sacrificed for us: therefore let us keep the feast. **O taste and see that the Lord is good: blessed is the man that trusteth in him.**

Ps. 116:12–13; 1 Co. 5:7–8; Ps. 34:8

156   With desire I have desired to eat this passover with you before I suffer [saith Jesus]: for I say unto you, I will not any more eat thereof, until it be fulfilled in the kingdom of God.

Lu. 22:15–16

157   The Spirit and the bride say, Come. And let him that heareth say, Come. And let him that is athirst come. And whosoever will, let him take the water of life freely.

Re. 22:17

Invocations

158   O God, who canst guide our feet into the sanctuary of thy presence: make ready, we beseech thee, our hearts to receive the sacrament of that love whereby thy Son hath redeemed us; through the same Jesus Christ our Lord. Amen.

John Wallace Suter

159   O Lord Jesus Christ, who gatheredst thy disciples about a table, and there didst open unto them the mystery of thy kingdom and lordship: constrain us, who are met to feast with thee; that we may heed such revelation of thyself as thou art bending to bestow, and may, with eager hearts, attend thy full commandments; through thy mercy, who livest and reignest with the Father and the Holy Spirit, even one God, world without end. Amen.

John Underwood Stephens

160   O God, who by the example of thy Son our Saviour Jesus Christ hast taught us the greatness of true humility, and dost call us to watch with him in his passion: give us grace to serve one another in all lowliness, and to enter into the fellowship in his sufferings; who liveth and reigneth with thee and the Holy Ghost, one God, world without end. Amen.

Divine Service

161   Our Father, who hast called us into the fellowship of thy Son: draw us closer to thee in this hour of meditation and communion. May our hearts be open to every holy affection and our minds ready to receive and cherish every sacred truth and serious impression. Enlarge our vision, deepen our loyalty, increase our faith, and enrich us anew with thine own divine love. We pray in Jesus' name. Amen.

Herman Paul Guhsé

Litany

(Boldface type indicates responses.)

162   Lord, if we have forgotten thee in the distractions of the workaday world and lost the sense of thy presence in the crowded hours of our days:
May we remember thee, O Lord.
If we have forsaken thine altars and turned our hearts from worship and our lips from praise:
May we remember thee, O Lord.

If we have withheld more than is meet and kept for ourselves what we should have given away:

May we remember thee, O Lord.

If thy service has made demands upon us which we have been slow to grant and the tasks of thy Kingdom have found us reluctant to assume them:

May we remember thee, O Lord.

If we have looked only upon our own things and not upon the things of others and so shortened our vision that we could not see the white fields of the world ready to harvest:

May we remember thee, O Lord.

O Lord, as we sit together in the gracious fellowship of this communion hour, with hearts that are one in aspiration and in hope, help us to recall that thou hast said:

This do in remembrance of me.

As we search our hearts, that we may worthily partake of these emblems of the eternal Love, hallowed by the devotion of the ages, may we with one accord accept the Master's commandment:

This do in remembrance of me. Amen.

Author Unknown

Prayers

163   Eternal God, who didst send thy Son to be our Saviour and our Friend: help us now to enter into deep and holy fellowship with him. Bring to remembrance all that we owe to him, and help us to treasure every gift from his hand. As we commemorate his last supper with his disciples, may we strive to be worthy of a place at his table. Deliver us from every selfish thought and low desire, and prepare our hearts for communion with one another and with thee.

We praise thee, O God, for the life of our Lord, and we give thanks for the faithfulness with which he faced suffering and death. As the shadows gather about him, and the hatred of men makes heavy his heart, may we see more clearly the beauty of his forgiveness and the radiance of his love. Reveal to us the sinfulness of our own lives, and so release us from our bondage to evil that we may press on renewed in our loyalty to him.

Upon our world in need send thou forth thy light and thy truth, and cause all thy people to be lifted to new heights of dedication and service. Help us with contrite hearts so to share our Lord's sufferings that we may be worthy to share also in his triumph over sin and death. Prepare us for our own Gethsemane, and give to us that complete surrender to thy holy purpose which shall enable us also to say, "Thy will be done." These things we ask in Jesus' name and for his sake. Amen. *Phillips P. Elliott*

164 Almighty God and Father of our Lord Jesus Christ, we come into thy presence in this service, with a feeling both of humility and triumph. We are humiliated when we remember that human sin brought thy Son to Calvary and forced the sacrifice that these symbols so vividly portray. Humbly we confess that all we too "like sheep have gone astray." These very moments bring memories of his sacrifice which throw all too clear a light upon our sin and selfishness. In so far as we truly repent, we pray thy forgiveness. May our hearts be freed from all pride and self-seeking, all bitterness and love of sin, that we may worthily enter into this upper room and commune with thee in all sincerity.

But we come into this experience also in a mood of holy triumph. Here we realize that through thee we can conquer our sins, and that they may be taken away from us the while thy eternal power flows into us to cleanse and strengthen us. As we enter within the sacred precincts of this Lord's table, we understand with a deeper understanding that thou, the Eternal God, canst commune with us and we with thee, through thy Son our Lord; that as the bread and the fruit of the vine minister to our bodies, so thou canst enter our spiritual beings and make them truly thy dwelling place. Help us now, therefore, to throw open the portals of our souls and let thee enter in as our "King of Glory," so that we may go from this service with the light of thy indwelling presence transfiguring us. This is the prayer we make in the name of him who himself blessed the bread and the wine and bade us unite with each other and with him in communion with thee. May he be one in our midst, we beseech thee. Amen. *Albert W. Beaven*

165 O thou who hast consecrated for us a new and living way, even Jesus Christ our Lord: grant unto us who are here met, so to partake of this bread and this cup that our hearts and lives may be truly yielded to the sway of his spirit. And here we offer and present unto thee, O Lord, ourselves, our souls and bodies, to be a reasonable, holy, and living sacrifice unto thee. Now, as we commemorate his last supper with his disciples, and his offering of himself in the sacrifice of the Cross, we humbly beseech thee to grant thy Holy Spirit, and to sanctify this bread and wine, that they may become unto us symbols of the body that was broken and of the blood that was shed for us. May they beget in us penitent hearts and a quickened faith, and may we receive this holy sacrament to our comfort; through Jesus Christ our Lord. Amen. *Boynton Merrill*

166   O most gracious Father, look upon us and enlighten our hearts, we pray thee, as we approach the sacrament to which, in his love, thy dear Son has called us. We come in obedience to his last request, to offer the memorial which his church has presented before thee during all the years since he offered himself for the sins of men. We come to receive his life within us and to plead the life he laid down for us. Cleanse us by thy visitation, that with hearts illumined and consciences undefiled we may approach these holy mysteries, with such reverence and contrition, such faith and purity, such love and devotion, as may bring to us the full power and virtue of the sacrament. May thy dear Son find in us a mansion prepared for his coming, and so fill us with his grace that we may minister to others even as he ministered, and be Christ-bearers to them even as he comes to us through earthly and material symbols in this sacrament. And grant that as we here receive him beneath the veil of the material, so we may at length behold him with unveiled face, in his eternal and glorious majesty, who now reigns, with thee and the Holy Spirit, one God, one world without end. Amen.   *Charles Fiske*

167   Heavenly Father, we thank thee we are called to be children of the light. Even though we have been children of the darkness, and have loved the ways of error rather than of truth, and of sin rather than of holiness, thou art calling us to the light of eternal day. We would answer thy call in penitence, and we would return to thee like wayward children who are coming home again. We do not ask to lose the sense of our shame, but we ask to taste the sweetness of thy forgiveness. We do not ask to forget our rebelliousness, but we ask to be assured that we are reconciled to thee. We would sit at thy table and receive the bread of life. We would worship at thy feet and receive the baptism of the Holy Spirit. We would stand before thee with our feet shod with the shoes of readiness, willing to go out on errands of Christian love and service. If we are inclined to frivolity may we become inclined to be serious and reverent. If we are heedless may we become fired with heavenly ambition and spiritual devotion. Redeem us from the littleness of selfishness and lift us into the blessed communion of our fellow-men. Give us a wide and generous outlook upon human affairs. Endow us with the sympathy that rejoices with them who are rejoicing and that weeps with them that weep. If thou art leading us through the gloom of adversity, may we find that even the clouds drop fatness. If thou art leading us through the green pastures and by the still waters, may we recognize the presence of the great Shepherd and may our hopes be sanctified. Hallow all our experiences, we humbly pray thee, and may we all become branches in the vine of our Lord. Amen.

John Henry Jowett

Poems

168   *From THE REPENTANCE OF PETER*

Without the High Priest's court with aching heart,
His sturdy shoulders bent, eyes wet with tears,
The man whom once his Lord had called a rock
Is seen alone in prayer, as daylight nears.

And with the rising sun and kindling hopes,
In his repenting heart a fairer morn,
Unseen by human eyes, steals o'er his soul,
And in its blaze of light a saint is born.

George W. Wiseman

169   *BE KNOWN TO US*

Be known to us in breaking bread,
But do not thou depart;
Saviour, with us abide, and spread
Thy Table in our heart.

There sup with us, in love divine;
Thy body and thy blood,
That living bread, that hevenly wine,
Be our immortal food.

James Montgomery

170   *DRINK YE ALL OF IT*

Drink ye all of it, all, not just a sup—
Drink my faith, my love, said Jesus,
Drink the fullness of my cup.

Drink ye all of it, all, not just my peace—
Drink my dangerous living, dying—
Drink my fearless, glad remorse.

Drink ye all of it, all, not just the sweet—
Drink my bitter tears of anguish—
Drink the dregs of my defeat.

Drink ye all of it, all, not just my pain—
Drink my joy of life abundant—
Drink my triumph, drink my reign!

E. Dent Lackey

171   BREAD

He knew what hunger a man can feel,
  So he broke the fishes and bread
That the weary thousands who followed him
  Might be strengthened and fed.

He knew what hunger a soul can feel,
  Sharing the husks with swine,
So he gave his broken body and blood
  For bread and wine.

Leslie Savage Clark

172   ON THE SACRAMENT

He was the Word, that spake it;
He took the bread and brake it;
And what that Word did make it,
I do believe and take it.

John Donne

173   FAITH

It is the road, the chart,
The wafer and the wine;
Who lives by faith
Shall find life good
And clutch the things divine.

Christ and his word shall be
Their sustenance till breath
Slips from the clay—
Who lives by faith
Shall never taste of death.

John Richard Moreland

Topics, Texts and Themes

174   THE LORD'S DESIRE

With desire I have desired to eat this passover with you before I suffer.
LU. 22:15

If the Saviour with desire desires to eat this passover with us, shall there be
no corresponding desire in our heart? Will there be no answering response?
It is all he asks for—desire. If we come humbly because we need, because we
want, because we desire, he will fulfil the desire of them that fear him. It is
not only that he gives gracious gifts for our need in sorrow or temptation
or sin, and not only that he gives love, but also that he gives himself. When we
can say, "There is none on earth that I desire besides thee," we are on the
way to be satisfied.

                                                                Hugh Black

175   THE GRACE OF THE SACRAMENT
           Not discerning the Lord's body. 1 co. 11:29.

He is there not only to give us that inward light and quietness which come
with the forgiveness of our sins: he is there to give us of his own life, of his
own energy, to give us of himself. It is true that men have fallen into error
by leaning excessively upon the grace of the sacrament. Let us see that we do
not err by thinking too lightly of it. There is a carelessness about communicat-
ing in our day, an easiness and want of seriousness, which permits people to be
irregular at Communion, and to disregard the duty of preparation; and it all
means that we at any rate are in danger not of exaggerating the importance
of the sacrament, but of making little, indeed nothing, of it.

                                                            John A. Hutton

176   BEHOLD THE MAN

"Behold the man," *the* man, the hope of the world. As we celebrate the
sacrament, we should keep in mind that its meaning embraces the three dimensions of time. It is a memorial of the past, the recall of his earthly life with its
atoning summit upon the Cross. The bread and wine symbolize, too, his
continuing presence which nourishes the devout believer. The communion is
also an account of that which is to come. Says Paul in one of the earliest
accounts of the Lord's Supper, "As often as ye eat this bread, and drink this
cup, ye do show the Lord's death till he come." The sacrament is the symbol

of hope—that in Jesus Christ we have the one for whom the centuries are looking and whose coming, in the flesh or the spirit, marks the consummation of all our mortal striving.

F. Gerald Ensley

177 *FOR YOU*

This is my body which is given for you. . . . This . . . is . . . my blood, which is shed for you. LU. 22:19–20

"For you" are the words I should impress as we approach this sacred table. I would seek by this simple meditation to stand you alone before all the Cross of Christ can mean. You alone; and out of the dark of it all, and out of the agony of it all, and out of the death of it all, would have you hear these solemn words said by your divine Lord and Saviour: "This body is broken *for you!* This blood is shed *for you!*"

We lose much out of religious meaning by having it brought before us in general terms. We draw great wide horizons about our considerations. We speak broadly of races, and nations, and mankind. I am sure the whole fact of religion is suffering among us today, for the reason we have so largely lost the direct individual application.

Merton S. Rice

178 *COMMUNION WITH GOD*

The cup of blessing which we bless, is it not the communion of the blood of Christ? The bread which we break, is it not the communion of the body of Christ? For we being many are one bread, and one body: for we are all partakers of that one bread. I CO. 10:16–17

"The communion of the body of Christ." The observance of the Lord's Supper does not *make* that communion. It is the form, among many others, in which the idea of that communion is most vividly enshrined. But in enshrining that idea, it enshrines another and a higher one—communion with God.

Through our daily communion with Christ, of which this supper is not the cause but the symbol, we realize, more deeply than we could do had he not been among us, our communion with God. We understand, through Christ's perfect communion with God, that we are right in claiming our communion with God. And that is the foremost need of man. To strive to dwell in God, and to feel him dwelling in us, is at once the duty and the destiny of humanity.

Stopford A. Brooke

179   *A CUP IN HIS HAND*

Omar Khayyám feasts because life is not joyful; he revels because he is not
glad: "Drink," he says, "for you know not whence you come nor why. Drink,
because the stars are cruel and the world as idle as a humming top. Drink,
because there is nothing worth trusting, nothing worth fighting for. Drink,
because all things are lapsed in a base equality and an evil peace." So he stands
offering us the cup in his hand.

And at the high altar of Christianity stands Another in whose hand also
is the cup of the vine. "Drink," he says, "for the whole world is as red as this
wine, with the crimson of the love and wrath of God. Drink, for the trumpets
are blowing for battle and this is the stirrup-cup. Drink, for this is my blood
of the New Testament that is shed for you. Drink, for I know of whence you
come and why. Drink, for I know of when you go and where."

Gilbert Keith Chesterton

180   *THE ART OF REMEMBERING*

This do in remembrance of me. LU. 22:19.

In establishing this simple memorial service Christ ministered to one of
the deepest needs of human life: the need of remembering. Have you
ever thought what life would be without memory? What gravitation is to
matter, memory is to mind; without the former buildings would vanish
like mist, and the solid earth would disappear like a cloud; without the latter
mind would be a mockery and worse. Memory is to thoughts what the silken
cord is to the beads, holding them in place. The blood is the life of the body,
and memory is the life of the soul; and when memory becomes sluggish, the
powers are paralyzed. "This do in remembrance"—that you might keep alive
and vital and strong the God-life of your soul.

You wonder, perhaps, that he did not say, "Trust me, have faith in me,
hope for me, love me," at this last supper. You cannot trust, believe, hope, love,
what memory fails to represent to you. And when you remember him, you
cannot fail to trust, believe, hope and love. Christ bids us remember him, well
knowing that when his hand presses the keyboard of memory, the music of
faith, hope and love shall fill the soul.

Henry Hitt Crane

181   *WHAT IN REMEMBRANCE?*

This do in remembrance of me. LU. 22:19.

The Master was never much interested in ceremonies as such. He said some things to Scribes and Pharisees which prove his disdain of mere ceremony, and for thousands of Christians the communion feast has been just that— a beautiful, perfunctory ritual. But that his people should follow him in sacrificial service to God and man—ah, that is like Jesus. Indeed, he said so many times in other words, "If any man would come after me, let him deny himself daily, take up his cross and follow me. . . . Are ye able to drink the cup that I drink? . . . Blessed are they who are persecuted for righteousness' sake." Surely he is best remembered in the experience of self-giving such as his own. The true, living, vital communion is not the highly ritualistic mass with service of pure silver upon embroidery of silk; the true, living, vital communion is a life broken, a soul poured out in lowly service in memory of his sacrifice.

Frank B. Fagerburg

182   *CHRISTIAN OPTIMISM*

The Lord Jesus the same night in which he was betrayed took bread: and when he had given thanks, he brake it. 1 CO. 11:23–24.

In the assurance of ultimate triumph, the certainty that his work was finished, he gave thanks. For himself and for his little ones who believe and should believe on him, he gave thanks. That his Father in heaven had led him and brought him up to this last step, he gave thanks. He beheld Satan as lightning fall from heaven, and knew that his work was accepted and would go on to the final triumph. The climax of sin was also the climax of faith as well as of love. Faith found its assurance in God's redeeming love, and our Lord in his seeming defeat knew that the old word would be fulfilled, "He will swallow up death in victory; and the Lord God will wipe away all tears from off all faces."

Hugh Black

183   *HIGHER LEVELS*

Houses in Palestine were usually small affairs. One story, flat-roofed, what we call bungalows! Here was a home more spacious—it had upper rooms, spare rooms, a guest-chamber. The Master knew the owner of it, and when he was about to eat the Passover with his disciples for the last time, he said to them: "Go into the city and you will meet a man with a pitcher of water. Follow him into the house where he enters, and he will show you a large upper room, furnished." An upper room, away from the noise of the street, above those interests on the ground floor which are altogether of the earth, higher than the adjacent buildings, giving it a broader outlook! An upper room with a certain spiritual frontage—"there make ready" for the further tasks which await you. . . .

Why should not we go aloft and explore that upper world of spiritual reality which towers above the ordinary grind as the Matterhorn towers above the valley of the Rhone? We can do it if we will. No weight of years, no lack of bodily vigor, need hold us back from that quest. . . . The path of spiritual ascent is not far from any one of us. Why not lay aside every weight and the sins which so easily beset us, and climb with patience to those higher levels where we can see the glory of the Lord and the true meaning of human life? "He shall show you" higher levels of experience.

Charles R. Brown

F. GOOD FRIDAY

Good Friday, formerly called Holy Friday, may have originally been known as God's Friday. The day is widely observed by a mid-day local church or community-wide service marking the three hours of Christ's suffering on the Cross and centering in a meditation on and interpretation of the last seven words of Christ from the Cross. These are: (1) "Father, forgive them; for they know not what they do" (Lu. 23:34), (2) "Verily, I say unto thee, Today shalt thou be with me in Paradise" (Lu. 23:43), (3) "Woman, behold thy son. . . . Behold thy mother" (Jn. 19:26–27), (4) "My God, my God, why hast thou forsaken me?" (Mat. 27:46 and Mk. 15:34), (5) "I thirst" (Jn. 19:28), (6) "It is finished" (Jn. 19:30), and (7) "Father, into thy hands I commend my spirit" (Lu. 23:46). The homiletic possibilities suggested by these verses are numerous. Often those churches which hold no special Good Friday service invite parishioners and others to meditate individually in the sanctuary during the three memorable hours.

Calls to Worship

(Boldface type indicates response.)

184   If any man will come after me, let him deny himself, and take up his cross, and follow me. For whosoever will save his life shall lose it: but whosoever will lose his life for my sake shall find it.

Mat. 17:24-25

185   Christ also suffered for us, leaving us an example, that ye should follow his steps: who his own self bare our sins in his own body on the tree, that we, being dead to sins, should live unto righteousness.

1 Pe. 2:21, 24

186   Surely he hath borne our griefs, and carried our sorrows: yet we did esteem him stricken, smitten of God, and afflicted. But he was wounded for our transgressions, he was bruised for our iniquities: the chastisement of our peace was upon him; and with his stripes we are healed.

Let us therefore come boldly unto the throne of grace, that we may obtain mercy, and find grace to help in time of need.

Is. 53:4; He. 4:16

Invocations

187   Our Loving Father in heaven, as the darkness of Calvary once covered the whole earth from the sixth to the ninth hour, so the darkness of our sins seems now to have covered forever this world for which our Saviour died. But we know his love will never let us go. His light will follow us, his Cross uplift us, and his endless life blossom red again. Amen.

Edwin T. Dahlberg

188   Forbid, O God, that we should forget, amid our earthly comforts, the pains and mortal anguish that our Lord Jesus endured for our salvation. Grant us this day a true vision of all that he suffered, in his betrayal, his lonely agony, his false trial, his mocking and scourging, and the torture of death upon the Cross. As thou hast given thyself utterly for us, may we give ourselves entirely to thee, O Jesus Christ, our only Lord and Saviour. Amen.

Book of Common Worship (P)

189   O Christ, give us patience, and faith, and hope as we kneel at the foot of thy Cross, and hold fast to it. Teach us by thy Cross, that however ill the world may go, the Father so loved us that he spared not thee. Amen.

Charles Kingsley

Litany

(Boldface type indicates responses.)

190   All-loving and gracious God, who dost permit us at this time to draw nigh unto thee: dispose our hearts aright, that we may lift up prayer and praise to thee, trusting not in our well deserving, but in thy great mercy, through thine only begotten Son, Jesus Christ:

Bow down thine ear, O Lord, and answer us; for we are poor and needy.

Comfort the soul of thy servant; for thou, Lord, art good and ready to forgive:

Bestow upon us of thy loving-kindness and thy tender mercies, and heal us with thy holy presence.

We bless thee, O Lord, that in the life of Jesus Christ, our Lord, thou hast revealed thine immeasurable love to us:

We bless thee, O Lord.

That in his life, death and resurrection, he did not refuse to share the lot of common man, but humbled himself and became obedient unto death, even the death of the Cross:

We bless thee, O Lord.

That thou didst not leave thy Holy One to see corruption, but didst raise him by the right hand of thy power, to be unto us for evermore the promise of eternal life:

We bless thee, O Lord.

Grant that this day of holy memorial, when we recall his dying agony and his redeeming love, may be unto us, his disciples, for the renewal of our faith and the sanctification of our lives:

Hear us, O Lord.

For the forgiveness of our sins and for the cleansing of our hearts:

We pray thee, O Lord.

For that due preparation of heart and mind that shall enable us to receive the entrance of thy Holy Spirit:

We pray thee, O Lord. Amen.

Author Unknown

Prayers

191 Eternal God, our Father, who didst send thy Son to be the Saviour of the world: we wait before thee in the shadows of the Cross where he made the supreme sacrifice that lost men might find their way back to thee. We confess that the sins which killed him often besiege our own hearts. We see ourselves in the varied company around him on Golgotha. We know the mood of fear, jealousy, hatred, and love of power. Search us, O God, and reveal to us our evil ways that in full surrender to thee we may be cleansed of all that corrupts our souls and separates us from thee. Forbid that on this day of his great agony we should join the mob that watched him there in morbid humor and pagan cruelty. Deliver us from the passive curiosity that waits a sign and the hypocrisy which joins the crowd to hide its emptiness. May thy Spirit find us today where we really are in our human frailty, our lagging loyalty, and our lack of faith. May the Light that overcomes the darkness touch the unseen depths of our hearts and expel all cowardice and unworthy motive. May he who came to make all things new begin in us now, and continue with each passing day, that work of redemption which shall give us the right to share in his resurrection and make this earth at last the heaven for which he taught us to pray. Amen.

Oren H. Baker

192 Almighty Father, who in thy patience didst accept the sacrifices of men as a preparation for faith in the one offering of Jesus: we pray that this day may be a day of recollection of his passion and of thy redeeming love. May the grace of the Cross empower us to offer our bodies a living sacrifice, holy and acceptable, a spiritual service. May the great Sufferer's prayer for those who crucified him prevail this day on behalf of all who reject him and thus crucify him anew; for all whose lives contradict goodness and truth; for every prodigal who wanders from his Father's house. May the power of the Cross be manifest in burdened and suffering lives. May persons who are anxious and distressed on behalf of those whom they love know Jesus in the fellowship of his sufferings and in the power of his resurrection. May the cry of the wronged and the depressed rise into harmony with Jesus' words of resignation and trust. We would come to the Cross this day to do thy will, O God, as he came, joyous in tribulation through our conquering Christ. Amen.

Fitzgerald S. Parker

193 Our Father, we would thank thee for the gift of thy Son to be the Saviour of the world and for all he means, known and unknown, to those who would take him at his word, follow him without reserve, let loose their faith in him each day. We especially thank thee for his outpoured life on the Cross.

We would thank thee, our Father, for the very mystery of thy Son's Cross, for the depths in which we find ourselves lost in wonder, love and praise. We cannot understand all that his Cross may mean but, kneeling here, we feel thy hand upon us and we would give ourselves afresh to thee. Love so amazing, so divine, demands my life, my soul, my all.

O Christ, who didst give thy life to set men free from their sins, giving thyself as a ransom for many, grant us thy grace to live in this freedom and never again become the slave to sin, held captive by the power of evil.

O Christ, who dost govern the world from thy Cross, I surrender all to thy control holding nothing back of which I know. Draw out my worst confession; draw out my best in consecration. Bind my wandering heart to thee.

O Christ, when I kneel at thy Cross and realize to what boundless depths and lengths thou hast gone, I see again how much my life is worth in thy sight. Help me to live like that. "This hast thou done for me; what have I done for Thee?" In a world filled with crucifixion causes, enable me to give myself to such causes in my day and generation.

O Christ, who didst give thyself for me, for each one of us, help me to understand more and more fully what it means to have thee take my place. Keep me at one forever with thine and the Father's heart.

O Christ, who didst give thyself to draw men back to the Father, make me an instrument of reconciliation in my lifetime. May I so witness by word and action for thee that others may find harmony and peace with one another because they are bound back to thy heart forever. In thy name. Amen.

Oscar F. Blackwelder

Poems

194   *PRAYER ON GOOD FRIDAY*

Blood of Jesus, shed for me,
Cleanse my sin and make me free.

Let His life, so freely given,
Heal our world asunder riven.

Let His words of love and peace
Rule our lives till strife shall cease.

Let His faith, His grace and power,
Be our strength in this dark hour.

Cross of Christ, undimmed by wrong,
Be today my triumph song!

Georgia Harkness

195   *OBLIVION*

Upon a hill called Calvary
    A Man went forth to die;
He gave his body to a Cross;
    They built it huge and high;
They sent him to oblivion,
    With many a cruel cry!

Long years have passed since Calvary;
    Those cruel cries are dead;
Dead too the hands that pressed the thorns
    In torture on his head—
All gone into oblivion;
    He is alive instead!

Ralph S. Cushman

196   *HIS HANDS*

                     The hands of Christ
                         Seem very frail
                     For they were broken
                         By a nail.

                     But only they
                         Reach heaven at last
                     Whom these frail, broken
                         Hands hold fast.

                                        John Richard Moreland

197   *BETRAYAL*

                     Still as of old
                     Men by themselves are priced—
                     For thirty pieces Judas sold
                     Himself, not Christ.

                                        Hester H. Cholmondeley

198   *IDENTITY*

                     Betrayer of the Master,
                     He sways against the sky
                     A black and broken body,
                     Iscariot—or I?

                                        Caroline Giltinan

199   *GETHSEMANE*

                     All those who journey, soon or late,
                     Must pass within the garden's gate;
                     Must kneel alone in darkness there,
                     And battle with some fierce despair.
                     God pity those who cannot say:
                     "Not mine but thine"; who only pray:
                     "Let this cup pass," and cannot see
                     The purpose in Gethsemane.

                                        Ella Wheeler Wilcox

200   *GETHSEMANE*

There is a way which man hath trod
   For, lo, these thronging, countless years;
It is the way of life, of God;
   It is the way of night, of tears;
Its winding we may not foresee;
It is the way—Gethsemane.

It is the way whereby we know
   Life's larger meanings and its claims,
The fellowship of human woe,
   Our partnership with others' pains.
It is the way which seems to be
Life's only way—Gethsemane.

Charles Russell Wakeley

201   *ETERNAL HOPE*

Upon a life I have not lived,
Upon a death I have not died—
Another's life, Another's death,
I stake my whole eternity.

Author Unknown

202   *QUATRAIN*

Christ bears a thousand crosses now
   Where once but one he bore;
Each cruel deed unto his brow
   Adds one thorn more.

Charles G. Blanden

203   *From THE CATHEDRAL*

The Cross, bold type of shame to homage turned,
Of an unfinished life that sways the world,
Shall tower as a sovereign emblem over all.

James Russell Lowell

Topics, Texts and Themes

204   *GOOD FRIDAY*

To die is gain. PH. 1:21

The day we call Good Friday is dedicated to the splendor and beauty of
death; of death willingly claimed and endured for the sake of love. To part
from life for the sake of those we love at home, for friends who are dear
as light and air, is noble enough to move the heart of man. It is nobler to
die for one's country, since that is less personal. It is still better to die for
great causes and ideas of vital importance to the progress of mankind, for
the support of thoughts and feelings without which the soul of humanity
would starve; for the moral powers—justice, righteousness and truth; for
the spiritual powers—love, faith and hope; for all that abides in and makes
God the Father and the life of Christ. These universal interests least involve personal desire. Without their continued life in us man would be,
for all his intellect, no better than the worm. With them he claims kindred with
God. And to die on behalf of their continuance, borne on the tide of their
passion, which takes the whole human race into its movement towards God,
is to reach the highest glory and beauty of which man is capable. The ultimate
judgment, then, as to the nobility of any death, or any sacrifice, is given on the
grounds of how much love for man, beyond our self, there was in the sacrifice;
and the ultimate glory of death is when it is the highest form of love to mankind.
It was for this ultimate idea of perfect love that Jesus died, and his death was its
expression. He loved his mother, his brethren, his friends, his enemies. But
above all he loved mankind, his Father's child. And he manifested that love,
not only by his life, but, in concentrated expression of it, by dying for the ideas
and the truths on whose prevalence and power rests the moral and spiritual
progress to God of the human race. His death passed beyond all particular
forms of love into its universal form. There is, I repeat, no greater glory on
earth than such a death, nor any greater beauty. Humanity, in such a death, is
clothed with divinity; becomes at one with God.

                                                                    Stopford A. Brooke

205   *A LONG LOOK AT JESUS*

They crucified him . . . and sitting down they watched him. MAT. 27:35-36

Suppose we sit down today and take a long, long look at Jesus. There are
different ways of doing it. We might recall all that we have ever heard men say

about Jesus. We would look at the body of testimony and find in it a beautiful etching of Jesus. Or we might sit at a desk and have brought to us the various "lives" of Jesus, as, for instance, those of Papini, Geikie, Bowie, and Middleton Murry. With this extensive material before us we can have an even more complete picture—a picture of color, light and shadow. But the view that we are to take today is direct—free of personal bias and literary intrusions. Let us sit down before the Cross as it was nineteen hundred years ago, and, with the guarding soldiers, look at the man with the nails in his hands and feet and the crown of thorns on his head. We are filled with awe, for we behold the most moving scene in history. Here on Golgotha we, with the soldiers, see revealed in a mighty panorama the greatest drama the world has ever witnessed. We are caught up in the very progress of the universe.

Albert Buckner Coe

206   *CALVARY AND MAIN STREET*

The place where Jesus was crucified was nigh to the city. JN. 19:20

This is a simple statement of geographical fact in the account of the crucifixion of Jesus in the Gospel of John which has a wide spiritual suggestiveness. It is the incidental reference to the distance of Calvary from Jerusalem.

In the Gospel record, of course, there is no double meaning to this geographical information. It is just a plain statement of physical fact that Calvary was near to the city. It is a luminous symbol of the truth that the Cross of Christ is near to the city today.

Calvary was not far from the city on that day when Jesus traveled the short road between them bearing his Cross. Calvary is not far from the city today. The sacrifice of Christ has a vital relationship to all of the eager life of every Main Street—its hopes, its love, its joy, its toil, its burdens, its tragedies.

Halford E. Luccock

207   *THE SYMBOL*

These . . . are some of the meanings of the Cross to all who use it as a symbol:

1. The unfailing, unchanging, undying love of God. That love is with us in disappointment, defeat, and death, as well as in prosperity, joy, and abundant life.

2. The ability of man, in his dependence on and cooperation with God, to face life and death without faltering and without bitterness or despair. The spirit of man may be triumphant *in love*.

3. The awful results of actions, deliberate or otherwise, growing out of prejudice and hate, that are not in keeping with God's purpose of good and of respect for persons.

Those who use this symbol, the Cross, thereby declare that it is their deliberate purpose to live the adventurous life in mutuality with their fellows and with God.

Some people speak and sing about taking up the Cross as if it meant little more than pinning a decoration on one's coat. To take up the Cross means to live the adventurous life day by day. It means practicing faith in God and in his unchanging love and purpose for good; a deep and abiding faith in the intrinsic worth of every person, and in his ability to live and endure for God; and the determination to venture to live in this faith, to follow the way of love and of service at all costs, even to risking life itself in the defense of one's fellow men.

A. J. William Myers

208   THE MEANING OF THE CROSS

The Cross of Christ means three things. It shows up the sin of the world; it reveals the grace of God; and it exhibits fundamentally the meaning of discipleship. The evil that lurks in human nature is shown by what it led typical men, respectable business men and politicians and religious leaders, as well as the fickle mob, to do, in hounding to his death such a one as Jesus. When we see that it was God with Christ and in some sense God working in and through him that kept him steady even unto death in his loving, self-giving service to men, we have our most impressive individual revelation of the gracious attitude of God toward sinful men. And when we see what bearing the yoke of the will of God for the Kingdom's sake meant for Jesus as he endured the Cross and all that led up to it and went with it, we get an idea of what it is in principle and what it may mean in practice truly to take upon ourselves his yoke as our way of life.

Douglas Clyde Macintosh

209   THREE CROSSES

There are three Crosses which are our spiritual possession. There is a rough-hewn, rugged Cross which tells us that God shares the suffering of the world. It reminds us that love has in it the capacity to suffer. Infinite love has infinite capacity to bear the world's pain. Leslie Weatherhead says that "God is the greatest casualty in this or any war." His deep love intensifies his suffering.

There is also a crucifix. The impaled Christ will always mean that God bears the sin of the world. "He was wounded for our transgressions." *Our* makes it collective, corporate; he bears *our* sin; the word is distributive, he bears my sin, my neighbor's. "Refuse humans" we may be called, but in the light of this Cross we find ourselves redeemed and valuable.

There is, too, a Cross of victory. It is a post-resurrection Cross. Sometimes we ornament it with the monogram IHS—"In hoc signo"—"In this sign we conquer."

Three Crosses—the Cross of our healing, the Cross of our forgiveness, the Cross of our peace. A trinity of Crosses, a three in one, even the Cross of our Lord and Savior, Jesus Christ.

M. K. W. Heicher

210 THE CROSS AND GOD'S LOVE

On Calvary we learn that sin is more than an unfortunate slip, a foolish mistake, or even a grave misfortune. Sin—of which it is now unfashionable to speak—is the deliberate setting of our human wills against the will of God. There is, therefore, need of some unmistakable disclosure of the heart of God, to make us see sin for what it is. In the death of Christ, as nowhere else, we see the full shame and pain of sin. Just as any serious attempt to measure our lives over against the life of Christ convinces us that he is a direct gift of God, so any such comparison forces upon us a sense of the awfulness of sin and the need of forgiveness. And just as human forgiveness in its best forms is saved from any demoralizing consequence when the one forgiven has been made to see the pain which his sin has caused, so do we discover, at the Cross, in the supreme moment of pardon, that forgiveness is possible because at last we see sin through the eyes of God. The Cross of Calvary shows us the love of God, if we believe that the victim is a Divine Victim. If Jesus was but a man, then it is only the story of one more good man, apparently deserted by God in the hour of need; in which case it is something of a mockery to talk of God's love. If the Sufferer is really the Divine Son, then the Cross is the eternally repeated assurance that God does the uttermost love can do to bring us to himself.

Charles Fiske

211 THE UNIVERSALITY OF JESUS

And a superscription also was written over him in letters of Greek, and Latin, and Hebrew, This is the King of the Jews. LU. 23:38

It was the common custom in those days, when a criminal was executed, publicly to placard his crime. As the man on the center Cross on Calvary had been condemned for claiming kingly rights for himself, a claim which obviously neither Caesar nor Judaism could tolerate, the words of the charge stood written above his head: "This is Jesus the King."

But why the three languages? No doubt they were used, in the first instance, to make sure that everyone in the crowd—for Jerusalem in that Passover time was packed with visitors from all parts of the world—should be able to read and understand. But another hand than Pilate's had been working there. Providence had a hand in it. For Greek, Latin, and Hebrew were the three great languages of the world. Each of them represented a whole panorama of history. Each was the vehicle and expression of a great world movement. Each stood for a different, dominant idea, each was the servant of that idea. Each was a tide which carried the spirits of men. And each was at the Cross to proclaim it: "This is Jesus the King." Do you see what providence was intending? Everything that the Greek idea in history stood for—Jesus was king there. Everything that the Roman idea in history stood for—Jesus was king there. Everything that the Hebrew idea in history stood for—Jesus was king there. Verily, on his head are many crowns!

James S. Stewart

212 THE CROSS WE UNDERSTAND

One reason why the Cross of Christ has so wrought on the conscience of men is that it exhibits the true character of moral evil by expressing it in terms of suffering, which all can understand. The sins of men actually crucified Jesus—the sins of the Jewish Sanhedrin, which were jealousy and prejudice, the sin of Judas, who betrayed him, the sin of Peter, who denied him, the sin of Pontius Pilate, who found injustice easier than justice, the sin of Roman soldiers, who added mocking to his scourging and crucifixion. These are our sins as much as theirs—jealousy, prejudice, disloyalty, time-serving, pitilessness— though the consequences are not so clearly seen, when we are the sinners. Yet, in similar circumstances, without the light that history has flung upon the Cross, any of us might do like deeds. But just because the result of those ancient sins is revealed in the suffering of the Cross, we are made to see what sin really is Sin is something that can do things like that. *H. Wheeler-Robinson*

213 THE WAY OF THE CROSS

He stedfastly set his face to go to Jerusalem. LU. 9:51

The Cross has become the symbol of our faith. Like the altar to the Jews, it occupies the central place in our worship, veiling, as it does, the "dark mystery of sacrifice." It has produced a voluminous literature. It has inspired some of our most beautiful hymns. The deepest moments of worship are experienced when we share the sacramental act, which Calvary has made available. No one could estimate the solace and the power which the "green hill far away," yet ever near, has had and still exerts upon numberless lives.

But are we in danger here, too, of taking a partial view of Calvary's meaning? The Cross is not only historic. It is prophetic. We have worked out its theological assumptions, but have we adequately faced its sociological implications? We speak of it as a "great transaction" that is "done," but do we see its bearing on what remains to be done, and its place in the unfinished program of Christianity? One has no desire to belittle the significance of doctrine, but it can surely be said that no doctrine of the Cross that hides the Cross itself will save the world.

For the Cross is more than an historic fact. It is the revelation of an eternal process. It is more than something that was. It is. Jerusalem is not simply a physical location. It is a moral and spiritual condition which still makes, as of old, its ceaseless demands upon redemptive love. The truth is that it still costs to redeem the world. In the economy of God this price does not fluctuate. Jesus has not "paid it all" in the sense that he spares us the experience of heroic and sacrificial living. He is more than a substitute. He is an example. Too often, as another has reminded us, we have been tempted to leave it all "To one great priestly act, one baptism, one cup of woe, though at the heart of all our worship are the words, 'Drink ye all of it.'" He steadfastly set his face to go to Jerusalem. Shall we cautiously turn our heads away?

Harold Cooke Phillips

214   *THE SIGN OF THE CROSS*

For the preaching of the cross is to them that perish foolishness; but unto us which are saved it is the power of God. 1 co. 1:18

How varied are the views men have of the Cross! To many, it is but an ornament to be worn about the neck. To the architect it is a symbol, adorning churches. To the scholar it is a goad, driving him on in intellectual pursuits. To the preacher it is a sermon, filling the need of the hour—and of eternity. To the skeptic it is a superstition, clouding men's souls. To the Communist it is a narcotic, benumbing men's minds, an opiate of the people. To the Roman it was an instrument of execution, obnoxious and hated. To Constantine it was a sign in which to conquer, turning defeat into victory. To Paul it was a symbol of glory, pointing the way to heaven. To Mary it was a memory of agony, piercing her soul. To the Sanhedrin it was a token of victory, imaginary and short-lived. To the motley mob on Golgotha it was a holiday, carnal and cursed.

To one thief it was the door to perdition, horrible and eternal. To the other it was the gate to Paradise, wondrous beyond work of men or angels. To Christ it was a bier and a throne, paradox of time, predestined to eternity. To multiplied millions of storm-tossed souls it is an anchor, offering a haven of rest.

Herschel H. Hobbs

215 *WHO WILL BETRAY HIM?*

And as they sat and did eat, Jesus said, Verily I say unto you, One of you which eateth with me shall betray me. And they began to be sorrowful, and to say unto him one by one, Is it I? MK. 14:18–19

Betrayal was a dreadful thing where loyalty was everything. The more remarkable that each should have suspected himself. Suppose I had knowledge that some one here today had carefully planned some evil for this very night. And I said to you, I know some one here will do this awful deed. At once there would be a protest. "No! No! We are all good people. We would never do that." Or some might say to themselves: "I think I know whom he means. I wouldn't put that past him." While others might draw themselves instinctively away from the one who sits next to them, lest he be the one who planned this evil in his heart. But the disciples were different. They began to say one by one, "Is it I?"

What was the matter with these men? Where was their confidence, their self-respect? Didn't they have any backbone? Perhaps . . . these honest humble words, "Is it I?" are more becoming for the Christian, more certainly a proof of his inward strength and integrity than the high-sounding promise and the pious boast.

Harold Elliott Nicely

216 *DUTY BORN OF STRUGGLE*

Now is my soul troubled; and what shall I say? Father, save me from this hour: but for this cause came I unto this hour. Father, glorify thy name. JN. 12:27–28

It is a genuine history of a genuine struggle. It is a memory of the temptation, and an anticipation of Gethsemane. I love it for its genuineness; for if Christ's human life be the type of the life of all humanity, then this struggle of his must be the perfect struggle, representing ours. It must include the way in which all men, from the assertion of a human repugnance, pass by degrees into an anxiety that God should glorify his name. It teaches us in general the method of all duty, or the process by which any man is led from an unwillingness to a willingness to do or bear God's will. Let us give it our study today from this point of view. We are standing today, as it were, waiting by the Cross where Jesus died. If his death is to be indeed the inspiration of all the duty of our lives, we may not forget that both in him and in us duty comes out of struggle.

Phillips Brooks

G. EASTER

Easter, the day of days and queen of Christian festivals, is observed, according to a decision made by the Council of Nicaea in A.D. 325, on the first Sunday after the date of the first full moon that occurs on or after March 21, and, therefore, falls between March 22 and April 25. Three-fourths of the church calendar is determined by the date of Easter, and Christianity has little meaning apart from the significance which Easter represents. Paul's word, "Christ our Passover is sacrificed for us: therefore let us keep the feast" (1 Co. 5:7–8), suggests that Easter is not only the most important but also the first of all Christian festivals.

Christ's resurrection on the first day of the week made Sunday the holy day for all Christendom and gave a special meaning to every Sunday as "a little Easter" and the occasion for the remembrance of the resurrection life.

Sunrise services, beginning when it is yet dark after the implication of Jn. 20:1, offer inspiration for Christians of all ages. Baptism, the rising with Christ into the newness of life, has long been an expressive aspect of Easter worship. Sunday evening services on Easter frequently recapture the spirit of the conversation of Christ along the road to Emmaus.

The following materials indicate that the preaching and worship possibilities of the day are not necessarily to be limited to the subject of immortality.

Calls to Worship

(Boldface type indicates responses.)

217   O give thanks unto the Lord, for he is good: for his mercy endureth for ever.

Now is Christ risen from the dead, and become the firstfruits of them that slept.

This is the day which the Lord hath made; we will rejoice and be glad in it.

Alleluia: for the Lord God omnipotent reigneth. Let us be glad and rejoice, and give honor to him.

Ps. 107:1; 1 Co. 15:20; Ps. 118:24; Re. 19:6–7

218   O give thanks unto the Lord; for he is good: for his mercy endureth for ever. Blessed be the God and Father of our Lord Jesus Christ, which according to his abundant mercy hath begotten us again unto a lively hope by the resurrection of Jesus Christ from the dead, to an inheritance incorruptible, and undefiled, and that fadeth not away, reserved in heaven for you.

Ps. 136:1; 1 Pe. 1:3–4

219   We declare unto you glad tidings, how that the promise which was made unto the fathers, God hath fulfilled the same unto us their children, in that he hath raised up Jesus again. Because I live [saith Jesus] ye shall live also. If ye then be risen with Christ, seek those things which are above, where Christ sitteth on the right hand of God.

Ac. 13:32–33; Jn. 14:19; Col. 3:1

220   Now is Christ risen from the dead, and become the firstfruits of them that slept.

For since by man came death, by man came also the resurrection of the dead.

For this corruptible must put on incorruption, and this mortal must put on immortality.

O death, where is thy sting? O grave, where is thy victory?

1 Co. 15:20–21, 53, 55

Invocations

221   O God, Source of the life eternal we are permitted to share, Fountain of the light in whose radiance we are privileged to live: deliver us, we pray thee, from bondage to our dead selves and from the rock-bound tomb of our feeble faith and grant us the grace and courage to follow the Risen Christ into newness of life that we may be able, through his Spirit, to build a new world wherein dwell righteousness and peace. Through Jesus Christ our Lord. Amen.

Raymond C. Brooks

222   O Almighty God, hear thy people who are this day met to glorify the resurrection of thy Son our Lord and guide them on from this festival to eternal gladness, from the exacting joy of this solemnity to joys that have no end; for this is the day of man's resurrection, the birthday of eternal life, the day in which we have been satisfied with thy mercy in the morning, in which the blessed One who cometh in the name of the Lord and who is our God hath shone upon us. Amen.*

Gothic Missal

223   O thou who makest the stars, and turnest the shadow of death into the morning: on this day of days we meet to render thee, our Lord and King, the tribute of our praise; for the resurrection of spring-time, for the everlasting hopes that rise within the human heart, and for the Gospel which hath brought life and immortality to light. Receive our thanksgiving, reveal thy presence, and send into our hearts the Spirit of the Risen Christ. Amen.

William E. Orchard

224   O thou living God our Father, who by thy life-giving Spirit didst raise our Lord Jesus from the dead and who by that same Spirit dost give life to all who put their trust in thee: grant us today, we beseech thee, a new vision of thyself. May we see thee as thou art, in thy majesty, in thy holiness, in thy compassion and understanding love, that seeing thee we may desire thee, and desiring thee may surrender to thee, and surrendering to thee, body, mind and spirit without reserve, may find our lives transformed by thy Spirit into the likeness of Jesus Christ, thy Son our Lord. Amen.

William Adams Brown

Litany

(Boldface type indicates responses.)

225   From the dust of vainly traveled highways and the weariness of almost forgotten hopes:
Lift up our eyes to thee, O Lord.
From the mysteries of evil, and pain, and sorrow, and from the dark records of history and tradition:
Lift up our eyes to thee, O Lord.
From scenes of temporal power and splendor and from all evidences of human confidence in might, oppression, and the enslavement of mankind:
Lift up our eyes to thee, O Lord.
From the depths of our sin, the limitations of our vision, the failures of our will, the littleness of our experience in a vast and eternal world:
Lift up our eyes to thee, O Lord.
From the sway of the dictator, the injustice of human systems, the transiency of the material, the apparent control of death and selfishness:
Lift up our eyes to thee, O Lord.
That we may know life with its eternal setting and background and become new creatures with minds set on things above:
Grant us the victory, we pray.

That we may see fulfilled before our eyes the miracle of seed-growth and the recurring and symbolic miracles of nature:

Grant us the victory, we pray.

That we may have the power to do greater things, to suffer even a cross, to die that we might no longer be holden of death through the spirit in us:

Grant us the victory, we pray.

That we may burst asunder all tombs of selfishness, pride, unbrotherhood, and unworthiness, and attain unto thy fullness through his power:

Grant us the victory, we pray.

That we may transform every defeat into triumph, every opposition into a way of help, every sacrifice into a means of new attainment:

Grant us the victory, we pray.

That we may know life abundant and eternal, and face the mysteries beyond with radiant confidence and smiling hope unto the eternal day of brotherhood, peace, and fully spiritual living:

Grant us the victory, we pray.

Richard K. Morton

Prayers

226 Almighty and eternal God, who hast made us in thy image and breathed into us the breath of life: we thank thee for this day and for the assurance it brings of thy love and care. Especially do we thank thee for Jesus Christ, our Lord and Saviour, who conquered death and brought life and immortality to light. May that light shine in our hearts today with such clearness that we shall never again doubt the deathlessness of truth and love and the immortality of the human soul.

Forgive us that so often we have forgotten our heritage as sons of God and have lived as though this life were the only life. Forgive us our preoccupation with temporal things, our little faith, our sordid aims, our feverish efforts after material satisfactions, and our neglect of the things of the spirit. Lift us to higher levels, our Father, and grant that, appreciating our divine destiny, we may henceforth seek the things that are above. Assured that truth and righteousness are eternal, may we not lose heart nor falter in the fight against evil. In the black hour when the battle goes against us may the remembrance of Calvary and Easter morn rekindle our faith and steady our courage until, by thy grace, victory is secure.

On this blessed Easter day we give thee solemn thanks for all those valiant souls who, believing in the power of an endless life, have fought the good fight, have finished the course, and now reign with thee. Especially do we rejoice in the triumph of those near and dear to us, the companions of our hearts in other days, whose ennobling memory abides with us, a constant strength and stay. As we think of them may we realize that life is ever lord of death, and love can never lose its own.

O God of the living universe and the loving heart, help us to believe that with thee there is no death, and that if we put our trust in thee and live for thee nothing in heaven or earth shall have power to separate us from thy love. In that faith and by that love help us to walk until faith becomes sight and we behold thee face to face, through Jesus Christ our Lord. Amen.

James Dalton Morrison

227   Christ the Lord is risen today. How quick we are to affirm it, to refute the blindness that released Barabbas, thinking that death could hold prisoner the gentle and divine spirit who, but for the shouts of the multitude and the cowardice of a ruler, might have been set free. We would say it again in the face of the authorities of this world who today would condemn him to exile and set in his place greed and suspicion and anger as rulers of the hearts of men. We would also say it to the crowds of the world, crowds bewildered by conflicting counsels, crowds wandering homeless, despoiled and spiritless across a world void of pity and reckless of life. To them, as to ourselves we would cry with exultation, Christ the Lord is risen today: Alleluia.

But this word is to be spoken and sung today not alone to lift our spirits from sorrow to joy, but also to rebuke our sin. We have lifted our buildings until they seem to touch the sky; we have raised our stores of gold till our wealth towers above our wisdom to use it rightly; we have exalted our pride till we have forgot that we are the brothers of all men. Surely it is time that Christ the Lord be risen today, and by our several and united loyalties made to stand even higher than the achievements we have boasted. Do thou, eternal Spirit of God, the Father of all mankind, help us to make these words a recognition of our duty as well as a recollection of our Lord's triumph, that in every heart the experience of resurrection may be made a living, creative experience. Amen.

Edwin McNeill Poteat

228   We seek to come to thee in the spirit of this day and as children of the resurrection, who have been begotten again to a lively hope. Help us live remembering, and loving to remember, him who died for us and who rose again. May this be to us a day of brightness, of calmness, of joy, of humiliation, of contrition, of holy purpose. We seek to worship thee in simplicity through Jesus Christ, accepting him as the image of the Invisible God, the true revealer of thee the Father.

May we enter into that real communion with him by which we become members of Christ. May we feel this unity to be most real—a unity whose root is love, and therefore the best, which is eternal, and identifies us in all things with him. Enable us to realize some of the great things which are given to us in this union—the encouragement of knowing we are loved, of being accompanied through life by One who knows the way, and who has himself triumphed, who lived his life in evidence that the best things can be obtained. Especially he had a life in direct communication with thee the father; and this he gives to us—a life forgiven, at peace, an energetic and hopeful fulfilment of God's will. We desire truly to consecrate ourselves to thee. Put that heart within us which shall make this true, necessary, abiding.

When disheartened by our own guilt and weakness may we find consolation and renewal in thee, and may we be enabled to believe that we can be as truly nourished by Christ's life as each member is by the life of the body. And as he embraced all men in his love, and could leave none outside, so may we be emptied of self and filled with love to thee and to our fellow-men, doing good to all as we have opportunity. In all that we purpose may we set thee before us, and give us the assurance that all our plans are well-pleasing in thy sight. Amen.

Marcus Dods

229   We thank thee, O Lord, for the faith which overcometh the world. We thank thee for victory over life with its temptations, its failures, and its separations; that the dominant note of life is joy and its mightiest force is love and its last word is hope. We thank thee that in many a gray morning we have seen the stone rolled away from the heart sepulchres and an angel sitting on it; so that the sorrow and loss which seemed to have closed down upon us was not only rolled back but glorified, and what seemed an irreparable loss has become a guide or genius. We thank thee for the victory over life.

We thank thee, too, for the victory over death; that the tomb cannot hold our dead nor the grave enclose our beloved. We know not how thou dost bring them forth. We know not how thou canst lead these broken lives and severed loves of ours to the fulfillment they demand, but all we know of love in ourselves, all we see of it in other human hearts, makes us confident that thou willest this fulfillment, and what thou willest thou canst. Thine, O Lord, is the victory.

We thank thee that in the light of Easter even death, that was the king of terrors, has become a hallowed thing, the answer to our prayer for life, more life and fuller. Help us to think of death not as the end of being but as its true beginning; not as a wall against which which we dash our heads but as a door opening to a larger room of the Father's house, a room prepared for us and made home-like by those who have gone before. Give us the sure faith that looks beyond the grave and trusts the larger hope. May we trust faith more than sight, for our eyes have deceived us and things are not what they seem. But faith is what thou hast writ into the heart of man.

We thank thee that when thy children die it is into a Father's hand they commit their spirits, and that in thy hands they are safe. We thank thee for all our great and noble dead who have enriched the world evermore and being dead yet speak to us. We pray that the work they have passed on to us may be taken up and carried forward with a will, and may we walk from day to day as those who are engaged with affairs of eternity.

Strengthen thou, O Lord, the heart of those who weep by new-made graves and by graves that seem opened but yesterday though years have passed over them. Let none linger where they left their dead. May a voice speak to them in the garden and say: "Not here! Risen! Alive for evermore!" Amen.

Paul Moore Strayer

Poems

230   *EASTER LIGHT*

> Because upon the first glad Easter day
> The stone that sealed his tomb was rolled away,
> So, through the deepening shadows of death's night,
> Men see an open door—beyond it light.
>
> *Ida Norton Munson*

231   *AN EASTER CANTICLE*

> In every trembling bud and bloom
>   That cleaves the earth, a flowery sword,
> I see thee come from out the tomb,
>   Thou risen Lord.
>
> In every April wind that sings
>   Down lanes that make the heart rejoice;
> Yea, in the word the wood thrush brings
>   I hear thy voice.
>
> Lo! every tulip is a cup
>   To hold thy morning's brimming wine;
> Drink, O my soul, the wonder up—
>   Is it not thine?

❋

Thou art not dead! Thou art the whole
Of life that quickens in the sod;
Green April is thy very soul,
Thou great Lord God!

Charles Hanson Towne

232   *THOUGHT FOR EASTER*

There is no dark despair that cannot be
Evicted from the heart's Gethsemane;
For faith is always more than unbelief
And vibrant courage triumphs over grief.

Mary E. McCullough

233   *EASTER MORNING*

This is the beauty of our Easter morning:
In him humanity may now arise
Out of the grave of self, all baseness scorning;
The holy radiance of his glorious eyes
Illumines everywhere uplifted faces,
Touches the earthly with a heavenly glow,
And in that blessed light all human graces
Into divine beatitudes must grow.

Lucy Larcom

234   *GOOD FRIDAY IN MY HEART*

Good Friday in my heart! Fear and affright!
My thoughts are the disciples when they fled,
My words the words that priest and soldier said,
My deed the spear to desecrate the dead,
And day, thy death therein, is changed to night.

Then Easter in my heart sends up the sun.
My thoughts are Mary, when she turned to see,
My words are Peter, answering, "Lov'st thou me?"
My deeds are all thine own drawn close to thee,
And night and day, since thou dost rise, are one.

Mary Elizabeth Coleridge

235   *MIRACLE*

If I had never seen a tiny blade,
Pulsing with life,
Where yesterday was only naked soil,
I could but doubt.

But I have seen the eager green things come
Through bare, brown earth,
Taking the gift of life from Unseen Power,
And this I know:

The resurrection of the Christ is not
More miracle
Than that a little plant should start to grow
On Easter morn.

Gladys Shafer

236   *TOMBS*

Egyptian tombs hold priceless things,
Sceptres and crowns and rings,
And ornaments of cunning skill
To humor the imperial will
Of mummied potentates.
Full tombs,
Great corridors and rooms,
To tell of ancient powers and high estates.

And has an empty tomb no glory shed?
"He is not here; He is risen," angels said.

Louise Webster

237   *ALIVE FOR EVERMORE*

Whom God hath raised up, having loosed the pangs of death: because it
was not possible that he should be holden of it. AC. 2:24

His spirit lives; he died and is alive,
That pure will haunts this guilty world forever.

How could men's idle fury drive
That mighty shepherd from his sheep? Or sever
His heart from Mary's, Peter's? Or deprive
Iscariot and the thief of his blest rod,
Far in the ultimate night apart from God?
Never, never
Could death's thin shadows dim that ardent Sun!
He walks amid the Golden Candlesticks
Today, and lights all souls while time shall run,
Who on the Crucifix tree by his own troth affixed
Has knit the life of God and man forever.

Amos N. Wilder

238   *FOR RESURRECTION LIVING*

For resurrection living
    There is resurrection power,
And the praise and prayer of trusting
    May glorify each hour.
For common days are holy
    And year's an Easter-tide
To those who with the living Lord
    In living faith abide.

Author Unknown

Topics, Texts and Themes

239   *THE GLORIES OF EASTER MORN*

Made of the seed of David according to the flesh; and declared to be the
Son of God with power . . . by the resurrection from the dead. ro. 1:3-4

Easter Day was a new Christmas Day; it was the second birth of Christ. His
second birth was grander than his first. His first birth was under disadvantages. The disadvantages lay not in the manger, but in the royal lineage. The
swaddling bands that circumscribed him were not the facts of his poverty, but
the glories of his ancestors; the royal line of David separated him from the main
line of humanity. But when he came from the dead he changed his lineage.
He broke with the line of David—with all lines but the lowliest. His second
life was not from Bethlehem: it was from the common dust of all cities—from
the city of the dead. We think of him as nearer to us when a child. That is a

great mistake. As a child he was always the Jewish Messiah—nearer to the tribes of Israel than to the tribes of Man. But with Easter morn he came up from the *depths*—from the dust of death. He came from the place where all join hands; and that is the secret of his resurrection power. We all meet in the lowest valley. We do not all meet on the highest mountain, on any mountain. We are not made one by joy; the privilege of the Jew divides him from the Gentile. But calamity makes us one; sin and death make us one. Christmas morning was beautiful, but it came from the fields of gold; Easter morning is more precious, for it comes from the miry clay.

George Matheson

240   *EASTER DAY*

That I may know him, and the power of his resurrection. PH. 8:10

We celebrate on Easter day the rising of our Saviour from the tomb. For that the whole aspect of our thought and worship changes. Our sober churches burst out into flowers, our hushed voices break out into songs of praise, our whole religiousness puts on another robe—exultation instead of sorrow, "the garment of praise for the spirit of heaviness." And we go about with one another, heart saying to heart everywhere, "Christ is risen." And what makes that such a glad greeting is the assurance that is hidden in under it and is heard up through it: "We too shall rise." It is the assurance of our immortality bound up with Christ's, the certainty that because he rose we shall rise also, that makes the resurrection such a message of gladness to us all.

But is that all? Is this simple assurance of continued existence, that we are to rise from the dead and go on in some future state of existence—is this what Paul means by "the power of the resurrection"? It seems certainly evident enough that Paul meant more than this—that it was some great powerful change to be worked in and on him himself. On him—not merely on things about him. It was not simply that by Christ's death and resurrection the tyranny of the old law of decay had been broken, so that instead of living seventy years his life was to stretch out into eternity and never to end. It was evidently that the quality of the life itself was to be changed, that he was to be something new and different, and not that he was just to be the same old thing a little or a good deal longer, when he should know the power of the resurrection. This was what he prayed for. . . . The promise of resurrection finds its consummate satisfaction only in close union with the other promise of regeneration. The two must go together—the new world and the new man.

Phillips Brooks

241   *RESURRECTION*

And he saith unto them, Be not affrighted: Ye seek Jesus of Nazareth,
which was crucified: he is risen. MK. 16:6

The meaning of the Resurrection is not hard to trace. Hundreds of sermons
are preached each Easter on immortality, but mere immortality is not the
Easter message. The disciples themselves probably believed in some kind of immortality even before Jesus came—in Sheol, a pale and shadowy replica of our
life on earth. The mere continuance of our tragic life on earth is hardly "Good
News." Some religions, Buddhism among them, propose escape from immortality, and see oblivion as salvation from the endless wheel of life. No, the meaning of Resurrection is *resurrection*: not the interminable dragging on of an
old life, but a new life springing from death.

Thus the meaning is that the fetters of evil are broken. How could Peter live
with himself after having lied his way out of danger? How can any man, or
any generation, live with perpetrated lies? They are like chains fastened upon
us. But when Christ rose from the dead, his disciples knew that his whole life
and death were held in the life of God. There on Calvary God had dealings
with us. What dealings? The word of forgiveness spoken there by Jesus was
God's word held in God's power. The sufferings of Jesus there were God's
sufferings—the grief of the Holy Father for the sins of his children on earth.
The cry of Jesus, "It is finished!" meant that God's war with man's evil had
been fought and won in love. There was a Power now available, the presence
of the Risen Lord, stronger than all the bondage of our sins. That was the
meaning, and *is* the meaning of the Resurrection.

George Arthur Buttrick

242   *THE HEART OF CHRISTIANITY*

If ye then be risen with Christ. COL. 3:1

The heart of Christianity, its innermost sanctuary, its most dazzling glory,
and the chief source of its power is not even the Cross. It is the open grave.

To me, indeed, the Cross must always be a very central thing. Whenever I
wander far from Calvary I, for one, begin to lose sight of the Master, and have
to get back. And yet is there not real point in Michelangelo's indignant protest,
when he turned in his stormy way upon his fellow-painters and demanded:
"Why do you keep filling gallery after gallery with endless pictures of the one
ever-reiterated theme, of Christ in weakness, Christ upon the cross, Christ dying,
most of all Christ hanging dead? Why do you concentrate upon that passing

episode, as if that were the last word and the final scene, as if the curtain dropped upon that horror of disaster and defeat? At worst all that lasted for only a few hours. But to the end of unending eternity Christ is alive, Christ rules and reigns and triumphs." And, if we would help people to be valiant in their Christian living, it is that we should be ringing out over the world that Christ has won, that evil is toppling, that the end is sure, that nothing can for long resist our mighty and victorious Lord. That is the tonic that we need to keep us healthy, the trumpet blast to fire our blood, and send us crowding in behind the Master, swinging happily upon our way, ready and eager to face anything, laughing and singing and recklessly unafraid, because the feel of victory is in the air, and our hearts thrill to it.   *Arthur John Gossip*

243   *EASTER JOY*

Thou hast turned . . . my heaviness into dancing: thou hast put off my sackcloth, and girded me with gladness. PS. 30:11

Here is described a change, complete, and more or less sudden, from sadness to joy. David has escaped a danger which had brought him very near to death; and now he is thankful and exultant. His words are in keeping with what Christians feel, as they pass from the last days of Holy Week into the first hours of Easter. If Easter is associated predominantly with any one emotion, it is with that of joy. When Mary Magdalene and the other Marys had heard the words of the angel of the Lord, "They departed quickly from the sepulchre, with fear and great joy." When, on the evening of Easter day, Jesus stood in the midst of the assembled disciples, and showed them his hands and his feet, their joy was too great for the steady exercise of their understanding: "They believed not for joy, and wondered." In these first hours of ecstatic bewilderment, as St. John says, "The disciples were glad when they saw the Lord." Was it not his own promise of a joy which would be beyond the reach of outward circumstance, that had now become true? "Verily, verily, I say unto you, that ye shall weep and lament, but the world shall rejoice"—that was the hour of Calvary—"and ye shall be sorrowful, but your sorrow shall be turned into joy" —that was to be the radiance of Easter.   *H. P. Liddon*

244   *THE FELLOWSHIP OF THE HOPEFUL*

For we are saved by hope. RO. 8:24

This is Easter Sunday. All over the world men's thoughts are turning to the new life which faith in Christ makes possible. From the sorrow and tragedy and heart-break of the present we lift our eyes to the new possibilities to which our risen and triumphant Master points us. Of all the festivals of the Christian year, Easter is pre-eminently the festival of hope.

But Christianity, we must remember, has no monopoly of hope. Jesus came into a world in which he found men already looking forward. What he brought was a clear vision of the goal, a reinforcement of the grounds for believing its attainment possible, and, above all, the example of a faith which, faced with what seemed the certainty of failure, held steadfast and was justified by the event.

William Adams Brown

245 *DESIGN FOR LIVING*

There is a big mistake about Easter. The big mistake about Easter is imagining that its message is simply a bit of comfort for the dying. It is that, and every one of us here shall face the hour when such a comfort will be like drops of cool water upon the parched lips of a very thirsty man.

But most of us are not expecting to die today; we are expecting to live to-morrow and many tomorrows. Does Easter have anything to say to us? Indeed Easter's supreme message is for us who expect to live. Turn again to the fifteenth chapter of First Corinthians. It has been called Paul's great taunt song sung to Death. "This corruptible must put on incorruption, and this mortal must put on immortality. . . . Death is swallowed up in victory. . . . O grave where is thy victory?" And what is Paul's conclusion? At the end of this song of triumph does he say, "Therefore, don't be afraid to die"? Nothing of the kind. His application is, "Therefore, don't be afraid to live!" Moreover, "Don't be afraid to live for God." He is saying that the message of Christ's resurrection is that the universe is on the side of truth, goodness and love. You may give yourself to these values sure that such living cannot be wasted.

Frank B. Fagerburg

246 *THE MESSAGE OF EASTER*

Easter is the demonstration of God that life itself is essentially spiritual and timeless. Easter tells us that life is to be interpreted not simply in terms of things but in terms of ideals. Easter speaks of life not only by years but by yearnings also. Easter identifies life not only with decay and destruction, but with continuance and creation. Easter is God's way of saying that man through Christ shares the life of God now and forever.

Charles M. Crowe

247   THE CROSS OF VICTORY

It is startling to us who are so attached to the Cross as a symbol of Christianity and its all-conquering power to find no symbolic use of the Cross in the Catacombs, or elsewhere, for almost three hundred years after Christ's Ascension. When at last it does appear in the Catacombs, it is not the passion Cross nor the Cross of the Lord's suffering, but the resurrection Cross, the Cross of the Lord's victory, that we see. Christ is represented as coming forth from his tomb mightily bearing a Cross, a picture of the living Lord who has triumphed over death.

James G. K. McClure

248   A NEW AND GLORIOUS POWER

No question ever occurred to the early Christian mind as to any difficulty about the resurrection: the event was so new it would be like disputing the dew of the morning; there it was, the thing was immediately present; it was a new eye in the midst of things looking over all the cloud and through it, and testifying to a new and glorious power. Paul turned the resurrection of Jesus Christ into an argument, and into a poem, and into an inspiration. He lived on it, he risked the whole Christian fabric upon the resurrection: "If Christ be not risen from the dead, then is our preaching vain," and that would be nothing; but "your faith is also vain," you are harboring a dead trust, you are mocking your own soul.

Joseph Parker

249   ENLIGHTENED BY EASTER

Easter has been called "the flower of the year." It commemorates the crowning act in our Redeemer's earthly life and guarantees the truth of our religion. "If Christ be not raised," says the apostle, "your faith is vain." If he still lives, here is the most significant fact ever revealed. It turns the tidings of Jesus into the good news of the Gospel. More is involved here than we can explain, but the multitudes who throng our sanctuaries this day are convinced that we are dealing with something basic and full of promise.

Easter heightens our appreciation of the fact that reality is more than obvious. . . . It testifies that life is more than mere duration. . . . It testifies that the soul is too big for earth. . . . It assures us that death has been conquered.

Teunis E. Gouwens

250 EASTER CONTRASTS

Out of the east comes new light after the darkness of night. And we call it morning. Out of the Easter morning came a wondrous new light—the light of life—after the darkness of sin's night. And it has been the first gleam of a morning, the morning of a new day, for all men.

Contrasts make things stand out. Black touching white seems blacker, and the white looks whiter. Sorrow makes joy seem gladder. Joy makes sorrow seem sadder. The deeper the sorrow, the greater is the uplift of joy following, after the first daze is over.

That first Easter morning stood in sharpest contrast with what went before. The greatest possible contrast is between life and death. All sorrow and darkness and heaviness brood in the black word—death. All gladness and brightness and lightness gather up at their best in that lightsome word—life.

S. D. Gordon

251 BEATITUDES OF THE RISEN LIFE

Blessed is the man whose heart today burns as he walks with Jesus by the way. Blessed is the man who having not seen, yet believes.

Blessed is the man who hears the voice of the Risen Lord saying, "Peace be unto you."

Blessed is the man who accepts the glorious Master, Jesus Christ, as his Lord and his God, and worships him.

Blessed is the man who thus lives the power of the endless life through fellowship with the Risen Lord.

Blessed is the man whose words and deeds are day by day and every day a witness to the living and loving Lord.

Blessed is the man who obeys the Risen Lord's last great command and commission, "Go ye into all the world and preach my gospel," for unto him shall be fulfilled the Lord's promise, "Lo I am with you always, even unto the end."

Oliver Huckel

RISEN OR REALIZED

Unto the measure of the stature of the fulness of Christ. EP. 4:13

The risen Christ has become in our minds the Christ of the theologians, the Christ of the ecclesiastic enthroned on altars and embalmed in sacraments, a venerated object of worship on the part of a religious cult that has grown up about him, a mystical strength and solace and assurance to adoring multitudes.

The realized Christ is a Christ incorporated into life, an incarnated spirit of love and good will, the embodied purpose to serve and to help, the urge in a man's breast which makes him assume burdens of responsibility for the weakness, the ignorance, the folly about him, girds him with sympathy and forgiveness, and makes him yearn somehow, somewhere, in his small way, to be a savior of mankind. The former is something to worship, to believe; the latter is something to live. The one is full often a selfish enjoyment; the other unfailingly an activity expressive and beneficent.

Carl Hopkins Elmore

253   *NATIONAL AWAKENING*

Arise, shine; for thy light is come, and the glory of the Lord is risen upon thee. IS. 60:1

What ought to happen in this concrete and confused world, if Christ rose from the dead, and if in him we shall all rise again? *He* conquered sin and death absolutely, and he conquered them representatively, potentially, for us. Can we set about to make conquest of the sin that is destroying the world about us today, and the death which is always its wages? Our light is come in the Risen Christ; the glory of the Lord is risen upon us. How may we as a people arise? How may this land of ours have a national resurrection? . . .

The first step is not resurrection, it is crucifixion. You never really get what Easter means if you haven't been through Good Friday with Christ. It is the crucifixion of pride, narrowness, stupidity, ignorant prejudice, intolerance, fixed viewpoints about other people, laziness, lack of vision, self-satisfaction, conventionality that we need. There is no resurrection without crucifixion. The reason Christ's Cross is so central is that there is a cross at the center of life anyway: either God's will is crucified on it so that our will may prevail; or our will is crucified on it so that God's will may prevail. . . .

You say, What can I do in national resurrection? I am only one person: it will take thousands. What can I do? . . . The first thing we can do is to face our own responsibility: admit that we make this country what it is, and might make it what it should be, if we would put behind us the practice of hoping somebody else would do it. . . . The next thing is that we recognize that only God can make us different. Only God can give us the sharpened sense of sin we need if we are to see wherein we are part of the world's need. . . . Third, many of us are in need of someone to help us see ourselves as we are, to see how we might become an answer instead of a problem in this nation. . . . Fourth, we need to make a decision. Christ in Galilee decided to go down to Jerusalem and risk death. In Gethsemane on Thursday night he decided he would go through with death for the sake of changing and redeeming the world. We have got to decide. . . . Fifth, we need training in the next steps of obeying God in everything, and so we need company. Only in companies can we work out our problems together, and only in companies can we make the world believe that God has the answer to its needs.

Samuel M. Shoemaker

254   THE INNER RESURRECTION

Because I live, ye shall live also. JN. 14:19

Christ is ever rising again. Day by day men seek to bury him under the debris of history, or embalm him in creed and phrase and definition, or immure him within the walls of churches and institutions, or smother him under a load of the cares and riches and pleasures of this life, or stab him to death with the daggers of their sins. But always he rises, phoenixlike, from the ashes of the fires of selfishness and carelessness in which we allow his power over our lives to be destroyed. Ever and again he is lifted up out of the common things of life, a vindication of his life and a triumph over the powers that did him to death, and all men are drawn to him as irresistibly as the earth is held in its orbit around the sun. The empty tomb opens before the world, telling us it is God who still has the last word, not ourselves; that on Easter day life looks forward, onward, upward, God-ward.

Elmer S. Freeman

255   THE EASTER SECRET

Death hath no more dominion over him. RO. 6:9

Jesus Christ is actually more alive today than he was before his death. He influences more people, he is better understood, he is more inspiring and comforting. It is pathetic to hear people repining that they did not live to know him in his physical lifetime, for it only means that they do not know that they have better opportunities to be acquainted with his whole life, and his purposes, and their significance for the world, than the most intimate of his disciples could possibly have had.

Edward Scribner Ames

256   *THE RESURRECTION OF THE SOUL*

> If we be dead with Christ, we believe that we shall also live with him.
> RO. 6:8

Charles Dickens' celebrated *Christmas Carol* is a Christmas story only in its setting; in theme it is actually an Easter carol, because it describes the resurrection of a dead soul. Scrooge was as mean and selfish an old skinflint as it is possible to imagine; his heart was cold to every generous impulse and kindly emotion. But in the course of the story he is led to see how hateful a being he has become, and in the end his old soul dies and a new soul rises within him. Scrooge inhabits the same body, but he is no longer the same man. Instead of being a withered old miser, he is a kind-hearted, charitable gentleman. And this is clearly a story which illustrates the truth of Easter.

When you and I come to church on Easter Sunday, what we want to know above everything else is how we may become new and better men and women. How can we conquer our evil passions; how can we master our tempers; how can we banish despair; how can we lay hold of joy? In other words, how can we make sure of eternal life here and now? That is the question fundamental to the question of immortality, because we know well enough that if we possess eternal life here, we need not trouble about immortality hereafter.

Charles H. Heimsath

257   *THAT UNESCAPABLE FUTURE TENSE*

We human beings live in three dimensions of time. We have memories of the past and experiences in the present, but Easter emphasizes the third, that unescapable future tense. The more worth while we are the more we possess that. It is low grade personalities who are pushed about by their past; it is the shiftless who live only in the present; but the creative spirits have always projected ahead their plans, purposes, aspirations, ambitions and ideals, until not alone the pressure of yesterday and the experience of today but the hope of tomorrow has been powerful in them. The more worth while we are the more important to us is that unescapable future tense and there in every man's future, obvious and certain, stands death.

Harry Emerson Fosdick

258 *THE FINAL TRIUMPH*

The last enemy that shall be destroyed is death. 1 co. 15:26

At the center of the Christian faith, there is the resurrection of Jesus. Some moderns have objected to the amount of space in the New Testament devoted to the Easter story. Why not spend more time discussing the life and teachings of Jesus? they say. Their assumption is that we are encouraged to spend too much time on what is secondary and we neglect the most important part of the Gospel. But such thinking is wrong. Those early Christians knew that the heart of their message was an announcement that the power of God has raised Christ from the dead. Admittedly, they did not know just what happened and some of their accounts seem confused. They could not find the precise words to express it and they fell back on symbolism to suggest their meanings. But the central truth of the experience they never doubted and they made it the center of their message.

Christians can never explain the resurrection because it is the resurrection that explains them. The rationalistic interpreters of Christianity can never find reasons convincing enough to be substituted for the resurrection. Their logic always has a gap in it. The whole Christian movement demands the resurrection in order to account for it. It is much more of a strain on our credulity to believe that our Lord was raised from the dead. I am frank to confess that I do not know the details of what happened on the third day. But I have been driven by the inadequacy of all other explanations, to believe that the Gospel which I have been called to proclaim, is rooted in Jesus Christ's victory over death.

Gerald Kennedy

259 *THE CONQUEROR OF DEATH*

Thanks be to God, who giveth us the victory through our Lord Jesus Christ.
1 co. 15:57

Grateful as we are for the blessings of peace, we are still confronted with the fact of death. Most of us try hard to keep thoughts of death from intruding upon us. In the ancient Greek legend the River Styx separated the region of the dead from the land of the living. And the name "Styx" comes from the verb "to hate, to loathe." From the days of the Greeks down to our own, the river of death has been regarded as a dark and fearsome stream.

Easter commemorates the day when Christ established a bridgehead on the other side of the River Styx. Christ, the Captain of our salvation, not only convinced his followers that he had effected a crossing of death's dark stream but also that he had gone to prepare a place for them. So confident are those who know him best that they shout with Paul, "Thanks be to God who giveth us the victory through our Lord Jesus Christ."

Ralph W. Sockman

H. UNIVERSAL WEEK OF PRAYER

Universal Week of Prayer, observed on an international basis during the first week of January, dates back to 1848 and appropriately inaugurates the New Year in the spirit of confession, petition, and intercession. Weekday services of devotion and instruction are often planned.

Other special occasions which unite all Christendom in prayer include Universal Day of Prayer for Students, usually assigned to the third Sunday in February and sponsored by the World's Student Christian Federation as an opportunity for college youth to profess their mutual concern and interest, and World Day of Prayer, celebrated now in more than one hundred countries on the first Friday in Lent and emphasizing the missionary witness of the church.

Calls to Worship

(Boldface type indicates responses.)

260   The Lord is nigh unto all them that call upon him, to all that call upon him in truth.

He will fulfil the desire of them that fear him: he also will hear their cry, and will save them.

Ask, and it shall be given you; seek, and ye shall find; knock, and it shall be opened unto you.

Ps. 145:18–19; Mat. 7:7

261   The Lord is in his holy temple: let all the earth keep silence before him. In every thing by prayer and supplication with thanksgiving let your requests be made known unto God. And the peace of God, which passeth all understanding, shall keep your hearts and minds through Christ Jesus.

Hab. 2:20; Ph. 4:6–7

262   They that wait upon the Lord shall renew their strength; they shall mount up with wings as eagles; they shall run, and not be weary; and they shall walk, and not faint. Wait on the Lord: be of good courage, and he shall strengthen thine heart: wait, I say, on the Lord.

Is. 40:31; Ps. 27:14

263   Who shall ascend into the hill of the Lord? or who shall stand in his
holy place?

**He that hath clean hands, and a pure heart; who hath not lifted up his
soul unto vanity, nor sworn deceitfully.**

Having therefore, brethren, boldness to enter into the holiest by the blood of
Jesus, by a new and living way, which he hath consecrated for us . . . let us
draw near with a true heart in full assurance of faith.

Ps. 24:3–4; He. 10:19–20, 22

Invocations

264   Our Father in heaven, we thank thee for the comradeship of prayer. As
we reverently wait before thee make us gratefully sensible of the great company,
to us unseen, who unite their prayers with ours. May we ask nothing for ourselves in which others may not be blessed; nor seek from thee any gain to their
loss. Multiply these hallowed moments of deep fellowship until they become
the bright day of brotherhood; for Jesus' sake. Amen.

Gaius Glenn Atkins

265   O Lord God, who never failest both to hear and to answer the prayer
that is sincere: let not our hearts be upon the world when our hands are lifted
up to pray, nor our prayers end upon our lips, but go forth with power to work
thy will in the world; through Jesus Christ our Lord. Amen.

Daily Prayer

266   Omnipotent and most merciful God, grant that we may diligently seek,
ardently desire, prudently examine, truly know and perfectly accomplish those
things which are pleasing unto thee; through Jesus Christ our Lord. Amen.

Thomas Aquinas

267   O God, crown with thy blessing the prayers of thy worshippers throughout the world. Give us grace to prepare our hearts, that we may serve thee with
reverence and godly fear. Grant us a true apprehension of thy divine majesty,
and a deep sense of our own unworthiness; that so, approaching thee with lowliness and devotion, we may commune with thee in the spirit of Jesus Christ
our Lord. Amen.

Anthology of Prayers for Public Worship

268   O Lord our God, who lovest the gates of Zion more than all the dwellings of Jacob, and who art ever nigh unto them that call upon thee in truth:

be merciful to us, we beseech thee, and make us joyful in thy house of prayer. Be pleased to shed thy Holy Spirit on all that are here assembled; that, being cleansed from sin and illumined by thy grace, we may worthily show forth thy praise, meekly learn thy word, render due thanks for thy mercies, and obtain a gracious answer to our prayers; through the merits of Jesus Christ our Lord. Amen.

Presbyterian Forms of Service

Prayers

269　Eternal Spirit, far above us and yet deep within us: we worship thee. The world is too much with us. We are distracted by its varying claims and tossed by its many winds. We would escape for a while from its clamorous noises into another and higher world where there are unity and purpose, sense and meaning, faith and hope. Clarify our minds, we beseech thee. Give us great ideas that we may strike our roots into them and be strong when the heavy winds descend. Clarify our hearts. Let the sediment settle. Save us from the folly of vindictiveness to the wisdom of magnanimity, and let goodwill have its way in our lives. Clarify our wills, we beseech thee. Save us from our cross-purposes and contradictory ambitions, and let some soul cry today, This one thing I do!

As we pray for ourselves, we know ourselves at one with all the souls of men. It is when we stand before the Eternal that we see of how little moment are the divisions of race and color, nation and speech, that separate man from man. Our souls are one; our deep needs are alike; our highest aspirations are the same. Thou hast made of one all mankind to dwell upon the face of the earth.

We lift our prayer today for those who forget to pray for themselves. If there are boys and girls offering no petitions for themselves, happy with the passing days, making no earnest supplication for their lives, we pray for them. Our hope is in them. Couldst thou, O Lord, lay thine hand on one of them, he might swing the gate of a new era for mankind. We lift up in our solicitous petition the youth of the world.

If there are churches that forget to pray for themselves, complacent and content, we pray for them. Thou didst give unto us so great a Founder, forgive us that we are so little worthy of him. Shame us in his presence. Impress his portrait on our imaginations that we may not forget him, that he may rebuke us constantly and then guide us toward that day when Christianity shall possess the quality of Christ.

We pray for those so harassed by difficulty and so lost to all high and vivid faith that they cannot pray for themselves. Grant to some such today such a vision of blue sky through the gathering clouds that they may be sure again that the sun is shining. Give us radiance instead of darkness; give us stability instead of bewilderment; and set some sore-stricken and shaken soul today upon such deep foundations that though the rains descend and the floods come and the winds blow and beat upon his house it shall not fall. In the name of Christ. Amen.*

Harry Emerson Fosdick

270   Our heavenly Father, we earnestly ask that this moment we spend in the attitude of prayer may also be spent in the spirit and knowledge of prayer. May it ever be such a definite and conscious fellowship of our hearts with thine that it shall become increasingly sweet and satisfying to all of us. May we ever find in the hour of prayer healing for our wounds, peace for our strife, wisdom for our problems, forgiveness for our sins, and blessedness for all of life.

In this moment of prayer we ask that we may all have an increased consciousness of the reality and abiding presence of God and of the transcendent value and supremacy of spiritual things. Help us, dear Lord, to set our affections not upon things below, but upon things above. We pray for such an intimate acquaintance with Christ and for such an acceptance of his spirit and program that our own lives may be fruitful in service to the world.

Give us, dear Father, such a quickened feeling of responsibility for our own surroundings as will lead us to the endeavor of their welfare. May we be more faithful to our vows and obligations to our country, our church, and our homes, that through these agencies we may so love and labor as to speedily bring in the reign of thy Kingdom. Amen.

Frank G. Smith

271   O thou who art the Creator of all mankind, we rejoice that in the mystery of thy wisdom thou hast made us in thine own spiritual image. And thou hast made us one! We know that thou hast made of one blood all nations and races of men to dwell on all the face of the earth. Into this great family of thy children we are born. Help us in our spirits and in our living to look upon all men everywhere as brothers who bear the stamp of thy creative handiwork.

Yet thou hast given us still closer bonds. For in thine infinite love thou hast sent thy Son for our redemption, and hast knit together in Christ's church those who bear his name and seek through him to serve thee. Into that great company of Christ's followers by thy mercy and grace we have come, and within this world-wide fellowship our spirits are heartened and made strong.

Grant us, O God, a keener sense of the bonds that unite us, a more loving spirit, a more steadfast determination to let no earthly barriers of nation, or race, or class, or household of faith divide us. Make us thy servants, that through us may come a greater measure of peace on earth, good will among men. We pray in the name of him who, on the night that he was betrayed, prayed for his followers that they might all be one. Amen.

Georgia Harkness

272 Holy, holy, holy, Lord God of hosts, all the earth is filled with thy glory. We rejoice to see thy majesty in the universe about us. We thank thee that we feel thy presence in the fellowship of kindred minds in the beauty of this thy sanctuary.

How we bless thee for the gracious privilege of prayer. How we thank thee that at thy slightest whisper our heart wings its way to thy golden throne. Thine ear is ever inclined to the prayers of thy earth-born children. Teach us, Lord, that there is no prayer that in thy wisdom is left unanswered. Thy denials to our requests spare our souls of leanness. Always thou dost answer in ways best for those who put their trust in thee.

On this day a multitude of believers are gathered in prayer circles large and small throughout the whole earth. For their faithfulness and consecration, we thank thee. May all who pray this day in the secret of their hearts, or with two or three of like mind, or in vast assembly know that thou art in their midst.

Bless thy church universal. Be with her representatives at home and those who labor in far and distant clime. May the glorious gospel of forgiveness, redemption and life everlasting in Christ Jesus our Lord be so lived and taught by those who have named his name that the whole earth may be filled with the knowledge of the Lord. Hasten the day when at the name of Jesus every knee shall bow and every heart confess that he is Lord of all, and we shall give only to thee the glory, world without end. Amen.

Hillyer H. Straton

273 Almighty and Eternal Father, thou hast openly shown thy righteousness in the sight of the heathen and all the ends of the earth have seen the salvation of our God.

On this day of world-wide prayer we are gratefully conscious of spiritual fellowship with thy people of every race and land. With them we join in prayer that thy truth and justice shall have dominion from sea to sea, and that all the nations shall learn to love and serve thee.

We praise thy name for the faithful missionaries whom thou hast called and sent by thy Spirit to far places. Humbly we confess that our share in their service has been small. We join with them, O God, in thanksgiving for thy children in every land who have heard the Gospel call and have responded to the challenge. We pray especially for those who stand in peril because of their faith and loyalty to thee. Protect, guide and sustain these our heroic brethren, dear Lord, and grant them thine aid and comfort.

We rejoice in the privilege of fellowship with those afar who pray for us and with us, even as we pray for them. May this day of universal intercession strengthen all Christian ties. We pray in the name of him after whom every family in heaven and earth is named and who himself prayed that we all might be one, even as he and his Father are one. Amen.

Ralph Walker

Poems

274   *THE UNSEEN BRIDGE*

> There is a bridge, whereof the span
> Is rooted in the heart of man,
> And reaches, without pile or rod,
> Unto the Great White Throne of God.
> Its traffic is in human sighs
> Fervently wafted to the skies;
> 'Tis the one pathway from despair;
> And it is called the Bridge of Prayer.

Gilbert Thomas

275   *THE PLACE OF PEACE*

> At the heart of the cyclone tearing the sky
> And flinging the clouds and the towers by,
>   Is a place of central calm:
> So here in the roar of mortal things,
> I have a place where my spirit sings,
>   In the hollow of God's Palm.

Edwin Markham

276   *From THE LITTLE GATE TO GOD*

> In the castle of my soul
> Is a little postern gate,
> Whereat, when I enter,
> I am in the presence of God.

In a moment, in the turning of a thought,
I am where God is,
This is a fact.
When I enter into God,
All life has a meaning,
Without asking I know;
My desires are even now fulfilled,
My fever is gone
In the great quiet of God.
My troubles are but pebbles on the road,
My joys are like the everlasting hills.

Walter Rauschenbusch

277   *From MORTE D'ARTHUR*

More things are wrought by prayer
Than this world dreams of. Wherefore, let thy voice
Rise like a fountain for me night and day.
For what are men better than sheep or goats
That nourish a blind life within the brain,
If, knowing God, they lift not hands of prayer
Both for themselves and those who call them friend?
For so the whole round earth is every way
Bound by gold chains about the feet of God.

Alfred Tennyson

278   *I NEED NOT LEAVE THE JOSTLING WORLD*

I need not leave the jostling world
Or wait 'till all my work is o'er
To fold my hands in secret prayer
Behind the silent, close-shut door.

There is a viewless, cloistered room
As high as heaven, as fair as day,
Where—though my feet must join the throng—
My soul can enter in and pray.

And people watching do not know
When I have crossed that threshold o'er,

But God himself who hears my prayer,
Perceives the shutting of that door.

Author Unknown

279   *From DIVINA COMMEDIA*

Oft have I seen at some cathedral door
    A laborer, pausing in the dust and heat,
    Lay down his burden, and with reverent feet
    Enter, and cross himself, and on the floor
Kneel to repeat his paternoster o'er;
    Far off the noises of the world retreat;
    The loud vociferations of the street
    Become an undistinguishable roar.
So as I enter here from day to day,
    And leave my burden at this minster gate,
    Kneeling in prayer, and not ashamed to pray,
The tumult of the time disconsolate
    To inarticulate murmurs dies away,
    While the eternal ages watch and wait.

Henry Wadsworth Longfellow

280   *From THE MEETING*

And so I find it well to come
For deeper rest to this still room,
For here the habit of the soul
Feels less the outer world's control;
For strength of mutual purpose pleads
More earnestly our common needs;
And from the silence multiplied
By these still forms on either side,
The world that time and sense have known
Falls off and leaves us God alone.

John Greenleaf Whittier

281   *TO THE SUPREME BEING*

The prayers I make will then be sweet indeed
If thou the spirit give by which I pray:

My unassisted heart is barren clay,
That of its native self can nothing feed:
Of good and pious works thou art the seed,
That quickens only where thou say'st it may:
Unless thou show to us thine own true way
No man can find it: Father! thou must lead.
Do thou, then, breathe those thoughts into my mind
By which such virtue may in me to be bred
That in thy holy footsteps I may tread;
The fetters of my tongue do thou unbind,
That I may have the power to sing of thee,
And sound thy praises everlastingly.

Michael Angelo, Tr. by William Wordsworth

282   *PERFECT DISENTHRALLMENT*

I, that still pray at morning and at eve

✻

Thrice in my life perhaps have truly prayed,
Thrice, stirred below my conscious self, have felt
That perfect disenthrallment which is God.

James Russell Lowell

Topics, Texts and Themes

283   *GOD-WARD SPEECH*

Prayer is man's side of converse with God; it is speech God-ward. Yes, prayer is speech God-ward, and worship is man's whole life of friendship with God, the flowing out, as it were, of all that tide of emotion and service which is love's best speech.

The essence of prayer is desire, forming itself into hope and aspiration, and mounting up into effort, in the direction of the unattained. Prayer is the address made by human personality to that with which it is desired to establish affiliations. It is a movement of the whole being which reaches after the heart's desire.

Prayer is the committal of our way unto the Lord, just as a deed of trust is the committal of our possessions to those who can handle them better than we. By living one day with God, preparation is made for living all days with God.

One may say that the real end of prayer is not so much to get this or **that** single desire granted, as to put human life into full and joyful conformity with the will of God.

Prayer is love melted into worship.

Charles H. Brent

284   *DIVINE-HUMAN FELLOWSHIP*

Prayer, whether it be the lisp of a little child or the wrestling of some great soul in desperate contest with the coils of habit or the evil customs of his generation, is a testimony to a divine-human fellowship. In hours of crisis the soul feels for its Companion, by a natural gravitation, as the brook feels for the ocean. In times of joy and strength, it reaches out to its source of life, as the plant does to the sun. And when it has learned the language of spiritual communion and knows its Father, praying refreshes it as the greeting of a friend refreshes one in a foreign land.

We ought not to expect that prayer, of the true and lofty sort, could be attained by easy steps. It involves appreciation of God and cooperation with him. One comes not to it in a day. Even human friendship is a great attainment. It calls for sacrifice of private wishes and for adjustment to the purposes of another life. One cannot be an artist or a musician without patient labor to make oneself an organ of the reality which he fain would express. He must bring himself by slow stages to a height of appreciation. Prayer is the highest human function.

Rufus M. Jones

285   *THE MOUNTAIN OF PRAYER*

And it came to pass about eight days after these sayings, he took Peter and John and James, and went up into the mountain to pray. And as he prayed, the fashion of his countenance was altered. LU. 9:28–29.

The purpose of the transfiguration has been variously stated, such as to establish Jesus as the Messiah, to confirm the status of Jesus in the presence of the laws and the prophets, to nerve and strengthen Jesus for the terrible ordeal ahead of him, and to reconcile his men to the approaching violence by revealing to them the glory that should follow. One wonders whether the real reason for the transfiguration is not stated for us so casually by St. Luke that, with the dramatic happenings described immediately, and in the midst of the pageantry, we miss his remark. It is that "Jesus went into the mountain to pray."

George Arthur Clarke

286   *PRAYER AS TAUGHT AND PRACTICED BY JESUS*

His prayer before temptation (Lu. 3:21; 4:1-13).

His prayer before appointing the twelve (Lu. 6:12-16).

His prayer before the Sermon on the Mount (Lu. 6:12, 17-49).

His practice of common prayer (Lu. 4:16-32; Mk. 1:21-22).

His teaching as to the manner of prayer (Mat. 6:5-8).

His teaching as to the matter of prayer (Mat. 6:9-15).

His teaching as to earnestness in prayer (Mat. 7:7-11; Lu. 11:5-10; 18:1-8).

His teaching as to the object of prayer (Lu. 11:11-13).

His prayer after serving the people (Mat. 14:22–23).

His prayer before his glory was manifested (Lu. 9:28-36).

His story about vain prayer (Lu. 18:9-14).

His prayer in joy (Lu. 10:17-24; Mat. 11:25-30).

His teaching as to the condition and power of prayer (Mat. 18:19-20; Mk. 11:22-25).

His warning concerning too much formal prayer (Lu. 20:45-47; Mat. 6:7-8).

His exhortation to vigilant prayer (Lu. 21:34-36; Mat. 24:32; 25:13).

His promises to the prayerful (Jn. 14:12-17; 15:7-10; 16:23-24).

His prayer for all Christians (Jn. 17).

His prayer for himself (Mat. 26:36-44).

His prayers from the Cross (Lu. 23:34, 46).

Thy Kingdom Come

287   *HOW TO PRAY AS A CHRISTIAN*

But thou, when thou prayest, enter into thy closet, and when thou hast shut thy door, pray to thy Father which is in secret; and thy Father which seeth in secret shall reward thee openly. MAT. 6:6

Jesus said to his disciples, "When ye pray." He did not say, "If ye pray." He presented no evidence to men that prayer was a scientific and an experimental fact. He never presented an apology for prayer. He took for granted that everywhere and always men sought after God, if haply they might find him. I take it that in the language of Jesus prayer is synonymous with faith and the desire to find religious reality. The greatest inquiry of the Christian heart is expressed in the words of the disciples' request to Jesus: "Lord, teach us to pray."

Hugh Thomson Kerr

288   *TAPPING LIFE'S RESERVES*

Men ought always to pray, and not to faint. lu. 18:1

Our Lord could have been thinking of our present-day world when he said
to his disciples, "Men ought always to pray, and not to faint," for his admonition presupposes a difficult time. Literally translated, his words are: "Men ought
always to pray, and not to fall out." We shall get the idea if we picture a column
of Roman soldiers on a gruelling march under the hot Syrian sun. If a soldier
weakens and falls out, he is walked over and left behind. In other words, Jesus
said, "When the going is toughest and life is the most exacting, men should
pray; then they will not fall out and be left behind."

Herschel H. Hobbs

289   *FAITH AND PRAYER*

There is a vast difference between prayer in faith and faith in prayer. Having
faith in prayer is believing that because certain prayers are offered certain results
will follow—that the praying will secure the thing prayed for. Praying in faith
comes of an abiding confidence in the Person prayed to; the confidence is in
him; it is based on a knowledge of what he is and on a conviction that he is in
every way worthy to be trusted. Praying in faith is the act of a simple-hearted
child of God.

H. Clay Trumbull

290   *THE PURPOSE OF PRAYER*

Prayer, which means the knowledge of God by firsthand *acquaintance* rather
than by mere *description,* is a turning away from self to the Divine Companion.
The purpose of prayer is not to change God's intention, which is already perfectly loving, but rather, by some mysterious process, which in our finiteness
we cannot understand, to open channels of grace and power which otherwise
are closed. If you can turn to God, at any time of day or night, as naturally and
unpretentiously as a child turning to his mother, you have found the secret of
the saints.

Elton Trueblood

291   *THE MANNER OF PRAYER*

Tell [God] all that is in your heart, as one unloads one's heart to a dear
friend. . . . Tell him your troubles, that he may comfort you; tell him your

joys, that he may sober them; tell him your longings, that he may purify them; tell him your mislikings, that he may help you to conquer them; talk to him of your temptations, that he may shield you from them; show him all the wounds of your heart, that he may heal them. Lay bare to him your indifference to good, your depraved tastes for evil . . . your instability. . . . If you thus pour out to him all your weaknesses, needs, and troubles, there will be no lack of what to say; you will never exhaust this subject, it is continually being renewed. People who have no secrets from each other never want subjects of conversation; they do not . . . weigh their words, because there is nothing to be kept back. Neither do they seek for something to say; they talk together out of the abundance of their heart—without consideration, just what they think. . . . Blessed are they who attain to such familiar, unreserved intercourse with God!

François Fénelon

292   THE IMPULSE TO PRAY

One can hardly imagine that there is any person in the world who does not, for one reason or another, feel like praying. The impulse to pray is as natural as breathing. On some occasion you are struck by the mystery of life. You ask yourself: "What is the meaning of life? Why am I here? What may I hope for?" At such a time you feel like praying in the hope, perhaps, that the mystery and meaning of life will be made clear.

Or one day you suddenly realize that you have been greatly misunderstood in something you have said or done. Your motives were pure, your intentions honest, and your heart set in the right direction. But folk unwittingly misjudged you and blamed you unjustly. In that hour you want to pray.

Or you have made a great mistake. You were faulty in your judgment. You look back upon the error with regret. You wish you could undo it, and you pray that the same blunder will not be made again. You want to pray, this time for forgiveness.

Or perhaps some unusual happiness has descended upon you. Some glad surprise has greeted you on your pathway. You feel as though you were a debtor to God and to all the world. Your heart sings, your voice rings with merriment, and you are thankful. Again prayer seems the proper expression.

Or in another situation life seems to pall on you. You have been enjoying the feast with few worries and obstacles. But one cannot live forever like that. You want to do something for somebody, and you look up for some guiding hand. You pray for a wider field of endeavor.

Eventually you find yourself in the presence of death. Death previously had come to others, but never touched you. But now the grievous event has happened. A loved one is taken. The light goes out in your sky. You wonder why, you are not prepared, and so you pray out of your distress.

Frederick Keller Stamm

293   *LIVING COMMUNION*

Religious persons and students of religion agree in testifying that prayer is the centre of religion, the soul of piety. The definition of the essence of prayer explains this testimony; prayer is a living communion of man with God. Prayer brings man into direct touch with God, into a personal relation with him. Without prayer faith remains a theoretical conviction; worship is only an external and formal act; moral action is without spiritual depth; man remains at a distance from God; an abyss yawns between the finite and Infinite. "God is in heaven and thou art on the earth." "We cannot come to God," says Luther, "except through prayer alone, for he is too high above us." In prayer man rises to heaven, heaven sinks to earth, the veil between the visible and the invisible is torn asunder, man comes before God to speak with him about his soul's welfare and salvation. "Prayer," says Mechthild of Magdeburg, "draws the great God down into a small heart; it drives the hungry soul up to God in his fulness." Similarly Johann Arndt says: "In prayer the highest and the lowest come together, the lowliest heart and the most exalted God."

Friedrich Heiler

294   *PHASES OF PRAYER*

Prayer may be only an act of confession, and occupy itself in a penitential rehearsal of one's sins and failings. There are moods and seasons in which this should be the burden of every Christian man's prayer, and there are some natures to whom this kind of prayer is more natural than any other.

Or, prayer may be an act of supplication; as when it occupies itself with solicitation for mercies or with deprecation of evils, beseeching the sending down of divine mercy or the averting of divine displeasure. This kind of prayer is very comprehensive. It stretches out with endless variation of detail. At times it is suitable for every one; but there are some natures that deal in it too exclusively, their experience in addressing God being almost wholly that of entreaty.

Or, prayer may be a more tranquil exercise of simple communion, in which a loving nature spreads before God the simple life of the hour, as children at evening converse with their parents, or as the disciples under the olive trees over against Jerusalem related to the Master the events of the day, and received instruction from his lips.

Or, prayer may be an act of thanksgiving, a recognition of God's goodness, an expression of gratitude for blessings received.

Or, finally, prayer may be the simple utterance of praise; as when the soul is made vividly to perceive the wisdom, the beneficence, or the glory of God, in providence or in grace, toward others or toward one's self, in respect to the past, the present, or the future.

While prayer may consist of any or all of these elements, ordinarily they mingle with or succeed each other, the soul ranging from one feeling to another. . . . In any comprehensive Christian experience that utters itself in prayer, confession, supplication, communion, thanksgiving, and praise come and go and blend to form the great whole, as do the tones of different instruments in a well-chorded orchestra. In other words, prayer is the simple interchange of thought and feeling with God; rising out of conscious sensuousness into spirituality; turning one's self away from the things of time, and standing upon the threshold of the eternal world.

Henry Ward Beecher

295   *HOW DOES ONE LEARN TO PRAY?*

First of all and fundamentally, by recognizing that the praying instinct which is native to each of us waits to be developed from an impulse into an exercise and from an exercise into an art. People complain of their disappointing experiences when they pray. Yet how much of the disappointment is due to the fact that they take for granted that they can become conscious of God at any time, in any mood, with any sort of moral life behind them. They are making a colossal mistake. It is impossible for a man who on his feet is superficial and selfish to become a saint on his knees. The apprehension of God is a moral and spiritual process and calls for purity of heart, singleness of mind, a disciplined will. Prayer is an exercise and an art as well as an instinct. It demands just as much patience, industry, and devotion as men give to painting, sculpture, or music. Mastery comes only with long practice. Proficiency cannot be picked up in a few short and simple lessons. Brother Lawrence spent ten years teaching himself to pray, ten years of quiet, resolute, unceasing effort. The chief reason why people give up praying is because of the difficulty of prayer, the practical far more than the theoretical difficulty. And back of the practical difficulty lies something deeper. Ali Ghazzali, the Moslem mystic, has a sentence that cuts like a knife. "If you are never alone with God, it is not because you are too busy; it is because you don't care for him, don't like him. And you had better face the facts." Let us be honest with ourselves about this. Do we really want to learn to pray? Are we prepared to pay the price which mastery of the art involves?

Robert J. McCracken

296   *PRAYER IN THE EXPERIENCE OF MEN*

To pray, for Luther, is "to come into God's Presence and to speak with him." On another occasion he expresses his amazement "that I who am only dust and ashes and full of sins should speak to the true, living, eternal God." This recognition of prayer as simple communion with God is likewise true of the other great leaders of the Protestant Reformation. To pray, for Calvin, is "a conversation with God"; for Zwingli, "to go to God," "to be acquainted with him and speak with him." Bunyan says, "By prayer is our most direct and immediate personal approach to the presence of God." This living communion with God is under the impulsion of the Holy Spirit. We might well describe the prayer of simplicity in Jude's phrase "praying in the Holy Spirit." Luther writes, "When the Holy Spirit specially touches and stirs the heart then prayer is wont to become very hot." George Fox says, "We pray publicly and privately as the Holy Spirit inspires us." John Bunyan states, "It is impossible for the heart to pour itself out without the Spirit's help."

Lynn James Radcliffe

297   *WHAT DO WE GET OUT OF PRAYER?*

All that ever you ask in prayer you shall have. MAT. 21:22 (Moffatt)

Prayer is not a laborsaving device but a task-producing one. The mystics called prayer the hardest kind of work. For when you really pray you have to do something about it! You get off your knees to get onto your feet! You learn to live hard! Prayer makes you feel a Presence that disturbs you with the toil of elevated tasks. It brings spiritual staying power, the perseverance of the saints. You become all atingle with expectancy over the outcome of the understanding at which God and you have arrived. Prayer sets up the inner sentinel. It eventuates in our saying, not in a tone of resignation but in a shout of resolution, "Thy will be done!"

When we pray aright we become able to pray, we become Amens to our prayers, we become answers to our prayers. When we are made answers to our own prayers, we make Amens of other folks. In prayer, then, we donate ourselves to God, renounce our own preferences, accept voluntarily the heroic impossibilities for which we pray! God, in answer to prayer, gives us the hidden manna. In the great old Calvinistic slogan, he does a work of grace in our hearts.

John M. Versteeg

298   *FRIENDSHIP WITH GOD*

Prayer is the homing of the soul, a fixed and deepest sense that guides us God-ward. Prayer is the postern gate to the City of Heart's Desire. For what do we most covet? Not any boon of hand or eye, nor any magic that could move rock mountains, nor any refuge from hardship which gives sinew and sight, nor any retreat from death. These are superficial hankerings soon outgrown. Our deepest yearning is for—God. Prayer is friendship with God. It is the same friendship whereby Jesus drew imperishable insight, lived with unwearied and unconquered love, and wrought with such power in human days (our days with their over-arching faithfulness and strange spurs of limitation) that he made of a Cross and a tomb his crown and our eternal gain.

George A. Buttrick

I. UNIVERSAL BIBLE SUNDAY

Universal Bible Sunday is generally held on the second Sunday of December and at the call of the American Bible Society. Through worship, preaching, discussion, and study the day makes possible a renewed appreciation of the influence of the Bible in individual lives and in world thought, and of its translation, publication, and distribution. The day falls at a midway point in a period, scheduled between Thanksgiving and Christmas, for private Bible reading. Continual reading of the Bible by church members is further emphasized in many denominations by the naming of Bible books to be studied each month or by schedules of day-to-day Bible lessons.

Calls to Worship

(Boldface type indicates responses.)

299   Receive with meekness the engrafted word, which is able to save your souls.

Search the scriptures; for in them ye think ye have eternal life: and they are they which testify of me.

These are written, that ye might believe that Jesus is the Christ, the Son of God; and that believing ye might have life through his name.

He that hath ears to hear, let him hear.

Ja. 1:21; Jn. 5:39; 21:31; Mat. 11:15

300   Thy testimonies are my delight and my counsellors.

Thy testimonies are wonderful: therefore doth my soul keep them.

The entrance of thy words giveth light.

O earth, earth, earth, hear the word of the Lord.

Ps. 119:24, 129-130; Je. 22:29

301   Thy word is a lamp unto my feet, and a light unto my path.

I have sworn, and I will perform it, that I will keep thy righteous judgments.

Quicken me, O Lord, according unto thy word.

Ps. 119:105–107

Invocations

302 Almighty and most merciful God, who hast given the Bible to be the revelation of thy great love to man, and of thy power and will to save him: grant that our study of it may not be made in vain by the carelessness of our hearts, but that by it we may be confirmed in penitence, lifted to hope, made strong to serve, and above all, filled with the true knowledge of thee and of thy Son Jesus Christ. Amen.

G. Adam Smith

303 O Lord, thy Word is before us: give us a meek and reverent and teachable mind, whilst we read and study it. Open to us its sacred truths and enable us to receive it, not as the word of men but as the Word of God, which liveth and abideth forever. Be thou, O blessed Spirit, our teacher. Enlighten our minds and prepare our hearts. Shine, O Lord, upon thine own sacred page and make it clear to us. What we see not show us, and where we are wrong correct us. Bring home some portion to our soul, and thus make us wise unto salvation; through Jesus Christ our Saviour. Amen.

Ashton Oxenden

304 Blessed Lord, who hast caused all Holy Scriptures to be written for our learning: grant that we may in such wise hear them, read, mark, learn, and inwardly digest them, that by patience, and comfort of thy Holy Word, we may embrace and ever hold fast the blessed hope of everlasting life, which thou hast given us in our Saviour Jesus Christ. Amen.

Book of English Collects

Litany

(Boldface type indicates responses.)

305 In the name of God our Father, source of all light and truth; and of Jesus Christ, our Teacher, Master and Saviour; and of the Holy Spirit that takes of the things of Christ and reveals them unto us:
We give thee thanks, O God.
For this Book, the charting of the way to God our Father wherein the children of Israel walked in ancient time, and which Jesus made so plain that the wayfaring man need not err therein; the proclamation of the truth, expounded in the Law and Commandments of Judaism, preached by the prophets and perfectly embodied in our Lord Jesus; and the unfolding of the life that is

eternal, the hope of raptured seers, the theme of the psalmists' hymns, and a reality to those who know the Christ:

We give thee thanks, O God.

For this Book, the inspiration of all our Christian education which nurtures children with spiritual food, which inspires youth to victorious living, and sustains age in faith and works:

We give thee thanks, O God.

For this Book, a standard for the Christian church whereby she may be corrected in error, healed in her divisions, and made one in Christ so that the world may believe:

We give thee thanks, O God.

For this Book, with its consolation in sorrow, hope in discouragement, light in darkness, truth in error, faith in doubt, victory in temptation, peace in turmoil, and strength in every need:

We give thee thanks, O God.

For this Book, the precious heritage of all mankind, a lamp unto our feet and a light unto our path, from youth to old age, in sickness and health, in plenty and in want, until the eternal Day breaks and the shadows flee away:

We give thee thanks, O God.

National Council

Prayers

306   O God, our Help in ages past, we thank thee for the Bible which, as it has been to our fathers, is still to us a lamp unto our feet and a light unto our path. We acknowledge with awe the marvelous leadership of thy Spirit in men's hearts and in thy church which has led to the creation and preservation of the literature of the Bible. We praise thee for the devotion of scribes who have transmitted to succeeding generations the manuscripts of Sacred Writ. We thank thee for the centuries of dedicated scholarship that have sought to recover the original words of Scripture. Our hearts thrill to the holy urge that has inspired men of every language and race to translate the Bible so that all men, each in his own tongue, might know the mighty words of God.

Bless the teachers of the Bible in seminary, college, and school. May the church school teachers read, mark, learn, and inwardly know the Scriptures and apply them wisely in every area of life. Inspire the preachers of today so to brood over the Scripture that the Bible may become again a fountain of light and a creative source of inspiration for the issues of today's life.

Arrest us with the prophet's passion for justice for all men. In days of international tensions lead us by the Bible's page of prophecy and its visions of apocalypse to see thee at work in the sweep of history with a mighty purpose that cannot be frustrated. Rekindle on the altars of our hearts the flames of religious devotion by contact with the psalmists of Israel. Teach us through the sages of Israel how to triumph over suffering and how to speak words of insight and sympathy to hearts racked by grief and pain.

Challenge us anew with the Gospel's story of Jesus. Lead us into an understanding of his teachings, and guide us as we seek to apply his Spirit to the life of our time. Fire our imagination with Jesus' world-embracing dream of the Kingdom of God, and fill us with the missionary zeal of his disciples and apostles. Imbue us with the Bible's undying hope and matchless courage, as in Christ's name and power we work for a better world; through Jesus Christ our Lord. Amen.

Elmer Leslie

307   O God, who hast uttered thyself supremely unto the world by the obedient life of thy Son, Jesus Christ, we thank thee for these records concerning him, whereby our wandering imaginations are curbed. Like Zacchaeus we are small of stature, and need to climb this tree of the gospels that we may see Jesus. We thank thee for the light from them that has dawned on countless souls throughout the world, speaking in various tongues.

As we study the things which eye-witnesses saw and heard concerning him, keep us reverent and humble before him. How should we presume to probe the depths of meaning in his words and acts, for our judgment is so warped by choosing lower ways of living than his? Yet we want to see his face as clearly as we may, and we ask the illumination of thy Spirit for this hour. And while we study may we remember that the way into his rest is not by talking about him, but by following him obediently and abiding in him, and so abiding in thee.

While we are musing may the fire burn, our will be stirred, our mind enlarged and our allegiance settled. Amen.

Private and Public Prayers

308   Almighty God, grant unto us such knowledge of the written and spoken word of God and man, as may give us understanding of the eternal Word which was with thee in the beginning, by which all things were made. May we, through the things that are made, oft-times pierce to the things of God, and by the very beauty of that which thou hast expressed, learn the eternal beauty and unbroken blessedness of him from whom it comes. May thy word and work alike conspire to teach us thy thoughts; that we may grow in wisdom and favor with God and man; and carry through this life, so often bowed down

by petty cares and troubles and by man's meanness, the heavenly beauty, the glory of paradise and the hope of restored glory. Grant to us such knowledge of thee, that we may shine with thy beauty; such communion with thee, as shall brighten our hope, strengthen our faith, increase our charity, and bring us at last through this life into the full peace of the life to come. Hear us, of thy mercy, through Jesus Christ our Lord. Amen.

George Dawson

309   Most gracious God, our heavenly Father, in whom alone dwelleth all fulness of light and wisdom: illumine our minds, we beseech thee, by thy Holy Spirit, in the true understanding of thy Word. Give us grace that we may receive it with reverence and humility. May it lead us to put our whole trust in thee alone, and so to serve and honor thee, that we may glorify thy holy name, and edify our neighbors by a good example. And since it hath pleased thee to number us among thy people, O help us to pay thee the love and homage that we owe, as children to our Father, and as servants to our Lord. We ask this for the sake of our Master and Saviour. Amen.*

John Calvin

Poems

310   *From THE MONASTERY* (Bk. 1, Ch. 12)

Within that awful volume lies
The mystery of mysteries!
Happiest they of human race,
To whom their God has given grace
To read, to fear, to hope, to pray,
To lift the latch, to force the way;
But better had they ne'er been born,
That read to doubt, or read to scorn.

Walter Scott

311   *From THE CHRISTIAN YEAR*

There is a book, who runs may read,
Which heavenly truth imparts,
And all the lore its scholars need,
Pure eyes and Christian hearts.

John Keble

312   *THE UNIVERSAL BOOK*

How many ages and generations
Have brooded and wept and agonized
Over this Book!
What untellable joys and ecstasies,
What support to martyrs at the stake!
To what myriads has it been
The shore and rock of safety—
The refuge from the driving tempest and wreck.
Translated into all languages,
How it has united this diverse world!
Of its thousands there is not a verse,
Not a word but is thick-studded
With human emotion.

Author Unknown

313   *THE BIBLE*

As to an ancient temple
Whose vast proportions tower
With summit inaccessible
Among the stars of heaven,
While the resistless ocean
Of peoples and of cities
Breaks at its feet in foam,
Work that a hundred ages
Hallow: I bow to thee.

David Levi

314   *GUIDE IN THE NIGHT*

The Bible? That's the Book. The Book indeed,
  The Book of books,
  Of which who looks,
As he should do, aright, shall never need
  Wish for a better light
  To guide him in the night.

Author Unknown

315   *From ON A PRAYER BOOKE SENT TO MRS. M. R.*

It is the armory of light;
Let constant use but keep it bright,
  You'll find it yields
To holy hands, and humble hearts,
  More swords and sheilds
Than sinne hath snares, or hell hath darts.

Richard Crashaw

316   *From MIRIAM*

We search the world for truth; we cull
The good, the true, the beautiful,
From graven stone and written scroll,
And all old flower-fields of the soul;
And, weary seekers of the best,
We come back laden from our quest,
To find that all the sages said
Is in the Book our mothers read.

John Greenleaf Whittier

317   *BIBLE READING*

Read then, but first thyself prepare
To read with zeal and mark with care;
And when thou read'st what here is writ
Let thy best practice second it:

So twice each precept read should be,
First in the Book and next in thee.

Author Unknown

318   *YOUR OWN VERSION*

You are writing a Gospel,
  A chapter each day,
By deeds that you do,
  By words that you say.

Men read what you write,
   Whether faithless or true;
Say, what is the Gospel
   According to You?

Paul Gilbert

319   *THE BOOK*

Softly I closed the Book as in a dream
And let its echoes linger to redeem
Silence with music, darkness with its gleam.

That day I worked no more. I could not bring
My hands to toil, my thought to trafficking.
A new light shone on every common thing.

Celestial glories flamed before my gaze.
That day I worked no more. But, to God's praise,
I shall work better all my other days.

Winfred Ernest Garrison

320   *BIBLE IN THE HEART*

He knew the book from A to Z;
   His mind had mastered every part;
A fine achievement, but alas!
   It never got into his heart.

C. W. Vandenbergh

321   *From BIBLIOLATRES*

Slowly the Bible of the race is writ,
And not on paper leaves nor leaves of stone;
Each age, each kindred, adds a verse to it,
Texts of despair or hope, of joy or moan.
While swings the sea, while mists the mountains shroud,
While thunder's surges burst on cliffs of cloud,
Still at the prophets' feet the nations sit.

James Russell Lowell

Topics, Texts and Themes

322   *THE BIBLE*

Born in the East and clothed in Oriental form and imagery, the Bible walks
the ways of all the world with familiar feet and enters land after land to find its
own everywhere. It has learned to speak in hundreds of languages to the heart
of man. It comes into the palace to tell the monarch that he is a servant of the
Most High, and into the cottage to assure the peasant that he is a son of God.
Children listen to its stories with wonder and delight, and wise men ponder
them as parables of life. It has a word for the time of peril, a word of comfort
for the time of calamity, a word of light for the hour of darkness. Its oracles are
repeated in the assembly of the people, and its counsels whispered in the ear
of the lonely. The wicked and the proud tremble at its warnings, but to the
wounded and penitent it has a mother's voice. The wilderness and the solitary
place have been made glad by it, and the fire on the hearth has lit the reading
of its well-worn pages. It has woven itself into our dearest dreams, so that
love, friendship, sympathy and devotion, memory and hope, put on the beautiful garments of its treasured speech, breathing of frankincense and myrrh. No
man is poor or desolate who has this treasure for his own. When the landscape
darkens and the trembling pilgrim comes to the valley named of the shadow,
he is not afraid to enter; he takes the rod and staff of Scripture in his hand, he
says to his friend and comrade: "Goodbye, we shall meet again," and comforted
by that support, he goes toward the lonely pass as one who walks through
darkness into light.

Henry van Dyke

323   *A BIBLE FAITH*

The grass withereth, the flower fadeth; but the word of our God shall
stand for ever. is. 40:8

Christianity is frankly and unashamedly a Bible religion. Christian beliefs
about God, about God's purpose for the world, and about the nature and calling
of man, are derived from the Bible. Christians are rightly accustomed to
measure the value of novel doctrines by the Bible. Are they or are they not in
harmony with the revelation which is therein contained?

It will not do simply to argue as was once argued by an enthusiastic but
narrow-minded Moslem soldier about the value of a famous library. "These
books," he said, "either contain the same teaching as the Koran, in which case
they are unnecessary, or they contradict the Koran, in which case they are

erroneous. Let them all be burned." The comparison is not so simple as all that. What is meant by measuring new doctrine against the Bible is this: not every-thing in the Bible is decisive, or even acutely relevant. Much of it may be neglected. Some must be set aside as due to inadequate understanding by human minds of the divine purpose. Yet there is a faith for which the Bible stands. The Bible contains the revelation of the living God, the God who acts, who has a purpose for the world and carries it forward in what men call history.

S. E. Carpenter

324 *BIBLE VISTAS*

The Bible is not only many books, it is a literature. History, poetry, prophecy, philosophy, theology, oratory, humor, sarcasm, irony, music, drama, tragedy, strategy, love tales, war tales, travelogues, laws, jurisprudence, songs, sermons, warnings, prayers, all are here. Was there ever such a literature? The Bible begins with a garden and ends with a city. It starts with a morning followed by a night and ends with a day that shall know no night. It breaks the silence with: "In the beginning God," and it hushes the universe to sleep with: "The grace of our Lord Jesus Christ be with you all." It finds man at the shut gates of the lost Eden, and leaves him before the open door at the top of the road. It begins with: "Thou art cursed," and it ends with: "Whosoever will may come." On its first page is condemnation. On its last page is invitation. At the shut gate stands an angel with drawn sword, and at the open door the Spirit and the bride wait to welcome all who would enter the door which no man can shut.

The Bible breaks at dawn with God's voice saying: "Let there be light." It sets at dusk with God's truth proclaiming: "Let there be life." Between the two speak all voices that can breathe a prayer, plead a need, confess a sin, utter a warning, sob a sorrow, or sigh a penitent's tear. Between the two are the tragedies of hate, the follies of fear, the stain and shame of sin, the paralysis of doubt, the torment of despair, and the choke of the fog that ends it all. Between the two are the stories of nations, the acclaim of heroes, the fall of empires, the rise of kingdoms, the decline of dynasties, the tramp of armies, the crack and crash of civilizations, and the coming of him who is "the bright and morning star."

James I. Vance

THE LIVING BIBLE

Surely it is not without significance that of the twelve historical religions
which are dead—the ancient Egyptian, the Peruvian and Mexican, Mithraism,
Manichaeism, the Babylonian, Phoenician, and Hittite, the Greek, the Roman,
the early Teutonic and Scandinavian—not one of them, according to Robert
Ernest Hume, "possessed anything which might be called a canon of sacred
Scriptures," whereas every one of the eleven living religions—Hinduism,
Jainism, Buddhism, Sikhism, Confucianism, Taoism, Shinto, Judaism, Zoro-
astrianism, Mohammedanism, and Christianity—"do possess definite sets of
documents which are regarded as conveying unique divine truths which need
to be known." There is power in the Book from which God speaks.

And what if the Book happens to be that crown of all the others, the Book
in which it is set down that the God who is speaking is not the God merely
of this tribe or that cult, but the Father of every human individual born into
the world! *That* Book was rediscovered at the dawn of the Reformation after
its long sleep in Latin. Wycliffe's translation into English, though only in
manuscript, swept like earthquake tremors through the kingdom, and with
something like the same results. A considerable sum was paid even for a few
sheets of it; a load of hay became the price for permission to read in it one
hour a day for a period; and some learned sections of it by heart to recite to the
throngs who gathered to hear. The readers of it went to their death when captured by the authorities, who were afraid of the power of it; they were hunted
down like wild beasts and burned with copies of it round their necks. But the
Bible won its own way; it changed the lives of those who listened for God's
word in it; eventually it revolutionized Europe.

Douglas Horton

BOOK OF OUR FATHERS

There is none that ever made an end to learning it, and there is none that
will ever find out its mysteries. For its wisdom is richer than any sea,
and its work deeper than any abyss. ECCLESIASTICUS 24:28–29

A house in which a family has lived for two generations or more becomes
filled with associations. . . . So, too, in a direct and real fashion the family
Bible sustains each new generation. Not in the old way of family worship, perhaps. But this is the book which father quoted on occasion—and to the point;
this is the book which mother was often seen to read. The children carried
copies of it to Sunday school and off to college. Yes, and a little New Testa-

ment was slipped in the overnight bag when any member of the family went to the hospital for an operation. It *has* been a family standby and, therefore, it *is* a family standby. Somehow the Bible is not just one more book in a book-filled world. It's the only book we have ever read which we know for sure our grandparents read, too; and their grandparents; and theirs. . . . It's a family book.

Margueritte Harmon Bro

327   *THE PERSONALITY OF THE WORD OF GOD*

Beginning at Moses and all the prophets, he expounded unto them in all the scriptures the things concerning himself. LU. 24:27

A modern novelist has described the presence of a Greek Testament in the room of a man tempted to his undoing. How often does the mere presence of the Divine Word make itself felt till the Book becomes no more a thing but a person! A glance at it, and though time and custom and sin have checked the old feelings, they are at once unsealed. The volume is not dumb. It speaks, appeals, warms, solicits, in the voice that floated along our dreams in childhood. It takes on an aspect sometimes terrible, as when it gleams like the flashing of a shield, sometimes tender as if it carried in it all the loving remonstrance of the past. The tendency to pass into personality characterizes things that greatly command us. . . . Most of us have pictures whose eyes follow us, rebuking and warning where we would err, smiling and restful as we strive up the heights. So it is with books, but especially with the Word of God. We come upon it suddenly as it lies upon the table, and it meets us with almost the full shock and passion of flesh-and-blood reality.

William Robertson Nicoll

328   *THE CALL OF THE BIBLE*

The Bible is largely the story of the "call" of men to do God's will on the earth. There is Abraham going out to seek a new land "not knowing where he went," finding God and being found of him. There is Moses hearing God say, "What is that in thine hand?" and being used of God as the great deliverer of his people. There is Amos the herdsman hearing the voice of God amid the lowing of the cattle. There is Isaiah the young priest hearing with bowed head the voice that cried, "Who will go for us?" and answering, "Here am I, send me." There is John the Baptist in the wilderness, with his heart aflame with a fiery passion for righteousness. There are Peter and Andrew, James and John, mending their fishing nets and hearing Jesus say, "Follow me." There is Saul of Tarsus on the road to Damascus, with hate in his heart, finally in humbleness of spirit, saying, in answer to a voice that spoke to him, "Lord, what wilt thou have me to do?" The record of men who have been called of God to do "many mighty works" is found not only in the Book. Wander through the centuries and hear them calling. Is it Luther? Is it Knox? Is it Lincoln? Is it Wilfred Grenfell? Is it Albert Schweitzer? Or is it the multitude of others, inconspicuous or undistinguished, who have made their witness and "kept the faith"? *You* answer!

Ray Freeman Jenney

329   *WHY MEN TREASURE THE BIBLE*

Why is it that men treasure the Bible? The ready answer may be that it is the Word of God and must, therefore, be eternal and commanding. But so easy an explanation does not satisfy. The Word of God is an eternal word because it gives an answer to questions that are eternally rising in the minds and souls of men. As time moves on, we are confronted ever and anon with the most pressing and poignant human problems. Man must be forever trying his spirit against the spirit of the world. Calamity smites him; confusion overtakes him; fortune smiles and then suddenly frowns upon him. Out of all this welter of conflicting emotions he cries for a sure word of direction, a solace to his wounded spirit, a light amid his surrounding darkness. These he must have or perish. With grateful heart he finds them unerringly in the Bible. It speaks his language; it "finds" him where he is, and points him to the place to which he wishes to go. It thus is born anew as the vivid and satisfying answer to the need of every generation. As long as men desire Reality and seek for God, they will turn wistfully the pages of this immortal epic of the soul.

Paul B. Kern

330   *BIBLE HORIZONS*

Study the Bible. Here is the double record of God's search for man and man's search for God. It is a plain-spoken old Book, with unvarnished sinners and back-sliding saints in it from cover to cover. Its peaks of spiritual insight and experience have never been surpassed, but it makes no excuse for human weakness nor attempt to hide it. We keep reading it because in it we keep seeing ourselves. The times, the clothes, the customs change: the people, the situations, human nature—not much! In the Psalms, for instance, you will find just about every mood that man can feel—exalted, rebellious, unselfish, forgotten, devout, cynical, tender, cruel. The words themselves are like drains in a wound; they canalize for us the emotions which, without them, could hardly find such full expression. Here is no serene book of pleasant affirmations: the peak of the Old Testament is the looking for a Suffering Servant, and the peak of the New Testament is the Suffering Servant himself, living as the lowliest among the lowly, and crucified on a Cross. Strange how in him people have found the deepest peace and joy this world has ever known! The more our minds feed in this rich pasture, the stronger will our spirits be.

Samuel H. Shoemaker

331 *STEPS TO GET MOST OUT OF THE BOOK*

In order to get the most out of the Book take these steps: (1) *Come to the Word expectantly*. This Book is alive with meanings. "For the word of God is living and active" (He. 4:12 RSV). Expect it to speak and it will. Faith is expectancy—according to your expectancy, be it unto you.

(2) *Come surrendering to the truths here revealed*. "He that is willing to do shall know." In a moral universe the key to knowledge is moral response. The moment we cease to obey, that moment the Revelation ceases to reveal.

(3) *Come expecting to use the truths here revealed*. Not only receive the truths revealed, but make yourself the channel of those truths to others. Nothing will come in that can't get out.

(4) *Come unhurriedly*. If you stalk through a forest, you will probably see and hear little. But sit down and the squirrels will come out, the birds draw near, and everything will speak to you since you are quiet and receptive. Get quiet and receptive and the Word will become alive with meaning.

(5) *Come with a proper emphasis*. Since the Old Testament is not Christianity, but a period of preparation for Christianity—Christianity is Christ—then spend about one fourth of your reading time in the Old Testament and three fourths in the New. Otherwise you'll be an Old Testament Christian, which means that you'll be sub-Christian.

(6) *Come to it even if nothing apparently comes from your coming*. The very fact that you have exposed yourself to the Word is infinitely worth while. For where Love is, silence may be the only language. To be with him, though unseen and unheard, is the reward.

E. Stanley Jones

332 *INTERPRETING THE BIBLE*

The Holy Scriptures will interpret themselves in spite of our human limitations. We need only dare to follow this drive, this spirit, this river, to grow out beyond ourselves toward the highest answer. This daring is faith; and we read the Bible rightly, not when we do so with false modesty, restraint, and attempted sobriety, for these are passive qualities, but when we read it in faith. And the invitation to dare and to reach toward the highest, even though we do not deserve it, is the expression of grace in the Bible. The Bible unfolds to us as we are met, guided, drawn on, and made to grow by the grace of God.

It is not right human thoughts about God which form the content of the Bible, but the right divine thoughts about men. The Bible tells us not how we should talk with God but what he says to us; not how we are to find the way to him, but how he has sought and found the way to us; not the right relation in which we must place ourselves to him, but the covenant which he has made with all who are Abraham's spiritual children and which he has sealed once and for all in Jesus Christ.

Karl Barth

333   *TO READ BELIEVINGLY*

Professor L. Leenhardt calls attention to three ways of reading the Bible. Taking his start from the words of Jesus—"It is the spirit that quickeneth; the flesh profiteth nothing: the words that I speak unto you, they are spirit, and they are life. But there are some of you that believe not" (Jn. 6:63–64)—he shows that they apply to the whole Bible. The first type of reader regards only the history contained within the Bible. He may submit the facts of the Bible to the same tests of knowledge found in other volumes. He may be said to "know" the Bible's events. In the second place, there is the man who regards the Bible as a book which deals with human reality. The Bible "speaks to us of man's depths of being." To read the Bible thus means to "understand" its personal encounters. The depths of man's being are probed. Thus he understands himself better, because he meets men as they really are—who do not live the life of pretense. In learning what man is, he discovers what it means to be "man." But there is a third type of reader, who may be called a "believing" reader. He reads the Bible and sees the relation of its characters and events to *God*. There is no chapter in their lives where God does not appear. "Sometimes in the inner life, sometimes in exterior events, the presence of God asserts itself; whether they obey or disobey, their life always appears as the reaction provoked by *God's* action." Now the reader is probing not into historical events, nor into man's inner being, but into that divine aspect of the Book which makes it universal. Differences in culture and mentality fall away, and he is in the presence of the God of the Bible. He is brought face to face with God's message, and he finds himself in the critical position in which "the irruption of an en-

tirely heterogeneous element places all men and all human history." He then
does not face a human opinion, but the God who speaks to men in concrete
situations.

If we grant that it is God who speaks, then we are reading the Bible in faith,
"believingly"—by the power of the Spirit in faith.

Elmer George Homrighausen

334   *READING THE BIBLE*

Bible, wonderful book, teacher of mankind, foundation of our spiritual
being! Thou art like that serene City of God, set upon earth's towering mountain tops, touching the heavens. The peoples of the world look to thee and
drink of the living waters of thy streams. Whole generations may turn from
thee and think nought of thee, because they know thee not; but mankind ever
turns back again to thee.

For more than two centuries man has striven to understand the Scriptures;
but who dare say that he has plumbed those deeps. Every century has seen
them in new light. To our forefathers they were one, a single word out of the
mouth of God. To us it has been given to read the manifold history of which
they are the record. Those who came before us have dipped impartially into
these writings, and have found again in them what was deepest and best in
themselves. We who come after them strive with care to catch the spirit of the
various times in which they were written, and to discover what the authors
themselves meant to say; and in no wise do we yield to our forefathers in our
reverence and love for this majestic book. In fact the story, so human, so divine,
as we begin to be able to see it in the Bible, is deeper and more precious than
anything our forefathers thought they found therein.

Hermann Gunkel

335   *LIFE PRINCIPLE*

Inspiration means to "inbreathe." The Bible is literature "inbreathed" by the
Holy Spirit. A professor of biology held a little brown seed in his hand. He
said: "I know just exactly the composition of this seed. It has in it hydrogen,
carbon, nitrogen. I can make a seed exactly like this seed that I hold in my
hand, but the seed I would make and plant lacks what we call the 'life principle.' The seed I would make would rot and die, but the seed God made gives
life and reproduces itself." The Bible has in it the "life principle." Simply plant
it in your heart and see what happens. That will prove the divine authorship of
the book. Let a man read it, it will lead him to God; let a man study it, he

will know the heart of God. Let a man ask his questions and he will find his answers. Let him test the Christ of these pages and he will find the power that Christ has to give.

Louis H. Evans

336   *WHAT THE BIBLE CAN DO FOR US TODAY*

The Bible can give us the wholesome pleasure of reading good literature. In simpler form than modern literature, but with all the qualities that make writing great in any age or language, the stories and poems and letters and sermons of the Bible make interesting reading. The fact that they come from a distant country and a bygone time gives them at times something of the character of the Arabian Nights; other parts are more like Homer's epics, while still other parts preserve the simple conversation and correspondence of every-day life.

The Bible can help us to understand human nature in ourselves and in others. Its frank, clear pictures of character and inner motives show human nature as it is. The very distance in time and space between us and the ancient Hebrews and the early Christians only brings out the fundamental unity of man's thinking, feeling and behavior. In Jacob, David, Paul, Esther, or Ruth we can see ourselves and our fellows, or what we should aspire to be, or what we must beware of becoming.

The Bible can help us to understand many practices and ideals of our present social order by showing us their roots and how they came to be. Our civilization is largely based upon the Bible. Many of our customs and conceptions, to be sure, are very different from those of the Hebrews, but others, which have been handed down to us without our knowing why, owe their existence, indirectly or directly, to the fact that the Bible has been the Sacred Book of our ancestors for many centuries.

The Bible can correct and elevate our ideals and our faith by its strong and noble expression of the noblest faith and ideals ever given to man. When life becomes almost too much for us, and our faith and hope grow weak or we are tempted to lower our ideals and be conformed to this world, the high, clear challenge of the Bible helps us to be transformed by the renewing of our minds. The Spirit within bears witness, and our consciences respond, "Yes, after all, that must be so!"

The Bible can help us to live worthily through the inspiration of the great examples it sets before us. Confronting the heroes and heroines of the faith, and most of all the Son, who was well pleasing to the Father and who was tempted in all points as we are, yet without sin, we are ashamed of our unworthiness and encouraged to press on toward the goal for the prize of our high calling in Christ Jesus.

American Bible Society

337   *YOUR BIBLE WAITS*

It is a devastating thought of how little is left of the greatness when all that our Bible has inspired vanishes. The most thrilling part of any spiritual enterprise is never statistical, and yet I find myself attracted in passing to look upon the labor which someone has undertaken to tell us about the Bible. The Sacred Writ contains 3,566,480 letters, 773,692 words, 31,173 verses, 1,189 chapters, and 66 books. The middle verse, he says, is Psalm 118:18. The longest verse is Esther 8:9, the shortest John 11:35.

In a busy day like ours modern man would find a set of statistics showing him how he could read these great truths to be of much more value than their technical aspects. Here is one method, not necessarily the best, but at least one set of statistics showing how a busy person can gain a knowledge of the Bible.

There are 929 chapters in the Old Testament, and 260 chapters in the New Testament. This makes our previous accounted total of 1,189 chapters in the entire Bible. If a person will read three chapters every day and five chapters each Sunday, he can finish reading the entire Bible in just one year. Or, if a man desires to read the New Testament alone, and reads two chapters a day, he can finish it in less than twenty weeks. If he reads only on Sunday, completing five New Testament chapters each Sunday, he will finish it on the fifty-second Sunday. In one afternoon a person can begin with Luke's Gospel and at one sitting read the remainder of the New Testament to be thrilled forever with its moving story of power.

J. Richard Sneed

J. REFORMATION SUNDAY

Reformation Sunday is celebrated in Protestant churches on the Sunday nearest to October 31, the anniversary of the day in 1517 when Martin Luther posted his Ninety-Five Theses on the door of the castle church at Wittenberg. The day is devoted to a restatement and reaffirmation of Protestant doctrines and to thanksgiving for the heroic men of Christian history. Community services are frequently scheduled for Reformation Day.

The materials in this section may be useful for other days which highlight the history, mission, and work of the church. These include: Pentecost or Whitsunday, the fiftieth day after Easter and the birthday of the Christian church as recorded in Ac. 2; Christian Unity Sunday; Church Loyalty Sunday; and Roll Call Sunday.

Calls to Worship

(Boldface type indicates responses.)

338   One thing have I desired of the Lord, that will I seek after; that I may dwell in the house of the Lord all the days of my life, to behold the beauty of the Lord, and to inquire in his temple.

I will come into thy house in the multitude of thy mercy: and in thy fear will I worship toward thy holy temple.

Ps. 27:4; 5:7

339   The Lord is in his holy temple: let all the earth keep silence before him.

Surely the Lord is in this place. . . . This is none other but the house of God, and this is the gate of heaven.

Let the words of my mouth, and the meditation of my heart, be acceptable in thy sight, O Lord, my strength, and my redeemer.

Hab. 2:20; Ge. 28:16–17; Ps. 19:14

340   I was glad when they said unto me, Let us go into the house of the Lord. For my brethren and companions' sakes, I will now say, Peace be within thee. Because of the house of the Lord our God I will seek thy good.

Ps. 122:1, 8–9

153

341   Seeing we . . . are compassed about with so great a cloud of witnesses, let us lay aside every weight, and the sin which doth so easily beset us, and let us run with patience the race that is set before us, looking into Jesus the author and finisher of our faith; who for the joy that was set before him endured the cross, despising the shame, and is set down at the right hand of the throne of God.

He. 12:1–2

Invocations

342   Almighty God, who, through the preaching of thy servants, the blessed reformers, hast caused the light of the Gospel to shine forth: grant, we beseech thee, that, knowing its saving power, we may faithfully guard and defend it against all enemies, and joyfully proclaim it, to the salvation of souls and the glory of thy holy name; through Jesus Christ, thy Son, our Lord. Amen.

Book of Worship (ER)

343   Most gracious Father, we humbly beseech thee for thy church. Fill it with all truth; in all truth with all peace. Where it is corrupt, purge it; where it is in error, direct it; where anything is amiss, reform it; where it is right, strengthen and confirm it; where it is in want, furnish it; where it is divided and rent asunder, make up the breaches of it, O thou Holy One of Israel. Amen.

William Laud

344   O Lord, we beseech thee to maintain thy church in truth and patience; that her clergy may be faithful, her watchmen vigilant, her flock loyal, her camp united, her war spiritual, her weapons heavenly, her lamps burning and shining; and as thy Son Jesus Christ hath given so great a price for us, let us not count it a hard thing to give up all for him, and to spend and be spent for the souls he hath redeemed; through Jesus Christ our Lord. Amen.

A Chain of Prayer

345   O thou, who hast set thy church in the valleys of our beloved land to be a bulwark and a sanctuary, and upon the hills to be a belfry and declarer of thy truth: make strong her walls, wide her gates, fearless her witness; may her chief effort be to discern thy will and faithfully to proclaim it; through him who came to show forth thy truth and love, even Jesus Christ our Lord. Amen.

Boynton Merrill

Prayers

346   Eternal God, the Father of all mankind, we thank thee for the opportunity of free worship in a free land on this Reformation Sunday. We thank thee for the great moral and spiritual reformers of the past who purified religious practice and gave us new churches and creative Christian principles. We thank thee for the Reformation and for all the good which it has offered to the passing centuries.

Forgive us, we pray thee, for not always being true to the religious heritage of our fathers. Many times we have lost thee as we have debated fine points of theology. We have often failed to see Jesus as we have looked for our brother's weaknesses. And we have hurt and divided our own hearts as we have established churches competing one with another. We have injured our souls as we have erected selfish barriers around the Table of the Lord. Forgive us and lead us forward toward a great new spiritual reformation which will lift, bring light, and save.

Help us, our Father, to look upon the Reformation as a yet unfinished opportunity. Help us to read the Bible as a living Book, to seek thee through prayer as a living Saviour, and to find liberty and truth and adventure in the local church. Help us to accept our church membership with loyal devotion and to grow in grace as we serve our Master day by day.

May we as Protestants pass from negative criticism to creative discipleship. May we not merely be protesters but stand firmly for positive principles which will lead to spiritual discovery, to freedom and to brotherhood.

Bless us, bless our church, anoint with power the church universal, on this hallowed day; in Christ's name. Amen.

Stanley I. Stuber

347   Eternal God, in whose name our fathers founded this church long ago, we pray that the spirit that kindled their lives may burn within us. We thank thee for every memory which this day revives of strong faith, humane service, and Christian character, and for the cloud of witnesses from days gone by that surround our worship here. Deepen our gratitude for sacrifices made by those who have gone the King's highway before us, and who have found in thy church refreshment and comfort, peace and restoration, challenge to service and strength to render it. Give us grace to see the need of our children, and our children's children, and let not the heritage of the Gospel fail them because of our slackness or infidelity.

Almighty God, who in the former times didst lead our fathers forth into this land, give thy grace to us, their children, in this nation now, that we may prove ourselves a people mindful of thy favor and glad to do thy will. Bless our land with honorable industry, sound learning, and pure religion. Defend our liberty and preserve our unity. Save us from violence, discord, and confusion, from pride and arrogance, and from every evil way. Fashion into one people the multitudes brought hither of many kindreds and tongues. Endue with the spirit of wisdom those whom we entrust with authority in these troubled days, to the end that there may be peace at home and that we keep a place among the nations of the earth. In the time of prosperity fill our hearts with thankfulness, and in the day of disaster suffer not our trust in thee to fail.

We pray thee for this church. May its enlarging past be an encouragement to the present and a prophecy of the future. For thy church throughout all the world we pray, set today amid the perplexities of a changing order, and face to face with new tasks. Make us and all churches true homes of the Divine Spirit, fruitful sources of great character, and an inspiration to world-wide service. For little children who enter these doors, for youths who seek here their inspiration, for all homes whose hopes are in the sanctuary, for this company, and all absent friends whose prayers are with us, we lift our supplication. Make us, O God, worthy of thy church, and make thy church worthy of thy Christ. Amen.*

Harry Emerson Fosdick

348 O God of the marching years, we thank thee that thou art also the God of the ages and that thy purposes, which are eternal, give meaning to our swiftly passing days. Thou Lord of history and mankind, we praise thee for the blessed Reformers that thou didst raise up to witness for thee and that through them thou didst cause the light of the Gospel to shine forth. We would praise thee for all the benefits to mankind which have flowed through them.

For the simple trust of thy children in thy grace as the one hope of life and living; for the worth and dignity of each individual life as his own priest before thee, O God; for the ennobling of family life and the establishment of the Christian parsonage; for the privilege of having thy Word to us in our own hands and tongues; for the opportunity of sharing more fully in Christian worship through music and both elements of Holy Communion; for the growth in thy way of life through Christian education; for the awakening of the democratic spirit in the aspiration of men who would be free, praise be to thee, O God.

O Lord of redemption, life and liberty, we would practice the heritage of the Reformation more earnestly than ever and fulfill the vocation of good priests whatever our work and life calling may be. O Spirit of truth, sanity and peace, may we follow in the footsteps of the Reformers where they followed thee.

For the redemption of men everywhere, we make our prayer. For our own justification by faith through thy grace, we pray. Set free troubled men who would be faithful and harassed nations which would be makers of good will, we pray.

In the name of him who is above all other names, even Jesus Christ our Lord, we make our prayer. Amen.

Oscar F. Blackwelder

349   Almighty, eternal God! what a strange thing is this world! How doth it open wide the mouths of the people! How small and poor is the confidence of men toward God! How is the flesh so tender and weak, and the Devil so mighty and so busy through his apostles and the wise of this world! How soon do they withdraw the hand and whirl away and run the common path and the broad way to hell, where the godless belong. They look upon that which is splendid and powerful, great and mighty, and which hath consideration. If I turn my eyes thither also it is all over with me; the bell is cast and judgment is pronounced.

Ah God! Ah God! O thou my God! Thou my God, stand thou by me against the reason and wisdom of all the world. Do thou so! Thou must do it. Thou alone. Behold, it is not my cause but thine. For my own person I have nothing to do here before these great lords of the world. Gladly would I, too, have good quiet days and be unperplexed. But thine is the cause, my Lord; it is just and eternal. Stand thou by me, thou true, eternal God!

I confide in no man. It is to no purpose and in vain. Everything halteth that is fleshy, or that savoreth of flesh. O God! O God! Hearest thou not, my God? Art thou dead? No! Thou canst not die. Thou only hidest thyself. Hast thou chosen me for this end? I ask thee. But I know for a surety that thou hast chosen me.

Ah! then may God direct it. For never did I think, in all my life, to be opposed to such great lords; neither have I intended it. Ah! God, then stand by me in the name of Jesus Christ, who shall be my shelter and my shield, yea! my firm tower, through the might and strengthening of thy Holy Spirit. Lord! where stayest thou? Thou my God! where art thou? Come, come! I am ready, even to lay down my life for this cause, patient as a little lamb. For just is the cause.

So will I not separate myself from thee forever. Be it determined in thy name. The world shall not be able to face me against my conscience, though it were full of devils. And though my body, originally the work and creature of thy hands, go to destruction in this cause—yea, though it be shattered to pieces—thy Word and thy Spirit they are good to me still! It concerneth only the body. The soul is thine, and belongeth to thee, and shall also remain with thee forever. Amen. God help me. Amen.

Martin Luther (Prayer before the Diet of Worms)

Poems

350   THE STREAM OF FAITH

From heart to heart, from creed to creed,
  The hidden river runs;
It quickens all the ages down,
  It binds the sires to sons,—
The stream of faith, whose source is God,
  Whose sound, the sound of prayer,
Whose meadows are the holy lives
  Upspringing everywhere.

And still it moves, a broadening flood;
  And fresher, fuller grows
A sense as if the sea were near,
  Towards which the river flows!
O thou, who art the secret Source
  That rises in each soul,
Thou art the Ocean too,—thy charm
  That ever-deepening roll!

William C. Gannett

351   SONG OF A PILGRIM-SOUL

March on, my soul, nor like a laggard stay!
March swiftly on. Yet err not from the way
Where all the nobly wise of old have trod—
The path of faith, made by the sons of God.

Follow the marks that they have set beside
The narrow, cloud-swept track, to be thy guide:
Follow, and honor what the past has gained,
And forward still, that more may be attained.

Something to learn, and something to forget:
Hold fast the good, and seek the better yet:
Press on, and prove the pilgrim-hope of youth:
The creeds are milestones on the road to Truth.

Henry van Dyke

352 *LATIMER'S LIGHT*

In Oxford town the faggots they piled,
With furious haste and curses wild,
Round two brave men of our British breed,
Who dared to stand true to their speech and deed;
Round two brave men of that sturdy race,
Who with tremorless souls the worst can face;
Round two brave souls who could keep their tryst
Through a pathway of fire to follow Christ.
And the flames leaped up, but the blinding smoke
Could not the soul of Hugh Latimer choke;
For, said he, "Brother Ridley, be of good cheer,
A candle in England is lighted here,
Which by grace of God shall never go out."
And that speech in whispers was echoed about—
Latimer's Light shall never go out,
However the winds may blow it about;
Latimer's Light is here to stay
Till the trump of a coming judgment day.

Author Unknown

353 *From "BEHOLD, THE FIELDS ARE WHITE"*

Where prophets' word, and martyrs' blood,
And prayers of saints were sown,
We, to their labors entering in,
Would reap where they have strown.

O thou whose call our hearts has stirred!
To do thy will we come;
Thrust in our sickles at thy word,
And bear our harvest home.

Samuel Longfellow

354   *From INHERITANCE*

As flow the rivers to the sea
Adown from rocky hill or plain,
A thousand ages toiled for thee
And gave thee harvest of their gain;
And weary myriads of yore
Dug out for thee earth's buried ore.

The shadowy toilers for thee fought
In chaos of primeval day
Blind battles with they knew not what;
And each before he passed away
Gave clear articulate cries of woe:
Your pain theirs of long ago.

A. E. (George William Russell)

355   *From HOW AMIABLE ARE THY TABERNACLES*

Thou, whose unmeasured temple stands,
   Built over earth and sea,
Accept the walls that human hands
   Have raised, O God! to thee.

*

May erring minds that worship here
   To find the better way,
And they who mourn and they who fear
   Be strengthened as they pray.

May faith grow firm, and love grow warm,
   And hallowed wishes rise,
While round these peaceful walls the storm
   Of earth-born passion dies.

William Cullen Bryant

356   *WHAT IS THE CHURCH?*

The church is man when his awed soul goes out,
In reverence to a mystery that swathes him all about.

When any living man in awe gropes God-ward in his search;
Then in that hour, that living man becomes the living church,
Then, though in wilderness or in waste, his soul is swept along
Down naves of prayer, through aisles of praise, up altar-stairs
    of song.
And where man fronts the Mystery with spirit bowed in prayer,
There is the universal church—the church of God is there.

Sam Walter Foss

357   *MY CHURCH*

My church to me means life;
A more abundant faith, enlarged, full-grown;
Unchanging in a swiftly moving age
When hope has flown.

My church to me means love;
An all-embracing love, secure, serene,
With hands outstretched to help the passing throng;
With self unseen.

My church to me means rest;
A quiet, peaceful rest, calm and complete;
Unbroken by the din of worldly strife;
The soul's retreat.

My church to me means home;
A happy, cheerful home, within whose walls
An undivided circle kneels in prayer,
As evening falls.

My church to me means hope;
A never-failing hope when light descends,
For in that hour it lights the evening lamp
And comfort sends.

My church to me means faith;
Triumphant faith, clearing the cluttered way
Toward that City where for us awaits
Eternal day.

My church to me means service;
A place to serve with others day to day,
Remembering always how the Master toiled to win
Men to the Way.

Author Unknown

358   *THE CHURCH OF MY DREAMS*

This is the church of my dreams:
The church of the warm heart,
Of the open mind,
Of the adventurous spirit;
The church that cares,
That heals hurt lives,
That comforts old people,
That challenges youth;
That knows no divisions of culture or class,
No frontiers, geographical or social;
The church that inquires as well as avers,
That looks forward as well as backward,
The church of the Master,
The church of the people,
High as the ideals of Jesus,
Low as the humblest human;
A working church,
A worshiping church,
A winsome church,
A church that interprets the truth in terms of truth;
That inspires courage for this life and hope for the life to come;
A church of courage,
A church of all good men,
The church of the Living God.

John Milton Moore

Topics, Texts and Themes

359   *THE GREATNESS OF THE REFORMATION*

The Reformation of the sixteenth century is, next to the introduction of
Christianity, the greatest event in history. . . . It was not a superficial amend-
ment, not a mere restoration, but a regeneration; not a return to the Augus-

tinian, or Nicene, or ante-Nicene age, but a vast progress beyond any previous
age or condition of the church since the death of St. John. It went, through
the intervening ages of ecclesiasticism, back to the fountain-head of Christianity
itself, as it came from the lips of the Son of God and his inspired Apostles.
It was a deeper plunge into the meaning of the Gospel than even St. Augustine
had made.

Philip Schaff

360   *THE HOPE OF PROTESTANTISM*

As in all Christianity from the beginning, continuing and growing vitality
depends upon the degree to which Protestantism is a channel of the eternal
Gospel. Protestantism came into being chiefly because through its great spirits
the Gospel found fresh outlet. The revivals which have marked the course of
Protestantism have sprung primarily from the same source. Other factors, some
political, some economic, some personal, have been partly accountable. The
most powerful and the one without which the others would have been
impotent is the Gospel. In a continuing and growing loyalty to the Gospel
in understanding and in full and joyous commitment is the hope of Protestantism. If Protestantism embodies the Gospel it will go on and grow. If it loses it
or becomes too stereotyped to give it free expression it will dwindle and the
eternal life in the Gospel will break out elsewhere and create for itself fresh
channels.

Kenneth Scott Latourette

361   *A DEFINITION OF PROTESTANTISM*

It is not a new form of the scribe's literal knowledge of a book. It is not the
rejection of sublimity and imaginative splendor in public worship. It is rather
a religion that affirms a historical foundation, and then a spiritual principle.
The historical foundation is that the Eternal has given us an actual revelation
of his will in Jesus Christ, and the spiritual principle is that the service of the
Eternal, after the manner of Christ, is direct, personal, immediate. A person,
not a rite nor an institution, is the first principle of Protestantism. Just as the
evolutionary process reaches its apex in an individual who lives; just as the
historical process reaches its apex in a man who is not an anonymous unit
in a mass, but stands erect, personal and free; so, says Protestantism, the
spiritual process reaches its apex in a developed spirit which stands face to face
with God. No system, no institution can be substituted for the spirit or for
God. Protestantism is a religion of transfigured and glorified individuality.

It is a high and exacting faith—possibly, it may prove too high and exacting, as it attempts to build a transfigured society on the transfigured individual. But there is a chance of triumphant life, even through pain and grief and death. The infinite spirit, the filial soul, the Christ as living grace and witness of the union of the two—such is Protestantism, and all disputes on texts or ordinances are non-essential compared with that.

William L. Sullivan

362 *THE BASIS OF PROTESTANTISM*

The truth is that Protestant religion is only possible on the condition that it is profoundly religious. It is only possible on the condition that a man's private judgment is continuously, anxiously, sincerely and humbly submitted, in prayer and thought and study and self-abnegation, to the will of God, as he is given light to discern that will and grace to obey it. Protestant religion, in short, is only possible on the basis of obedience—an obedience more complete and self-surrendering than that of the Catholic because it must be accompanied by the reasoned inward assent of the disciple. He knows he must obey God. He knows also that he must obey reason and conscience. Does this mean that he must necessarily experience a clash of loyalties? No. In the Protestant view of things nothing that clashes with reason and conscience can be thought of as having anything to do with God. If it is a church tradition it must go. If it is a majority vote in a religious assembly it must go. Even if it is a text of Scripture (or, rather, a text of Scripture as traditionally or usually interpreted) it must go. It may be said without irreverence that the Protestant Christian has not only to choose daily whether he will obey God or not; he also has to choose daily what God he will obey.

Ernest H. Jeffs

363 *JUSTIFICATION BY FAITH*

Carlyle said the greatest moment in the modern history of man was Luther at the Diet of Worms. You remember Luther in the monastery at Erfurt had reduced himself by his misery and despair almost to death itself, when the Vicar-General visited him, and said, "Luther, repeat the creed," and when Luther came to the line, "I believe in the forgiveness of sins" he realized that his sins were included there, and relief came to him. And then he was summoned to Rome, and he climbed the stairs of St. John's Church.

I have seen long processions of people there, climbing those steps on their hands and knees hoping thereby to obtain forgiveness of sins. And as Luther was thus climbing these stairs there flashed in upon him, by the light of the Spirit of God, the words: "The just shall live by faith," and he sprang to his feet, and said: "I defy all those who deny that a man is saved by faith." He realized that it was the doctrine that brought light and liberty and joy and power to all who accepted it.

You and I know what it is to be justified by faith, to be forgiven, to be accepted of God, and to experience joy and peace in believing. It was that doctrine that brought Luther to the Diet of Worms. That was a great moment: with all the power of the church, and all the power of the world on one side, and he, standing alone, on the other. "Recant, and you are forgiven: fail to recant, and death." Luther begged for time to consider, and the next day, after a night of prayer he was himself again, yea, more than himself. "Convince me," he said, "by plain reason, or by this Word of God, and I will recant."

John Wilson

364   *MAKING OUR ANCESTORS OUR CONTEMPORARIES*

And these all, having obtained a good report through faith, received not the promise: God having provided some better thing for us, that they without us should not be made perfect. HE. 11:39-40

The Christian tradition . . . comes to us most potently as the gift of twenty centuries of dead men. For Christianity includes all that it has done for men during the last two thousand years. It includes all that men have become through the influence of Jesus Christ. It includes all that men have done under his inspiration. You cannot deprive the Apostle Paul of the right to vote at any Christian convocation because he is dead. And Boniface from the German forests, and the monk Augustine in early England, and Patrick in Ireland, and Carey in India, and Livingstone in Africa belong to every Christian assembly. And Origen from Alexandria, and Chrysostom from Constantinople, and the great Bishop of Hippo from Africa, and Anselm from eleventh-century England, and Saint Francis from thirteenth-century Italy come to do commerce with us today. It takes everything that has ever happened to all the saints and martyrs and thinkers and men of action inspired by Christ to make up the Christian Church. From every Christian century they come hurrying to councils vaster and more potent than Nicaea. And as we allow them all to speak, and as we allow them all to vote, we begin really to understand the quality and the meaning of the Christian religion. It is only when all our Christian ancestors are allowed to become our contemporaries that the real splendor of the Christian faith and the Christian life begin to dawn upon us.

Lynn Harold Hough

365 *THE WITNESS OF THE CHURCH*

Wherefore of these men which have companied with us all the time that the Lord Jesus went in and out among us, beginning from the baptism of John, unto that same day that he was taken up from us, must one be ordained to be a witness with us of his resurrection. . . . And they gave forth their lots; and the lot fell upon Matthias; and he was numbered with the eleven apostles. AC. 1:21–22, 26

The essential duty of the ministry is still to bear witness. We are entrusted with a life-saving and life-giving truth and charged to carry it to others. Of course, in a sense we are still truth-seekers. We are constantly finding new meanings in the teachings of our Lord. We must be growing into new appreciations and larger apprehensions of the religion we would commend to the world. We are constantly trying to apply Christianity to the social, economic, industrial, national and inter-national problems of the day. We must endeavor to express the truth in the language of our own generation. We must show its power to satisfy the desires and remedy the evils of this present age.

But—the real strength of our witness lies in the fact that we are already, in heart and mind, convinced of the truth that is in Christ Jesus and feel an irresistible impulse, or summons, or call, to bear witness to this truth as a way of salvation for individuals, for communities, for the world. We speak, of course, that which we ourselves know, but we speak not simply as those who make their own assertions, but as representatives of a long line of witnesses whose testimony we have tested and accepted. We are not merely individuals giving voice to our own thoughts—though, of course, we do speak with this personal testimony—but we are representatives of a society which has wrought out the truth through an age-long experience. When we speak we believe that behind our words are the deep convictions of the saints of all ages, who have had their rich part in this experience, into whose thought and devotion we have entered and through which we have found life. In word, as well as in sacrament, ours is a representative priesthood.

Charles Fiske

366 *From THE EPISTLE TO DIOGNETUS*

Christians are not differentiated from the rest of mankind either by country, language, or customs. For they neither dwell in any cities of their own, nor employ any unusual dialect, nor practice any strange mode of life. Nor do they possess the kind of knowledge that is discovered by any device and ingenuity of inquisitive men; nor are they, like some, advocates of human philosophic dogma.

While they dwell in both Greek and non-Greek cities, according to individual circumstances, and follow native customs in clothing and food and other phases of life, yet they set forth a marvelous and confessedly incredible type of citizenship for themselves. They live in their native countries, but as sojourners; they participate in all activities as citizens, and endure all things as strangers. Every foreign land is their fatherland, and every fatherland is foreign. They marry like all other men and beget children, but they do not expose their offspring. They share a common table, but not a common bed. They are in the flesh, but do not live according to the flesh. They abide on earth, but live as citizens of heaven. They obey the established laws, and in their own lives they surpass the laws. They love all men and are persecuted by all. They are unrecognized, and yet they are condemned. They are put to death, and they have an increase in life. They are poor, yet they bestow riches on many. They suffer the want of all things, and they superabound in all things. They endure indignities, and they are glorified in their indignities. They are slandered, and they are justified. They are abused, and they bless. They are scoffed at and they show reverence. While they perform good deeds they are punished as evildoers. When punished they rejoice as attaining unto life. They are warred against as aliens by the Jews and are persecuted by the Greeks, yet those who hate them are unable to state the cause of their hatred. In brief, what the soul is to the body Christians are to the world.

367   *TESTIMONY*

This seems a cheerful world, Donatus, when I view it from this fair garden under the shadow of these vines. But, if I climb some great mountain and look out over the wide lands, you know very well what I would see—brigands on the road, pirates on the high seas, in the amphitheatres men murdering each other to please applauding crowds, under all roofs misery and selfishness. It is really a bad world, Donatus—an incredibly bad world. Yet, in the midst of it, I found a quiet and holy people. They have discovered a joy which is a thousand times better than any pleasure of this sinful life. They are despised and persecuted—but they care not. These people, Donatus, are the Christians, and I am one of them.

From a letter by Cyprian, bishop of Carthage (248–258)

368 *WHAT IT MEANS TO BE A CHRISTIAN*

They took knowledge of them, that they had been with Jesus. AC. 4:13

Our personalities are made up of convictions and desires and actions. One can have convictions that are Christlike, but if his desires or his actions are not Christlike, he is not worthy to be called a Christian. Or one could have a wishful attitude toward the things which Christ desired, but if he did not have the convictions Jesus had, or if he did not follow his desires with an action that was consonant with his profession, he could not be called a Christian. Or if he, puppetlike, simply went through the activities that Christ went through, and had neither the desire nor the conviction that Christ had, he could not be called a Christian. But if one believes what Christ believed and one desires what Jesus desired and one seeks to do what Jesus did and taught other people to do, we do not need to look at the name above the church where he worships; we do not need to study the ritual he follows. A person who has taken Jesus as a worthy interpreter of life and put his whole personality into Jesus' keeping, whose convictions, desires, and activities are in harmony with his—that person is a disciple of Jesus.

Paul Quillian

369 *WHY TO ATTEND CHURCH?*

There are various reasons why one should go to church. One of these is that if you do not attend—and not merely attend but enter into its ongoing life —you are a parasite! The church is the chief conserver of spiritual values, and it is the institutional embodiment of our Christian heritage. During the Dark Ages it preserved not only religion but civilization; it has fostered the spread of educaton throughout the centuries; it has nourished the spirit of democracy; it has built moral attitudes into the lives of millions of persons; it has made people more humane in their treatment of the weak and underprivileged; it has goaded consciences to abolish slavery; it has lifted the position of women and children. We are the inheritors of this freedom and this humanization, in which the church has not been the sole but has been the chief agent. To turn our backs on the church is to cast off our cultural parentage.

A second reason why you need to go to church is that the church needs you. . . . Its major need is for active and intelligent leadership, in congregations as in pulpits. It has done great things; it can do greater. . . .

The basic reason for attending church is that it offers you corporate worship of God in the name of Christ. Churches are not cinemas, soda-fountains, or concert-halls, and are not to be judged by the amount of entertainment they provide. They are places of worship, for the nourishment of the good life, and for Christian fellowship. Conceivably one might maintain a growing religious experience without the church . . . but not many people do.

Georgia Harkness

370   *A GREAT CHURCH*

The expression "a great church" is used so frequently by so many people that the true significance of it is often overlooked. Really, what constitutes "a great church"?

A church is great in the sight of God when it is:

Great in spirit. When its warmth of fellowship is apparent to all who worship there. It possesses a warmth which blesses all who come.

Great in love. Its love abounds toward Christ and toward sinners. The members love one another with deathless devotion.

Great in compassion. Its heart reaches out to suffer with those who need its ministry. Only by having compassion of heart can a church be great. As one well said, "A passionless church is a passing church."

Great in consecration. It withdraws itself from the world with its fashions and its fads; its members live a consecrated life; it has no place for worldliness and for human aspirations.

Great in loyalty. It is loyal to Christ. It is loyal to his word. It is loyal to "the faith once for all delivered unto the saints." Its members are loyal to the Lord and to his church by their dedication of time, of talents, and of treasure.

Author Unknown

371   *THE CHURCH*

The living source of teaching about God and religion.

The center for corporate worship and the inspirer of private worship.

The trainer of the young in the Christian life.

The representative of the Christian to the community at large.

The fellowship for mutual strengthening of those who have a common Christian faith and purpose.

The instrument for common Christian action.

The only organization devoted to ideals which parallels in size and scope the national and world problems which need those ideals.

The friend of the stranger and the friendless in the cold modern community.

The immediate source of healing influences which keep people going amidst the difficulties, frustrations, and tragedies of life.

The only institution which is concerned with the whole of life in a day of specialization, when education is secularized and departmentalized.

The most flexible institution which can take on new activities until the need for them is recognized by the community.

The home in which pioneers, prophets, radical minorities are developed even though they abandon it.

The freest platform for the prophet and a sounding board for his message.

Author Unknown

372   *THIS IS MY CHURCH*

My church is an inheritance, the result of struggle and sorrow, through which multitudes passed in other days.

My church is an entrustment and I must pass on a richer, more spiritual organization to the next generation.

My church is the church of my brother, and I must live in helpful relationship to him.

My church is the church of a group, and I must relate myself to their opinions and decisions.

My church worships, and I must join others in prayer and praise.

My church is an evangelist, and I must take part in its program to win others.

My church requires money, and I must contribute toward its support and advancement.

My church can only be held together by love, and I must seek to practice and inspire others to live this "more excellent way."

Charles P. MacGregor

373   *MY CHURCH*

Before I was born, the church gave to my parents ideals of life and love that made my home a place of strength and beauty. In helpless infancy the church joined my parents in consecrating me to Christ and in baptizing me in his name.

The church enriched my childhood with the romance of religion and the lessons of life that have been woven into the texture of my soul. Sometimes I seem to have forgotten and then, when else I might surrender to foolish and futile ideals of life, the truths the church taught become radiant, insistent, and inescapable.

In the stress of adolescence the church heard the surge of my soul and guided my footsteps by lifting my eyes toward the stars. When first my heart knew the strange awakenings of love, the church taught me to chasten and spiritualize my affections; she sanctified and blessed my home.

When my heart was seamed with sorrow, and the way ahead was not clear, the church drew me to the Friend of all the weary and whispered to me the hope of another morning, eternal and tearless.

When my steps have slipped and I have known the bitterness of sin, the church has believed in me and wooingly she has called me back to live within the heights of myself.

My church calls me to her heart. She asks my service and my loyalty. She has a right to ask it! I will help her to do for others what she has done for me. In this place which I live, I will help her keep aflame and aloft the torch of a living faith.

Deep in my heart I know that the church is of God. That in spite of human frailties, she has brought blessings untold to all generations including our own. That she has made my community and my country a better place in which to live, to work and to establish a home. That I would not want to live in a land where no church spires point its people heavenward. I also know that the church continues to live triumphantly even when men and nations reject her by indifference or open hostility. In this knowledge I gladly give myself to my church and offer her my loyal support by intelligent membership, regular attendance, generous giving, ardent prayer and devoted service.

William Henry Boddy

II. The Christian Mission

A. MISSIONARY SUNDAY

Christian missions is not a concern which can be limited to a single day or season, for it is implicit in all of the work and ministry of the church. A particular occasion, however, is frequently designated as Missionary Sunday. Other days may specifically celebrate foreign missions or home missions. Many churches devote a series of programs, such as a School of Missions, to the study of mission history and biography and to the presentation of need and achievement of modern missions. Men and Missions Day, observed in connection with Churchmen's Week and held annually on the second Sunday in October, enlists the support of men for world missions.

This section contains materials appropriate also for financial appeals in behalf of missions, worship programs of women's missionary societies and Sunday school and youth groups, and missionary commissioning services.

Calls to Worship

(Boldface type indicates response.)

374 [Jesus saith] I have set thee to be a light of the Gentiles, that thou shouldest be for salvation unto the ends of the earth.

They shall come from the east, and from the west, and from the north, and from the south, and shall sit down in the kingdom of God.

Ac. 13:47; Lu. 13:29

375 O Zion, that bringest good tidings, get thee up into the high mountain; O Jerusalem, that bringest good tidings, lift up thy voice with strength; lift it up, be not afraid; say unto the cities of Judah, Behold your God!

Is. 40:9

376 From the rising of the sun even unto the going down of the same my name shall be great among the Gentiles [saith the Lord]. [Jesus saith] Other sheep I have, which are not of this fold: them also I must bring, and they shall hear my voice; and there shall be one fold, and one shepherd.

Mal. 1:11; Jn. 10:16

377 God so loved the world, that he gave his only begotten Son, that whosoever believeth in him should not perish, but have everlasting life. The harvest

truly is plenteous, but the laborers are few; pray ye therefore the Lord of the harvest, that he will send forth laborers into his harvest.

Jn. 3:16; Mat. 9:37-38

Invocations

378   Almighty and all-merciful God, help the church of Christ throughout the world to arise to the meanings of thy purpose which beat like wings about thy throne. Lead us from height to height, from vision to vision, from truth to truth, until at last we enter into that broad place where thy purpose shall be our purpose, and thy will, our will. Amen.

W. S. Archibald

379   Grant thy servants, O God, to be set on fire with thy Spirit, strengthened by thy power, illuminated by thy splendour, filled with thy grace, and to go forward by thine aid. Give them, O Lord, a right faith, perfect love, true humility. Grant, O Lord, that there may be in us simple affection, brave patience, persevering obedience, perpetual peace, a pure mind, a right and honest heart, a good will, a holy conscience, spiritual strength; through Jesus Christ our Lord. Amen.

Gallican Sacramentary

380   Almighty God, whose compassions fail not, and whose loving kindness reacheth unto the world's end: we give thee humble thanks for all the great things thou hast done and art doing for the children of men; for the opening of distant lands to the light of thy truth; for making paths in the deep waters and highways in the desert; for knitting nation to nation in the bond of fellowship, and for the planting of thy church in all the earth. O merciful Father, in whom the whole family in heaven and earth is named, fill full our hearts with grateful love for this thy goodness, granting us grace henceforth to serve thee better and more perfectly to know thee; through Jesus Christ our Lord. Amen.

Prayers for the Church Service League

Prayers

381   Most gracious God who hast sent thy Son to be the Saviour of the world, we praise thee for the transforming power of the gospel, and for those heroic souls whom thou hast sent forth into all lands to lay deep and strong the foundations of the Christian church. We praise thee for a spiritual fellowship which transcends all bounds of birth and race and clime, and for a prophetic vision of the glorious city of God in the light of which all peoples yet shall rejoice.

We render our humble thanks to thee for all the blessings and brightness brought into our lives by the knowledge of Christ and by the power of his Spirit; but do thou guard us from selfish enjoyment and bounded horizons. Make us to share the sympathy of the Master who when he saw the multitudes was moved with compassion for them because they were distressed and scattered as sheep not having a shepherd. Help us so to see the struggling and bewildered masses of this stricken world. Stir within us an eager desire to bring them under the guidance of the Good Shepherd who alone can lead them in right paths and can give rest to their souls.

Follow with thy favor and thy protecting care those our friends serving as ambassadors of Christ in distant fields beyond the seas. Sustain them in loneliness and peril, in weariness and pain. Show them precious fruits of their labors, assure them of the certain triumph of their Lord. Give unfailing courage and fortitude to the followers who in their native lands are witnessing to fellow countrymen concerning the redeeming grace and power of Christ. May they be used to introduce kindlier customs, purer laws and nobler lives. If persecuted and tormented, may they be faithful unto death, expecting from thee a crown of life. Control the rulers and leaders of the nations. Bring to an end the thousand wars of old. Bring in the thousand years of peace. Bring in the Christ that is to be.

We ask this in his name. Amen.

Charles R. Erdman

382   Most gracious and blessed God, we adore thee for thy gracious purposes for a lost world, and bless thee that thou dost permit men to share with thee in thine infinite plan of mercy and grace.

We thank thee for the prophets and apostles and martyrs, and for the noble company of disciples in all the centuries, who, endowed and inspired by thyself, laid their lives on the altar of sacrifice and service. We bless thee for the multitudes who today, in so many lands, have entered into the fellowship of this ministry and are seeking to live the Christlife, to publish the glad news, and to bring men everywhere to know Jesus Christ as the only Saviour of mankind. Thrust forth, we pray thee, more laborers into the fields that are white unto the harvest, that all open doors may be entered speedily and that the day may soon dawn when all nations shall own him Lord.

Enrich the missionary servants continually, we pray thee, with fresh baptisms of the Holy Spirit, that their ministry may be in the demonstration of the Spirit and of power. May they be living epistles, written by the Spirit of God, known and read of all men. So open their eyes to the riches of the glory of the inheritance in Christ that they shall endure gladly the present trial, in view of the exceeding and eternal weight of glory. May the great cloud of witnesses, the innumerable company of those who have gone before and entered into rest, be to them even now an inspiration and a joy. Make them to sing thy song, to walk in thy light, and to know thy joy and thy peace.

All these things we ask in the name of Jesus Christ our Lord. Amen.

R. P. Mackay

383   O thou who rules by thy providence over land and sea, defend and guide and bless the messengers of Christ; in danger be their shield, in darkness be their hope; enrich their word and work with wisdom, joy and power, and let them gather souls for thee in far fields white unto the harvest.

O thou who by thy Holy Spirit workest wonders in secret, open the minds that dimly look for light to see the day-star in Christ; open the minds that seek the Unknown God to know their heavenly Father in Christ; open the hearts that hunger for righteousness to find eternal peace in Christ. Deliver the poor prisoners of ignorance and captives of idolatry, break down the bars of error, and dispel the shadows of the ancient night; lift up the gates, and let the King of Glory and the Prince of Peace come in.

Thy Kingdom, O Christ, is an everlasting Kingdom! Strengthen thy servants to pray and labor and wait for its appearing; forgive our little faith and the weakness of our endeavour; hasten the day when all nations shall be at peace with thee, and every land and every heart throughout the world shall bless the name of the Lord Jesus, to the glory of God the Father. Amen.

Henry van Dyke

384   Almighty God, who by thy Son Jesus Christ didst give commandment to the holy apostles that they should go into all the world and preach the Gospel to every creature; grant to us whom thou hast called to follow thee, a ready will to obey thy will, and fill us with a hearty desire to make thy way known upon earth, thy saving health among all nations. Look with compassion upon all who are living without thee, and on the multitudes who even in this land are scattered abroad as sheep having no shepherd, or who in strange lands are far from the church of their fathers. Visit them with thy salvation. O heavenly Father, Lord of the harvest, have respect, we beseech thee, to these our prayers, and send forth laborers into thy harvest. Fit and prepare them by thy grace for the work of their ministry. Give them the spirit of power, and of love, and of a sound mind. Strengthen them to endure hardness, and grant that both by their

life and doctrine they may set forth thy glory and set forward the salvation of
all men; through Jesus Christ our Lord. Amen.

Prayer Book of the Church of Ireland

Poems

385   *From FOREIGN MISSIONS IN BATTLE ARRAY*

An endless line of splendor,
These troops with heaven for home,
With creeds they go from Scotland,
With incense go from Rome.
These, in the name of Jesus,
Against the dark gods stand,
They gird the earth with valor,
They heed their King's command.

❋

What is the final ending?
The issue, can we know?
Will Christ outlive Mohammed?
Will Kali's altar go?
This is our faith tremendous,—
Our wild hope, who shall scorn,—
That in the name of Jesus
The world shall be reborn!

Vachel Lindsay

386   *THE MISSIONARIES*

O missionaries of the Blood! Ambassadors of God!
Our souls flame in us when we see where ye have fearless trod
At break of day; your dauntless faith our slackened valor shames,
And every eve our joyful prayers are jeweled with your names.

Robert McIntyre

387   *WHERE SHALL I WORK?*

"Master, where shall I work today?"
And my love flowed warm and free.
Then he pointed out a tiny plot,

And he said: "Work there for me."
But I answered quickly: "Oh, no, not there!
  Not any one could see,
No matter how well my task is done—
  Not that small place for me!"
And his voice, when he spoke, it was not stern,
  But he answered me tenderly:
"Disciple, search that heart of thine.
  Are you working for them, or for me?
Nazareth was just a little place,
  And so was Galilee."

Author Unknown

388   *STIR US, OH, STIR US, LORD*

Stir us, oh, stir us, Lord, we care not how,
But stir our hearts in passion for the world;
Stir us to give, to go, but most to pray;
Stir till the blood-red banner be unfurled
O'er lands that still in heathen darkness lie,
O'er deserts where no Cross is lifted high.

Author Unknown

389   *BECAUSE I LOVE THEE*

Because I love thee, I would go
To Afric's suns, or Greenland's snow;
I'd press to India's coral strand,
Or unto China's sin-swept land;
I'd gladly go the world around,
Wherever mortal man is found.

Author Unknown

390   *WHEN THE DAYLIGHT WANES*

No more in Galilee we look for thee,
  O Risen Lord;
In every land and on each moonlit sea
  Thy voice is heard;

And when thy saints are gathered in thy Name,
Closer thou art to each than fire to flame.

Thomas Tiplady

391 *IS THERE SOME DESERT*

Is there some desert or some pathless sea
Where thou, good God of angels, wilt send me?
Some oak for me to rend; some sod,
Some rock for me to break;
Some handful of his corn to take
And scatter far afield,
Till it, in turn, shall yield
Its hundred fold
Of grains of gold
To feed the waiting children of my God.
Show me the desert, Father, or the sea.
Is it thine enterprise? Great God, send me.

Edward Everett Hale

Topics, Texts and Themes

392 *COME—GO*

Jesus says, "Come to me," in order that he may say, "Go ye therefore." We cannot go unless we come to Jesus and put ourselves under his yoke of humanity's wretchedness and woe. Nor can we come to Jesus unless we also go. We cannot find rest to our souls unless we take his yoke upon us. It is only as we become "meek and lowly in heart," asking nothing for ourselves but to share the yoke with Jesus, giving our lives as he gave his to teach that best and happiest way of living which is the Kingdom of God, that we really discover what it means to come to Jesus.

Jesus invites us to come in order that we may go. We come to him that we may go for him and with him to lift the yoke of superstition and error, of a guilty conscience and an evil life, of misfortune and despair from the necks of boys and girls and men and women of every race, and color, and creed. We come to him that we may go for him and with him to bring in the Kingdom of God.

Harold McA. Robinson

393　　　　　　　　*THE OUTREACH*

Go ye into all the world, and preach the gospel to every creature. MK. 16:15

As one seeks to examine the causes that have undergirded, and still underlie our missionary effort, at least two settled convictions suggest themselves as being a part of the deep out of which these tides of missionary effort have come, and do come.

One of those things is the belief which, rightly or wrongly, Christian people have always held, namely that the truths of Christianity should gain universal acceptance. When one speaks of Christianity as a religion that should become universal he arouses very honest objections. Surely, in saying this, one is not implying that there is nothing good or true or beautiful in other religions. The day for such bigotry has passed. He is rather saying that the best in other religions is found in Christianity, and in addition something more which other faiths do not possess.

And what is that something more? In a word, it is Christ—Christ who comes not to destroy, but to fulfill. . . .

There is another motive that prompts us to go into all the world and preach to every creature. And that is the belief that Christ is the very best that the West has, and we should give our best, not our worst. . . . Surely no sober student of our Western civilization will deny that the greatest values of our civilization have sprung from the life and teachings of Jesus; nor can it be doubted that the most wholesome and helpful contacts that we make with other lands grow out of those personal relationships established by our missionaries. They go not to get, but to give; not for personal gain, but for social good. . . . They are messengers of mercy. They have won the confidence of those to whom they minister, and their good will. They are Christian missionaries, taking the best our civilization has to offer, not its worst.

Harold Cooke Phillips

394　　　　　　　*THE CHRISTIAN COMPULSION*

He that hath sent me is with me; he hath not left me alone; for I do always the things that are pleasing to him. JN. 8:29 (RV)

The Christian compulsion is threefold: (1) A sense of direction—to "do always the things that are pleasing to him." Nothing can transcend the example and practice of our Lord Jesus Christ. Among all treatises on personal relationship and conduct, there can be found no more reliable guide in matters of faith and conduct than that afforded in this simple and vital summary—that is, that we occupy ourselves with doing (not just contemplating) the things pleasing to Christ, "always."

(2) A sense of mission. Note that Christ recognized and accepted his divine mandate. With him the task was not a self-appointed one, but rather he was conscious of divine compulsion. "He *sent* me." So it must be with all who bear his name.

(3) A sense of companionship. Christ reiterates this fact of the divine presence. "He hath not left me alone." Supremely important is this reassurance.

John R. Mott

395   *WORLD WIDE MISSION*

The field is the world. MAT. 13:38

Jesus offered a pattern of life to be lived out in this present world as we find it. Self-exalting nationalism and isolationism, then and now, find no support from him. Mediaeval monks withdrew from an evil world and lived unnatural and unproductive lives but they had no commission nor approval of Jesus. The field, the soil and substance of our lives, is around about us and the Gospel is framed for men who live in the world as it is and have to deal with its wheat and tares, its soil and stones, and good and evil, as all in the day's work. The setting for God's eternal purposes is the world, the whole wide world as the material home of all men of every race and country. In this age of totalitarian states and God-defying dictators, Jesus again is reminding us that his plans are for all humanity and that race prejudices have no place in Christian attitudes. The breadth and scope of Jesus' program forever goes out beyond "the township mind" to "every creature" and every human life and problem.

George A. Miller

396   *CHRIST AS A MISSIONARY*

Christ was a home missionary in the house of Lazarus.

He was a foreign missionary when the Greeks came to him.

A city missionary when he taught in Samaria.

A Sunday school missionary when he opened up the Scriptures and set men to studying the Word of God.

A children's missionary when he took them in his arms and blessed them.

A missionary to the poor when he opened the eyes of the blind beggar.

A missionary to the rich when he opened the spiritual eyes of Zaccheus.

Even on the Cross Christ was a missionary to the robber, and his last command was the missionary commission.

Amos R. Wells

397   *THE BIBLE AND FOREIGN MISSIONS*

Every book in the New Testament was written by a foreign missionary.

Every epistle in the New Testament that was written to a church was written to a foreign missionary church.

Every letter in the New Testament that was written to an individual was written to the convert of a foreign missionary.

Every book in the New Testament that was written to a community of believers was written to a general group of foreign missionary churches.

The one book of prophecy in the New Testament was written to the seven foreign missionary churches in Asia.

The only authoritative history of the early Christian church is a foreign missionary journal.

The disciples were called Christians first in a foreign missionary community.

The language of the books of the New Testament is the missionary language.

The map of the early Christian world is the tracings of the missionary journals of the apostles.

The problems which arose in the early church were largely questions of missionary procedure.

Of the twelve apostles chosen by Jesus every apostle except one became a missionary. That one became a traitor.

Only a foreign missionary could write an everlasting gospel.

According to the apostles the missionary is the highest expression of the Christian life.

William Adams Brown

398   *THE FIRST-CENTURY CHURCH—*
          ITS MISSIONARY PASSION

Neither is there salvation in any other: for there is none other name under heaven given among men, whereby we must be saved. AC. 4:12

What was it in the heart of the church of the first century that made it supremely missionary and drove the early followers of Christ to witness everywhere concerning the "good news"? To assess the motives and passion in that early day of great danger should help us of the modern church to face our sinister times with a confident and eager message. Let us inquire into the missionary zeal of the ancient church.

The early church was sensitive to the Christian imperative to go into all the world. . . . Missionary work received the stamp of God's approval. . . . The early church and missions were identical. . . . The early missionaries saw the urgency of their times.

Stephen J. Corey

399   *THE MISSION SPIRIT*

Thou hast done well that thou art come. Now therefore are we all here present before God, to hear all things that are commanded thee of God. AC. 10:33

In the conversion of Cornelius we have an instance of successful evangelism. Such work would be just as successful today if the same conditions were fulfilled: a proper evangelist willing to go, "Thou hast done well that thou art come"; a congregation gathered through the efforts of a layman, "Cornelius had called together his kinsmen and near friends"; people disposed to listen, "We are all here present before God to hear"; and a clear Gospel message.

Robert Valenzuela

400   *ACCEPTING A LARGE TASK*

In 1771, an English soldier-preacher who was being sent to the colonies in response to young Asbury's urgent pleading for more preachers, received a stirring letter:

Dear George,
    The time has arrived for you to embark for America. You must go down to Bristol where you will meet with T. Rankin, Capt. Webb and his wife. I let you loose, George, on the great continent of America. Publish your message in the open face of the sun, and do all the good you can.
    I am, dear George, yours affectionately,

John Wesley

On a continent for a parish—and a message worthy of being published in the open face of the sun! They had large aims in those days. The first sermon preached by the great evangelist Rankin after he reached America was on a text from Revelation: "I have set before thee an open door, and no man can shut it."

Margueritte Harmon Bro

401   *RELIGION TO POSSESS AND TO SHARE*

Paul clearly realized that the very nature of living religion is such that *you only possess it as you share it*. If you are dealing with material things, the more you give them away the less you have them. If you are dealing with ideas, the more you pass them on the more you own them. Your clarity and sureness of grasp are increased by the very activity of exposition. And if you are dealing with great ideals, the more you give them to others the more you possess them yourself. But these parallel activities scarcely go to the root of the matter. For in a very singular and a very potent sense religion springs into new life in your own personality every time you share it with another. It becomes more your own every time it is given to another. It becomes more your own every time it is given to some one else. There is something creative about the very act of giving. . . . The Christianity which is shared is the Christianity which is convincing.

Lynn Harold Hough

402   *HOW TO PAY DEBTS*

Hundreds of years ago an ardent Christian wrote a sentence which has puzzled me ever since I first read it. Paul said: "I am debtor both to the Greeks, and to the Barbarians; both to the wise, and to the unwise. So . . . I am ready to preach the gospel to you that are at Rome also." It seems like an absurd way for a man to pay debts. He confessess that he owes much to Greeks and Barbarians. Yet he does not attempt to pay *them*. He knows that he cannot. The only recourse he has to make his payments to the *Romans*. So far as we know, he owes the Romans nothing. But he really owes it to them to pay them for what he has received from the Greeks and Barbarians. It is the only way to pay debts after all.

The only way to be truly grateful for the America which we inherit is to pass on a better America to our children. The only way to pay for the Gospel is to scatter the Gospel gladly over all the world. The greatest mistake in the world of economics is made by the man who insists that he will enjoy nothing for which he does not directly pay, and will pay for nothing that he himself does not enjoy. He could not conscientiously ride a mile on a railroad, buy a single copy of a newspaper, or eat a slice of bread, or come to church. These things cannot be done. We are irrevocably bound together. For better or worse, we depend upon one another.

Bernard C. Clausen

403   *OUR DEBT TO THE MISSIONARIES*

How then shall they call on him in whom they have not believed?
and how shall they believe in him of whom they have not heard? and how
shall they hear without a preacher? and how shall they preach, except they
be sent? RO. 10:14–15

If there never had been any missionaries . . . Have you ever tried to imagine
what the world would be . . . what America would be . . . what you would
be, if those first disciples had not obeyed Jesus? There might have been a
Columbus, but he would have brought no Cross to the new world. There
would have been no Pilgrims to land at Plymouth Rock. There would have
been no Judson to make the name of Baptists glorious. There would have been
no Samuel F. Smith to write "America," and no Lincoln to give us the gospel
of our democracy. And, too, have you ever thought what sort of person you
would be? What strange gods would you worship? What thoughts would you
think—if there had been no missionaries to tell the Good News? Can you imagine a musician who does not believe in music? an American who does not
believe in freedom? a scholar who does not believe in books? a physician who
does not believe in hospitals? Can you imagine a true Christian who does not
believe in missions?

                                                        Everett C. Herrick

404   *SACRIFICE AND PRIVILEGE*

For my own part, I have never ceased to rejoice that God has appointed me
to such an office. People talk of the sacrifice I have made in spending so much
of my life in Africa. Can that be called a sacrifice which is simply paid back as
a small part of a great debt owing to our God, which we can never repay? Is
that a sacrifice which brings its own blest reward in healthful activity, the consciousness of doing good, peace of mind, and a bright hope of a glorious destiny
hereafter? Away with the word in such a view, and with such a thought! It is
emphatically no sacrifice. Say rather it is a privilege. Anxiety, sickness, suffering, or danger, now and then, with a forgoing of the common conveniences
and charities of this life, may make us pause, and cause the spirit to waver, and
the soul to sink; but let this be only for a moment. All these are nothing when
compared with the glory which shall hereafter be revealed in, and for, us. I
never made a sacrifice. Of this we ought not to talk, when we remember the
great sacrifice which he made who left his Father's throne on high to give

himself for us; "who being the brightness of that Father's glory, and the express image of his person, and upholding all things by the word of his power, when he had by himself purged our sins, sat down on the right hand of the Majesty on high."

David Livingstone

B. WORLD WIDE COMMUNION SUNDAY

World Wide Communion, observed internationally since 1938 on the first Sunday in October, stresses the world fellowship and unity of all Christians in Christ and the oneness of Christ's followers at the his Table. A special missions offering is sometimes received at this service. Particular effort is made to secure a complete representation at communion of all members. Communion is offered to shut-in and hospitalized members.

Calls to Worship

(Boldface type indicates response.)

405 The cup of blessing which we bless, is it not the communion of the blood of Christ? The bread which we break, is it not the communion of the body of Christ?

For we being many are one bread, and one body: for we are all partakers of that one bread.

1 Co. 10:16–17

406 Christ our passover is sacrificed for us: therefore let us keep the feast, not with old leaven, neither with the leaven of malice and wickedness; but with the unleavened bread of sincerity and truth.

1 Co. 5:7–8

407 If any man be in Christ, he is a new creature: old things are passed away; behold, all things are become new. And all things are of God, who hath reconciled us to himself by Jesus Christ, and hath given to us the ministry of reconciliation.

2 Co. 5:17–18

Invocations

408 Grant, O Son of God, that as thou and the Father are one, so we thy people may be bound together in thee. Unite in mutual forbearance, loyalty and brotherly kindness thy brethren who are fellow-guests at this thy table, that we, being moved by the common impulse of thine eternal purpose, may promote the peace of thy Kingdom in the daily interminglings of our common life; whom with the Father and the Holy Ghost we worship and glorify as God forever and ever. Amen.

Charles H. Brent

409　O thou great Friend of all the sons of men, the Comrade of the beaten and broken, of the young and old, the valiant and the timid: bring us within the circle of thy love and power and wisdom, that we may be to others what thou art to us, the unfailing Companion, the cup of strength to souls in need, the reconciling Friend. As we sit at thy table and meditate upon thy love for all the world, let our holy communion be in truth within the world-wide community of thy holy church. Draw us closer to thyself and so closer to one another in Jesus Christ thy Son our Saviour. Amen.

David A. MacLennan

410　Son of the living God, who, being the true bread of life, dost feed and satisfy with thy body and blood all troubled souls, all restless consciences, all hungry and thirsty hearts, and dost invite all men to this heavenly meal: receive us also graciously; feed and quicken our needy souls with thy true body and blood unto everlasting life. Amen.

St. Augustine

Prayers

411 O thou who hast broken the Bread of Life for a hungry world, and satisfied its thirst with the Water of Life: grant to us, as we remember thee, all that makes life worth while. We thank thee that it has been made wonderful because thou didst live it so wonderfully. We bless thee for this table around which the whole world may sit down and feel the Brotherhood, as from thy hand it receives the token of thy oneness with the human race. Take out of our hearts at this time and place the narrow and bitter feeling of superiority and pride. Make us humble in the presence of that Personality that, although divine, knelt to wash the feet of common men. Make us to feel the majesty of that divine act of service which even after the resurrection with thine own hands prepared a meal for hungry fishermen as they came in from the night's toil. And from this table may we all arise to go out into the world of action to follow thee, cheered by the eternal Presence, and fed by the abundant Life. Amen.

Charles M. Sheldon

412   Grant forgiveness, O God, for all acts of malice and uncharitableness, blindness and hardness of heart. Give us the spirit of true charity which alone is true wisdom, and grant that we may come to this sacrament of holy communion in charity with each other and with all; determined henceforth to feel for each other and with each other; to put ourselves in our neighbors' places; to see with their eyes, and feel with their hearts; to make allowances for their mistakes and failings; to give and forgive, even as thou dost give and forgive, that so we may indeed be thy children, O heavenly Father, whose name is Love, and indeed discern the Lord's body—that it is a body of union and sympathy, of mutual trust and help and affection, and once again, with all contrition and humility, in spirit and in truth, claim and obtain our share in the body and the blood, in the spirit and in the mind, of him who sacrificed himself for a rebellious world. Amen.

Charles Kingsley

413   Pour out, we beseech thee, O Lord, thy spirit upon thy church, that to its members may come new visions, new life, new fellowship with Christ, its living head. Send us out, if thou wilt, and through us send out many another to work for the extension of thy Kingdom throughout the world. Open our hearts that we may see Christ with hands outstretched to bless. Do with us what thou wilt and as thou wilt. So shall the earth be filled with the knowledge of thyself as the waters cover the sea. And to thee be the glory and praise, now and forevermore. Amen.

Author Unknown

Poems

414   *COMMUNION*

I would be one with Thee.
And is thy brother near?
He would not come with me.
Go, thou, and bring him here.
And if he does not come?
Then come not thou to me;
We must be Three in One,
Thyself and he in Me.

Loren W. Burch

415   *BENEATH THE FORMS OF OUTWARD RITE*

Beneath the forms of outward rite
Thy supper, Lord, is spread
In every quiet upper room
Where fainting souls are fed.

The bread is always consecrate
Which men divide with men;
And every act of brotherhood
Repeats thy feast again.

The blessed cup is only passed
True memory of thee,
When life anew pours out its wine
With rich sufficiency.

O Master, through these symbols shared,
Thine own dear self impart,
That in our daily life may flame
The passion of thy heart.

James A. Blaisdell

416   *From THE VISION OF SIR LAUNFAL*

And the voice that was calmer than silence said,
"Lo, it is I, be not afraid!
In many climes, without avail,
Thou hast spent thy life for the Holy Grail;
Behold, it is here,—this cup which thou
Didst fill at the streamlet for me but now;
This crust is my body broken for thee,
This water his blood that died on the tree;
The Holy Supper is kept, indeed,
In whatso we share with another's need;
Not what we give, but what we share—
For the gift without the giver is bare;
Who gives himself with his alms feeds three—
Himself, his hungering neighbor, and me."

James Russell Lowell

417   *COMMUNION*

> *I am the bread of life,* the Saviour said,
> And with the loaves, and words,
> Men were fed;
> *I am the vine,* God's Son taught,
> *My Father is the husbandman—ye, branches,*
> *Which he wrought.*
>
> *This is my body, broken for thee,* the Master said,
> While breaking in his hands
> The apostles' bread;
> *This my blood was shed for thee*—he took the cup,
> Bidding his friends take theirs, too, and
> With him sup.
>
> O Broken Bread, broken for me, O Living Bread!
> O Bruiséd Vine, bruiséd for me, Sustaining Vine!
> Let me take up the cup—remembering
> A hungry world, broken and unfed,
> People athirst for thee, adrift, misled,
> Needing, as Galileans needed, thee! . . . O living
> Vine and Bread!

Mary Dickerson Bangham

418   *THE CROSS*

> Our Saviour's cross, begilt with guiltless blood,
> Was framed (as some write) of four kinds of wood,
> Palm, cedar, cypress, olive; which might show
> That blessings thence to the four parts should flow
> Of the vast world, and from the four winds should
> Christ's flock be fetched to his thrice-blessed fold.

Thomas Bancroft

419   *From "BEHOLD I MAKE ALL THINGS NEW"*

> From hand to hand the greeting flows,
> From eye to eye the signals run,

From heart to heart the bright hope glows;
  The seekers of the Light are one,—

One in the freedom of the Truth,
  One in the joy of paths untrod,
One in the soul's perennial youth,
  One in the larger thought of God,—

The freer step, the fuller breath,
  The wide horizon's grander view,
The sense of life that knows no death,—
  The Life that maketh all things new.

Samuel Longfellow

420   *THE TRIMMED LAMP*

I dare not slight the stranger at my gate—
Threadbare of garb, and sorrowful of lot
Lest it be Christ that stands, and goes his way
Because I, all unworthy, knew him not.

I dare not miss one flash of loving cheer
From alien souls, in challenge fine and high:
Ah,—what if God be moving very near—
And I, so blind, so deaf—had passed him by?

Laura Simmons

Topics, Texts and Themes

421   *THE PLACE WHERE WE MAY WELL BE AT ONE*

Nevertheless, whereto we have already attained, let us walk by the same
rule, let us mind the same thing. PH. 3:16

The sacrament of the Lord's Supper is something, at least, which all the
churches of Christendom have in common. Perhaps it will be by the simple
acceptance of the ideas and beliefs which are embodied in that sacrament, that
the divided and broken church may one day return to unity. For though the
great divisions of Christendom—Catholic, Orthodox, Evangelical—surround
this sacrament with practices which differ, and approach it with differing expectations, it is possible, when one brings sympathy and charity, to find that
beneath the surface they mean the same.   *John A. Hutton*

422   *THE TABLE OF UNITY*

There is at least one point at which all Christians are united. There is at least one common element in our religion which runs through all the differing units, holding us in common unity, making us one faith, one body, one church. That point of union, that binding factor is the central sacrament of holy communion, the Lord's Supper. To be sure, there may be minor variations of administration of the sacrament's inner meaning and in our acceptance of its social implications.

As to the inner meaning of the sacrament, we Christians are agreed, first, that the sacrament begins with the open humility of admitting one's sins and being repentant for them. Unless we first have attained the purging humility of the honestly contrite heart, the sacrament will never be able to bestow its blessing upon us.

Christians agree, secondly, on the spiritual meaning of the sacrament, that mystic union of partaker and Master when by submitting ourselves to him, his Spirit becomes our spirit, his aims our aims.

And thirdly, we agree on the rededication of will. This must always happen in the sacrament so that we arise from the table "intending to lead a new life, following the commandments of God." These are inner meanings of the sacrament, and these we all accept.

Christians are equally united, however, in their acceptance of the outer or the social implications of the sacrament. For instance, we do not dare to come to the table except we first are "in love and charity with our neighbors." That is, as preparation for the sacrament we must be willing to accept and must be committed to achieve a life of conscious Christian brotherhood in this world, with all that its achievement implies. We know that in this modern world, such achievement is difficult, to say the least. Yet living in love and charity with one's neighbors is the inescapable prerequisite.

Hear again the words of the general invitation which set the requirements all over the world: "Ye that do truly and earnestly repent of your sins, and are in love and charity with your neighbors, and intend to lead a new life, following the commandments of God . . . draw near with faith and take this holy sacrament. . . ." Here is the heart of the Christian religion, here is the binding element which makes us all one.

Harry V. Richardson

423   *ONE IN CHRIST*

For ye are all one in Christ Jesus. GA. 3:28

Paul is speaking here about the Christian community spirit. He means that world-wide community of members of the Christian fellowship who look to Christ as life's great example. Such a spirit involves several things:

Interdependence, which is the watchword of our generation. We depend upon each other economically, culturally, spiritually. Our modern world has shrunk in size with rapidity of communication and travel. *Brotherhood,* which is at the heart of the Christian spirit, as it is in the message and life of Jesus. It demands a life, freed from hatred and prejudice and filled with love and active good will. *Unifying faith,* which is the main bond that unites men across the world. Our common faith in Christ brings unity, which neither war nor scourge nor death can dissolve. It is common—unity. One comman faith makes "all one in Christ Jesus."

Hoover Rupert

424   *THE FELLOWSHIP OF KINDRED MINDS*

That I may know him, and the power of his resurrection, and the fellowship of his sufferings. PH. 3:10

The world needs some great unifying experience, and such an experience is presented to us in "World Communion." Christian people differ widely in their thinking, but we are all one in the acceptance of Christ as our Lord and Master. In the communion service our thoughts are centered on the Cross, and there is real value in having one service in the year when multitudes of Christians have their hearts united before that Cross.

Suffering is a unifying experience. When one suffers for others, all who benefit from that suffering are bound together by their devotion to him. Many illustrations of that fact might be cited, but the most significant illustration is the death of Christ on the Cross. He died for all of us.

Paul's desire to know the fellowship of Christ's suffering might well be our prayer. If all Christians were to share in that fellowship, Christ's prayer for the unity of his followers would be realized. We would then be united in him and in the Father.

A. W. Fortune

425   *AN UNBROKEN BOND*

Here at the Table of the Lord we perceive in a mellow light those words of Holy Scripture that God hath made one all nations of men who dwell on the earth. The inclusive nature of the Supper is impressive. When it was instituted, Jesus invited the twelve including Judas; not one was left out. The family aspect of the Lord's Supper is revealing. The idea of an unbroken bond that shall in time include all nations, tongues, tribes, is most inspiring. At the Lord's Table, divisions, schisms, cliques, and coteries, seem mean and contemptible. Sectarianism and denominational pride shrink and shrivel. In their place comes the picture of the shepherd who, having a hundred sheep and one of them lost, found no rest of body or peace of mind until the lost sheep was found, lifted upon his shoulder, and brought back with rejoicing to the fold. . . .

The equality of all believers before God at the Lord's Table signifies the equality of all believers everywhere, a doctrine we have preached but fail to practice. The Lord's Supper is not a service; it is the inspirer of service. It is not a rite; it may be an aid to right living. The Lord's Supper is not a magical experience, though it is not without mystery. It is the soul seeking God and perceiving him in symbols of life and ministry, faith, hope, and love. To receive the symbols of his body and his blood and not perceive their relation to human society, the hopes and dreams, the fears and tears of the multitude, is to company with the betrayer who left the Lord's Table that night of nights and went out to bargain for his delivery into the hands of his enemies.

Edgar DeWitt Jones

426   *THE BROKEN BODY AND THE UNITED CHURCH*

Our sectarianism has . . . reduced the Lord's Supper to a sentimental act of individual memory, instead of the sacramental act of communion of the whole Body of Christ in which each member participates. The *broken* body, symbolized by the breaking of bread, is—strange paradox—the *united* body of the church! The broken bread spells the unbroken body. It can be received only by the unbroken body. And a church in schism can receive it in truth only as it deliberately and by conscious intention confesses the incompleteness of its offering so long as it is in schism, and enlarges its communion beyond the boundaries of its own sect, so as to embrace, potentially, all those who belong to the Lord Jesus Christ. The Lord's Supper belongs to the church's catholicity, it is a function of catholicity, and it cannot be fully complete until its every celebration is an act of a church that is holy and catholic.

Charles Clayton Morrison

427   *THE FELLOWSHIP OF COMMUNION*

God is faithful, by whom ye were called unto the fellowship of his Son Jesus Christ our Lord. 1 co. 1:9

In the observance of holy communion there is a definite experience and expression of fellowship. The church acknowledges the sacramental significance of this service. In a very special manner, designed by Christ himself, this service is a unique means of grace to quicken, nourish and strengthen the spiritual life of the participant. The manner and measure of the meditation of this grace is, however, differently interpreted. There are those who believe this is accomplished through a physical sharing, others through a veiled physical presence, others through a spiritual sharing. But all accept this service as a unique impartation of redemptive grace and power. Whatever the interpretation, the Lord's Supper is accepted by the Christian church as a service of fellowship. It is a witness to the truth that fellowship is real.

John S. Stamm

428   *THE COMMON TABLE*

When you partake of the Lord's Supper have you thought that the bread had a direct connection with the loaf that Jesus blessed and broke? As the whole human family is interrelated and can be traced back to one common source, so the vegetable kingdom is likewise related. The grains of wheat sown today have come from similar grains in Christ's time. So we all sit at a common table. When he said, "This is my body," he was partaking of that which gave him life. When the minister today says, "Take, eat," he is passing to us that which will give us life. We are all members of this one body. That makes us brothers.

J. P. Hauser

429   *BREAD OF THE UPPER ROOM*

And as they were eating, Jesus took bread, and blessed it, and brake it. MAT. 26:26

In so simple a way the greatest of the Christian sacraments was instituted. How the table became an altar or the bread the "real presence" belongs to the theologian: the bread blest and broken belongs to life. For whatever love and sacrifice have consecrated is thereafter a sacrament: the outer and evident sign of an inner and spiritual grace.

Surely if bread is to become a sacrament, the labor that baked it, the mill which ground the flour, the field which grew the grain, the toil that sowed it, and the rain and sunshine which quickened it should all be sacred.

There is in this sacramental conception of all material things and all labor a power, if we will permit it, to make our fields altars, all toil holy, and deliver us from the blindness which finds no sanctity anywhere. Beneath Jesus' touch all right ways of life are transformed, our very tools transfigured. Bread lovingly baked and served makes every table an altar.

Gaius Glenn Atkins

430   ON THE MEANING OF THE LORD'S SUPPER

It is an ironical fact that the sacrament which epitomizes the unity of Christendom is at the same time one of the most serious obstacles to unity. Often the theological arguments we use against each other seem quite secondary. For behind the arguments stand various forms of pride and pettiness. We may have to expect this sort of thing in ordinary human affairs; but we make a mockery of ourselves and of our religion when we bring such traits to the communion table. Indeed, it calls for a very solemn ecclesiastic, who has lost his sense of the ludicrous, to issue an invitation to this table of our Lord's words and then to withhold the invitation from multitudes of his fellow Christians. And all of us will continue to be a bit ludicrous, at least in God's sight, until the barriers which divide us have been broken down.

Nevertheless, rising above these barriers, everyone in the world who believes in Christ can have fellowship with him and participate in the body of the church through this common service. This is a fact which even our bumbling ecclesiasticism cannot undermine. And it is upon this fact that our minds and hearts should dwell. We must have doctrine, we must have church organizations, we must have private devotions, we must have Christian social action. But in the sacrament of the Lord's Supper the meaning of our faith is drawn together and expressed as in no other way. And it is possible to characterize this meaning without becoming embroiled in controversy or in partisan interpretation. All we need do is to meditate upon the amazing contrast between what we bring to the table and what we receive from it.

David E. Roberts

431   THE SACRAMENT OF MAN

The Lord's Supper should be the rallying place for all the good activity and worthy hopes of men. It is in the power of this great Christian sacrament, this great human sacrament, to become that rallying place. It would be the evidence of the world's transformation if to this great "sacrament of man" all classes of

people—the mystic, the seeker after truth, the student, the schoolboy, the legis-
lator, the inventor, men, women and children—were to come, meeting in a
great host at the table of the Lord, owning themselves his children, claiming
for themselves his strength, and thence go forth to their work. The communion
service would lift up its voice and sing itself in triumph, the great anthem of
dedicated human life.

Phillips Brooks

432   *THE APPREHENDED PRESENCE*

Here is a symbolic act that brings home, as no mere words can do, the great
affirmations of the Christian faith. Here is a celebration that proclaims the possibility of forgiveness for sin, healing for sorrow, strength for the day, and peace
within even amidst the most adverse conditions. Here for those who "draw near
with faith" is the apprehension of a divine presence and power whereby the
heart is cleansed, renewed, and comforted. Here is opportunity for self-com-
mitment: "We offer and present unto thee, O Lord, our selves, our souls and
bodies, to be a reasonable, holy, and living sacrifice unto thee."

Broken bread and poured-out wine are most meaningful symbols. They
recall and make real the life and love and death of Christ and all that his coming has meant to the world. This symbolism has been overlaid with dogma. It is
open to doubt that eucharistic dogma has enhanced the spiritual value of the
Lord's Supper. For many Christians, most probably an increasing number, the
doctrine of transubstantiation is impossible. Not only can they not believe that
the elements of bread and wine in the Mass become the actual body and blood
of Christ, but they protest the underlying assumption that salvation can come
by quasi-magical and mechanical means.

What is essential to the spiritual value of this sacrament is apprehension of
the presence of Christ, personal response to the will of God revealed in him,
and hearty participation in the fellowship which he brought into being. Apprehension of the presence of Christ is not dependent upon the belief that he is
physically present in the elements of bread and wine. These do not serve to
make real a divine love and power that is always and everywhere accessible
but, alas, not always apprehended.

Spiritual communion with Christ involves that we will share his love to God
and men. "If a man goes out from his communion to love and serve men better
he has received the Real Presence. If he feels every thrill and tremor of devotion,
but goes out as selfish as before, he has not received it. It was offered, but he
did not receive it."

The early Christians, if we may judge from 1 Co. 11:17–34, combined the eucharist with a meal taken in common. This association was the most natural thing in the world, since the historic Last Supper was itself a meal taken in common. And indeed one of the most notable results of Christ's coming was a mutual interest and devotion among his followers that led a pagan world to exclaim: "Behold how these Christians love one another!" It belongs to the initial idea of Holy Communion that Christians by means of the sacred elements should come into fellowship with Christ *and with one another*. What an irony of Christian history it then is that this sacrament, instead of being a means of fellowship, should all too often—and notably at ecumenical conferences—be the occasion for separation of Christians one from another because of differences of belief as to eucharistic doctrine.

Ernest Fremont Tittle

C. CHRISTIAN UNITY SUNDAY

Christian Unity Sunday, sometimes scheduled on the Sunday following Pentecost, the birthday of the Christian church, interprets the great common concerns and beliefs of all Protestants and strives for a growth in mutual tolerance and understanding. Plans for the day may include union services, or pulpit exchange on an inter-church basis, or the meetings of young people with groups from other churches. The day suggests possibilities for the enlistment of community support for the churches on a co-operative basis.

Calls to Worship

433 Fulfil ye my joy, that ye be likeminded, having the same love, being of one accord, of one mind. . . . That at the name of Jesus every knee should bow, of things in heaven, and things in earth, and things under the earth.

Ph. 2:2, 10

434 When they prayed, the place was shaken where they were assembled together; and they were all filled with the Holy Ghost, and they spake the word of God with boldness. And the multitude of them that believed were of one heart and of one soul.

Ac. 4:31-32

435 If two of you shall agree on earth as touching any thing that they shall ask, it shall be done for them of my Father which is in heaven. For where two or three are gathered together in my name, there am I in the midst of them.

Mat. 18:19-20

Invocations

436 O Lord God Almighty, look down upon thy church and people throughout the whole world; enable them everywhere to witness by their lives to the worthiness of thy name, and the greatness of thy power. Knit them together in love, peace, and in wise and mutual sympathy. Send upon all the enlightening gift of thy most Holy Spirit, that as there is one body and one spirit, they may attain the one hope of their calling; through Jesus Christ our Lord. Amen.

Boyd Carpenter

437   In thy house, O Lord, let us dwell in peace and concord: give us all one heart, one mind, one true interpretation upon thy Word; that all who believe in thee may together extol thy name: O Lord God, most glorious and excellent over all. Amen.

Godly Prayers (1552)

438   O God our Father, good beyond all that is good, fair beyond all that is fair, in whom is calmness and peace: do thou make up the dissensions which divide us from each other, and bring us back into an unity of love, which may bear some likeness to thy divine nature. Grant that we may be spiritually one, as well in ourselves as in each other, through that peace of thine which maketh all things peaceful, and through the grace, mercy and tenderness of thine only Son. Amen.

Jacobite Liturgy of St. Dionysius

Litany

(Boldface type indicates responses.)

439   We give thanks to Almighty God, Father, Son and Holy Spirit, that we are one in our Lord Jesus Christ; not by the agreement of our minds or the consent of our wills, but by that which he, in his infinite grace, has done for us in his incarnation, death and resurrection, and by the gift of the Holy Spirit:
We thank thee, O God.
We give thanks for the knowledge that though we are divided in outward form we all are the objects of the love and grace of God:
We thank thee, O God.
We give thanks for the joy that we have found in sharing the treasures of worship and devotion that we even now hold in common:
We thank thee, O God.
We acknowledge that our understanding of the truth as it is in Jesus has been limited by our pride, wilfulness and narrowness of mind, and that our witness to the world is weakened by our divisions:
Lord, have mercy upon us.
We pray that all men everywhere, in a world distracted and divided, may turn to Christ, who makes us one in spite of our divisions; that he may bind in one those whom many worldly claims set at variance; and that the world may at last find peace and unity in him; to whom be glory for ever.
Lord, hear our prayer.

World Council of Churches

Prayers

440 Eternal Father of mankind, guide thou our spirits as we pray for thy church in these tragic days of its helplessness to stay the fires and flames of passion that have submerged our world.

Deliver us from the self-confidence, intellectual pride, and sense of spiritual satisfaction, from the selfishness of our temperaments and desires, which have wrought division among us.

May we seek the childlike simplicity of thought which our Master has revealed in us and taught us as the way into the Kingdom of heaven on earth.

Help us to magnify the things that unite us, as we repent of our common consciousness of our sin and failure, with its sense of a need which all our churches share.

May we be diligent in judging ourselves rather than in passing judgment on our fellow men. Deliver us from all censoriousness of spirit, and vainglory.

Help us, with sympathy and humility, to enter into the lives and thoughts of those who differ from us, in their symbols and in their ways of expressing truth through their minds and human reason, that we may understand the motives of their hearts and the spiritual realities they seek to put into failing human speech.

May our churches not become so involved in the machinery and administration of their tasks, as to lose sight of the intangible realities of spiritual life. Reveal to them the standards of value that will lift them to heights above our humanistic waywardness.

Teach us to search for the calm, the strength and the fearlessness which we have lost, not in the vain efforts of our minds to fathom the unsearchable depths of thy truth, but in our humble dependence and perfect trust in thee.

Unite our hearts in a sense of brotherhood through our common acknowledgment of thy divine Fatherhood and our consciousness of the sonship which we share with thy Son, our Lord and Master.

Guide by thy Holy Spirit, we pray thee, all our efforts to restore our lost unity, in these hours of crisis throughout the world, as we realize that the church itself has shared in the divisiveness that has brought disaster to mankind.

Help thy church in our nation, and throughout the world, to become the true body of our divine Redeemer. To this end impart the mind to us as it was in Christ Jesus, that we may be one with thyself, one with him, and one in the fellowship of one another, that in the midst of a humanity that has lost its way, the church shall be the bearer of an abiding light to all mankind; in our Lord's name. Amen. *Charles S. Macfarland*

441   Eternal Father, who leavest not thy children homeless, but providest, here and hereafter, their nurture and protection: we thank thee for thy holy church, reaching unto us across the ages, circling earth, and encompassing heaven. We praise thee for communion therein, with those we love, both who are with us now, and who have gone before; and with saints, apostles, prophets, martyrs, of every time and place; and with the great Head of the church, even Christ our Lord, who blesseth us with grace upon grace; and with the Holy Spirit, who daily laboreth within us, guiding, purifying, perfecting, and binding us together into one; and with thyself, who art over all, our Creator and our God. Let not those, who wait for thee, through us be put to shame. Thy name be praised in every mouth, both now and evermore. Amen.

John Underwood Stephens

442   O God, who hast made of one blood all the nations of mankind, so that all are children and members one of another: how is it that we are so slow to trace the family likeness, so reluctant to claim our common kinship? We pray thee, O our God, to make the peoples one.

We pray for the church of Christ so broken, scattered and dismembered, that none would think we followed all one Lord and held a common faith. Purge away the vanity, intolerance, and unforgiving spirit which keep us far apart. May the seamless robe not be utterly rent, nor the body any longer broken.

We pray that since man's need is one, we all may find the one way to thee, the one God. Forbid that in our highest things we should find fellowship impossible. May the spirit of Christ break down all barriers and answer the desire of all nations.

We pray for a union so deep and universal that it shall gather all within one fold: those who pray and those who cannot; those whose faith is firm, and those whose doubt is slow to clear. May we never be content with aught that excludes another from the fullness of thy grace, a single soul from the welcome of thy heart. Amen.

William E. Orchard

Poems

443   *GATHER US IN*

Gather us in: thou Love that fillest all;
    Gather our rival faiths within thy fold;
Rend each man's temple veil, and bid it fall,
    That we may know that thou hast been of old.

Gather us in: we worship only thee;
  In varied names we stretch a common hand;
In diverse forms a common soul we see;
  In many ships we seek one spirit-land.

Some seek a Father in the heavens above;
  Some ask a human image to adore;
Some crave a spirit vast as life and love;
  Within thy mansions we have all and more.

George Matheson

444   *A CREED*

  There is a destiny that makes us brothers:
    None goes his way alone:
  All that we send into the lives of others
    Comes back into our own.

  I care not what his temples or his creeds,
    One thing holds firm and fast—
  That into his fateful heap of days and deeds
    The soul of man is cast.

Edwin Markham

445   *THE CHURCHES*

  Two, in the darkness, sought the Cross,
  But in their blindness found it not;
  This way and that, in dole and loss,
  They sought the Cross, but found it not.

  "This way!"—the one insistent cried;
  "Nay, this!"—the other quick replied;
  And each the other's hope denied.

  "I tell you, my way is the right!"
  "Nay then, you stumbler in the night,
  My way alone leads to the light!"

"*Perverse!—Go then your own wrong road!*"
"*I go—for my way leads to God.*"
And each his own way brusquely strode.

And up above, upon the Tree,
Christ's wounds broke in fresh agony.

John Oxenham

446   *THE GOAL*

All roads that lead to God are good;
   What matters it, your faith or mine;
   Both center at the goal divine
Of love's eternal brotherhood.

A thousand creeds have come and gone;
   But what is that to you or me?
   Creeds are but branches of a tree,
The root of love lives on and on.

Though branch by branch proves withered wood,
   The root is warm with precious wine;
   Then keep your faith, and leave me mine;
All roads that lead to God are good.

Ella Wheeler Wilcox

447   *FORGIVE*

Forgive, O Lord, our severing ways;
The rival altars that we raise,
The wrangling tongues that mar thy praise.

Thy grace impart; in time to be
Shall one great temple rise to thee—
One church for all humanity.

White flowers of love its walls shall climb,
Soft bells of peace shall ring its chime,
Its days shall all be holy time.

A sweeter song shall then be heard,
Confessing, in a world's accord,
The inward Christ, the living Word.

That song shall swell from shore to shore,
One hope, one faith, one love restore
The seamless robe that Jesus wore.

Based on lines by
John Greenleaf Whittier

448   *BOUNDARIES*

Man cannot look round the roadway's curve
    Or beyond a mountain see,
And yet he dares to fashion creeds
    And bound eternity.

Catherine Cate Coblentz

449   *CREEDS*

How pitiful are little folk—
They seem so very small;
They look at stars, and think they are
Denominational.

Willard Wattles

450   *From THE VICAR*

And when religious sects ran mad,
    He held, in spite of all his learning,
That if a man's belief is bad,
    It will not be improved by burning.

Winthrop Mackworth Praed

451   *RELIGIOUS UNITY*

Yes, we do differ when we most agree,
For words are not the same to you and me,
And it may be our several spiritual needs
Are best supplied by seeming different creeds.

>   And, differing, we agree in one
>   Inseparable communion,
>   If the true life be in our hearts; the faith
>   Which not to want is death;
>   To want is penance; to desire
>   Is purgatorial fire;
>   To hope is paradise; and to believe
>   Is all of heaven that earth can e'er receive.

Hartley Coleridge

Topics, Texts and Themes

452   *THAT THEY MAY BE ONE*

And now I am no more in the world, but these are in the world, and I
come to thee. Holy Father, keep through thine own name those whom thou
hast given me, that they may be one, as we are. JN. 17:11

On this particular occasion Jesus is not praying, as many have imagined, that
all peoples on earth may live as one single family. Jesus has just said, "I pray for
them [my followers] not for the world, but for those whom thou hast given
me do I pray." Just as a father may love the members of his family and pray
for them without any the less loving his native land and praying for it, so
Jesus at this time prays for those who are his followers.

Secondly, Jesus is not praying that all his followers may be one numerically,
in one institution or in one church, as they have argued. The oneness for which
he prays has a much deeper significance than either of these interpretations
suggests.

Jesus' meaning is in the following four words "as we are one." Jesus prays that
all men whose lives are committed to his way of life, may be one, as he and
God, the Father, are one. The essence of this oneness is love. This is the life
of supreme harmony amid enriching differences, as the glorious music of a
Bach chorale unites many musicians with different instruments into one meaningful theme. The Christian's oneness with God and with fellow Christians is
a unity of life which even physical death cannot destroy.

Charles W. Kegley

453   *UNITY IN CHRIST*

The church may be united, though it may appear to be superficially divided.
In my judgment, and I make this the basis of my teaching, the church of
Christ is united. When people are talking about the reunion of Christendom, I

do not understand their foreign language. Christendom was never divided, except in a nominal, formal way, in a way quite mechanical. It has never been divided so long as it has held to the Christ. It is not the creed, but the Christ that unites men in one massive and indestructible church. We must allow each other his way of looking at things. Every man must read the Bible according to his own capacity, his own intelligence, and his own opportunity. The point at which we are united is not in our commentaries, but in our inquiry and searching into the mystery of the divine Word. If we are all really in quest of the revelation, we shall soon see that merely literary and scholastic questions adjust and determine themselves. All the denominations are one, yet no two of them are alike, and they are utterly diverse one from another as to framework and purpose and methods of doing things. Find the unity in the Christ, not in the formula or the ritual. . . . We are appointed to different functions, we are gifted in different degrees and measures; but there is one Lord, and he must judge and settle all.

Joseph Parker

454   *EDINBURGH AFFIRMATION OF UNITY*

We are one in faith in our Lord Jesus Christ, the incarnate Word of God. We are one in allegiance to him as Head of the church, and as King of kings and Lord of lords. We are one in acknowledging that this allegiance takes precedence of any other allegiance that may make claims upon us.

This unity does not consist in the agreement of our minds or the consent of our wills. It is founded in Jesus Christ himself, who lived, died and rose again to bring us to the Father, and who through the Holy Spirit dwells in his church. We are one because we are all the objects of the love and grace of God, called by him to witness in all the world to his glorious Gospel.

We humbly acknowledge that our divisions are contrary to the will of Christ, and we pray God in his mercy to shorten the days of our separation and to guide us by his Spirit into fullness of unity.

We desire also to declare to all men everywhere our assurance that Christ is the one hope of unity for the world in face of the distractions and dissensions of this present time. We know that our witness is weakened by our divisions. Yet we are one in Christ and in the fellowship of his Spirit. We pray that everywhere, in a world divided and perplexed, men may turn to Jesus Christ our Lord, who makes us one in spite of our divisions; that he may bind in one those who by many worldly claims are set at variance; and that the world may at last find peace and unity in him; to whom be glory for ever.

Second World Conference on
Faith and Order (1937)

455   *GOD'S DESIGN*

All Christians believe in the church. Though they may believe many different things about it, they are agreed that the church is indispensable. Christianity is a social religion. . . . The church is the principal agency of that fellowship. It furnishes the place, the conditions, and the means of worship, Christian nurture, the preaching of the Gospel and administration of the sacraments, and the continuous ministration of God's grace to men. The church in which all these things are possible, and actual, is something not of man's invention but of God's design.

Winfred E. Garrison

456   *UNITY IN DIVERSITY*

Now there are diversities of gifts, but the same Spirit. 1 CO. 12:4

Daniel Webster said: "Liberty and union are one and inseparable." . . . The great orator declared a universal truth. Diversity in unity is the law of freedom and of all reasonable life. The secret of progress lies in finding the unity which underlies diversity.

So it is in science. The primitive mind, like that of the child, stresses differences. The history of science is a record of the discovery of unifying principles. Before Newton no one imagined that an apple which fell and moon which didn't were equally under the control of gravity.

Again, in the relations of society, progress depends upon finding and placing in operation the underlying identity of interests. Otherwise the schisms between labor and management, between racial groups, between the poor and those who live sumptuously, drive fatal wedges which split the Commonwealth.

The principle holds also in the realm of religion. It requires four gospels to give the full portrait of the Master. Paul and Peter, James and John, contrasting characters, give us in their writings differing facets of truth. These are not in opposition; they complement each other. One writer is the apostle of faith, another of hope, another of works, and another of love.

While honest seekers for truth may be as distinct as the waves, they are one as the sea; different as the colors of the rainbow, they are as truly one as the pure white light into which these colors fuse. The mountain of truth has many trails but all climbers meet at the top.

Daniel Russell

457   *CHRISTIAN CONTROVERSY*

Speaking the truth in love. EP. 4:15

Amid all the diversity of operations in the church there is one body, and one Spirit, one Lord, one faith, one baptism, one God and Father of all, who is above all and through all and in all. The different gifts possessed by different members of the church are all designed for the one sole end, for the perfecting of the saints, for the edifying of the body of Christ. The whole church is meant to be carried forward and upward in the unity of the faith to a higher level of Christian living and Christian character. Christ is the beginning, and Christ is the end. He is the source of the unity, and he is the fulfilment for which it is designed. We are expected to grow up out of all the immaturity and fickleness of childhood to full-grown men, grow up into him in all things who is the head, even Christ.   *Hugh Black*

458   *THE INEXHAUSTIBLE CHRIST*

Some indeed preach Christ even of envy and strife; and some also of good will. . . . What then? notwithstanding, every way, whether in pretence, or in truth, Christ is preached. PH. 1:15, 18

The Kingdom of God on earth is not the divided force that it so often seems to be. We are a thousandfold nearer to those with whom we differ than we realize. Like air and water and fire, the Christ spirit in the lives of men differs only in superficialities. Names and creeds are only colors and flavors. Would God that we were broad enough to ask of men about us, only this: Does the air you breathe in your thought of Christ, whatever its odor, give life? Does it urge you constantly to new effort of self-sacrificing love? Does the water that you drink in the name of Christ, however it be tinged, quench the thirst of your immortal soul? Down in your heart, whether it smolder or blaze, is there a fire of loyalty and devotion to him that you call Master? Then our eyes would be opened and we should see all around us the marching brotherhood of a triumphant army and we would sing from the depths of our hearts, "We are not divided, all one body, we."

                                                       Carl Hopkins Elmore

459   *TOWARD REUNION*

One of the most frequent complaints against the church refers to the unhappy divisions of Christendom; but to what do we owe the movement for unity but to the church itself? Division came because the church had become secularized and corrupted and had to be reformed. In the effort to establish truth, men became enamored of meticulous doctrinal expositions of the faith, and the process of fission went madly on. But it is the church, not its critics, which is leading the return to unity and fellowship, and leading it with right motive, not as an economic consolidation, but as a unity of evangelical purpose, with true understanding of the mind of Christ. Nothing in our present age is so indicative of the recuperative power of the church as the strength of this movement toward reunion.

Charles Fiske

460   *A CALL FOR INTERPRETERS*

Love is . . . always eager to believe the best. 1 co. 13:6–7 (Moffatt)

One of the most significant and useful services which a Christian can render for Christ today is to stand as an interpreter between divergent groups who do not understand each other; to help one group appreciate the other group more sincerely; to assist each group to understand something of the difficulties and handicaps under which the other group works; and slowly, but surely, to bring them together in one great fellowship in Christ.

Edward Hughes Pruden

461   *WESLEY'S COVENANT*

John Wesley once felt the need of closer sympathy among the ministers, and, together with twelve others, he signed the following covenant:

It is agreed by us whose names are underwritten:

First, that we will not listen or willingly inquire after any ill concerning each other;

Secondly, that if we do hear any ill of each other, we will not be forward to believe it;

Thirdly, that as soon as possible we will communicate what we hear by speaking or writing to the person concerned;

Fourthly, that until we have done this, we will not write or speak a syllable of it to any other person whatsoever;

Fifthly, that neither will we mention it, after we have done this, to any other person;

Sixthly, that we will not make any exception to any of these rules, unless we think ourselves absolutely obliged to do so.

462   *EMPHASES*

Get religion like the Methodists
Be loyal to it like the Baptists
Pay for it like the Presbyterians
Witness for it like the Salvation Army
Keep it democratic like the Congregationalists
Make it historic like the Lutherans
Intellectualize it like the Unitarians
Worship in it like the Episcopalians
Plead for it like the Disciples
Organize it like the Roman Catholics
And enjoy it like the Negroes.

Edgar DeWitt Jones

D. WORLD ORDER DAY

World Order Day and such occasions as World Peace Day, Human Rights Day, World Community Day, and United Nations Week emphasize the role of the church and Christian citizens in applying Christian principles to the problems of war and peace. The day recognizes the church's insistence that Christ must be a participant in international relations and highlights the social responsibilities and obligations which his followers must assume. This day is frequently observed on the third Sunday in October and climaxes United Nations Week.

Calls to Worship

(Boldface type indicates response.)

463   Come, behold the works of the Lord. . . . He maketh wars to cease unto the end of the earth; he breaketh the bow, and cutteth the spear in sunder; he burneth the chariots in the fire. Be still, and know that I am God: I will be exalted among the heathen, I will be exalted in the earth.
The Lord of hosts is with us; the God of Jacob is our refuge.

Ps. 46:8, 9-11

464   God was in Christ, reconciling the world unto himself . . . and hath committed unto us the word of reconciliation. How beautiful upon the mountains are the feet of him that bringeth good tidings, that publisheth peace; that bringeth good tidings of good, that publisheth salvation.

2 Co. 5:19; Is. 52:7

465   [Thus saith the Lord] I will give peace in the land, and ye shall lie down, and none shall make you afraid. In everything by prayer and supplication with thanksgiving let your requests be made known unto God. And the peace of God, which passeth all understanding, shall keep your hearts and minds through Christ Jesus.

Le. 26:6; Ph. 4:6

Invocations

466   Almighty God, from whom all thoughts of truth and peace proceed: kindle, we pray thee, in the hearts of all men the true love of peace, and guide with thy pure and peaceable wisdom those who take counsel for the nations of the earth; that in tranquillity thy Kingdom may go forward, till the earth is filled with the knowledge of thy love; through Jesus Christ our Lord. Amen.

Francis Paget

467   God, our Father, give to the nations of the world a new heart of comradeship, the old man of ignorance being done away and the new man put on, renewed in knowledge to strengthen and serve the brethren; that every people may bring its tribute of excellence to the common treasury, without fear, and without the lust of domination; and all the world may go forward in the new and living way which Christ has consecrated for us, who liveth and reigneth with thee and the Spirit of Truth, one God, world without end. Amen.

Percy Dearmer

468   Almighty God, our heavenly Father, guide, we beseech thee, the nations of the world into the way of justice and truth, and establish among them that peace which is the fruit of righteousness; that they may become the Kingdom of our Lord and Saviour, Jesus Christ. Amen.

Edward L. Parsons

Litany

(Boldface type indicates responses.)

469   O Father of all men, we pray for the realization of brotherhood among the nations, a brotherhood rooted in thy Fatherhood. May each nation find its own freedom in giving itself to world comradeship, and in rendering service to the good of all:

Hear our prayer, O Lord.

Unite all peoples of the world in an order of peace. Destroy the influences which create bitterness and division. Purge diplomacy and commerce of all that is base and mean, and hasten the day when nation shall not lift up sword against nation, nor learn war any more:

Hear our prayer, O Lord.

O thou whose service is perfect freedom, loosen, we beseech thee, the fetters of the hindered races of the earth; deliver them from galling bonds and heal their wounds. May their rights and liberties be protected by the great nations of mankind; and grant that each tribe and people, freed by justice to do justly, and by mercy to be merciful, may find its soul in the unity of love, and do its part in thy world family:

Hear our prayer, O Lord.

Save the world from unholy ambition, from the lust of power, and from armed enmity among the nations; and prosper those who seek to check the beginnings of discord and to spread the message of goodwill:

Hear our prayer, O Lord.

Intercession Services

Prayers

470   O God of wisdom, what is man that thou art mindful of him? We have boasted of our learning when all of our knowledge is as a grain of sand upon an endless shore.

We inherit the dreams of past ages; the gates of heaven are open to our wings, and through the depths of the sea our message is carried across the floor of the ocean. Treasures of forest and of mountain are our possession, while the forces of the lightning and the cataract do our bidding.

We are rich beyond the dreams of ancient kings; we are wise in our own conceit, but we have failed to live by the light of thy word. We have not cared enough for our brothers to use our knowledge and power for peace and equal justice to all men. We prepare machines for the slaying of our fellows, and we fill our hearts with fears.

Stir up in us, O Lord, a protest against such betrayal of our heritage; quicken within us a deeper sense of our responsibility to others. Forgive us that we made the hope of a dying world the sport of our party politics and, secure in our own false prosperity, turned our ways toward self-seeking.

Remind us of our citizenship in the Eternal City, and make us responsive to a higher wisdom than that of earth. With our increasing knowledge of science, our spirits need far more to be freed from bondage to material gain, lest we destroy others and ourselves.

Renew in us our sense of immortality and our ultimate responsibility to thee, in whose name our fathers endured much that we might be free to serve. Amen.

S. Ralph Harlow

471   O God, who hast made of one blood all nations of men for to dwell on the face of the earth; God of love, wonderful Counsellor, mighty God, everlasting Father, Prince of Peace, upon thy shoulder shall be the government, world without end.

Forgive us that in our day the nations have gone after strange gods, worshiping the state and offering human sacrifice to war. Rebuke, O God, the price of race and clan, the vainglory of men, and the lust for empire which lead to war. Make the nations to know themselves to be but men. Teach us that the wages of sin is death. May we repent and turn again. Though our sins be as scarlet, forgive us, O God, and cleanse our ways from war. For against thee, and thee only, have we sinned, and done this even in thy sight.

O God of love, unite in opposition to war all those who worship thee throughout the world. Grant that each may love his native land, and obey her laws up to the point where obedience to man would be disobedience to God. Give us ever the higher courage to take our stand with thee. If men persecute us and say all manner of evil against us, let us rejoice in the divine comradeship of the Cross, as we follow in nearer company with Christ in the redemption of the world.

Send now thy Holy Spirit upon us. Grant us wisdom in our time to build a warless world. Help us to search out and to remove the causes of war. Teach us so to control our economic life that profit in arms, pressure for markets and materials, and selfish interests of finance shall no longer destroy the peace of the world.

Help us to build the instruments of peace in court and covenant and league, in the parliament of man and the federation of the world. Give us grace to use these means not alone for prevention of war, but in brotherly provision for the economic needs of all nations in a new brotherhood of man.

Our Father, remove now from our hearts the very seeds of war, all enmity and selfishness and strife. Give us humility, and goodwill toward every man. May thy Kingdom come within us, that we may bear more moving witness to thy ways of love and peace. In the name of Jesus Christ our Lord. Amen.

James Myers

472   *PRAYER FOR THE UNITED NATIONS*

God of the free, we pledge our hearts and lives today to the cause of all free mankind. . . .

Grant us honor for our dead who died in the faith, honor for our living who work and strive for the faith, redemption and security for all captive lands and peoples. Grant us patience with the deluded and pity for the betrayed. And grant us the skill and valor that shall cleanse the world of oppression and the old base doctrine that the strong must eat the weak because they are strong.

Yet most of all grant us brotherhood, not only for this day but for all our years—a brotherhood not of words but of acts and deeds. We are all of us children of earth—grant us that simple knowledge. If our brothers are oppressed, then we are oppressed. If they hunger, we hunger. If their freedom is taken away, our freedom is not secure.

Grant us a common faith that man shall know bread and peace—that he shall know justice and righteousness, freedom and security, an equal opportunity and an equal chance to do his best, not only in our own lands, but throughout the world. And in that faith let us march toward the clean world our hands can make. Amen.

Stephen Vincent Benét

Poems

473   *HE SHALL SPEAK PEACE*

Hatred and greed and pride shall die,
Cannon and swords shall prostrate lie;
Warring shall end, the world shall cry—
    For he shall speak peace.

Rivers shall nevermore run red,
Terror shall hide his bloody head,
Life shall no more for lust be shed—
    For he shall speak peace.

They shall not strive in earth again,
Honor will come to dwell with men;
Children shall bide in safety then—
    For he shall speak peace.

Desolate plains, now bleak and cold,
Burst forth again in green and gold;
Birds of the trenches sing, as of old—
    For he shall speak peace.

Thomas Curtis Clark

474   *From THE CHRISTIAN SOLDIER*

Peace does not mean the end of all our striving,
Joy does not mean the drying of our tears,

Peace is the power that comes to souls arriving,
Up to the light where God himself appears.

G. A. Studdert-Kennedy

475   THE MEN OF EARTH SAID

The men of the earth said: "We must war,
    As men of the earth have warred;
'Tis ours to wield on the battlefield
    The unrelenting sword."
But they who had seen the valiant die,
The fathers of men, they answered, "Why?"

The men of the earth said: "We must arm,
    For so we would reveal
The nobler part of the human heart,
    The love of the nation's weal."
But they who had sung their lullaby,
The mothers of men, they answered, "Why?"

The men of the earth said: "We must fall,
    And falling build the road
O'er which the race with quickening pace
    Can find its way to God."
But down from a Cross uplifted high,
The Savior of men, he answered, "Why?"

Robert Freeman

476   From *MY COUNTRY*

My country is the world; I count
    No son of man my foe,
Whether the warm life-currents mount
    And mantle brows like snow
Or red or yellow, brown or black,
The face that into mine looks back.

My party is all human kind,
    My platform brotherhood;
I count all men of honest mind

Who work for human good,
And for the hope that gleams afar,
My comrades in this holy war.

My heroes are the great and good
    Of every age and clime,
Too often mocked, misunderstood,
    And murdered in their time,
But spite of ignorance and hate
Known and exalted soon or late.

My country is the world; I scorn
    No lesser love than mine,
But calmly wait that happy morn
    When all shall own this sign,
And love of country as of clan
Shall yield to worldwide love of man.

Robert Whitaker

477   *From THE FATHERLAND*

Where is the true man's fatherland?
    Is it where he by chance is born?
    Doth not the yearning spirit scorn
In such scant borders to be spanned?
Oh, yes! his fatherland must be
As the blue heavens, wide and free!

Is it alone where freedom is?
    Where God is God and man is man?
    Doth he not claim a broader span
For the soul's love of home than this?
Oh, yes! his fatherland must be
As the blue heavens, wide and free!

Where'er a human heart doth wear
    Joy's myrtle-wreath or sorrow's gyves,
    Where'er a human spirit strives
After a life more true and fair,

There is the true man's birthplace grand,
His is a world-wide fatherland!

James Russell Lowell

478   *THE MARCH OF TIME*

The Sphinx, the Iliad, Christ upon the Tree—
The past is in these three.
World peace, world brotherhood, Love's hero themes—
Of these the future dreams.

Edwin Markham

479   *From WAR AND HELL*

The old, old dream of empire—
The dream of Alexander and Caesar, of Tamerlane and Genghis Khan—
The dream of subject peoples carrying out our sovereign will through fear—
The dream of a universe forced to converge upon us—
The dream of pride and loftiness justified by strength of arms—
The dream of our arbitrary "Yea" overcoming all "Nays" whatsoever—
The dream of a cold, stern, hated machine of empire!

But there is a more enticing dream:
The dream of wise freedom made contagious—
The dream of gratitude rising from broken fetters—
The dream of coercion laid prostrate once for all—
The dream of nations in love with each other without a thought of a common
hatred or danger—
The dream of tyrants stripped of their tyrannies and oppressors despoiled of
their prey—
The dream of a warm, throbbing, one-hearted empire of brothers!

Ernest Crosby

480   *From LOCKSLEY HALL*

Men, my brothers, men the workers, ever reaping something new;
That which they have done but earnest of the things they shall do.

For I dipt into the future, far as human eye could see,
Saw the Vision of the world, and all the wonder that would be;

Saw the heavens fill with commerce, argosies of magic sails,
Pilots of the purple twilight, dropping down with costly bales;

Heard the heavens fill with shouting, and there rain'd a ghastly dew
From the nations' airy navies grappling in the central blue;

Far along the world-wide whisper of the south-wind rushing warm,
With the standards of the peoples plunging thro' the thunder-storm;

Till the war-drum throbb'd no longer, and the battle-flags were furl'd
In the Parliament of man, the Federation of the world.

There the common sense of most shall hold a fretful realm in awe,
And the kindly earth shall slumber, lapt in universal law.

Alfred Tennyson

Topics, Texts and Themes

481   *THE WAY OF PEACE*

Thou . . . shalt be called the prophet of the Most High . . . to guide our
feet into the way of peace. LU. 1:76-79 (ARV)

While men long for peace, they often hesitate, even refuse, to walk in the
way of peace. Peace is more than an order established through military power,
power politics, social and economic systems, or even the organization of an
agency for cooperative fellowship. Peace is a moral and spiritual relationship.
Unless there is an order and motive of righteousness in all human relationships,
there will be no peace. The prophet Isaiah pointed this out when he said, "The
work of righteousness shall be peace; and the effect of righteousness, quietness
and confidence for ever." Peace is more than the absence of conflict and war. It
is more than a political structure. Peace is an order of relationship in terms of
living. It is a way of life. Peace will never be established through external controls. Such controls are needed but in themselves will never secure peace. If
there is to be peace, there must be a mind for peace and the willingness to walk
in the way of peace.

John S. Stamm

482   *WORLD UNITY BASED ON LOVE*

Our idea of God's power depends upon our ideas of God's purpose, and we
cannot have a clear conception of his power until we perceive with heart and

mind that the purpose of God is Brotherhood, the creation of "Man," the making of a united family of human beings.

When we have really got that perception clear and clean in our hearts and minds, then we begin to see that for God's purpose, which is the creation of man, the human family or unity, there is, and can be, only one power, and that is Love. For that purpose force is not power; it is a weakness. A unity of human beings is an imperfect unity just so far as it is based upon force and fear. That is the lesson that the history of these last strange years should have blasted into our minds. How much we hoped from the unity of the classes and nations in time of war, and how bitterly our hopes have been disappointed! It was a weak and superficial unity, because it was not based upon Love.

G. A. Studdert-Kennedy

483   *WE HAVE THE SOLUTION*

He has . . . broken down the barrier that kept us apart . . . in order to . . . create out of the two partiess one new man by uniting them with himself. EP. 2:15 (Goodspeed)

There may have been times in the past when it would have been excusable for a Christian to think of his faith in personal and provincial terms, but the kind of world in which we are living today requires of us a Christian faith that possesses definite world-wide implications and significance. The terrible events that are taking place all around us remind us that we are world citizens with inescapable interests and responsibilities. We must put into our expression of Christianity that universal note which was sounded by the angel in announcing our Savior's birth: "Behold, I bring you good tidings of great joy, which shall be to all people"; and the best translations of the song of the heavenly host leave us in no doubt that they sang of a peace that would come to all men of good will, irrespective of race or nationality. Those who became the first disciples of Christ believed that the life and influence of him who moved among them would one day bring glory to God in heaven and provide a means whereby peace should be realized among men on earth, and we share that belief today.

Edward Hughes Pruden

484   *THE MEANING OF PEACE*

Peace is an ever-present condition of living, rather than the abstract condition to be devoutly wished for in some distant utopia. Peace is normal, as health is normal. We have to have a philosophy in which we believe that peace is positive and not merely the absence of conflicts and wars—a negative ideal. Peace is rich, peace is satisfying, peace is growth and movement and action and life. Peace is as natural as harmony because it is the normal way of man; man rejects war as he intuitively rejects discord or dissonance in music. And the psychology of domestic peace, national peace, and world peace cannot be very different—it is merely the harmony of social relationships. For that harmony of social relationships there is a technique. Human philosophy should occupy itself exclusively with that technique of social harmony.

Lin Yutang

485   AMERICAN HISTORY IN THREE WORDS

World (1492–1776)—America like other countries had its origin in the family of nations from which it drew its life.

Self (1776–1890)—Then followed the period of self-development during which America considered itself largely independent of the rest of the world.

World (1890–   )—Arriving at maturity, America reintegrated with the family of nations, gradually taking world responsibilities.

I. D. Taubeneck

486   From *THE BOOK OF THE PEOPLE*

Your task is to form the universal family, to build the City of God, and by a continuous labor gradually to translate his work in humanity into fact.

When you love one another as brothers, and treat each other reciprocally as such; when each one, seeking his own good in the good of all, shall identify his own life with the life of all, his own interests with the interests of all, and shall be always ready to sacrifice himself for all the members of the human family— then most of the ills which weigh upon the human race will vanish, as thick mists gathered upon the horizon vanish at the rising of the sun.

Robert de Lamennais

487   THE GREAT SOCIETY

All great wars are now civil wars. They are not battles against an alien foe but internecine struggles within one closely related, intricately interdependent community. Modern war tears apart huge populations which have become dependent upon one another for the maintenance of their standard of life—in some degree, for the maintenance of life itself. That is why modern war is so devastating to victor and to vanquished alike. That is why war can no longer be employed successfully as an instrument of national policy. That is why those who preach and provoke war are regarded as rebels against the peace and order of the community of peoples, and why, in attacking their prey, they arouse the encircling hostility of that whole community of nations. That is why pacifism has so recently ceased to be an other-world aspiration and has become the working doctrine of practical men. For it was in the nineteenth century that the self-sufficiency of nations, of local communities, and of individuals, gave way to a deep and intricate interdependence. Men found themselves living in a Great Society.

Walter Lippmann

488   THE PEACE WE WANT

Not an idle dream, but an energizing reality.
Not mere cessation from strife, but ardent, courageous fellowship.
Not born of fear and cowardice, but begotten of hope and sacrifice.
Not negative, anemic, passive, but positive, vital, passionate.
Not based on policy and selfishness, but the fruit of conviction and service.
Not bought at any price, but won at heavy cost.
Not the submission of the weak, but the bestowal of the strong.
Not just conserving moral values, but achieving spiritual victories.
Not the peace of man, but the peace of God.

George Ashton Oldham

489   VICTIMS OF VIOLENCE

A cursory glance at human history reveals that men have sought for countless generations to bring peace into the world by the instrumentality of violence. The fact is significant because it is tried repeatedly and to no basic advantage. The remark which someone has made, that perhaps the most important fact we learn from history is that we do not learn from history, is very much to the point. Violence is very deceptive as a technique because of the way in which it comes to the rescue of those who are in a hurry. Violence at first is very efficient, very effective. It stampedes, overruns, pushes aside and carries the day. It becomes the major vehicle of power, or the radical threat of power. It inspires resistance and fear. The fact that it inspires resistance is underestimated, while the fact that it inspires fear is overestimated. This is the secret of its deception. Violence is the ritual and the etiquette of those who stand in a position of overt control in the world. As long as this is true, it will be impossible to make power —economic, social or political—responsive to anything that is morally or socially motivating. Men resort to violence when they are unable or unwilling to tax their resourcefulness for methods that will inspire the confidence or the mental and moral support of other men. This is true, whether in the relationship between parents and children in the home or in great affairs of the state involving the affirmation of masses of the people. Violence rarely, if ever, gets the consent of the spirit of men upon whom it is used. It drives them underground, it makes them seek cover, if they cannot overcome it in other ways. It merely postpones the day of revenge and retaliation. To believe in some other way, that will not inspire retaliation and will curb evil and bring about social change, requires a spiritual maturity that has appeared only sporadically in the life of man on this planet. The statement *may* provide the machinery, but the functioning of it is dependent upon the climate created by the daily habits of the people.

Howard Thurman

490   *LIVING LIKE HUMAN BEINGS*

God hath tempered the body together, with a special dignity for the obscure parts, so that there may be no disunion in the body, but that the various members should have a common concern for one another. If one suffer—all suffer; if one is honored—all share its honor. 1 co. 12:24–26

We differ; different members of the same body; yet all bound together. How glorious it is that I may think one way and you may think another and yet we may love each other and find a unity in the whole body of our humanity. . . .

The scriptural foundation . . . is a clause out of that great parable by the Apostle Paul: "That there may be no disunion in the body, but that the various members should have a common concern for one another."

This is Paul's parable of variety in unity, representing man's peculiar human paradox. We love order and peace and regular development. We love quietness. We do not like to be disturbed, and yet we have an instinct for revolt. Every time a situation becomes too static or too sure we revolt against it. Strange human paradox—a love of order and an instinct for revolt.

Frederick B. Fisher

491   *THE CHURCH AND THE INTERNATIONAL MIND*

God hath given to us the ministry of reconciliation. 2 co. 5:18

The church of Christ is not in politics; that is to say, it is not concerned with the controversies of parties or the ambitions of persons. But its sphere is the whole of life, nothing less; its specific task to make vivid in thought and controlling in action the principles which in a Christian civilization must govern all human relations. If it fail to touch with redemptive power any bit of human life; if any group of relations—domestic, social, industrial, political, national, or international—is untouched by its influence, in so far it fails of its function, in so far it fails in loyalty to its great Master, to whom nothing human was foreign.

Alexander MacColl

492   *THE NEED OF COURAGE*

It is the church's privilege and duty to speak from outside society, free to praise and free to rebuke. It can build the inter-nation through representing the super-national element in the heart of citizens—also super-class, super-race, super-status. The church should be in its own life, not a kindly reproach, but an authoritative denunciation of the compromises and cruelties of our massive national self-righteousness, of the hideous indiscriminacy of our own methods of warfare, of the abysmal wickedness of revenge among nations, of punishment inflicted in the wrong generation, of seeking security through the death of an ex-enemy nation, of the lingering brutalities of maintaining racial dominance at home or abroad through racial degradation, of the radical sin of failure to love one's neighbor across group boundaries. The church is "good"; but what it has still to do for human morality is to touch moral necessity, far below the level of sagacity: it needs the courage of its own function.

William Ernest Hocking

493   *A UNITED PEOPLE*

A day will come when a cannon will be exhibited in public museums, just as an instrument of torture is now, and people will be astonished how such a thing could have been. A day will come when those two immense groups, the United States of America and the United States of Europe, shall be seen placed in presence of each other, extending the hand of friendship across the ocean, exchanging their produce, their commerce, their industry, their arts, their genius, clearing the earth, peopling the deserts, improving creation under the eye of the Creator, and uniting, for the good of all, these two irresistible and infinite powers, the fraternity of men and the power of God. Nor is it necessary that four hundred years should pass away for that day to come. But French, English, Germans, Russians, Slavs, Europeans, Americans, what have we to do in order to hasten the advent of that great day? We must love each other! To love each other is, in this immense labor of pacification, the best manner of aiding God!

Victor Hugo

494   THE WORLD CITIZEN

There can be no democratic world order without a democratic world citizen, any more than there can be a democratic American order without a democratic American citizen. What is more, we cannot be the protagonists of such a democratic world order if we are not prepared to be such world citizens ourselves. This will involve very great efforts and sacrifices on our own part. These sacrifices are part of establishing the world order we want to live in. The only basis on which we can ask other people to share the four freedoms and to be willing to accept their guarantees through effective world government is our own use of them. This means that our own policies and commitments must be such as to help other people to prosper. Carl Schurz once said: "If you want to be free, there is but one way: it is to guarantee an equally full measure of liberty to all your neighbors. There is no other."

We cannot hope to go forward by ourselves, either materially or spiritually, on this planet. And when we say this, we are not thinking of this year or next year, but of the generation now in the making. The citizen of the past was a national citizen. It was a question of turning folks from many lands into Americans. The citizen of the future will be a world citizen, or there will be no democratic world order. Frankly, I believe that this building of world citizenship has to begin right here in America.

Carl J. Friedrich

495   THE TRIED AND THE UNTRIED

The Tried
   To build a world of brotherhood by the machinery of war;
   To establish fellowship by feeling racial rancor—by
      keeping the Negro and immigrant in place;
   To use force and violence in guaranteeing national
      security;

To dispose of the criminal by a prison system;

To put money first in the purpose of life; and

To be a Christian without following Christ.

The Untried

To build a friendly world by faith and understanding—to
   put love where there is now hate;

To lead the race toward a juster, wiser and more merciful
   social order, where each individual is evaluated in terms
   of his true worth;

To fortify the nation by the armaments of faith and the
   long range cannons of love;

To give guidance to those who err and in time redeem the
   environment of every little child;

To work for the good of all—not for the gain of wealth; and

To make an earnest trial of Jesus' way of life.

                                                    Roy A. Burkhart

496   *FOUNDATION FOR COOPERATION*

Whatever the superstructure may be, a *foundation* for world-wide cooperation has been built, and never before has such a foundation existed.

It is not as if we were starting from the beginning. Ever since the Renaissance
the process has been at work. Slowly and almost without our knowing of it,
the intellectual life of the world has been largely internationalized, and a
definite pattern of unity has been woven into human society. There is not an
area of activity in which this cannot be illustrated. In World War II, an
American soldier wounded on a battlefield in the Far East owed his life to
the Japanese scientist, Kitasato, who isolated the bacillus of tetanus. A Russian
soldier saved by a blood transfusion was indebted to Landsteiner, an Austrian.
A German soldier was shielded from typhoid fever with the help of a Russian,
Metchnikoff. A Dutch marine in the East Indies was protected from malaria
because of the experiments of an Italian, Grassi; while a British aviator in
North Africa escaped death from surgical infection because a Frenchman,
Pasteur, and a German, Koch, elaborated a new technique.

In peace, as in war, we are all of us the beneficiaries of contributions to
knowledge made by every nation in the world. Our children are guarded from
diphtheria by what a Japanese and a German did; they are protected from
smallpox by an Englishman's work; they are saved from rabies because of a
Frenchman; they are cured of pellagra through the researches of an Austrian.
From birth to death they are surrounded by an invisible host—the spirits of

men who never thought in terms of flags or boundary lines and who never served a lesser loyalty than the welfare of mankind. The best that every individual or group has produced anywhere in the world is available to serve the race of men, regardless of nation or color.

Raymond B. Fosdick

E. WORLD TEMPERANCE SUNDAY

World Temperance Sunday, often observed on the last Sunday in October, is an occasion when the church underscores and reaffirms its message in regard to the relationship of temperance to individual and national welfare.

Calls to Worship

(Boldface type indicates response.)

497   Trust in the Lord, and do good; so shalt thou dwell in the land, and verily thou shalt be fed. Delight thyself also in the Lord; and he shall give thee the desires of thine heart. Commit thy way unto the Lord; trust also in him; and he shall bring it to pass. And he shall bring forth thy righteousness as the light, and thy judgment as the noonday.

Ps. 37:3-6

498   Lord, I cry unto thee: make haste unto me; give ear unto my voice, when I cry unto thee. Let my prayer be set forth before thee as incense; and the lifting up of my hands as the evening sacrifice. Set a watch, O Lord, before my mouth; keep the door of my lips. Incline not my heart to any evil thing, to practice wicked works with men that work iniquity.

Ps. 141:1-4

499   The fruit of the Spirit is love, joy, peace, longsuffering, gentleness, goodness, faith, meekness, temperance: against such there is now law.
If we live in the Spirit, let us also walk in the Spirit.

Ga. 5:22-23, 25

Invocations

500   We worship thee, O God, in thy church throughout the world, in the Holy Spirit who guides us into all truth in every holy impulse and every holy life, in every victory over evil within and without, in every outgoing of love, service and devotion, in every vision of thy purpose and thy Kingdom on earth. Amen.

Richard Roberts

501   Most merciful God, Author of all good things, who hast given unto us thy holy commandments whereby we should direct our life: imprint them in our hearts by thy Holy Spirit; and grant that we may so renounce all our fleshly desires, and all the vanities of this world, that our whole delight may be in thy law, and that we, being always governed by thy holy Word, may in the end attain unto that eternal salvation which thou hast promised; through Jesus Christ thy Son. Amen.

Scottish Collects

502   O Lord our God, teach us temperance and self-control, that we may live unto the spirit and be mindful of all that Jesus endured and sacrificed for our sakes, and how he was made perfect through suffering; and help us so to keep the fast that thou hast chosen, that we may loose the bands of wickedness, undo the heavy burdens, and let the oppressed go free; through the grace of Christ Jesus, our crucified and risen Saviour. Amen.

Henry van Dyke

Prayers

503   O Lord, we praise thy holy name, for thou hast made bare thine arm in the sight of all nations and done wonders. But still we cry to thee in the weary struggle of our people againts the power of drink. Remember, Lord, the strong men who were led astray and blighted in the flower of their youth. Remember the aged who have brought their gray hairs to a dishonored grave. Remember the homes that have been made desolate of joy, the wifely love that has been outraged in its sanctuary, the little children who have learned to despise where once they loved. Remember, O thou great avenger of sin, and make this nation to remember.

May those who now entrap the feet of the weak and make their living by the degradation of men, thrust away their shameful gains and stand clear. But if their conscience is silenced by profit, do thou grant thy people the indomitable strength of faith to make an end of it. May all the great churches of our land shake off those who seek the shelter of religion for that which damns, and stand with level front against their common foe. May all who still soothe their souls with half-truths, saying "Peace, peace," where there can be no peace, learn to see through thy stern eyes and come to the help of Jehovah against the mighty. Help us to cast down the men in high places who use the people's powers to beat back the people's hands from the wrong they fain would crush.

O God, bring nigh the day when all our men shall face their daily task with minds undrugged and with tempered passions; when the unseemly mirth of drink shall seem a shame to all who hear and see; when the trade that debauches men shall be loathed like the trade that debauches women; and when all this black remnant of savagery shall haunt the memory of a new generation but as an evil dream of the night. For this accept our vows, O Lord, and grant thine aid. Amen.

Walter Rauschenbusch

504 Our sovereign Lord and righteous Father, who proclaimest liberty to the captive and opening of prisons to those who are bound: in humility and confidence we come to thee on behalf of the multitudes of our unfortunate brethren who are enslaved to intemperance, who dwell in the prisons of degenerative habits, and are blinded by the disease of alcohol.

Give us divine wisdom and courage to know how to conquer the evil of intemperate living and to set at liberty our brothers and sisters and our boys and girls who are hypnotised and bound in its tyranny. Help us to point them to the secret of self-control until they may become victors through the healing power of our risen Lord and Saviour. Thy hand, O Lord, is not shortened that it cannot save, and thine ear is not heavy that it cannot hear.

Give the church and the forces of temperance wisdom to build constructive programs and to develop techniques to counteract all social evil. Help our local and national governments to plan more wholesome social environments that shall encourage the growth of stalwart citizenship and the abundant life which Jesus came to offer.

Awaken Christian people everywhere to their responsibility and save them from self-complacent indifference until the prayer of our Lord Jesus Christ shall become their passion to see thy will be done on earth as it is in heaven. This we pray in the name of the Great Physician and the world's Emancipator, Jesus Christ. Amen.

Gordon Palmer

505 Almighty God, giver of every perfect gift, we thank thee for thy many benevolences. Thou hast supplied bountifully for every human need, light for our darkness, rest for our weariness, food for our hunger, drink for our thirst. We rejoice in the healthy satisfactions of thy food and drink that makes glad the heart of man.

Forgive us, O Lord, when we have made our appetite an end in itself. By thy grace help us to avoid the allurement of appetite except as it fills legitimate need. Teach us the satisfaction of temperance in food and drink.

Withhold not thy holy wrath from all who exploit their felows, who traffic in human weakness, and turn aside when lives are wrecked, homes are broken, chastity is flouted, and work neglected. Give voters and legislators courage to curb selfish gain at the expense of human sorrow. May we realize how ephemeral is the moment's joy and how brief the surcease gained through alcohol.

We pray for all lives damaged by intemperance. Restore unto them the will to abstinence. Help us to help them. May their plight be to us a solemn warning of the cup whose sting is like an adder and whose end is death.

May there ever reign in our hearts the truth of thy holy Word that we are our brothers' keeper, and that we cannot pass unconcerned when our brethren stumble and fall. We pray this in the name of thy Son, Jesus Christ our Lord, who taught that it were better for a mill stone to be hanged about our necks than that we cause one of thy little ones to stumble, and who died that men might be free from the curse of sin and death. Amen.

Hillyer H. Straton

506   O God, Source of all harmony and strength: we bow our heads in loving devotion unto thee and lift our voices in praise and thanksgiving unto thy holy name. Enable us to know thee better, O our Father, that thy will may be done in us. Temper us by thy health-giving spirit that our bodies may be disciplined that we may know the radiant vitality that comes from true obedience to thy will. Save us from surrender to vicious appetites that weaken and destroy, separating us from one another and from thee. Restrain us, O God, from the selfish use of our powers and impulses, and free us from all enslavement save to thee alone. Fill us, our Father, with that life which is from thee that we may appreciate those things which are good for us and for all people.

May food and drink, the good fruits of thy good earth, remain ever our servants and never our masters, that our bodies may be efficient and our minds sensitive to thy truth and our souls responsive to thy redeeming love. May our lives truly become temples of thy spirit. Grant us to know by experience the harmonious way of living that enlarges thy image in us and brings that peace which passeth all human understanding. In the name of Jesus Christ, thy Son, our Saviour, whom we would have live in us and work through us in thy holy service, we offer unto thee our earnest prayer. Amen.

Lee C. Sheppard

Poems

507   *AN ADAGE FROM THE ORIENT*

At the punch-bowl's brink,
Let the thirsty think
What they say in Japan:
"First the man takes a drink,
Then the drink takes a drink,
Then the drink takes the man!"

Edward Rowland Sill

508   *From THE EVERLASTING MERCY*

"Saul Kane," she said, "when next you drink,
Do me the gentleness to think
That every drop of drink accursed
Makes Christ within you die of thirst,
That every dirty word you say
Is one more flint upon His way . . .
Another nail, another cross.
All that you are is that Christ's loss."

John Masefield

509   *From THE GOLDEN LEGEND*

Touch the goblet no more!
It will make thy heart sore
To its very core!
Its perfume is the breath
Of the Angel of Death,
And the light that within it lies
Is the flash of his evil eyes.
Beware! Oh, beware!
For sickness, sorrow, and care
All are there!

Henry Wadsworth Longfellow

510   *From COMUS*

> Impostor do not charge most innocent Nature,
> As if she would her children should be riotous
> With her abundance; she, good cateress,
> Means her provision only to the good
> That live according to her sober laws,
> And holy dictate of spare Temperance.

John Milton

Topics, Texts and Themes

511   *THE QUESTION OF TEMPERANCE*

John the Baptist came neither eating bread nor drinking wine; and ye say,
He hath a devil. The Son of man is come eating and drinking; and ye say,
Behold a gluttonous man, and a wine bibber. LU. 7:33-34

The Scriptures class drunkenness with other sins, and refuse to put it in a category by itself. Current custom today, unfortunately, takes a very different attitude. It singles out this particular sin as though it were something exceptional —exceptional either in the irresistible quality of its temptation, or exceptional in the fact that it is not really as mortal an offense as the others alongside which it is named. There are a dozen euphemisms for being drunk. Every other sin is called by its own name; it is not disguised by some gentler term. Theft is theft, lying is lying, and adultery is adultery; but in common speech there are a dozen terms for being drunk, which do not altogether convey the idea that a man who gets drunk is guilty of a moral fault. The Scriptures never make this mistake. They call the evil by its right name, and class it with other sins for which the sinner himself is responsible. The popular way of dealing with this produces two evils. In the first place, it breaks down the moral resistance of the person who is tempted, if it is intimated to him that he is a "poor victim of drink," especially if it is intimated that he is the unfortunate possessor of an inherited appetite. He very quickly takes the kind-hearted but foolish reformer at his word, and regards himself as a victim rather than a sinner. In the second place, popular speech directs the public indignation against the wrong party. If one tenth of the public abuse which is addressed to the liquor dealer were brought to bear upon the liquor drinker, the evil, if not eradicated, would be greatly lessened. For, after all, the man who sells the liquor is not the criminal. At most he is only an accessory before the fact. We do not pity the man who commits burglary, and fine and imprison the man who sells him the jimmy. It would be just as wise to do so, as to pity the fellow who gets drunk and fine the dealer who sells him the liquor. . . .

What does Christianity provide in the way of incentive or in the way of restraint? The chief thing is the simple teaching of the New Testament as to the value, the destiny, and sanctity of the human body. It says to every follower of Christ, "Your body is a temple of the Holy Spirit." If you abuse it you commit not only a physical fault, but an offense which is in its nature sacrilege. "Know ye not that your body is the temple of the Holy Ghost?" Your bodies are members of Christ.

S. D. McConnell

512   *IS DRINKING A RELIGIOUS PROBLEM?*

No one denies . . . that drinking is a health, an economic, and a law-enforcement problem of gravest proportions. Yet it is denied by many that it is a moral and religious problem! What they mean, to put it simply, is this: It is their own business if, when, where, and how much they drink. They contend that it concerns them and no one else, whether God or man. This is precisely the point with which I wish to take issue, and to do so in terms of reasons drawn up and stated by Dr. Haven Emerson, who for many years has been one of the foremost medical scientists in the study of the meaning of alcohol in human life.

Among the fourteen basic facts which he gives about the meaning of alcohol, four have an especial bearing on the problem of whether it is a moral and a religious problem. (1) "Alcohol is a narcotic which, by depressing the higher centers removes inhibitions; (2) By releasing inhibitions, it makes for social ease and pleasure, and herein lies one of its great dangers; (3) It impairs reason, will, self-control, judgment, physical skill and endurance; (4) It is used primarily for its psychological effect as a means of escape from unpleasant reality." Yet some claim that the habit which produces these effects in human life lies beyond the concern of religion! The religious implications of reasons like these are written in letters so large that even he who runs may read. . . .

For these reasons, the Christian church as a social institution, committed to the achievement of the abundant life for all men, includes in her legitimate concern for all human problems the problem of drinking.

We have a right to be concerned about the sick—and drinking is related to mental, physical, and social disease. We have a right to be concerned about the poor—and drinking is intimately related to much of the poverty in the land. We have a right to be concerned about disillusionment—and disillusionment runs rife, and many seek courage by means of drink. We have a right to be concerned about the criminal—and drinking is related to the extent and type of crimes actually being committed today. We have a right to be concerned about broken homes—and drinking is a prolific cause of domestic unhappiness and catastrophe. We have a right to be concerned with any business which systematically educates our children for vice—and the liquor business does just that! Therefore, we say to those who might wish us to keep silent on matters like these: Drinking, seen through the eyes of what it does to men, is a religious problem of major magnitude; we therefore call upon our people, individually and collectively, to face it as a major personal and social problem.

Harold A. Bosley

513   *ON BEING A BROTHER'S KEEPER*

Am I my brother's keeper? GE. 4:9

Of course, you are. There is no escape. The obligation is written into the very constitution of life. The fact of the fatherhood of God and the brotherhood of man makes such a relationship inevitable. The privileges and obligations, the rights and responsibilities of belonging to God's great family are ours. We cannot have one without the other.

In no sphere of present-day life is there a greater appeal for consideration of others than in that of the use of beverage alcohol. We cannot "do as we please," and "take our liquor or let it alone" with no concern for the rest of God's great family. We are bound together for weal or woe. We cannot go on our own self-gratifying way because we are strong, and say, "Our pleasures cannot be denied us, because there are some weak and foolish people who cannot handle their liquor." One of those may prove to be your son, your daughter, your husband or your wife, any one of whom may make a start toward becoming an alcoholic by taking the social glass.

Wilbur E. Hammaker

514   *WHY PEOPLE DRINK*

Why do people turn to alcohol? (1) They may have inherited an unbalanced nervous equipment from alcoholism in their family. Then someone starts them off and away they go plunging down hill like a loosely balanced stone kicked by a careless foot. (2) Folk are frightened by life. They don't look as though they are because we all wear masks. But we are frightened, and we are weak, and things look threatening and things go wrong. Then alcohol for a little time makes us feel twice our size. (3) We are shy and we are lonely. We may be sexually tormented. We are very conscious of being inferior, life catches us some very hard smacks, and alcohol helps us to forget for a little. (4) We have no plan for life. We are lost on the road, quite forlorn, and very bored. We have done something wrong, or failed in something and the memory haunts us like a ghost.

McEwan Lawson

515   THE METHOD OF ALCOHOLICS ANONYMOUS

(1) We admitted we were powerless over alcohol—that our lives had become unmanageable. (2) We came to believe that a Power greater than ourselves could restore us to sanity. (3) We made a decision to turn our wills and our lives over to the care of God *as we understood him.* (4) We made a searching and fearless moral inventory of ourselves. (5) We admitted to God, to ourselves, and to another human being the exact nature of our wrongs. (6) We were entirely ready to have God remove all defects of character. (7) We humbly asked him to remove our shortcomings. (8) We made a list of all persons we had harmed and became willing to make amends to them all. (9) We made direct amends to such people wherever possible, except where to do so would injure them or others. (10) We continued to take personal inventory and when we were wrong promptly admitted it. (11) We sought through prayer and meditation to improve our conscious contact with God *as we understood him,* praying only for knowledge of his will for us and the power to carry out that will. (12) Having had a spiritual experience as a result of these steps, we tried to carry this message to alcoholics and to practice these principles.

E. Stanley Jones

516   SUMMING UP

William E. Gladstone frequently handed to his neighbors at Hawarden, England, printed slips reading:
Drunkenness expels reason.
Drowns the memory.
Distempers the body.
Diminishes strength.
Inflames the blood.
Causes internal and external wounds.
It's a witch to the senses.
A devil to the soul.

A thief to the purse.

A beggar's companion.

A wife's woe and children's sorrow.

It makes a man become a beast and self-murderer. He drinks to others' good health and robs himself of his own.

F. STEWARDSHIP SUNDAY

Christian stewardship is more inclusive, of course, than the budget emphasis of this section. Every pastor realizes the necessity of an occasional fund-raising or financial enlistment sermon. A particular day or period is frequently designated by a national denominational group for an Every Member Canvass. The United Church Canvass, representing a simultaneous and concerted effort by all churches in a community or area, is widely observed.

The materials which follow may be useful for programs concerned with the raising of funds for missions, the work of the Sunday school and other church educational projects, church building and improvement campaigns, and the dedication of tithes and offerings.

Calls to Worship

(Boldface type indicates responses.)

517   What shall I render unto the Lord for all his benefits toward me?

I will take the cup of salvation, and call upon the name of the Lord. I will pay my vows unto the Lord now in the presence of all his people. I will offer to thee the sacrifice of thanksgiving, and will call upon the name of the Lord. I will pay my vows unto the Lord now in the presence of all his people, in the courts of the Lord's house, in the midst of thee, O Jerusalem.

Ps. 116:12–14, 17–19

518   Rejoice in the Lord, O ye righteous: for praise is comely for the upright.

It is a good thing to give thanks unto the Lord, and to sing praises unto thy name, O most High.

For thy lovingkindness is before mine eyes: and I have walked in thy truth.
Ps. 33:1; 92:1; 26:3

519   Give unto the Lord, ye kindreds of the people, give unto the Lord glory and strength.

Give unto the Lord the glory due unto his name: bring an offering, and come before him: worship the Lord in the beauty of holiness.

Let the heavens be glad, and let the earth rejoice: and let men say among the nations, the Lord reigneth.

1 Ch. 16:28–29, 31

Invocations

520 O Son of God, who by thy lowly service hast made manifest the royalty of service: teach us, O Lord, that it is better to give than to receive, better to minister than to be ministered unto; after thine own example, who now livest and reignest in the glory of the eternal trinity, world without end. Amen.

Daily Prayer

521 O Lord, who hast taught us that all our doings without charity are worth nothing, and that it is more blessed to give than to receive, pour into the hearts of thy people that most excellent gift of charity, and incline them to liberal offerings for the extension of thy church and the salvation of mankind; and, thus bringing forth the fruit of good works, may they by thee be plenteously rewarded, and be made partakers of thy heavenly treasure; through the merits of Jesus Christ, our most blessed Lord and Saviour. Amen.

Book of Worship (ER)

522 O God, who in thine infinite love didst send thy Son to bring light to all that are in darkness: fill us with thine own love for men; and, since thou hast entrusted to us both the knowledge of thy truth and the gifts of thy bounty, help us to use them as good stewards, giving liberally, praying instantly, and working diligently, that we may be sharers in bringing all men to thy light and hastening the coming of thy Kingdom. Amen.

Prayers for the Christian Year

Prayers

523 O God, we acknowledge thee as the Fountain of all good, the Giver of every perfect gift. For all thy bounty and love we are humbly grateful.

Forgive us for our selfishness. We so often forget that truly "all things come of thee." We confess to our inordinate use of "my" and "mine." We are guilty of undue preoccupation with things. Help us to correct our thoughts and ways by believing assuredly that "the earth is the Lord's and the fulness thereof." Save us from being spiritual robbers.

Help us to accept and use our treasure, time and talents as a sacred trust. Save us from the love of money. Keep us from wasting our time. Inspire us to use our talents with such fidelity that we shall enter even now into the joy of our Lord.

Grant, O loving Father, in this time of desperate need that we shall have the compassion and vision of Christ. By his example and teachings lift us into a life of lasting concern and glad sharing. Yielded to thee in body, mind and spirit, empower us with all our gifts to honor thee and advance thy Kingdom.

In making this prayer with our lips, arouse us to do our part in answering by our lives. These things we ask in the name of thy Unspeakable Gift. Amen.

John S. Land

524   O God, the Father of our Lord Jesus and Father of all who have believed on the name of thy holy Son: we thank thee that we have been daily recipients of thy great bounty. We do not ask thee to increase our blessings, but to make us worthy of the least of thy gifts. Enable us to rejoice in the privilege which is ours of honoring thee with our substance and with the first-fruits of all our increase. Keep us from wasting thy benevolences in worldly endeavour.

May we remember that the tithe is thine, and that it is holy unto thee. Since we have so freely received from thee, may we as freely give to thee. Whatever we give, may we give with cheerful hearts and willing hands, not grudgingly or with coercion, for thou dost love a cheerful giver.

O God, make us mindful of thy truth that he which soweth sparingly shall reap also sparingly. Help us to hold in our hearts thy precious truth that thou art able to make all grace to abound toward us that we, always having all sufficiency in all things, may abound unto every good work.

We would love thee with our creative skills and with the rewards of our effort, even as we love thee with our hearts. We remember the words of Jesus that it is more blessed to give than to receive. May we not forget that he taught that a man's life consisteth not in the abundance of things which he possesseth. Give us wisdom to heed his injunction not to lay up treasure on earth where moth and rust corrupt and where thieves break through and steal, but to lay up treasure in heaven. Help us to make money serve the causes of Christ until he comes, or until the pierced hands that opened to us the gates to grace shall open to us the gates of glory. In the holy and blessed name of our Lord Jesus Christ, we make our prayer. Amen.   *Robert G. Lee*

525   Almighty God, from whom we come and unto whom our souls return, we acknowledge that all we have is thine. Our souls and bodies, our time and talents, our money and goods, even our children are thy possessions and we but stewards and keepers for a brief span of years.

When we act selfishly, forgive us; when we are careless and indifferent keepers, reprove and instruct us; when we try to be faithful stewards, assist and inspire us. Too often, our Father, we confess that we have used the good earth which thou hast formed for our needs mainly for fleeting pleasure, or for selfish power, or to feed our vanity. For this sin, forgive us, O God. Even as Jesus Christ resisted the temptation to use the earth for his own power, help us to resist the temptation to use the small part we have solely for ourselves. Keep us aware that somewhere hungry children cry for bread, and that everywhere men's souls hunger and thirst for Christ's Gospel. May we know that whether their yearnings are satisfied depends on the manner in which we share our blessings.

Fill us, O God, with the mind of Christ that we shall gladly give ourselves in service as he gave himself on the Cross. We pray in the name of him who gave us an example that we should love and serve and sacrifice for mankind, even Christ Jesus our Lord and Saviour. Amen.

Graham R. Hodges

Poems

526 WORLD SYMPATHIES

He is dead whose hand is not open wide
  To help the need of a human brother;
He doubles the length of his lifelong ride
  Who gives his hand to another.
And a thousand million lives are his
Who carries the world in his sympathies.

Author Unknown

527 SHARING

Hast thou plenty? Then rejoice;
  Rejoice and freely share.
Hast thou scanty store? E'en then,
  A little thou canst spare.

Be the portion small or great,
  The loving, generous heart
Will always find it large enough
  To give away a part.

Anne Emelie Poulsson

528   *GIVING*

To give a little from a shining store,
Is that to give? To give and feel no loss,
Is that to give as Christ gave on the Cross?
To share the crumbs of happiness we gain
With those who weep apart, to give our best
Of healing sympathy to hearts in pain,
To give our labor when we fain would rest,
This is the charity men knew when he
First breathed that word by starlit Galilee!

William F. Kirk

529   *IT IS NOT THE DEED*

It is not the deed that we do,
    Tho' the deed be never so fair,
But the love that the dear Lord looketh for,
    Hidden with loving care
    In heart of the deed so fair.

Yes, love is the priceless thing,
    The treasure, our treasure must hold,
Or ever the Master receives the gift,
    Or tells the weight of the gold,
    By the love which cannot be told.

Author Unknown

530   *WE GIVE THEE BUT THINE OWN*

We give thee but thine own,
Whate'er the gift may be;
All that we have is thine alone,
A trust, O Lord, from thee.

May we thy bounties thus
As stewards true receive,
And gladly, as thou blessest us,
To thee our first-fruits give.

William Walsham How

531   *A MODERN HAMLET SOLILOQUIZES*

To pledge or not to pledge—that is the question.
Whether 'tis nobler in a man
To take the Gospel free and let another foot the bill,
Or sign a pledge and pay toward church expenses!
To give, to pay—aye, there's the rub. To pay,
When on the free-pew plan, a man may have
A sitting free and take the Gospel, too,
As though he paid, and none be aught the wiser
Save the Finance Committee, who—
Most honorable of men—can keep a secret!
"To err is human," and human, too, to buy
At cheapest rate. I'll take the Gospel so!
For others do the same—a common rule!
I'm wise, I'll wait, not work—I'll pray, not pay,
And let the other fellow foot the bills,
And so I'll get the Gospel free, you see.

Author Unknown

532   *ONCE THERE WAS A CHRISTIAN*

Once there was a Christian,
    He had a pious look;
His consecration was complete—
    Except his pocketbook.

He'd put a nickel in the plate,
    And then with might and main
He'd sing, "When we asunder part
    It gives us inward pain."

Author Unknown

Topics, Texts and Themes

533   *THE FINER SPIRIT OF TRUSTEESHIP*

The individual never sees life in the radiant glow of its greatness, its dignity and its privilege until he realizes it as trusteeship. Life itself is but the individual trusteeship of time. Man does not truly own even his own life; he has merely a life-interest in it, and sometime he must surrender it.

In the truest sense, man owns nothing absolutely, to do with precisely as he pleases; over all his possessions ever breathes the spirit of trusteeship. His time, his money, his health, his mind, his character, his business, his worldly goods, his opportunities, his influence—all that he is, and has, he holds but as trustee for his higher self, the world around him, and humanity itself. These possessions are all covered by a first mortgage of the rights of others.

Trusteeship is one of the great words of life because it concentrates in a single expression the essence of all true living. It inspires man with the revelation of his constant relation to himself, to all others and to the Infinite. It gives a royal dignity to life, making man, not a mere isolated individual, but interblended with other lives and an indispensable factor in the whole scheme of living.

William G. Jordan

534   *ON THE USE OF MONEY*

Have you observed that all Christ's main teachings by direct order, by earnest parable, and by his own permanent emotion, regard the use and misuse of money? We might have thought, if we had been asked what a divine teacher was most likely to teach, that he would have left inferior persons to give directions about money; and himself spoken only concerning faith and love, and the discipline of the passions, and the guilt of the crimes of soul against soul. But not so. He speaks in general terms of these. But he does not speak parables about them for all men's memory, nor permit himself fierce indignation against them, in all men's sight. The Pharisees bring him an adulteress. He writes her forgiveness on the dust of which he had formed her. Another, despised of all for known sin, he recognized as a giver of unknown love. But he acknowledges no love in buyers and sellers in his house. One should have thought there were people in that house twenty times worse than they; Caiaphas and his like—false priests, false prayer-makers, false leaders of the people—who needed putting to silence, or to flight, with darkest wrath. But the scourge is only against the traffickers and thieves. The two most intense of all the parables: the two which lead the rest in love and in terror (this of the Prodigal, and of Dives) relate, both of them, to management of riches. The practical order given to the only seeker of advice, of whom it is recorded that Christ "loved him," is briefly about his property. "Sell that thou hast."

John Ruskin

535   *BASES OF GIVING*

This poor widow hath cast in more than they all. LU. 21:3

Some of us have got to the point of giving generously; or so we think. But do we ever stop to consider how much we retain for ourselves? According to Jesus the acid test is not how much is given but how much is retained. In his eyes a "big giver" is not necessarily one who makes a large contribution but is a man or woman whose contribution, whether large or small, represents real sacrifice.

As a fact, most of us have only begun to give, and some of us haven't got even that far. True, we worry about giving. "It's getting to be something awful," we say. "Why I never open my mail any more without finding a begging letter. If it isn't the Community Chest, it's the church or old alma mater or the Red Cross or the lame, the halt, or the blind." We fret and suffer about giving, but not to the point of parting with anything. Like the man who confided to a friend: "It's terrible the way my wife is always wanting money—one dollar for this, five dollars for that, ten dollars for something else. There is simply no end to it." The friend, all sympathy, asked: "How do you handle her?" and was told: "Well, of course, I never give her anything."

We cannot be lectured into giving. There is no use telling us that we ought to give. We know it, but can always find plausible reasons for withholding. One thing only will avail, and that is wholehearted acceptance of the principle of stewardship. Let a man come to regard his income as a trust fund to be administered for the glory of God and the good of men, and he will need no one to tell him that he ought to give or to suggest what would be an appropriate amount. He will give as a matter of course—and give serious thought to the matter, with a view to putting his money where it may do the most good.

Ernest Fremont Tittle

536   *THE DEDICATION OF SUBSTANCE*

2 K. 4:38–44

Here is a man recognizing the sacredness of his substance. He saw the seal of the Lord upon his harvest, and he offered the first-fruits in token of its rightful Owner. Men go wrong when the only name upon their field is their own. "*My* power, and the strength of *my* hand hath gotten me this wealth." It matters nothing what the wealth may be—material substance, mental skill, or business sagacity. It becomes unhallowed power when we attach our own label to it, and erase the name of God.

This man dedicated his substance, and the hunger of his fellows was appeased. That is a great principle in human life. One man's satisfaction is dependent on another man's fidelity. His want is to be filled with my fulness. If I am selfish he remains hungry. If I acknowledge "the rights of God," and therefore "the rights of man," he has "enough and to spare." If I hoard my treasure I rob both God and man.

John Henry Jowett

537   *CONCERNING THE COLLECTION*

Concerning the collection. 1 co. 16:1

What a seeming anti-climax to the great resurrection argument of the fifteenth chapter. Yet that chapter ends with a noble "Therefore." Doctrine always points to duty, and creed is consummated in deed. So, right in sight of the open grave of Jesus, Paul calls attention to the collection.

To many folks money is a tenderly delicate theme; their spiritual sensibilities are so sweetly seraphic that they forever soar above so sordid a subject! But, really, it is only very cheap folks who can be drawn to church by the notice, "No collection." God makes no apologies for talking about it in his Book, nor does his apostle Paul for exhorting concerning it. The church ought not to have to discuss finance, and would not if all life was conceived as stewardship.

Giving is a positive duty . . . Giving is a personal duty . . . Giving is a duty of Christian partnership . . . Giving is a periodic duty . . . Giving is a primary duty . . . Giving is a pious duty . . . Giving is a proportionate duty.

George Elliott

538   *THE PAY CHECK AND RELIGION*

Where your treasure is, there will be your heart be also. lu. 12:34

One of the most frequently overlooked fundamentals of religion is the relation of the pay check to spiritual life. The first impulse, which often becomes a deep conviction, is that there is no relation between a man's pay check and his spiritual life; or if there be any relation, it is detrimental; the less a man pays out of his pay check for religion the more spiritual he becomes; while the more he pays out the less spiritual he becomes. This is a mistake. . . . Push your treasure out ahead of you toward God, and see how your heart will follow your treasure toward him.

Walter R. Fruit

539   *WASTING OR SPENDING*

[He] wasted his substance with riotous living. . . LU. 15:13
I will very gladly spend and be spent for you. co. 12:15

There are three things a man can do with himself and his possessions. He
may selfishly hoard them; he may lavishly waste them; he may intelligently
spend them.

There can be no question as to which method religion calls on every man to
follow . . . If he tries to hoard it he only fixes his attention on the sure day
when he shall lose it all—without profit to himself or others. For the miser is
one of the most wretched of men. If he dissipates it in riotous living he shall
speedily find himself (aided and abetted by various sorts of human harpies) in
bitter want of even the humblest necessities of life. Only if he spends it freely
and gladly for the purposes of his soul may he experience the full meaning of
life and say at the end:

Glad did I live and gladly die,
And I laid me down with a will.

For of what value is strength of mind or body, or what is the significance of
worldly possessions save as they are spent for the release of spiritual powers?

Henry and Tertius van Dyke

540   *CHRISTIAN STEWARDSHIP*

Christian stewardship is something more than a habit, an attitude, a technique or a phase of religious experience. These things are all involved.

Christian stewardship is really a philosophy, a way of life resulting from a
commitment to a great end, the accomplishment of the will of God on earth.
It is no surface adjustment but an inner conviction expressed in outer relationships.

It has been defined as "Christian materialism," that is to say, the Christian
philosophy with reference to possessions or things. This definition does not
tell the whole story, for stewardship also implies the idea of commitment and
action. It is not an intellectual conception alone. It is motivation as well. It involves dedication and sacrifice.

Herman C. Weber

541   *PRINCIPLES OF STEWARDSHIP*

1. God is the sovereign owner of all things.

2. Man is a steward, and must give an account for all that is entrusted to him.

3. God's sovereign ownership and man's stewardship ought to be acknowledged.

4. This acknowledgment requires, as its material expression, the setting apart, as an act of worship, of a separated portion of income.

5. Biblical history records the setting apart of the tenth of income as that acknowledgment.

6. This separated portion ought to be systematically administered for the Kingdom of God, and the balance treated as no less a trust.

Ralph S. Cushman

542   *STEPS OF CHARITY*

There are eight degrees or steps in the duty of charity:

The first and lowest is to give, but with reluctance or regret. This is the gift of the hand but not of the heart.

The second is to give cheerfully, but not proportionately to the distress of the sufferer.

The third is to give cheerfully and proportionately to the distress of the sufferer.

The fourth is to give cheerfully, proportionately, and even unsolicited; but to put it in the poor man's hand, thereby exciting in him the painful emotion of shame.

The fifth is to give charity in such a way that the distressed may receive the bounty and know their benefactor, without their being known to him. Such was the conduct of some of our ancestors who used to tie up money in the corners of their cloaks, so that the poor might take it unperceived.

The sixth, which rises still higher, is to know the object of our bounty, but remain unknown to them. Such was the conduct of those of our ancestors who used to convey their charitable gifts into poor people's dwellings; taking care that their own persons and names should remain unknown.

The seventh is still more meritorious, namely to bestow charity in such a way that the benefactor may not know the relieved persons, as was done by our charitable forefathers during the existence of the Temple. For there was in that holy building a place called the Chamber of the Silent, wherein the good deposited secretly whatever their generous hearts suggested; and from which the poor were maintained with equal secrecy.

But the eighth and most meritorious of all is to anticipate charity by preventing poverty; namely, to assist the reduced fellow-man, either by a considerable gift or sum of money, or by teaching him a trade, or by putting him in the way of business, so that he may earn an honest livelihood, and not be forced to the dreadful alternative of holding out his hand for charity.

This is the highest step and the summit of charity's golden ladder.

Ben Maimon

543 *SEVEN WAYS OF GIVING*

First—*The Careless Way:* To give something to every cause that is presented, without inquiring into its merits.

Second—*The Impulsive Way:* To give from impulse—as much and as often as love and piety and sensibility prompt.

Third—*The Lazy Way:* To make a special offer to earn money for benevolent objects by fairs, festivals, etc.

Fourth—*The Self-denying Way:* To save the cost of luxuries and apply them to purposes of religion and charity. This may lead to asceticism and self-complacence.

Fifth—*The Systematic Way:* To lay aside as an offering to God a definite portion of our gains—one-tenth, one-fifth, one-third, or one-half. This is adapted to all, whether rich or poor, and gifts would be largely increased if it were generally practiced (1 Co. 16:2).

Sixth—*The Equal Way:* To give to God and the needy just as much as we spend on ourselves, balancing all our personal expenditures by our gifts.

Seventh—*The Heroic Way:* To limit our own expenditures to a certain sum and give away all the rest of our income. This was John Wesley's way.

A. T. Pierson

544 *MY MONEY CREED*

1. To spend my income rightly, is one of my first tasks as a Christian. Until I settle this, my prayers and confessions will be like saying, "Lord, Lord," and not doing the will of my Father.

2. I should set aside a definite proportion of my income for the church and the service of others. I do this in acknowledgment of God's sovereignty over all my material possessions. I do this because it is businesslike. Giving on impulse and without system does not accord with the importance of this work.

3. The proportion to be set aside for these purposes should not be less than one-tenth of my income. The Old Testament enjoined the tithe in ancient Israel, and surely I am receiving far more from God than did the men of any former generation. Nevertheless, one-tenth is not to be the limit of my giving. . . . I should begin with not less than one-tenth. I ought to give more, if I am able.

Harris Franklin Rall

545   *ACTION/REACTION*

I am a firm believer in tithing as the best beginning for a system of giving to the cause of God. The one-tenth figure must have a peculiar appropriateness to the average life, as the history of the tithe would show. When cleared of certain mechanical features which relate it too closely to legalism, tithing does great work in two directions:

1. Its *action* is remarkable. It would finance the Kingdom plenteously. If its practice were general, we would be embarrassed with a surplus of funds until such time as we extended our religious work to fit our larger treasuries. We would banish "rummage sales" and "nickel socials" and other humiliating methods of securing funds for the good Father's work; and we would accordingly dignify the church.

2. The *reaction* would be even more remarkable. It is the universal experience that the person who begins to tithe grows in vision and grace. Even as God used the tithe to educate the race on toward Christ, so he will now use the tithe to educate individuals on toward Christian generosity. The adoption of the one-tenth figure of income by the majority of our church members, as the start, and not the goal, of systematic Christian giving, would again open the windows of heaven, and the old promise of blessing would be modernly fulfilled. As the tendency of a properly used Sabbath is to consecrate all time, so the tendency of conscientious tithing is to consecrate all property to God.

Edwin H. Hughes

546   *TITHING IN THE LIGHT OF HISTORY*

In the history of the Church in the first centuries we have abundant evidence that the tithe had not been discontinued. Clement (30–100 A.D.) and Justin Martyr (110–165 A.D.) were very clear in their teachings concerning the offerings that were due to God. Irenaeus (120–202 A.D.) speaks of "the obligation of Christians to render tithes unto God." Neander declares, "The duty was also embodied in the Apostolic canons, a complication of laws in force among the

Christian churches about the close of the second century." The tithe was declared as a Christian duty by Origen (185–254), by Cyprian (200–258), by Jerome (345–420), by Ambrose (340–397), who said, "God has reserved the tenth part to himself, and therefore it is not lawful for a man to retain what God has reserved for himself." Augustine (354–430) declared, "Our ancestors used to abound in wealth of every kind for this very reason that they used to give tithes, and pay the tax to Caesar." And he goes on to say that because they have "been unwilling to share the tithe with God now the whole is taken away." He urges the giving of the tenth, and used these two strong expressions: "The scribes and Pharisees gave tithes, for whom Christ had not yet shed his blood. But yet I cannot keep back what he who died for us said whilst he was alive, 'Except your righteousness shall exceed the righteousness of the scribes and Pharisees, ye shall in no case enter into the kingdom of heaven.'"

The tithe was enjoined by the Council of Tours in A.D. 567, by that of Macon in 585, of Rouen in 650, of Nantes in 660, and of Metz in 756. For centuries it was the prevailing custom throughout all Christendom. Bingham in his *Christian Antiquities* says, "This was the unanimous judgment of the Fathers, and the voice of the church uncontradicted for more than a thousand years, or until the usages of the church were alienated and perverted by the papal hierarchy during the dark ages."

It is a well recognized principle of law that when once a law has been in force, and the conditions which called it forth still exist, the law is binding until it is repealed. History shows that the law of tithing, while merged into the ceremonial law, has never been repealed, and the need for its enforcement has never been greater than at the present time.

John Y. Aitcheson

III. The Christian Home

A. FESTIVAL OF THE CHRISTIAN HOME

The Festival of the Christian Home stresses the importance of the church in family life and the significance of the family in the life of the church and community. This day falls on the second Sunday in May and concludes National Family Week. In some churches this occasion has replaced days specifically dedicated to mothers and fathers.

Many other activities in the church year relate to the Christian family. Some of these include: family life and home planning courses, family night dinners, banquets for fathers and sons and mothers and daughters, training conferences for engaged and recently married members, and such particular days as Couples Sunday and Homecoming Sunday.

Calls to Worship

547 He that dwelleth in the secret place of the most High shall abide under the shadow of the Almighty. . . . Because thou hast made the Lord, which is my refuge, even the most High, thy habitation; there shall no evil befall thee, neither shall any plague come nigh thy dwelling.

Ps. 91:1, 9–10

548 Lord, thou hast been our dwelling place in all generations. Before the mountains were brought forth, or ever thou hadst formed the earth and the world, even from everlasting to everlasting, thou art God.

Ps. 90:1–2

549 Wherefore come out from among them, and be ye separate, saith the Lord, and touch not the unclean thing; and I will receive you, and will be a Father unto you, and ye shall be my sons and daughters, saith the Lord Almighty.

2 Co. 6:17–18

Invocations

550 Grant unto us, O Lord God, that we may love one another unfeignedly; for where love is, there art thou; and he that loveth his brother is born of thee, and dwelleth in thee and thou in him. And where brethren do glorify thee with

one accord, there thou dost pour out thy blessing upon them. Love us, therefore, O Lord, that we may love thee, and our brethren in thee and for thee, as all children to thee; through Jesus Christ our Lord. Amen.

Author Unknown

551   O thou Christ of Galilee, who didst go into the homes and the hearts of many folk and kindle there a light which has burned through all the centuries: make each of us a humble sharer of thy glory and goodness, that so we may find a purpose and meaning in life. Teach us to speak and act so that we may cheer and help men. Grant us love for all, that we may everywhere see thy children and heed their cries. Amen.*

Floyd Tompkins

552   Make thy tranquillity, O Lord, to dwell amongst us, and thy peace to abide in our hearts. May our voices proclaim thy truth, and may thy Cross be the guardian of our souls. Account us worthy, O Lord, with the boldness which is of thee, to offer unto thee of thy grace a pure and holy prayer, through Jesus Christ our Lord. Amen.

Liturgy of the Nestorians

Litany

(Boldface type indicates responses.)

553   O God, our heavenly Father, whose goodness loved us into life, and whose mercies never fail: we commend to thee all who have a place in our hearts and sympathies; all who are joined to us by the sacred ties of kindred, friendship and love; keep them outwardly in their bodies and inwardly in their souls. Bless all little children, dear to us and dear to thee; and grant that love may reign in our homes, uniting us together and to thee; in Jesus Christ our Lord.

(*Silent prayer*)

Most gracious Father, sanctify the ties that bind us to friends and kindred; and so fill us with love, gentleness and forbearance that we may live together in peace and joy. May we love thee supremely and abide in thy love, that we may be comforters and helpers one of another unto the end:

We beseech thee to hear us, O Lord.

Grant unto us a revival of the simplicity and purity of home life; may parents bring up their children in the nurture and admonition of the Lord, and children love and reverence their parents:

We beseech thee to hear us, O Lord.

Stir up in the young a zeal for whatever things are beautiful and true and

good, that they may bravely witness for thee; and keep the hearts of the aged
fresh with sweet affection and quiet trust, that at their eventide there may be
light:

We beseech thee to hear us, O Lord.

For the careless and the wayward that they may be delivered from the bonds
of iniquity; for all who are beset by passionate temptations that thy mercy may
be their salvation; and for all who are lonely and sad in the midst of others'
joy that they may know God as their Friend and Comforter:

We beseech thee to hear us, O Lord.

Intercession Services

Prayers

554 .O thou Father of every family, we lift up to thee the family life of our
nation. We thank thee for all Christian homes where each is loved by all and
all by each, and each and all in thee; where the lovely things grow and flourish;
and where evil tempers wilt and wither and die; where difficulties are solved,
and irritation melted in an atmosphere of good will and good humor; where
little children laugh and live without fear, and where young people grow into
manhood and womanhood in freedom and in joy.

We pray for all broken homes that they may be repaired in spirit as well as
in outward appearance. We pray for all little children wounded in their very
souls by quarrelsome parents and for all parents who grieve over children who
care nothing for the sacred word "home."

Give us today a new ideal of what our homes might be, that putting away all
nagging and unkind criticism, all jealousy and suspicion, all desire to dominate
and rule another's life, the family life of our land may be that wholesome basis
of the life of a nation which thou canst use. O God, bless the families of
America and of the world. Through Jesus Christ our Lord. Amen.

Author Unknown

555 Father,
Grant unto us true family love,
That we may belong more entirely to those whom thou hast given us,
Understanding each other, day by day, more instinctively,
Forbearing each other, day by day, more patiently,
Growing, day by day, more closely into oneness with each other.

Father,
Thou too art love:
Thou knowest the depth of pain and the height to glory

Which abide continually in love:
Make us perfect in love for these our dear ones,
As knowing that without them we can never be made perfect in thee.

Father,
Bring to full fruit in us thine own nature—
That nature of humble redemptive devotion,
Which out of two responsive souls,
Can create a new heaven and a new earth,
One eternal glory of divine self-sharing. Amen.

John S. Hoyland

556   Lord Jesus, our great Elder Brother, who didst know on earth the love
of father and mother, and didst share a home with brothers and sisters: teach
us thy way in our own homes. May we not reserve our best faces for strangers
and relieve our feelings at the expense of those we love. Save us from the false
bashfulness that holds back words of affection or acknowledgment of mistakes.
Remind us of chances for unaccustomed bits of helpfulness. Shame us out of
words of impatience before they are spoken. Give us understanding hearts,
eternal vigilance against selfishness and irritation, and the love that envieth not,
vaunteth not itself, seeketh not its own, is not provoked, never faileth. Amen.

Frank J. Scribner

Poems

557   *THE MAIN AIMS*

Happy is the family
  Whose members know what a home is for,
And keep the main aims in view;

Who give more thought to affection
  Than to the shelter that houses it;
And more attention to persons
  Than to the things amid which they live.

For a home is a shelter for love
  And a setting for joy and growth,
Rather than a place to be kept up.

It is a hallowed place,
    To which its members shall turn
With a lifting of the heart.   *Leland Foster Wood*

558   *O HAPPY HOME*

O happy home, where thou art loved the dearest,
    Thou loving Friend, and Saviour of our race,
And where among the guests there never cometh
    One who can hold such high and honored place.

O happy home, where two in heart united
    In holy faith and blessed hope are one,
Whom death a little while alone divideth,
    And cannot end the union here begun.

O happy home, where thou art not forgotten
    When joy is overflowing, full, and free;
O happy home, where every wounded spirit
    Is brought, Physician, Comforter, to thee.

United at last, when earth's day's work is ended
    All meet thee in the blessed home above,
From whence thou camest, where thou hast ascended,
    Thy everlasting home of peace and love.
                                    Karl J. P. Spitta

559   *From DOMESTIC LOVE*

How lovely is domestic harmony,
Where mind on mind and heart on heart repose
Undoubting; and the friends, whom Providence
Has cast together, sharing each with each
Their hopes, their joys, their cares, appear to live
One common life, and breathe one common will!
So beautiful is this; and where the love
Of God is added to this love of man,
Somewhat of heaven itself to earth descends.
For what is heaven but one immortal home,
Where all are brother, parent, child, or friend?
                                    Henry F. Lyte

560   *BEATITUDES FOR THE HOME*

Blessed are they who rejoice in their children;
To them is revealed the Fatherhood of God.
Blessed are they who know the power of love;
They dwell in God, for God is love.
Blessed are the songful of soul;
They carry light and joy to shadowed lives.
Blessed are they that see visions;
They shall rejoice in the hidden ways of God.
Blessed are they that have understanding hearts;
To them shall be multiplied kingdoms of delight.
Blessed are the childless, loving children still;
Theirs shall be a mightier family—even as the stars of heaven.
Blessed are they whose memories we cherish;
Our thoughts add jewels to their crowns.

John Oxenham

561   *HOME*

Home is where
You hang
Your memories.

Home is the
Conscience of age,
The melody
At the end of
Eternity.

Home is truth
Guiding youth.
Home is the regret
In every madness.

Home is where
You begin again
To dream again.

Charles Angoff

562   *SO LONG AS THERE ARE HOMES*

So long as there are homes to which men turn
At close of day,
So long as there are homes where children are—
Where women stay,
If love and loyalty and faith be found
Across those sills,
A stricken nation can recover from
Its gravest ills.

So long as there are homes where fires burn
And there is bread,
So long as there are homes where lamps are lit
And prayers are said;
Although people falter through the dark
And nations grope,
With God himself back of these little homes
We still can hope.

Grace Noll Crowell

563   *HOME DEDICATION*

We build an altar here, and pray
    That thou wilt show thy face;
Dear Lord, if thou wilt come to stay,
This home we consecrate today
    Will be a holy place.

Author Unknown

564   *HOUSE AND HOME*

A house is built of logs and stone,
    Of tiles and posts and piers;
A home is built of loving deeds
    That stand a thousand years.

Victor Hugo

565   *MARVEL*

I marvel at what tact, what force,
What wisdom from some hidden source,
What superhuman understanding,
What genius for adroit commanding,
What sympathy, what wit, what prayer,
What saintly patience, selfless care
It takes to bring up, fair and mild,
A wholly ordinary child.

Mabel Kelley

566   *EMPHASIS*

We flatter those we scarcely know,
  We please the fleeting guest,
And deal full many a thoughtless blow
  To those we love the best.

Ella Wheeler Wilcox

567   *SON OF MAN*

He often spoke of things of home,
  Of linen white as snow,
Of platters cleansed inside and out,
  Of leaven hid in dough,
And lost coin sought with broom and lamp.
  Was he wistful, he
Who walked, alone, the road toward death,
  Homeless in Galilee?

Leslie Savage Clark

Topics, Texts and Themes

568   *JESUS AT HOME*

Nazareth stands for the home life. It contains the greater part of his great
career. By far the greater number of years was spent here. Here were more praying for others and over the life plan, more communing with the Father, more
battling with temptation and narrow prejudice, and ignorance than in the few

years of public service. Here were more purity of life and steadiness of purpose, more wisdom in action and patience in touch with others and with the knotty little problems of daily life, more of all this being lived than could ever find outlet at his lips. . . . Those three years and odd of public life all grew out of this Nazareth home life. They are the top of the hill; Nazareth is the base and bulk; Calvary the tip-top where every victory had already been won. The public life was built on home life. Under the ministering to crowds, healing the sick, raising the dead, and patient teaching of the multitudes, lay the great strong home life in its purity. Calvary was built on Nazareth.

S. D. Gordon

569   *HOUSE OR HOME*

Anyone can build an altar; it requires a God to provide the flame. Anybody can build a house; we need the Lord for the creation of a home. A house is an agglomeration of bricks and stones, with an assorted collection of manufactured goods; a home is the abiding-place of ardent affection, of fervent hope, of genial trust. There is many a homeless man who lives in a richly furnished house. There is many a fifteen-pound house in the crowded street which is an illuminated and beautiful home. The sumptuously furnished house may only be an exquisitely sculptured tomb; the scantily furnished house may be the very hearthstone of the eternal God. Now the Christian religion claims to be able to convert houses into homes, to supply the missing fire, and to bring an aspiring flame to the cold and chilling heap. The New Testament does not say very much about homes; it says a great deal about the things that make them. It speaks about life and love and joy and peace and rest! If we get a house and put these into it, we shall have secured a home.

John Henry Jowett

570   *THE MEASURE OF A HOME*

A London magazine one time asked its subscribers to define a home. Out of the nearly one thousand replies six were selected as the best definitions of a home:

Home—a world of strife shut out, a world of love shut in.

Home—a place where the small are great, and the great are small.

Home—the father's kingdom, the mother's world, and the child's paradise.

Home—the place where we grumble the most and are treated the best.

Home—the center of our affection, round which our heart's best wishes twine.

Home—the place where our stomachs get three square meals a day and our hearts a thousand.

A home is all this, but a great deal more. It is important that newspapers and advertisers center the attention of people on the home. It is very much more important that the church magnify the Christian measure and meaning of home life. For the American home, the guardian of much that we hold dear, is seriously threatened and needs the moral and spiritual undergirding of the Christian gospel.

Charles M. Crowe

571   *HOW TO BUILD A HOUSE*

The walls of a house are not built of wood, brick or stone, but of truth and loyalty.

Unpleasant sounds, the friction of living, the clash of personalities, are not deadened by Persian rugs or polished floors, but by conciliation, concession, and self-control. . . .

The house is not a structure where bodies meet, but a hearthstone upon which flames mingle, separate flames of souls, which, the more perfectly they unite, the more clearly they shine and the straighter they rise toward heaven.

Your house is your fortress in a warring world, where a woman's hand buckles on your armour in the morning and soothes your fatigue and wounds at night.

The beauty of a house is harmony.

The security of a house is loyalty.

The joy of a house is love.

The plenty of a house is in children.

The rule of a house is service.

The comfort of a house is in contented spirits. . . .

The maker of a house, of a real human house, is God himself, the same who made the stars and built the world.

Frank Crane

572   *MY HOME*

(A Paraphrase of 1 co. 13)

My home may be made beautiful by the wealth of the world, but if it has not love, it is only an empty shell.

My home may be the rendezvous of the witty and the meeting place of the wise, but if it has not love, it is only a noisy house.

My home may distribute its welcome to men of every estate, my home may toil for the betterment of all mankind, but if it has not love its influence will soon vanish.

The spirit of a true home is very patient, very kind, it knows no jealousy, makes no parade, gives itself no airs, is never rude, never selfish, never irritated, never resentful. It is never gladdened when sorrow comes to another home, is made happy by goodness, always slow to talk with others about the intimacies of the home, always eager to believe the best, always hopeful, always enduring. The home will never disappear. As for civilizations, they will be superseded; as for knowledge, it will grow out of date; as for institutions, they will cease. For we only know a little now and we can see only dimly into the future, but when the spirit of a true home rules the affairs of this earth, then will be established the perfect Kingdom of God. Thus faith and hope and love last on forever in our homes, these three, but the greatest of all is love.

Robert W. Burns

573   *OUR HOME*

We believe that our home has a personality. It is not the wood and the stone that makes a home, but the folks who live within—the way they live together, the way they live with their neighbors, the way they live with God. This constitutes the personality of the home.

We believe that the keystone which holds our home together is the spirit of true love, a love that will deepen and broaden through the years. Without this love, the windows will be dark, and no fire will burn within.

We believe that wisdom and common sense should help true love govern our home. Love alone may often be blind, but wisdom and common sense furnish two good eyes that help love find the right pathway.

We believe that our home should be honest. It is not a place for sham or make-believe living. Genuineness and sincerity should be practiced by those within and seen by those without.

We believe that our home should be a place in which peace and harmony touch all lives that step over the threshold. Harsh words, uncontrolled temper, sullen dispositions—all these are unwelcomed guests.

We believe that our home is one of the important departments in this great school called life. It is here that we first learn the fine art of living together. Those who cannot learn how to live together within the home will find the world too crowded outside.

We believe that our home can be a temple made holy by the spirit of the living God, and blessed by the presence of Jesus Christ. Then, and then only, will a warm light glow within and all the storm from without will not destroy our home.

Quentin T. Lightner

574   *FOUNDATION OF HOME*

Christ at the marriage altar.
Christ on the bridal journey.
Christ when the new home is set up.
Christ when the baby comes.
Christ when the baby dies.
Christ in the pinching times.
Christ when the wedded pair walk
        toward the sunset gates.
Christ for time, Christ for eternity—
    This is the foundation of home.

Protestant Episcopal Marriage Commission

575   *AN EVERLASTING ANCHORAGE*

When a man achieves a fair measure of harmony within himself and his family circle, he achieves peace; and a nation made up of such individuals and groups is a happy nation. As the harmony of a star in its course is expressed by rhythm and grace, so the harmony of a man's life-course is expressed by happiness. . . .

At the end only two things really matter to a man, regardless of who he is; and they are the affection and understanding of his family. Anything and everything else he creates are insubstantial; they are ships given over to the mercy of the winds and tides of prejudice. But the family is an everlasting anchorage, a quiet harbor where a man's ships can be left to swing in the moorings of pride and loyalty.

Richard E. Byrd

576   *CHARLES KINGSLEY'S HOME LIFE*

Home [writes his wife] was to him the sweetest, fairest, most romantic thing in life; and there all that was best and brightest in him shone with steady and purest luster. I would speak of his chivalry—for I can call it nothing else— in daily life—a chivalry which clothed the most ordinary and commonplace duties with freshness and pleasantness. No fatigue was too great to make him forget the courtesy of less wearied moments, no business too engrossing to deprive him of his readiness to show kindness and sympathy. To school himself to this code of unfaltering high and noble living was the great work of a self-discipline so constant that to many people, even of noble temperament, it might appear quixotic. He always seemed content with the society he was in, because he educated himself to draw out the best of every one, and touch on their stronger, and not weaker, points. Justice and mercy, and that self-control which kept him from speaking a hasty word or harboring a mean suspicion, combined with a divine tenderness, were his governing principles in all his home relationships.

577   *PERFECT PICTURE OF A HOME*

Give me the privilege of reading the names of your guests, the friends whom you delight to have in your house, the privilege of seeing the titles of the books on the shelves of your library, the magazines you permit to come into your home, to listen to your conversations when you do not know you are being overheard, allow me to say a word or two, to put a pointed question to the servants in your household. Then permit me to talk to your chosen friends. And then I will give you a perfect picture of your home, though I may not be personally acquainted with you. I will tell you what you have been in the past, what you are at the present, and what you will be in the future. What you have in your home really determines what your home is.

J. Wilbur Chapman

578   *THE LOVE WITHOUT DEMAND*

What does it mean, to love? It means to place another at the center of one's life. Do I love my child? I do if my child matters to me more than I matter to myself, if I regard myself as existing to make it possible for the child to come to a good maturity. If this desire is lacking in me, if what I chiefly desire is rather that my child shall amuse me and serve me, or, even worse, that my child shall not bother me, shall not prevent my doing as I please, when I please, then I do not love my child; I love myself. Do I love my friend? I do if I am willing to be to that friend a servant of that friend's sustenance, looking on that friend with thought not of what that friend may do for me but of what I may do for that friend. Do I love my wife or husband? Only on terms of self-investment does even conjugality release me from that enslavement to myself which is the chief cause of human woe, which is indeed the essence of damnation.

In our day the word "love" is greatly abused. "I am in love," we say, and mean by this that we wish to be loved. Now being loved is a pleasant experience, but it is not a necessary one. "To be loved"—that is passive voice. I do nothing. I sit serene, complacent, somnolent, while some one loves me. To love is not a passive thing. "To love" is active voice. When I love I do something, I function, I give. I do not love in order that I may be loved back again, but for the creative joy of loving. And every time I do so love I am freed, at least a little, by the outgoing of love, from enslavement to that most intolerable of masters, myself.

My beloved, my parent, my child, my friend, my mate, may or may not love me in return, or may once have loved me in return but have ceased to love me in return. That does not fatally matter. If he or she does not love in return, I still can love. "If ye love only them that love you, what profit is that to anyone?" asks Jesus. "I say to you, Love even them that are your enemies, them that reject you, treat you with contempt. So shall you become the children of the Eternal Father." *No one can take away from me the one great treasure, the love I bear without demand of love.* The beloved may reject, hate, kill; but there is one thing the beloved who spurns my love can never do. He or she can never break my heart. When one cries out that the beloved has broken one's heart, it is not love that has caused the heartbreak. It is rather disappointed self-esteem.

Bernard Iddings Bell

579   MARRIAGE MUDDLES

[The] twain shall be one flesh. MAT. 19:5

A marriage may be a masterpiece, a mixture or a muddle. Most marriages are mixtures, too many are muddles and some are tragedies. A marriage rests on the love of a man and woman, and the kind of people they are.

The things that make marriage a muddle are the things that make life itself a muddle. Only in marriage they are more acutely felt, because marriage is the most consecrated form of human fellowship. It is a school of character, a test of living, and only adults should undertake it.

Joseph Fort Newton

580   DOMESTIC SYMBOLISMS

The home, first of all, is God's theological seminary. It is here that he most fittingly and powerfully explains himself. He takes the relationships of the home and makes them the tutors and teachers of his own character and personality. "Like as a father pitieth his children . . ." and we understand the pity of God in a father's love, his easy forgiveness of our mischief, his constant daily provision and the fact that his heart is like a barometer indicating all the storms that touch our lives. "As one whom his mother comforteth, so will I comfort you . . ." and through a mother's compassion and understanding we better see and understand the illimitable love of God. Christ "sticketh closer than a brother," and it is true that through the unselfish, fraternal love of the household we understand that unquenchable love of Christ. "Husbands love your wives, even as Christ also loved the church and gave himself for it." We should be able, through the experience of marriage, to come to an appreciation of the high relationship that Christ sustains to his church. To some this relationship thus becomes beautiful; to others it has become a chamber of horrors. You see that by domestic symbolisms God wishes to explain himself. Therefore, when you destroy a home you destroy a theological seminary, a university in which the soul goes to school to God.

Louis H. Evans

581 *THE CHURCH IN THY HOUSE*

I do not know why it is that many of us are so terribly afraid of sharing any religious experience with those we love best. I suppose it is in part a natural unwillingness to bare our deepest thoughts to anyone and in part a fear that knowing what we actually are, the family will find incredible what we tell God we really want to be. But whatever the reason for our reluctance, with the rarest of exceptions we shall not reach our full stature in the Christian life until we reach it in the company of those most near and dear to us. Something happens when the members of a family lift their hearts to God in prayer together, when each member takes his turn in voicing to God the deepest yearning of his soul for each of them and all of them. Something happens when the members of a family read the Bible together, when they discuss the Christian faith together, when they speak together of the life which God wants each of them to live. In his letter to his well-beloved brother Philemon, Paul sends his greeting to the "church in thy house," and that is what the Christian family ought itself to be. It ought to be a church in your own house —a worshiping church, a learning church, a serving church, a church whose members are together moving ever forward in the knowledge of God and the love of God.

Roy M. Pearson

582   *TEN COMMANDMENTS FOR MODERN PARENTS*

I. Give your children the support of love and confidence, with appreciation of the individuality of each. This will provide for them a firm foundation of faith in you, in themselves and in life.

II. Plan for good times with your children and try always to realize how things seem to a child. This will create a pleasant home atmosphere and a pattern for happy family life.

III. Give your children a share in the tasks, plans and creative activities of the home. Through taking responsibilities in accordance with their strength they will grow in character and increase in resourcefulness.

IV. Look for good which you can praise more than for faults which you must condemn. Children generously encouraged try to improve still more, but those too much condemned lose heart and expect little good of themselves.

V. Value curiosity in your children and stimulate in them the love of all things true and beautiful. By rewarding their inquiries and developing their appreciations you inspire them to a larger growth.

VI. Teach your children to convert obstacles into opportunities. Strength develops by firm purpose and by creative conquest of difficulty.

VII. Develop in yourself such qualities as you want your children to have. Honesty, considerateness, courage—such virtues come mainly by example and contagion. You want vital growth not mere conformity.

VIII. Make your home a center of friendship and good neighborliness. Its ties of comradeship will prepare members for good citizenship in the community, the nation and the world.

IX. Share with your children in the fellowship of the church. This will give them the sustaining strength of a community of faith and love which extends across the ages and embraces all peoples.

X. Lead your children into faith in God through discipleship to Jesus Christ that they may be workers with God in overcoming evil and promoting the good. This will be aided by thought-sharing, religious interpretation and worship in the home, and by living in the great purposes of the Kingdom of God.

National Council

583   *THE FATEFUL MISSION OF THE HOME*

The arresting and somewhat terrifying fact about the home is that in it new human beings are wholly at the disposal of the old. The child may come trailing clouds of glory; but what happens to these largely depends upon the adults who have the child in their control: who both lay down the initial rules for his behavior and build his first expectations about life.

No social institution is more fateful for the human race than the home. In it the primary shaping of character takes place. In a good home, maturing gets quickly under way: the child is helped to grow from stage to stage of confidence, skill, affection, responsibility, and understanding. The "light of common day" into which he grows has its own permanent radiance: it does not dissipate his clouds of glory.

Harry A. Overstreet

584 *JESUS AND THE FAMILY*

Jesus' teaching on the family may be summarized as follows:

(1) The family is an institution ordained of God (Mk. 10:6–9).

(2) Divorce is not permissible (Mk. 10:11–12; Mat. 5:32; Lu. 16:18). The exception made in Mat. 5:32—"except on the ground of unchastity" (RSV)— is probably a later interpolation.

(3) Duty to parents demands that they shall be cared for in old age; this is a prior responsibility (Mk. 7:9–13).

(4) Supreme loyalty belongs to God, not to family (Mat. 10:37; Lu. 14:26).

(5) Those are kindred who "hear the word of God and do it." They are united in the bonds of a common faith and devotion.

Ernest Fremont Tittle

B. MOTHER'S DAY

Mother's Day was first celebrated in Philadelphia in 1908. By 1914 it had become a national day for the honoring of mothers. It seems proper that the Festival of the Christian Home should be observed at the same services which single out the mothers for special tribute.

Calls to Worship

(Boldface type indicates responses.)

585　I will extol thee, my God, O king; and I will bless thy name for ever and ever.
Every day will I bless thee; and I will praise thy name for ever and ever.
Great is the Lord, and greatly to be praised; and his greatness is unsearchable.
One generation shall praise thy works to another, and shall declare thy mighty acts.

Ps. 145:1-4

586　Hearken unto me, ye that know righteousness, the people in whose heart is my law. My righteousness shall be for ever, and my salvation from generation to generation.

Is. 51:7-8

587　This is my commandment, That ye love one another, as I have loved you. Greater love hath no man than this, that a man lay down his life for his friends. Ye are my friends, if ye do whatsoever I command you.

Jn. 15:12-14

Invocations

588　O God, who hast built up thy church through the divers gifts and graces of thy faithful servants: we give thee humble thanks for the example of devoted women, and especially, this day, for our mothers; and we beseech thee to maintain among us the shelter of a mother's love and the protection of a mother's prayer; in the name of thy Son, Jesus Christ our Lord. Amen.

Author Unknown

589   Almighty God, of whose love our love was born, and in whom they dwell who dwell in love: grant, we beseech thee, that love may furnish us with heavenly understanding, and understanding lift and purify our love; that our hearts in truth may be thy temple, and our homes may glorify thy name; through Jesus Christ our Lord. Amen.

John Underwood Stephens

590   Our Father, varied are thy calls that surely lead us to thee, and set our feet upon life's upper paths, amid exalted bliss. We praise thee for hallowed moments, and holy places, and sacred bonds. This morning the tender and loving call of mother sends forth its rapturous note. By everything that is divine and undying—in the wide sweep and intimate grip of motherland—enkindle our minds, warm our hearts, flood our souls, and quicken the spiritual pulse of our better natures; in Jesus' name. Amen.

Herman Paul Guhsé

Litany

(Boldface type indicates responses.)

591   Almighty and everlasting God, before whom stand the spirits of the living and the dead, Light of lights, Fountain of wisdom and goodness, who dwellest in all brave and generous souls:
Hear thou our prayer of praise.
For the women who have gone before us, seers of visions and doers of deeds, pioneers of freedom and pathfinders of humanity, leaders of a great cause, builders of a better world:
We praise thee, O God.
For their clear vision of the wrong of all distinction because of color, creed or sex, their righteous anger against all oppression of the weak and exploitation of the helpless, their stern struggle against all injustice and hardness of heart:
We praise thee, O God.
For their passionate pity for the joyless, their compassion for all scorned and crushed, their swift responsiveness to every cry of need:
We praise thee, O God.
For the inspired audacity of their ambitions, the sturdy wisdom of their endeavors, the abiding values of their achievements:
We praise thee, O God.
For their deathless spirits, living still in poem and story, statue, painting and song; for their sense of the beauty and meaning of life expressed in glorious form and symbol:

We praise thee, O God.

For homes they have made, for their gifts to little children, and to family joy; for their daily lives, obscure and unknown, renowned and reverenced:

We praise thee, O God.

For their perseverance amid discouragement and failures, their steadfastness amid misunderstanding and ridicule, their dauntless courage amid loneliness and the contempt of men:

We praise thee, O God.

For all the blessings that we know today, for freedom and knowledge, for opportunity and responsibility, for all our experience of abundant life, for which they paid the price:

We praise thee, O God.

That we may be humble in the consciousness of how much we have received, how little we have given; that we may be contrite in the memory of our failures and the knowledge of our temptations to cowardice and ease; that we may ever seek the things that are before, with courage and devotion:

We earnestly pray thee.

That we may think bravely, love widely, witness humbly, build greatly:

We earnestly pray thee. Amen.*

A Book of Services for Group Worship

Prayers

592   Our heavenly Father, our prayer today is one of thanksgiving for the dearest of all thy blessings and gifts to us—for the dear mothers whose love, of all human loves, is most like thine own divine love.

We pray that whatever our mothers may need in body, mind and spirit to enable them to perform faithfully their sweet and loving duties to their children may be given to them; and hasten thou the day when all the children of earth shall have the blessing of true Christian mothers.

For the beauty and fragrance of the red and white roses that bloom in our gardens, we thank thee, but infinitely more do we thank thee for those dear ones whose moral beauty and purity are symbolized in these sweet flowers which we wear as emblems of love and remembrance today.

Nor do we forget to remember in this our prayer our fathers and brothers and sisters, and to beseech thee to help us all so to live that our family circles shall at the last be complete in heaven, and that we may find where God and our loved ones are our happy and eternal home. These and all our blessings we ask in Jesus' name. Amen.

Wilbur F. Tillett

593 O God, who didst create mothers to a high and holy duty, we thank thee for the example of the beautiful life of the mother of the Savior and for the example of Christ's devotion to his mother. Open the eyes of mothers everywhere that they may see not only the drudgery of housework and the exacting demands of rearing children, but especially the blessed privilege that is theirs in the opportunity of making the next generation more Christian than theirs and in bringing little ones to thee and to the Savior. Where we as children have failed to heed the Christian counsel of our parents, or have refused to walk the Christian way they showed us how to walk, forgive us for Jesus' sake. Where we as parents have failed to teach our children of thee as a loving Father, of Christ as a forgiving Savior, and of thy will, forgive us for Jesus' sake. Comfort the parents whose hearts are grieved by wayward children and let such children quickly see the folly of their ways. Let mothers and children who are separated find comfort in the knowledge that thou dost watch over them all. Bless all mothers richly and let them be a blessing to their children; through Jesus Christ our Lord. Amen.

Armin C. Oldsen

594 Our Father God, may the altar flowers be theirs today. Thou hast let them share with thee in the mysterious labor of creation and entrusted them with an indestructible love resembling thine.

Throughout all time thou hast taught them to bear the dread and agony of their life-giving task without complaint. Thou hast endowed them with divine sympathy to understand childhood's foolish fears, flashing rages, dismaying greeds, and careless responses to costly devotion. At thy feet they have interpreted the mounting insubordination of their liberty-questing sons and the smiling condescensions of their flowering daughters, aware that each passing generation must quickly yield its scepter to another in the cause of progress.

We thank thee for the valor displayed by mothers in bewildered eras when the keepers of the house tremble. We rejoice in the prescience with which they discern new duties in new occasions. Hearten them, we beseech thee, in this troubled time. With faith-empowered poise may they soothe their children's unrest. Grant them the greatness of heart to glimpse a rescuing justice in the impending redistribution of human privileges. Enable them to teach their ambitious sons that comfort for many is better than luxury for some.

At this hour when, indignant over age-old hypocrisies and long-sanctioned shams, the new generation clamors for truth and candor, make all mothers keenly sensitive to the embarrassing demands of integrity. Strengthen their passionate cries for peace. Reassure them that all things work together for good in the lives of those who love thee. And make their calmness ours. Amen.

Lloyd C. Douglas

595   We bless thee for the great and precious ideal of motherhood. We praise thee for the present joy and the lasting influence of all good mothers. We think of the noble women all over the world and in all times who have prayed God to bless them with children, and then have prayed him to bless their children. We thank thee, our heavenly Father, for the mothers who freely offered themselves that we might live. We think of their love and their loyalty, their gentleness and their strength, their kindness and care, their sacrifice and patience. Help us, O God, to honor them by our thoughts, by our words, by our actions, by our appreciation and by our gratitude. Help us so to learn and grow and live that we may become the fulfilling of our mother's desires and prayers for us. May we be kind to them as they have been kind to us; may we help them as they have helped us. Amen.

Songs of Work and Worship

Poems

596   *THE MOTHER IN THE HOUSE*

For such as you, I do believe,
Spirits their softest carpets weave,
And spread them out with gracious hand
Wherever you walk, wherever you stand.

For such as you, of scent and dew,
Spirits their rarest nectar brew,
And where you sit and where you sup
Pour beauty's elixir in your cup.

For all day long, like other folk,
You bear the burdens, wear the yoke,
And yet when I look in your eyes at eve
You are lovelier than ever, I do believe.

Hermann Hagedorn

597   *From LOVE'S LANTERN*

Because the way was steep and long,
And through a dark and dreary land,
God set upon her lips a song
And placed a lantern in her hand.

Joyce Kilmer

598   *TRIBUTE*

    Thine is the strong and solemn glow,
    Thine is the sweet transcendent grace,
    Of her whose love, through weal and woe,
      Lights her transfigured face.
    Where hope is high and thought is free,
    Where life is brave and death is true,
    Where duty unrelenting leads
    To tasks of pain forever new
    The heart that triumphs while it bleeds,
      Mother, thy face we see.
                       LeBaron Russell Briggs

599   *From THE PRINCESS (Pt. 7)*

               I loved her, one
    Not learned, save in gracious household ways,
    Not perfect, nay, but full of tender wants,
    No angel, but a dearer being, all dipt
    In angel instincts, breathing Paradise,
    Interpreter between the gods and men,
    Who look'd all native to her place, and yet
    On tiptoe seem'd to touch upon a sphere
    Too gross to tread, and all male minds perforce
    Sway'd to her from their orbits as they moved,
    And girdled her with music. Happy he
    With such a mother! faith in womankind
    Beats in his blood, and trust in all things high
    Comes easy to him, and tho' he trip and fall
    He shall not blind his soul with clay.
                         Alfred Tennyson

600   *THE PARTNERSHIP WITH GOD*

  The partnership with God is Motherhood,
    What strength, what purity, what self-control,
  What love, what wisdom shall belong to her
    Who helps God fashion an immortal soul.
                       Author Unknown

601   *THE HOLY WOMEN*

I have seen Mary at the Cross
    And Mary at the tomb
And Mary weeping as she spread her hair
    In a leper's room.

But it was not in Bethany
    Or groping up Calvary hill
I learned how women break their hearts to ease
    Another's ill.

Compassionate and wise in pain,
    Most faithful in defeat,
The holy Marys I have watched and loved
    Live on our street.

William Alexander Percy

602   *THE MOTHER'S HYMN*

Lord who ordainest for mankind
    Benignant toils and tender cares!
We thank thee for the ties that bind
    The mother to the child she bears.

We thank thee for the hopes that rise,
    Within her heart, as, day by day,
The dawning soul, from those young eyes,
    Looks with a clearer steadier ray.

And grateful for the blessing given
    With that dear infant on her knee,
She trains the eye to look to heaven,
    The voice to lisp a prayer to thee.

Such thanks the blessed Mary gave,
    When from her lap the holy Child,
Sent from on high to seek and save
    The lost of earth, looked up and smiled.

All-Gracious! grant to those who bear
A mother's charge, the strength and light
To lead the steps that own their care
In ways of Love and Truth and Right.
William Cullen Bryant

603   *THE HOUSEWIFE*

Jesus, teach me how to be
Proud of my simplicity.

Sweep the floors, wash the clothes,
Gather for each vase a rose.

Iron and tend a tiny frock,
Keeping one eye on the clock.

Always having time kept free
For childish questions asked of me.

Grant me wisdom Mary had
When she taught her little Lad.
Catherine Cate Coblentz

Topics, Texts and Themes

604   *MOTHERS OF THE BIBLE*

Did you ever notice the way in which the Bible honors the mothers of men?
They are placed in a hall of fame all their own. No matter whether he was a
wise or a foolish, a righteous or an evil king, his mother's name is set down.
It all runs something like this: His mother's name was Jochebed. His mother's
name was Jehoaddan. His mother's name was Zibiah. His mother's name was
Jecholiah. His mother's name was Jerusha. His mother's name was Abi. His
mother's name was Hephzibah. His mother's name was Hamutal. His mother's
name was Jedidah. His mother's name was Micaiah. His mother's name was
Elizabeth. His mother's name was Mary. You will remember that it was a
mother who said, "Grant that these my two sons may sit, the one on thy right
hand, and the other on the left, in thy kingdom." It is always so. Who else but
a mother has a right to demand that her children shall sit on thrones and be

wreathed with crowns? It is also important for us to remember that Jesus did not deny the plea, but promised to grant the request if her children would prove worthy. Sometimes a mother's prayers fail, not because of what she has been or done, but because of the unworthiness of those who refuse the crown with which their mother would crown them.

Hugh Thomson Kerr

605 GREAT HOMES OF THE BIBLE

1. The home of the independent religious leadership, Jos. 24:15. It is a great hour in a home when someone with spiritual leadership says, "We worship God; we confess Christ; we go to church."

2. The home of dedication of children to God, 1 S. 1:27–28. It would be impossible to estimate the influence for Christ and the church that has come where parents have dedicated their children to God.

3. The home of the Christian lineage, 2 Ti. 1:5. "From generation to generation," is a phrase of immortal significance. It is an unbroken line holding fast for God and his people.

4. The home of triumphant faith, Mat. 15:21–28. The mother's faith overcame silence, a strange opposition, unexpected exclusion, and pride.

5. The home near the church, Ac. 18:7. This old-time family of Titus Justus does not need any other testimony as to its relation to the house of God. Geography is not the most important matter, but spiritual nearness and sacrifices and love cover long distances and are always "near the church" today.

6. The home of Christian hospitality, Jn. 12:1–2. When every other home was closed to Jesus, the home in Bethany was always open. Christian hospitality sheds its radiance everywhere.

7. The home of salvation, Lu. 19:9. "Today is salvation come to this house." This is both the beginning, the continuing, and the never-ending blessing Christ gives to any home that looks in faith to him.

G. B. F. Hallock

606 MOTHERHOOD AND ITS IDEAL

Honour thy mother. EX. 20:12

This precept of the Decalogue has its perpetual echo and long development in the Scriptures at large. One after another there the forms of noble women, seen distinct or dim, but all beautiful with wise and honored motherhood, pass by before us. We see Hannah, and Elisheba, and the lady of Shunem, and her who taught virtue to King Lemuel; and then Elizabeth and Salome, and the

Scripture-loving Eunice with her Timothy at her knee, while white-haired Lois, the grandmother, groups herself the third with the two over the oracles of God. Supreme among them all, we contemplate the maternal Maid of Nazareth, the crowning flower of womanhood for ever, her through whom God the Son of God entered man's life and a human home, and to whom he was subject there.

Full of the mother's honor is the great book of Proverbs, that luminous manual of godly living, with its character-building power. "I was my mother's son"; "Forsake not the law of thy mother"; "A foolish man" (and only he, the witless victim of his own self-will, for such is "the fool" of the Proverbs) "despiseth his mother."

In one wonderful prophetic utterance the mother's strong consoling tenderness is taken up by the Eternal himself as the only worthy image of his own. He clasps to his infinite heart the tired and broken hearts of his human children. And lo! an ineffable maternity is found to live, and breathe, and burn in the depth of the Almighty Father's love: "As one whom his mother comforteth, so will I comfort you."

Handley C. G. Moule

607   *From THE SKETCH BOOK*

There is an enduring tenderness in the love of a mother to her son that transcends all other affections of the heart. It is neither to be chilled by selfishness, nor daunted by danger, nor weakened by worthlessness, nor stifled by ingratitude. She will sacrifice every comfort to his convenience; she will surrender every pleasure to his enjoyment; she will glory in his fame, and exult in his prosperity: and, if misfortune overtake him, he will be the dearer to her for misfortune; and if disgrace settle upon his name, she will still love and cherish him in spite of his disgrace; and if all the world beside cast him off, she will be all the world to him.

Washington Irving

608   *MOTHER OF THE WESLEYS*

Take her for all and in all, I do not believe that any human being ever brought into the world, and carried through it a larger portion of original goodness than my dear mother. Everyone who knew her loved her, for she seemed to be made to be happy herself, and to make everyone happy within her little sphere. Her understanding was as good as her heart; it is from her that I have inherited that alertness of mind and quickness of apprehension without which it would have been impossible for me to have undertaken half of what

I have performed. God never blessed a human creature with a more cheerful disposition, a more generous spirit, a sweeter temper, or a tenderer heart. I remember that when I first understood what death was, and began to think of it, the most fearful thought it induced was that of losing my mother; it seemed to me more than I could bear, and I used to hope that I might die first.

John Wesley

609   *From A BEATITUDE FOR MOTHERS*

Blessed are the mothers of yesterday, for their memories shall be called beautiful and beneficent. They are like flowers growing by sunken gardens and beside still waters and in green fields, for they are like soft winds that blow with peace and love on wistful wings.

Blessed are the mothers of today, for they have the keeping of tomorrow in their hands and in their hearts; and the destiny of nations, hearts and homes.

Blessed are the mothers of tomorrow, for they have been summoned to a great and heroic hour. For they shall be called the mothers of men, who shall make miracles of human life. The mothers of tomorrow shall breed a race of giants who handle lightning as a little thing, and make the clouds and thunder obey their wills. Blessed are the mothers of tomorrow.

Blessed are the mothers of scientists and statesmen; of laborers and poets; of preachers and prophets; of teachers and dreamers; for dreams and visions and prophecies and the glow and glory of creation is born in the hearts of mothers.

Blessed are the mothers, for they are conservers of the human race. Blessed are the mothers, for they forced the nomadic tribes to settle in a permanent community that the young might be served and saved. Blessed are the mothers, for they taught barbarian ancestors to grow grains and build shelters. Blessed are the mothers of the world, for they have conserved the spiritual things of life for the sake of their children.

Blessed are the mothers of the earth, for they have combined the practical and the spiritual into one workable way of human life. They have darned little stockings, mended little dresses, washed little faces, and have pointed little eyes to the stars, and little souls to eternal things. Blessed are the mothers.

William L. Stidger

610   *A MOTHER'S CREED*

I believe in the eternal importance of the home as the fundamental institution of society.

I believe in the immeasurable possibilities of every boy and girl.

I believe in the imagination, the trust, the hopes and the ideals which dwell in the hearts of all children.

I believe in the beauty of nature, of art, of books and of friendship.

I believe in the satisfactions of duty.

I believe in the little homely joys of every-day life.

I believe in the goodness of the great design which lies behind our complex world.

I believe in the safety and peace which surround us all through the over-brooding love of God.

Ozora Davis

611   *THE DIVINE MOTHERHOOD*

But Mary kept all these things, and pondered them in her heart. LU. 2:19

Motherhood, even on the subhuman levels, has elements of nobility and beauty. The bird hovering over its nest in the fields, the very tiger in the jungle, will reveal the passionate devotion of the mother to the young which risks life itself in order that its young may be protected. All along the march of evolution motherhood behaves that way. It can be tender and fierce, protecting and passionate. When it loves, it does not count the cost. It risks anything, dares anything, gives everything. On the human level, most men know that about their mothers. She is the one who has loved them beyond all question of whether they have deserved her love. She is the one who unfailingly will stand by them, no matter which others fail.

But it is also true that the highest type of motherhood is that into which the religious element enters. The mere instinct of motherhood may fail. Everyone has seen some woman treat a child with petulant anger—seen a woman snatch her child after her on the street when the child lagged behind to look at something in a shopwindow, slap a child on the subway or on a railroad train because it fretted, shake a child and scream threats into its ear if it has disobeyed. A woman who is a mother only in the biological sense may defend her child in a crisis, but be stupid and unimaginative and unconsciously cruel in ordinary times. It takes religion to lift motherhood into dependable beauty, for religion gives the background of divine consciousness against which the life of a child is set. Religion makes the mother know that her child is a soul, sensitive to blessing, sensitive to hurt. Religion gives reverence for personality because the child is accounted as a gift from God. To the uninspired mother the child may seem no more than a bundle of annoying appetites and restless energies. It is only the mother whose soul is disciplined before the highest who can be gentle and patient through times of annoyance and weariness. For such a mother a child's needs and a child's demands do not produce irritation. They send her to the source from which she finds her strength.

Walter Russell Bowie

612   THE MOTHERHOOD OF GOD

As one whom his mother comforteth, so will I comfort you. is. 66:13

"Father" is the usual term which expresses for us God's tenderness and love. Isaiah's word is not, however, a unique one. The same thought appears elsewhere in Scripture. In Deuteronomy it is the mother eagle who beareth her young upon her wings. The sheltering, shadowing wings in the Psalms is a mother figure. The literal rendering of Acts 13:18 is: "About the time of forty years he fed them as a nurse feedeth her child."

God comforts and instructs with a mother's patience. Like a mother, he stoops to the child mind. Where he cannot teach us to read he gives us picture books, setting before us a snow-crowned mountain, a "flower in the crannied wall," an altar of gold and white, a communion table. He comforts with a mother's partiality for the neediest.

He has a mother's patience for the erring. When a man goes wrong—yes even if he were to be "hanging on the highest hill"—his mother waits and hopes. God's love is like that, but goes beyond. "When my father and mother forsake me, then the Lord will take me up."

One would scarcely expect Paul to see the mother side of God, yet he writes to the Thessalonians: "Them also which sleep in Jesus will God bring with him." Like tired children at the close of day, they are hushed to sleep in mothering arms and laid in bed—until morning.

"As one whom his mother comforteth," such is our assurance of the divine compassion.

Daniel Russell

613   JESUS' ATTITUDE TOWARD WOMEN

One side of the work of Jesus must never be forgotten. His attitude to woman has altered her position in the world. No one can study society in classical antiquity or in non-Christian lands with any intimacy and not realize this. Widowhood in Hinduism, marriage among Mohammedans—they are proverbs for the misery of women. Even the Jew still prays: "Blessed art thou, O Lord our God! King of the Universe, who hast not made me a woman." . . .

There is no reference made by Jesus to woman that is not respectful and sympathetic; he never warns men against women. Even the most degraded women find in him an amazing sympathy; for he has the secret of being pure and kind at the same time—his purity has not to be protected; it is itself a purifying force. . . .

Critics have remarked on the place of woman in Luke's Gospel, and some have played with fancies as to the feminine sources whence he drew his knowledge—did the women who ministered to Jesus, Joanna, for instance, the wife of Chuza, tell him these illuminative stories of the Master? In any case Jesus' new attitude to woman is in the record; and it has so reshaped the thought of mankind, and made it so hard to imagine anything else, that we do not readily grasp what a revolution he made—here as always by referring men's thoughts back to the standard of God's thoughts, and supporting what he taught by what he was.

T. R. Glover

C. CHILDREN'S DAY

Children's Day is usually the second Sunday in June and focuses attention not only on the work with children in the local church but also the church's ministry to children throughout the world. The day is particularly appropriate for the dedication and baptism of children and for the promotion of children from one department to another in the Sunday school.

Calls to Worship

614   Give ear, O my people, to my law: incline your ears to the words of my mouth . . . which we have heard and known, and our fathers have told us. We will not hide them from their children, shewing to the generation to come the praises of the Lord, and his strength, and his wonderful works that he hath done.

Ps. 78:1, 3-4

615   Verily I say unto you, Except ye be converted, and become as little children, ye shall not enter into the kingdom of heaven. Whosoever therefore shall humble himself as this little child, the same is greatest in the kingdom of heaven. And whoso shall receive one such little child in my name receiveth me.

Mat. 18:3-5

616   If any man desire to be first, the same shall be last of all, and servant of all. And he took a child, and set him in the midst of them: and when he had taken him in his arms, he said unto them, Whosoever shall receive one of such children in my name, receiveth me: and whosoever shall receive me, receiveth not me, but him that sent me.

Mk. 9:35-37

Invocations

617   Almighty God, our heavenly Father, who hast committed to thy holy church the care and nurture of thy children: enlighten with thy wisdom those who teach and those who learn, that, rejoicing in the knowledge of thy truth, we may worship thee and serve thee from generation to generation; through Jesus Christ our Lord. Amen.

John Wallace Suter

618 O Lord Jesus, thou great Shepherd of the sheep: look on these thy children; embrace them with the arms of thy mercy, pour on them the riches of thy blessing, and so fill them with thy manifold gifts of grace that they may continue thine for ever; to the honor and glory of thy name. Amen.

Book of English Collects

619 O Saviour, meek and lowly of heart, let not our pride refuse thy bidding, to become as little children, in joy and simplicity, in trustfulness one toward another, in lowliness of heart; and by this thine own glory, bring us unto ours; for thy majesty and thy mercy's sake. Amen.

Cambridge Bede Book

Litany

(Boldface type indicates responses.)

620 O God of love, we come to thee this day as children to a loving Father. As in the days of long ago Jesus laid his hands on little children and blessed them, so bless each one of us. Bless all children in lands far and near who have not heard of thee. Make thyself known to them that they may not grow up in fear and ignorance and sin:

Hear us, heavenly Father.

Forgive us for the evil we have thought and said and done. Sometimes we think unkindly of others, speak angry words, and do things that are mean and selfish. Help us to remember that these things grieve thee and sadden others. Make us sorry for our sins and help us to grow wiser and better:

Hear us, heavenly Father.

We thank thee for sending Jesus Christ to reveal thy love, and to show us how we may serve thee. We thank thee for his teaching and the beauty of his life. May we learn of him, follow him, and, by the help of thy Spirit, become more like him!

Hear us, heavenly Father.

We praise thee for our happy homes, for this favored land in which we live, and for all the brave, wise, and good men and women through whose service and sacrifice our country has been made great and free. Teach us to love their memory, and, like them, to strive earnestly for that which is true and right. God bless our President and all who are chosen to govern us, and make this nation a blessing to all the nations of the earth:

Hear us, heavenly Father.

Father of all, in our health and gladness we would remember the many who are sorrowful and those who suffer pain. We pray for all sick children, for children who have neither father nor mother to love them, and for all men and women who are in trouble. In thy great kindness, comfort and help them as thou knowest best:

We beseech thee, hear us, heavenly Father.

Intercession Services

Prayers

621 Almighty and most merciful Father, who claimest the children for thy heritage: bless, we beseech thee, these boys and girls who have come to thy house this day. As they take part in this service may they feel that thou art near them and art their Friend. In the days of their youth may they remember thee, and as the years multiply may they grow in the knowledge of thee and of thy Son Jesus Christ. Help them to choose the better way which Jesus revealed, that both in this life and in the life to come they may know the joy and peace which come to those who walk with thee. Bless us who have traveled farther along life's way. Renew in us the faith and the purity of childhood that we may enter again, in some measure at least, into the world of wonder and purity which is theirs. Amen.

James Dalton Morrison

622 O thou Ruler of the universe, Maker of suns and stars, Creator of the myriad forms of life that dwell upon the earth and throng the sea: we, humbled by the majesty of thy creation, come seeking thee. We are deeply conscious of our need of thee—thy wisdom, thy patience, and thy understanding love. For we, too, O God, are creators. We are parents. We have dared to cause a child to live. Upon the road of life we have placed its feet; into its tiny body we have put our physical weakness and our strength; even into its mind and soul have gone the tendencies that mark our own; the language we speak, our race, our color, even the creed that we profess, we have bequeathed to our child.

Standing in the presence of thy creation thou hast no fear, for thou art God. But as we look upon this our child whom we have made to live, our hearts are often fearful. What if we fail him? What if we prove false guides, and following us he misses the way?

Guide us, O our God. For this child's sake, take from our hearts all selfishness and false ambition; give us courage to follow high ideals of truth and honor; help us daily to surround him with sympathy and security that he may know the joys of happy childhood and enter upon the pathway of youth with enthusiasm and confidence.

O God, for the sake of this child whom we have created, help us to make a world in which he can find justice, freedom and peace. Give us unflinching courage as we battle against man's greed for goods and gold, and his passion for power. Help us, we pray, to face bravely the truth that only as all childhood is happy and free in a world of good will, can life at its best be the certain possession of this our child.

In the spirit of our Lord Jesus Christ who has revealed to us thy loving concern for all they creation, we come to thee, our Creator and our God. Amen.

Margaret Slattery

623   We praise thee, O God, for the little children given into our keeping. For their purity of heart, their constant simplicity, their natural and trusting affection, and for the wonderful comfort and joy they bring to us, we praise and bless thy glorious name. Continue, we beseech thee, thy protection to them; and grant to us such a measure of thy Spirit that we may work together with thee for their good.

We remember before thee the many children who are now denied a fair chance in life, all who are hindered by a bad environment, all who are made to toil at an early age, all who are unwanted, neglected, and ill-treated. Make haste, O Lord, for the help of these thy little ones. Suffer us not to add to their burden, or to leave them without a champion for their cause. Fill us with thy holy wrath toward the things whereby they are bruised and afflicted, and by thy great compassion bring us swiftly to their aid. All which we ask in the name of him who took little children in his arms and laid his hands upon them in blessing, thy Son Jesus Christ our Lord. Amen.

Ernest Fremont Tittle

624   *A BOY'S PRAYER*

Give me clean hands, clean words, and clear thoughts; help me to stand for the hard right against the easy wrong; save me from habits that harm; teach me to work as hard and play as fair in thy sight alone as if all the world saw; forgive me when I am unkind; and help me to forgive those who are unkind to me; keep me ready to help others at some cost to myself; send me chances to do a little good every day, and to grow more like Christ. Amen.

William DeWitt Hyde

625   *A PARENT'S PRAYER*

I have a boy to bring up:

Help me to perform my task with wisdom and kindness and good cheer. Help me always to see him clearly, as he is. Let not my pride in him hide his faults.

Let not my fear for him magnify my doubts and fears until I make him doubting and fearful in his turn. Quicken my judgment so that I shall know how to train him to think as a child, to be in all things pure and simple as a child.

I have a boy to bring up:

Give me great patience and a long memory. Let me remember the hard places in my own youth, so that I may help when I see him struggling as I struggled then. Let me remember the things that made me glad, lest I, sweating in the toil and strain of life, forget that a little child's laughter is the light of life.

I have a boy to bring up:

Teach me that love that understandeth all things; the love that knows no weakness, tolerates no selfishness. Keep me from weakening my son through granting him pleasures that end in pain, ease of body that must bring sickness of soul, a vision of life that must end in death. Grant that I may love my son wisely and myself not at all.

I have a boy to bring up:

Give him the values and beauty and just rewards of industry. Give him an understanding brain and hands that are cunning, to work out his happiness.

I have a boy to bring up:

Help me to send him into the world with a mission of service. Strengthen my mind and heart that I may teach him that he is his brother's keeper. Grant that he may serve those who know not the need of service, and not knowing, need it the most.

I have a boy to bring up:

So guide and direct me that I may do this service to the glory of God, the service of my country, and to my son's happiness. Amen.

Angelo Patri

Poems

626   *From CHILD-SONGS*

We need love's tender lessons taught
   As only weakness can;
God hath his small interpreters;
   The child must teach the man.

John Greenleaf Whittier

627   THE KINGDOM

"Where is the Kingdom?" asked the pompous priest,
Weighted with lore, and spent with fast and feast.
The lowly Christ on his pretensions smiled,
And simply said, "In the heart of a little child."

                                         Thomas Curtis Clark

628   *From* THE CHILDREN

They are idols of the hearts and of households;
    They are angels of God in disguise;
The sunlight still sleeps in their tresses,
    His glory still gleams in their eyes;
These truants from home and from heaven—
    They have made me more manly and mild;
And I know now how Jesus could liken
    The Kingdom of God to a child.

                                         Charles M. Dickinson

629   HIS MONUMENT

He built a house, time laid it in the dust;
    He wrote a book, its title now forgot;
    He ruled a city, but his name is not
On any tablet graven, or where rust
Can gather from disuse, or marble bust.

He took a child from a wretched cot,
Who on the State dishonor might have brought,
    And reared him in the Christian's hope and trust.
The boy, to manhood grown, became a light
    To many souls and preached to human need
The wondrous love of the Omnipotent.
The work has multiplied like stars at night
    When darkness deepens; every noble deed
Lasts longer than a granite monument.

                                         Sarah Knowles Bolton

630   *TO THE CHILD JESUS*

Could every time-worn heart but see thee once again
A happy human child, among the homes of men,
The age of doubt would pass,—the vision of thy face
Would silently restore the childhood of the race.

Henry van Dyke

631   *LITTLE BOYS IN CHURCH*

Small boys in the church pews grow
Very fast, the first you know
Ones only halfway up are older
And at their father's cheek or shoulder.

One day they are only bright
Heads that in the high church light
Look as if they were washed in dew,
Their ears and hair are all so new.

This Sunday only heads that dance,
Next Sunday heads and coats and pants,
All the boys have sprung uphill,
Heads are erect and ears stand still.

One week they are boys, and then
Next week they are slim young men
Standing very still and lean,
Perilously scrubbed and clean.

Enjoy each small boy while you can,
Tomorrow there will be a man
Standing taller than belief;
Little boys in church are brief.

Robert P. Tristram Coffin

632   *MARY, WHEN THAT LITTLE CHILD*

Mary, when that little child
    Lay upon your heart at rest,
Did the thorns, Maid-mother, mild,
    Pierce your breast?

Mary, when that little child
Softly kissed your cheek benign,
Did you know, O Mary Mild,
Judas' sign?

Mary, when that little child
Cooed and prattled at your knee,
Did you see with heart-beat wild,
Calvary?

Rose Trumbull

633   THE CHILD'S APPEAL

I am the Child.
All the world waits for my coming.
All the earth watches with interest to see what I shall become.
Civilization hangs in the balance,
For what I am, the world of tomorrow will be.
I am the Child.
I have come into your world, about which I know nothing.
Why I came I know not;
How I came I know not.
I am curious; I am interested.

I am the Child.
You hold in your hand my destiny.
You determine, largely, whether I shall succeed or fail.
Give me, I pray you, those things that make for happiness.
Train me, I beg you, that I may be a blessing to the world.

Mamie Gene Cole

Topics, Texts and Themes

634   THE HERITAGE OF OUR CHILDREN

The children ought not to lay up for the parents, but the parents for the children. 2 CO. 12:14

What are you laying up for your children? The query is in line with this text from Saint Paul. He never had little ones of his own. But, like many another childless minister, the apostle loved a host of human beings. He looked on them all as his children. In the letter before us he is explaining to his friends at Corinth how they ought to live in a worldly city. In the words surrounding our text he is making clear his personal attitude towards money. He shows that he loves people more than things, and that he enjoys giving far more than getting. He takes delight in giving himself and his heart's love. What a model for Christian parents! Surely we all are concerned about the heritage of our children.

Andrew W. Blackwood

635   *MY FAITH IN CHILDHOOD*

I believe that the child is supreme value; that the home, school, and church exist for the sake of the child; that the test of civilization consists in its provision for the physical and spiritual needs of its childhood; and that the child is created in the likeness of God and is a new revelation of God to man.

I believe that to be childlike is to be Christ-like; that childlikeness is a condition of entrance into the Kingdom of God; that childlikeness includes teachableness, trust, and sincerity; and that a little child may lead his elders into the very presence of God.

I believe that respect for a child is essential to the development of a wholesome personality and to the adult's understanding of the child; that the child manifests its most wholesome growth in an atmosphere of love and helpfulness; and that nothing can take the place of a Christian home in the religious nurture of the child.

I believe that Jesus' childhood and religious growth constitute the model pattern of religious experience for childhood today; that the child may grow normally and gradually into full religious maturity; and that the conservation of childhood and youth is the challenge to Christian education today.

I believe that Jesus gave the child a central place in his thought and program; that his birth and childhood hallowed childhood and parenthood; that Jesus enlarged and spiritualized the conception of the family into the Kingdom of God; that the child should be dedicated to God and that Christian nurture of childhood is the supreme privilege and major responsibility of the Christian church.

P. Henry Lotz

636   *A TRIBUTE TO CHILDHOOD*

When God made the child he began early in the morning. He watched the golden hues of the rising day chasing away the darkness, and he chose the azure of the opening heavens for the color of childhood's eyes, the crimson of the clouds to paint its cheeks, and the gold of the morning for its flowing tresses. He listened to the song of the birds as they sang and warbled and whispered, and strung childhood's harp with notes now soft and low—now sweet and strong.

He saw little lambs among the flock romp and play and skip, and he put play into childhood's heart. He saw the silvery brook and listened to its music and he made the laughter of the child like the ripple of the brook. He saw angels of light as upon the wings of love they hastened to holy duty, and he formed the child's heart in purity and love.

And having made the child, he sent it out to bring joy into the home, laughter on the green and gladness everywhere. He sent it into the home and said to the parents, "Nourish and bring up this child for me." He sent it to the church and said, "Teach it my love and my laws." He sent it to the state and said, "Deal tenderly with it and it will bless and not curse you." He sent it to the nation and said: "Be good to the child. It is thy greatest asset and thy hope."

George W. Rideout

637 *WHAT IS A BOY?*

He is a person who is going to carry on what you have started.

He is to sit right where you are sitting and attend when you are gone to those things you think are so important.

You may adopt all the policies you please, but how they will be carried out depends upon him.

Even if you make leagues and treaties, he will have to manage them.

He is going to sit at your desk in the Senate, and occupy your place on the Supreme Bench.

He will assume control of your cities, states and nation.

He is going to move in, take over your prisons, churches, universities, schools and corporations.

All your work is going to be judged and praised or condemned by him.

Your reputation and your future are in his hands.

All your work is for him, and the fate of the nation and of humanity is in his hands.

So it might be well to pay him some attention.

Author Unknown

638   *LESSONS DRAWN FROM CHILDHOOD*

Every reader of the Gospels has marked the sympathy of Jesus with children. How he watched their games! How angry he was with his disciples for belitting them! How he used to warn men, whatever they did, never to hurt a little child! How grateful were children's praises when all others had turned against him! One is apt to admire the beautiful sentiment, and to forget that children were more to Jesus than helpless gentle creatures to be loved and protected. They were his chief parable of the Kingdom of Heaven. As a type of character the Kingdom was like unto a little child, and the greatest in the Kingdom would be the most childlike. According to Jesus, a well-conditioned child illustrates better than anthing else on earth the distinctive features of Christian character. Because he does not assert nor aggrandize himself. Because he has no memory of injuries, and no room in his heart for a grudge. Because he has no previous opinions, and is not ashamed to confess his ignorance. Because he can imagine, and has the key of another world, entering in through the ivory gate and living amid the things unseen and eternal. The new society of Jesus was a magnificent imagination, and he who entered it must lay aside the world standards and ideals of character, and become as a little child.

John Watson

639   *THE CHILD AND THE KINGDOM*

Something in the spirit of childhood itself Jesus considers essential to one's discovery of truth. "Except ye turn and become as little children, ye shall in no wise enter the kingdom of heaven." What is there in the spirit of childhood that guides one to the discovery of truth? The cynic will say that Christ is making capital of the child's ignorance. The child lacks critical judgment. He believes in fairies and Santa Claus. To enter the Kingdom of God, become a child and leave your critical faculties at the door.

Let us, however, not be too hasty in our judgment. . . . For one thing, the child has not lost the capacity for wonder. Wonder is often the beginning of wisdom. . . . When Jesus said that unless we turn and become as little children we cannot enter the Kingdom of Heaven, perhaps he meant that the capacity to wonder at the mystery of life was essential to one's discovery of the truth about life. To lose the sense of wonder and mystery is to lose the capacity for reverence and "thought without reverence is barren, perhaps poisonous." . . .

There is another observation which should be briefly made. It is what Dean Sperry has in mind when he refers to the child as being "unself-conscious." An exaggerated self-consciousness is never a healthy condition. When we become absorbed with ourselves, usually what is worse in us engages our attention.

Harold Cooke Phillips

640   *MAGNIFICENT REVERSAL*

Except ye be converted, and become as little children, ye shall not enter into the kingdom. MAT. 18:3

What is there about a child which we must try to get back to in order to be a part of the Kingdom? A child is innocent, but that is both an impossible and undesirable thing for men and women. Lovely as innocence is, it is not as wonderful as character. Real character results from the push and pull of inner urges, temptations and decisions. Certainly Jesus did not want men either morally or spiritually naïve.

But there are margins and capacities in a child which are all but lost as the days creep along the years into manhood and womanhood.

A child has a capacity for learning which an adult easily loses. . . . As we grow older we become indolent and satisfied. Basically it is a matter of humility. A child is quite aware of his ignorance. He has not yet learned the words and phrases—or the silences—to cover it. But gradually as we come to know a few things, we become satisfied if not vain in our knowledge. But if we grownups could contrast our bit of knowledge with the great universe of truth, instead of with the child's ignorance, we should grow more humble instead of less. . . .

There is also in a little child a great capacity for idealism. Nothing is too big to expect of the world, the future, other people and from himself.

Frank B. Fagerburg

D. YOUTH SUNDAY

Youth Sunday may be held on one of the Sundays immediately following Easter, during National Youth Week which begins on the last Sunday in January, or at almost any other time in the church year. The day emphasizes the role of youth in the church, the responsibility of the church and community to youth, the training of youth for Christian citizenship, and the preparing of youth for Christian service. The work of such groups as Boy and Girl Scouts may be featured and the young people are sometimes invited to participate in the worship services of the church.

Calls to Worship

(Boldface type indicates responses.)

641   Remember now thy Creator in the days of thy youth, while the evil days come not, nor the years draw nigh, when thou shalt say, I have no pleasure in them. . . . Fear God and keep his commandments: for this is the whole duty of man. For God shall bring every work into judgment, with every secret thing, whether it be good, or whether it be evil.

Ec. 12:1, 13–14

642   Rejoice, O young man, in thy youth; and let thy heart cheer thee in the days of thy youth, and walk in the ways of thine heart, and in the sight of thine eyes. . . . Remove sorrow from thy heart, and put away evil from thy flesh.

Ec. 11:9–10

643   Let no man despise thy youth; but be thou an example of the believers, in word, in conversation, in charity, in spirit, in faith, in purity. . . . Neglect not the gift that is in thee.

1 Ti. 4:12, 14

644   Wherewithal shall a young man cleanse his way? by taking heed thereto according to thy word.
Thy word have I hid in mine heart, that I might not sin against thee.
I will meditate in thy precepts, and have respect unto thy ways.
I will delight myself in thy statutes: I will not forget thy word.

Ps. 119:9, 11, 15–16

Invocations

645 O God, who art the Fountain of all wisdom and Founder of all learning: breathe into our souls the spirit of understanding. Make us obedient to our prayers, dutiful to our teachers, loving to our school-fellows, full of reverence to old age, and brotherly towards all men. Bless us, O Lord, this day; guide our feet, direct our minds, bless our studies, govern all our actions according to the mind of Jesus Christ our Lord. Amen.

Book of Common Worship (CC)

646 Hear our prayers, O Lord Jesus, the everlasting Wisdom of the Father, who givest unto us, in the days of our youth, aptness to learn: add, we pray thee, the furtherance of thy grace, so to learn knowledge and the liberal sciences that, by their help, we may attain to the fuller knowing of thee, whom to know is the height of blessedness; and by the example of thy boyhood, may duly increase in age, wisdom and favor with God and man; who livest and reignest with the Father and the Holy Ghost, world without end. Amen.*

Desiderius Erasmus

647 Give us, O Lord, steadfast hearts, which no unworthy thought can drag downwards; unconquered hearts, which no tribulation can wear out; upright hearts, which no unworthy purpose may tempt aside. Bestow upon us also, O Lord our God, understanding to know thee, diligence to seek thee, wisdom to find thee, and a faithfulness that may finally embrace thee; through Jesus Christ our Lord. Amen.

Thomas Aquinas

Litanies

(Boldface type indicates responses.)

648 In these days of confusion and unrest, God calls us. Let us affirm our Christian faith and dedicate our lives to his service. We believe in Jesus Christ, that his life, his birth, his growth from childhood to manhood, his ministry, his love, his tenderness, his concern, his healing, his teaching and his sacrifice reveal the nature of God himself:

We believe in Jesus Christ.

We believe in the church, its divine origin, its inspired mission through the ages, its power expressed through the loyalty and unflagging zeal of its members who braved fire, sword and death for the Gospel's sake:

We believe in the church.

We believe in the Christian life, its beauty, simplicity, grandeur, its challenge to a better life, its triumph over self-centeredness, its promise of eternal existence:

We believe in the Christian life.

We believe in true justice, the way to live in peace and happiness with the people of the world, the way of honesty, equity, morality and truthfulness, the way of fair dealing with employee and employer, the way of integrity in all our relationships in the home, the school, the community:

We believe in true justice.

(Pause for brief, silent prayer of dedication)

Through the life of thy Son, O God, through thy church and through the lives of fellow Christians, we hear thy challenge to us. We answer thy call and with joy surrender ourselves to thy will.

National Council

649 O God, the Giver of all good things, we thank thee for our home and for our college and for the heritage that is ours. Bless this university. Grant that we may maintain every good tradition which our fathers have preserved and that we may press forward to the attainment of new truth.

Bestow upon us all the grace of honesty of mind. Teach us the hard discipline of scholarship. Give to us and to all other teachers and students the true love of knowledge which makes all study a satisfaction and delight. Bind us one to another with the spirit of loyalty; remove far from us the bitterness of rivalry; inspire us with the firm purpose to seek first, not our own advantage, but the common good.

Pour thy Spirit upon us and upon the students of other nations that we may devote ourselves to thy service and go forth into the world prepared and with a good courage.

Let us give thanks to God.

For his gifts of truth, wisdom and knowledge:

Thanks be to God.

For the scholars and sages and artists of the past:

Thanks be to God.

For those who provided for schools, colleges and other places of learning, especially for our benefactors:

Thanks be to God.

For the great opportunities that are opening before us:

Thanks be to God.

For parents and friends who are making it possible for us to use these opportunities:

Thanks be to God.

Let us give thanks to God for his gifts of wisdom and knowledge, for health and the zest of living, for sincerity and earnestness, for courage of mind and will as well as for physical courage, for whole-hearted devotion to a worthy cause:

Lord, hear our prayer and let our cry come unto thee.

O Lord, who didst thyself grow in wisdom and stature and in favor with God and man: grant that the mystery of such growth may operate in us that we may become thy true and faithful disciples. Amen.

Thomas L. Harris

Prayers

650   Our heavenly Father, Shepherd of the journeying generations, amid so much that changes and decays, we praise thy holy name that thou art the same yesterday, today and forever. The burden of our prayer is for our youth. We do not ask for sheltered or easy voyages for our sons and daughters; we pray for strength and fortitude, that they may face squarely every problem and danger and be given wisdom and determination to turn their "necessity to glorious gain." Deliver them from fear that paralyzes the will, and from doubt that breeds despair. May the joys of life not make them selfish, nor the sorrows of life make them bitter. May whatever disappointments that await them make them gentle and generous and sympathetic and strong. May victory make them grateful and humble. Below the wave-tossed surface of our wind-driven life, may the depths of loyalty and faith, generosity and unselfishness, in our homes and churches and schools, be undisturbed, so that when this present hurricane is over, we shall have preserved intact the great treasures of life; through Jesus Christ our Lord. Amen.

Richard C. Raines

651   O God, our Father, thou Searcher of men's hearts, help us to draw near to thee in sincerity and truth. May our religion be filled with gladness and may our worship of thee be natural.

Strengthen and increase our admiration for honest dealing and clean thinking, and suffer not our hatred of hypocrisy and pretense ever to diminish. Encourage us in our endeavor to live above the common level of life.

Make us to choose the harder right instead of the easier wrong, and never to be content with a half truth when the whole can be won. Endow us with courage that is born of loyalty to all that is noble and worthy, that scorns compromise with vice and injustice and knows no fear when truth and right are in jeopardy. Guard us against flippancy and irreverence in the sacred things of life.

Grant us new ties of friendship and new opportunities of service. Kindle our hearts in fellowship with those of a cheerful countenance, and soften our hearts with sympathy for those who sorrow and suffer. May we find genuine pleasure in clean and wholesome mirth and feel inherent disgust for all coarse-minded humor.

Help us, in our work and in our play, to keep ourselves physically strong, mentally awake and morally straight. All of which we ask in the name of the great Friend and Master of men. Amen.

West Point Cadet Prayer

652   Almighty Father, the Author of every good and perfect gift, whose care for thy childrn faileth not, neither groweth weary: we gather in thy house to lift up to thee the voice of our thanksgiving and praise.

We praise thee for our physical life, for the glow of health and the feeling of strength it may bring; for food and clothing and shelter, and all the innocent pleasures of sense.

We praise thee for our intellectual life, for the power to observe and think, plan and meditate, and to influence others by the energy of our minds; and for all wise and good books and teachers whose words quicken, enlarge and enrich our thought.

We praise thee for our moral life, that, notwithstanding our transgression and sin, conscience still speaks to us, and that we have still the power to choose the right and reject the wrong.

We praise thee for our social life, for all its beneficent fellowships and ministries, for home and friends, and all the things which give us strength and peace amid the disquietude and strife of our passing days.

We praise thee for our spiritual life, for our knowledge of thee and our communion with thee, and for the peace passing all understanding, which the prayer of trust and submission ever brings into our hearts and minds.

We praise thee for the hope of that life which is immortal, for the persuasion that the souls of the departed are in thy hand, and that only in the sight of the unwise do they seem to die. Amen.*

John Hunter

653   Strong Son of God, hear our prayer for the youth of our church. Give them the vision of the pure in heart, that the warfare of the spirit may be waged with unstained steel. Grant them the grace of humility, neither to spurn the treasured history of the past nor to sneer at the pageantry of present-day progress. Guard them with the whole armor of God, the girdle of triumphant truth, the breastplate of worthy righteousness, the sandals of perfect peace, the shield of saving faith, the helmet of holy salvation, the sword of the divine Spirit, the protection of persistent prayer, and the weapon of constant watchfulness, that they may be able to stand and withstand in the evil day. May the chivalry of knighthood, the loyalty of discipleship, the courtesy of noble character, and the bravery of fearless witness be the portion of our youth in extending the frontiers of the Kingdom of God. And may thy benediction abide in their hearts always. Amen.

John F. Fedders

Poems

654   *From MORITURI SALUTAMUS*

How beautiful is youth! how bright it gleams
With its illusions, aspirations, dreams!
Book of Beginnings, Story without End,
Each maid a heroine, and each man a friend!

❊

All possibilities are in its hands,
No danger daunts it, and no foe withstands;
In its sublime audacity of faith,
"Be thou removed!" it to the mountain saith,
And with ambitious feet, secure and proud,
Ascends the ladder leaning on the cloud!

Henry Wadsworth Longfellow

655   *MY TASK*

To be honest, to be kind;
To earn a little and to spend a little less;
To make upon the whole a family happier for his presence;
To renounce when that shall be necessary and not to be embittered;
To keep a few friends, but those without capitulation—
Above all, on the same grim conditions, to keep friends with himself—
Here is a task for all that a man has of fortitude and delicacy.

Robert Louis Stevenson

656　　　　　　　　　　*A YOUTH'S PRAYER*

To build a life that's clean, upright, secure,
God's temple that will through the years endure;
To walk courageously, steadfast and sure;
　　This is my prayer.

To teach a war-torn world the fruits of peace;
To plead that cruelty and hate must cease,
That earth might see goodwill and love increase;
　　This is my prayer.

To dedicate my life, my youth, my all
To Christ, and then in answer to his call,
Be faithful to each task—the large, the small;
　　This is my prayer.

　　　　　　　　　　　　　　　George W. Wiseman

657　　　　　　　　　　　*PRAYER*

Great God, I ask thee for no meaner pelf
Than that I may not disappoint myself,
That in my action I may soar as high
As I can now discern with this clear eye.

And next in value, which thy kindness lends,
That I may greatly disappoint my friends,
Howe'er they think or hope that it may be,
They may not dream how thou'st distinguished me.

That my weak hand may equal my firm faith,
And my life practise more than my tongue saith;
　　That my low conduct may not show,
　　　　Nor my relenting lines,
　　That I thy purpose did not know,
　　　　Or overrated thy designs.

　　　　　　　　　　　　　　　Henry David Thoreau

658   *TO ONE WHO DOUBTS THE WORTH OF DOING*
        ANYTHING IF YOU CAN'T DO EVERYTHING

You say the little efforts that I make
Will do no good: they never will prevail
To tip the hovering scale
Where justice hangs in balance.
   I don't think
I ever thought they would.
But I am prejudiced beyond debate
In favor of my right to choose which side
Shall feel the stubborn ounces of my weight.

Bonaro W. Overstreet

659   *FIRE MAKER'S DESIRE*

As fuel is brought to the fire
So I purpose to bring
My strength
My ambition
My heart's desire
My joy
And my sorrow
To the fire
Of humankind;
For I will tend
As my fathers have tended
And my fathers' fathers
Since time began
The fire that is called
The love of man for man
The love of man for God.

John Collier

660   *CHILD*

The young child, Christ, is straight and wise
And asks questions of the old men, questions
Found under running water for all children
And found under shadows thrown on still waters
By tall trees looking downwards, old and gnarled.

Found to the eyes of children alone, untold,
Singing a low song in the loneliness.
And the young child, Christ, goes asking
And the old men answer nothing and only know love
For the young child. Christ, straight and wise.

Carl Sandburg

Topics, Texts and Themes

661   *A YOUTH MOVEMENT*

> Now as he walked by the sea of Galilee, he saw Simon, and Andrew his brother, casting a net into the sea: for they were fishers. And Jesus said unto them, Come ye after me, and I will make you to become fishers of men.
> MK. 1:16–17

Youth, arising in each new generation, is the world's fountain-source of human advancement. Jesus inaugurated the most fruitful youth movement that man has witnessed; for he founded a worthy, constructive, growing, and permanent enterprise. How did he do this?

He selected twelve young men between the approximate ages of eighteen and thirty. They had time, resiliency, stamina, and capacity. They were not bound by the routine responsibilities of homes and organizations. They were not restricted by the fixed prejudices and provincial loyalties so common to old age. None was hindered by priestly or political ties or aspirations. Their capacity for God had not been crystallized. They were teachable; they were able to see the issues of life; they were able to hear the still, sad music of humanity; they were able to feel indignation and kindness; and they were able to recognize truth and submit themselves to its obligations. They were able, therefore, to grow in wisdom concerning God and man.

A. C. Reid

662   *JESUS AND YOUNG MEN*

If ever there were a cause in the history of the world which should attract young men, it is Christianity. Jesus was a young man. He died at 33. When the hymn, "When I survey the wondrous Cross," was first written, the second line ran like this: "Where the young Prince of Glory died." I have always been sorry that that beautiful phrase, "the young Prince of Glory," was cut out of later editions of the hymn. . . . Jesus called young men and young *laymen*. We parsons and professional ecclesiastics do not come into the picture very creditably in the Gospels. As far as we know, Jesus called no parsons at all, no old

men, no professional people. He called men who were simple-minded, like
Peter and James and John, the men who got their living by fishing in the
Galilean lake. Not because they were uneducated, but because young men, and
especially young men who work with their hands and have an unsophisticated
outlook, can change their ideas. They are not hidebound and conventional and
the victims of the etiquette and tyranny of their set, or their profession, or their
party. They are free to follow truth. New thoughts are not rejected by un-
trammeled young men because they are new, and new ways of looking at life
are welcome if there seems to be a promise that they will work.

Leslie D. Weatherhead

663   *THE GIFT OF YOUTH*

Let no man despise thy youth. 1 TI. 4:12

Only the foolish despise youth: only the foolish look down upon it and seek
ever to cramp and stifle it; though few even of the wise estimate aright the
glorious gift of youth. Poets and romancers sing the praises of youth, but often
only for its capacity of joy, as a wonderful time of abounding energy and fresh
optimism, a time of joy and hope and strength. Older men will sometimes envy
youth because of this, not for its opportunity, but for its capacity for enjoyment. Even for that it is not to be despised. The pleasures of health and strength,
the first delight in the world of nature; the pleasures of friendship, meeting in
the fresh glow of loyal feeling without suspicion, without self-interest, without
considering motives, without thought of anything but sympathy, and kindness,
and goodwill; the pleasure of acquiring knowledge, of finding new intellectual
interests; the pleasures of beginning work, of entering on a definite pursuit; the
pleasure of acknowledging greatness in others, ungrudgingly admiring and
loving some without thought of jealousy or envy or meanness—all these and
others have surely been the portion in some degree of all who remember their
youth.

Hugh Black

664   *THE YOUTHFUL MIND*

Youth is not a time of life; it is a state of mind. It is not a matter of ripe
cheeks, red lips, and supple knees; it is a temper of the will, a quality of the
imagination, a vigor of the emotions. It is a freshness of the deep springs of life.
Youth means a temperamental predominance of courage over timidity, of the
appetite of adventure over the love of ease. It sometimes exists in a man of fifty
more than in a boy of twenty. Nobody grows old merely by living a number

of years; people grow old only by deserting their ideals. Years wrinkle the skin but to give up enthusiasm wrinkles the soul. Worry, doubt, self-distrust, fear and despair—these are the long, long years that bow the head and turn the growing spirit back to dust. Whether seventy or sixteen, there is in every being's heart the love of wonder, the unfailing child-like appetite for what comes next, the joy of the game of life. You are as young as your faith, as old as your doubts; as young as your self-confidence, as old as your fear; as young as your hope, as old as your despair. In the central place of your heart there is a wireless station; so long as it receives messages of beauty, hope, cheer, courage, grandeur and power from the earth, from men and from the Infinite, so long are you young. When the wires are all down, and the central place of your heart is covered with the snows of pessimism and the ice of cynicism, then are you grown old indeed.

Frank Crane

665   *A CREED FOR YOUTH*

I believe in the energy and enthusiasm of youth. They are the dynamic power of the human race.

I believe in the dreams and aspirations of youth. They give vision to life.

I believe in the ideals of youth. They hold the human race to its goal.

I believe in the mistakes of youth. They are the furnace in which its gold is refined. Without the discipline of its mistakes, youth would often lose its balance.

But I know that the energies and enthusiasms of youth may be dissipated, that its dream and aspirations may be forgotten, that its ideals may be dimmed, its mistakes repeated. Such happens all too frequently, and it is the tragedy of humanity that it does.

Knowing this, I shall do my utmost to preserve these things of youth that I believe in, and to press home the lesson from each mistake so vividly that the same mistake need never be made again. I shall strive to teach my boy to direct his energy and enthusiasm into the right channel instead of wasting it, to realize his dreams and aspirations instead of forgetting them, to hold to his ideals, in spite of disillusionment.

This is no easy task that I have set for myself. I will need all the experience and judgment of mature years. I will need the systematic understanding of the problems of youth, an understanding that can come only from keeping in close touch with young hearts.

Lelia Munsell

666 . *THANK GOD FOR YOUTH*

Youth—heir of the sufferings, ministries, achievements of past generations; whose lifeblood is the very lifeblood of those who give them birth; whose intellectual grasp is the product of patient tutelage at home and at school; whose spiritual ideals root in the great souls of yesterday and today—youth, heir of all the past.

Youth—come into a wanton world created by the sin and stupidity of its elders; handicapped by the mistakes of well-meaning but blind generations; burdened but not overwhelmed by the immensity of the problems of the hour— youth, creature of the past but creator of the future.

Youth—energetic and dissatisified, sometimes moved by a reckless restlessness and again by a divine discontent; misguided and uncontrolled, at times, wasting its substance in riotous living; divinely motivated and sublimely purposed, at times, daring to attempt a perfection which seems, to cautious older minds, to be idealistic folly—youth, unwilling to accept the world as it is.

Youth—suffering deep pent-up sorrows, enduring well-nigh crushing defeats, hoping against tremendous odds, fighting cruel inner battles, winning unheralded but glorious triumphs—youth, victim and victor.

Christian youth—captured by the dream of the young Idealist of Nazareth, impelled by the lofty concerns which led him to Calvary; Christian youth, seeking to know and follow the will of God, embracing all human kind within the family circle; determined to rid the world of its besetting sins and unnecessary sorrow—Christian youth, with whom the name "Christian" takes on a new, and yet its oldest, meaning.

Christian youth—newly conscious of its potential power, impatient with the trivialities which divide the Church of Christ, accepting the responsibility to build a Christlike world, counting the possible cost of allegiance to Christ and increasingly ready to pay the price—Christian youth a dedicated minority, intent upon the world for which Christ gave his life.

Christian youth—aware of the limits of their own wisdom, taking counsel of the experiences of the past, seeking the help which comes from God alone, cherishing no fantastic thought that theirs will be a quick or easy victory— Christian youth who call Jesus "Master," who enlist in his cause for the duration of life, trusting the God of all power to give them strength for every need.

Thank God for youth!

Missionary Herald

667   *A LADDER FOR YOUTH*

As you start out in life, you will need five things: (1) A faith to live by. (2) A cause to serve. (3) A fellowship in which that faith can be nourished and through which that cause can be served. (4) A decision to accept that faith, serve that cause, and enter that fellowship. (5) A life dedication to that faith, to that cause, to that fellowship—now. Therefore, here and now accept that faith—Christ. Give yourself to that cause—the Kingdom of God. Enter that fellowship—the church, with a life dedication now. That means you have a life pattern.

                                                        E. Stanley Jones

668   *WHAT IT MEANS TO GROW UP*

Childhood with its carefree attitudes is so attractive that doubtless we all at times have wished we could be children again. Certainly we understand the sentiment in the familiar line, "Make me a child again, just for tonight!" One cannot seriously study the problem of being real persons, however, without encountering the fact that our neurological and psychiatric institutions, to say nothing of more familiar places, are filled with people who have offered that prayer too consistently and have had it altogether too well answered. They never have grown up. Their basic emotional reactions are infantile; they are still in the stage of childhood's tantrums or adolescent aimlessness; they do not know what mature personality means. One of the most tragic failures of personal life is the refusal to grow up.

                                                  Harry Emerson Fosdick

669   *"I AM JUST A YOUNG MAN"*

Scores say this: "I am just a young man."
In other words, what thousands of men today would like to be! A potentiality with his face to the East! A lifetime stretching ahead! The Book of Life with clean pages to be written on as he may elect! "Just a young man" in a time like this: in a land like this: in a world like this! Then he deprecates himself! In a land of opportunity where every chance beckons and every road invites! A road straight and clear, and the high peaks of achievement beyond—and oh! so few on them! To carve out of Life what one wills! How many men there are who would gladly give all they possess to have that chance once more!

                                                        Edward W. Bok

670   *THE CREATIVE USE OF LIFE*

Except a corn of wheat fall into the ground and die, it abideth alone: but if
it die, it bringeth forth much fruit. JN. 12:24

What a difference it makes when we are using life rather than having life
use us. When we, to a marked degree, are managing our moods, controlling our
emotions, making life meaningful, filling every day with the heights of Christian living, we may say with confidence that we are using life.

But when worry grips the mind and paralyzes the heart, or the dull edge of
sin robs life of radiancy, or fear grips our life, rather than an abiding faith, and
life runs out into a morass of doubt, disillusionment and despair, we know
that life is using us.

Frank A. Court

671   *ACCENT ON YOUTH*

Your young men shall see visions. AC. 2:17

It is noteworthy that in the first recorded instance of Christian preaching
there should be found, in the quotation from Joel, the mention of youth as receiving the outpouring of the Holy Spirit. It was in some degree a forecast of
that part that youth has played in the expansion of Christianity; a fitting expression of the real affinity which exists between the genius of Christianity and
the distinguishing qualities of youth.

Halford E. Luccock

E. CHRISTIAN EDUCATION WEEK

Christian Education Week begins on the last Sunday in September, a day frequently designated as Rally Day. It is a time when Sunday school workers are honored, when training courses for church workers are held, and when the needs of Christian schools and colleges are presented. Services of dedication and installation of Sunday school teachers and officers are widely scheduled for this week.

Calls to Worship

(Boldface type indicates responses.)

672 Great is the Lord, and greatly to be praised; and his greatness is unsearchable. One generation shall praise thy works to another, and shall declare thy mighty acts. I will speak of the glorious honor of thy majesty, and of thy wondrous works.

Ps. 145:3-5

673 Blessed be the name of God for ever and ever: for wisdom and might are his.

He giveth wisdom unto the wise, and knowledge to them that know understanding.

Seek ye the Lord while he may be found, call ye upon him while he is near.

For great is the Lord, and greatly to be praised.

Da. 2:20-21; Is. 55:6; 1 Ch. 16:25

674 I will instruct thee and teach thee in the way which thou shalt go [saith the Lord]. I will guide thee with mine eye.

Be glad in the Lord, and rejoice, ye righteous: and shout for joy, all ye that are upright in heart.

Ps. 32:8, 11

Invocations

675 O gracious and holy Father, give us wisdom to perceive thee, intelligence to understand thee, diligence to seek thee, patience to wait for thee, eyes to

behold thee, a heart to meditate upon thee, and a life to proclaim thee; through the power of the spirit of Jesus Christ our Lord.

St. Benedict

676   O God, who art nigh to all them that call upon thee in truth; who art thyself the Truth, whom to know is perfect knowledge: instruct us with thy divine wisdom, and teach us thy law; that we may know the truth and walk in it; through him in whom the truth was made manifest, even Jesus Christ thy Son our Lord. Amen.

Christian Prayers (1578)

677   O Lord Jesus Christ, who art the Way, the Truth, and the Life, we pray thee suffer us not to stray from thee, who art the Way, nor to distrust thee, who art the Truth, nor to rest in any other thing than thee, who art the Life. Teach us by thy Holy Spirit what to believe, what to do, and wherein to take our rest. For thine own name's sake we ask it. Amen.

Desiderius Erasmus

678   Almighty God, we beseech thee with thy gracious favor to behold our universities, colleges and schools, that knowledge may be increased among us, and all good learning flourish and abound. Bless all who teach and all who learn, and grant that in humility of heart they may ever look unto thee, who art the fountain of all wisdom; through Jesus Christ our Lord. Amen.*

Gelasian Sacramentary

Litany

(Boldface type indicates responses.)

679   Eternal God, who hast promised us the liberty who follow after truth: grant that, keeping the commandments of Christ, we may have the mind of Christ and be free, as he was free. For all who guard the truths which were known of old, that, as good stewards of that knowledge, they may confirm us in simple and righteous living:

We beseech thee to hear us, good Lord.

For those who seek for new truth, that, believing more light is yet to break, they may be sustained in their searching by the faith that thou art the rewarder of them that diligently seek thee:

We beseech thee to hear us, good Lord.

For all scientists, looking upon the face of nature, that they may see order in its variety and law in its constancy, and may teach men to live upon earth in confidence and without fear:

We beseech thee to hear us, good Lord.

For all historians, that, telling again the story of the past with sincerity and sympathy, they may bind the generations together in one communion of thy real sons:

We beseech thee to hear us, good Lord.

For all builders, poets, painters, and makers of music, that they may open our blind eyes and unstop our deaf ears to the beauty of thy world:

We beseech thee to hear us, good Lord.

For all who would lead man's long thoughts beyond the things that are known into the world which is unknown, that their faith may prepare for us a place in the infinite mystery:

We beseech thee to hear us, good Lord.

For all who unselfishly bring their knowledge to the service of the world, that they may prove their learning by their works, and give that vision without which the people perish:

We beseech thee to hear us, good Lord.

For ourselves in this society of the truth, that accepting with gladness the high offices of thought, that seeing clearly, and feeling deeply we may go forth to be in the world as those who serve, and may thus know that mind of Christ which we would make the manner of our thinking; and all these things we ask in his name, even Jesus Christ our Lord. Amen.

Willard L. Sperry

Prayers

680   Eternal God, our Father, we thank thee for thy continuing creation in each new life that comes into the world, for the renewing of thy purpose from generation to generation. We bring to thee those whom thou hast appointed to work with thee in the ministry to children. We pray for all parents. May they affirm their partnership with thee in nurturing the new life thou hast given and discern in each child the spirit which has its origin in thee. Grant to them a warm and active love which expresses thy presence in the relations and events of every day. Make them sensitive to the needs of growing minds. Give them vital faith in thy goodness and the wisdom to communicate it in ways that shall bring abiding strength to youth in the face of temptations and diversions from the path of duty and righteousness. Keep ever before all parents the goal of fulfillment and the joy of mature fellowship with thee.

We pray for those whom thou hast called to serve thee in the church through the work of teaching. Impart to them the spirit of the Master who saw in children and youth open doors to the Kingdom. Grant to all who are engaged in this ministry the art of access to young minds and the gift to bring in song and story and lesson the vision of the Christ who redeems and exalts all life by the power of the truth which sets men free. May all these, thy servants, so witness for him that at last he shall claim all children for himself in an ever-growing kingdom of eternal goodness. In the name of the Great Teacher, may they give themselves anew to this task. Amen.

Oren H. Baker

681   We thank thee, O God, for that great heritage of Christian learning by which our fathers lived and with which we have been entrusted in our time. For our Holy Bible, a lamp unto our feet and a light unto our path, we give thee thanks. For the Christian church, with its glorious company of saints, apostles, prophets, martyrs and an unnumbered host of faithful, humble Christians, we give thee thanks. For our heritage of Christian morality and the undergirding of our nation and common life by Christian ideals, we give thee thanks. Above all we thank thee for Jesus Christ our Lord, in whom we see thee as thou art and from whom comes all that is best and highest.

Grant, O Lord, thy guidance and thy strength to all who teach and to all who learn as we seek to pass on this heritage to each new generation. May our minds be ever responsive to thy wisdom, our hearts to thy love, our service to thy call. May the mystery of thy glory lift us, the knowledge of thy truth lead us. Let not our minds be darkened by prejudice and ignorance; let not our souls be dull to the glow of fellowship with thee. Help us to discover and to bring forth the best in each young life, that all may grow in Christian knowledge and in Christian living. Together we would see Jesus, and find in him the Way, the Truth, and the Life. In his name we pray. Amen.

Georgia Harkness

682   Eternal God, Friend of all ages, we seek renewal for our weary spirits. Here amid the hallowed memories and aspirations of many now gone from our presence, we recall thy power unto men of old. Yet art thou the same yesterday, today and forever. Thy strength, generously given, is never exhausted.

We remember this day all who have offered us a fuller life through thy church. For devoted church school teachers who have brightened our lives with fact and feeling about thy love for humankind, we give thee thanks. For church school administrators who with skill and consecration have created efficient patterns of organization, we recognize our indebtedness. For pastors who in countless ways influence growing life through their example and admonition, we raise our voices in praise. For denominational leaders who appreciate the role of religious instruction in the full program of the living church, we express our gratitude. For artists and writers who have wrought the materials of instruction and edification, we offer praise. For faithful parents at whose knees we first learned life's deepest meanings, we open our hearts in thanksgiving. Thanks be to thee, O God, for all who have taught and all who teach.

Grant thy church wisdom, our Father, that it may continue to teach children in the way they should go. Give to each of us the knowledge needed to join with church leaders in their effort to achieve thy Kingdom of truth and righteousness. These mercies we ask in the name of the Teacher sent from God, even Christ Jesus. Amen.

Herbert Stroup

683 Almighty God, we acknowledge thee to be the only wise God, the source of all wisdom, and our Father-God. We bless thee for the vision and inspiration of those who have established houses of instruction in which we may learn the good way of life and walk therein. We praise thee for thy providence, which preserves this heritage from generation to generation. Grant that we may enter into our high privilege with rejoicing in the things of wisdom; and guard us, we beseech thee, from the arrogance and vainglory of those who are wise in their own conceits. Consecrate us to the noble pursuit of sound learning, and may we truly love thee with all our mind. Send out thy light and thy truth; let them guide us. Send upon us the wisdom that is from above, which is first pure, then peaceable, gentle, easy to be entreated, full of mercy and good fruits, without partiality and without hypocrisy. By the guidance of such wisdom may knowledge grow from more to more, and greater reverence dwell in our midst, until we shall attain unto the measure of the fullness of Christ, the incarnate wisdom of God. Grant us the mind of Christ, for his name's sake. Amen.

Elmer W. K. Mould

684 We implore thy blessing, O God, on all the men and women who teach the children and youth of our nation, for they are the potent friends and helpers of our homes. Into their hands we daily commit the dearest that we have, and as they make our children, so shall future years see them.

Grant them an abiding consciousness that they are co-workers with thee, thou great teacher of humanity, and that thou hast charged them with the holy duty of bringing forth from the budding life of the young the mysterious stores of character and ability which thou hast hidden in them. Teach them to reverence the young lives, clean and plastic, which have newly come from thee, and to realize that generations still unborn shall rue their sloth or rise to higher levels through their wisdom and faithfulness.

Gird them for their task with thy patience and tranquillity, with a great fatherly and motherly love for the young, and with special tenderness for the backward and afflicted. Save them from physical exhaustion, from loneliness and discouragement, from the numbness of routine, and from all bitterness of heart.

We bless thee for the free and noble spirit that is breathing with quickening power upon the educational life of our day, and for the men and women of large mind and loving heart who have made that spirit our common possession by their teaching example. But grant that a higher obedience and self-restraint may grow in the new atmosphere of freedom.

We remember with gratitude to thee the godly teachers of our own youth who won our hearts to higher purposes by the sacred contagion of their life. May the strength and beauty of Christlike service still be plainly wrought in the lives of their successors, that our children may not want for strong models of devout manhood on whom their characters can be molded.

Do thou reward thy servants with a glad sense of their own eternal worth as teachers of the race, and in the heat of the day do thou show them the spring by the wayside that flows from the eternal silence of God and gives new light to the eyes of all who drink of it. Amen.

Walter Rauschenbusch

Poems

685   *THE CHURCH SCHOOL*

Here we shall seek for truth as a miner searches
    For gold in the far-off hills, and we shall find
Along clear rushing streams the shining nuggets
    To store in eager heart and seeking mind.
Our Leader is an able, wise prospector
    To guide where precious metal can be found.
Too long we have sought through barren, darkened lowlands,
    He goes before to lead to higher ground.

Seekers for truth, there are veins untouched, untested,
    There is gold still deep that our picks will yet unlease,
Dig earnestly along the upland channels
    That stretch afar, and lead the soul to peace.
In the Word of God with its precious, priceless gold
    Truly are mines with their glorious wealth untold.

Grace Noll Crowell

686   *SHEEP AND SHEPHERD*

O Lord, thy benediction give
    On all who teach, on all who learn,
That so thy Church may holier live,
    And every lamp more brightly burn.

Give those that learn the willing ear,
    The spirit meek, the guileless mind;
Such gifts will make the lowliest here
    Far better than a kingdom find.

O bless the shepherd, bless the sheep,
    That guide and guided both be one;
One in the faithful watch they keep,
    One in the joy of work well done.

John Armstrong

687   *THE LEADEN-EYED*

Let not young souls be smothered out before
    They do quaint deeds and fully flaunt their pride.
It is the world's one crime its babes grow dull,
    Its poor are ox-like, limp and leaden eyed.

Not that they starve, but starve so dreamlessly.
    Not that they sow, but that they seldom reap.
Not that they serve, but have no gods to serve.
    Not that they die, but that they die like sheep.

Vachel Lindsay

688   *THE PSALM OF THE GOOD TEACHER*

The Lord is my Teacher;
I shall not lose the way to wisdom.
He leadeth me in the lowly path of learning,
He prepareth a lesson for me every day.
He findeth the clear fountain of instruction—
Little by little he showeth me the beauty of truth.

The world is a great book that he has written,
He turneth the leaves for me slowly;
They are all inscribed with images and letters—
His voice poureth light on the pictures and the words.

Then am I glad when I perceive his meaning.
He taketh me by the hand to the hill-top of wisdom;
In the valley, also, he walketh beside me,
And in the dark places he whispereth in my heart.

Yea, though my lesson be hard, it is not hopeless,
For the Lord is very patient with his slow scholar.
He will wait a while for my weakness—
He will help me to read the truth through tears—
Surely thou wilt enlighten me daily by joy and by sorrow,
And lead me at last, O Lord, to the perfect knowledge of thee.

Henry van Dyke

689   *THE TEACHER'S PRAYER*

My Lord, I do not ask to stand
    As king or prince of high degree.
I only pray that, hand in hand,
    A child and I may come to thee.

Help me to share what thou dost give
    And be a friend, a trusted guide.
As in thy sight, oh, let me live.
    May selfishness be crucified.

Thou art the life, the truth, the way
    That leads to God, that saves from sin.
Oh, may my teaching, day by day,
    Help those in need, thy life to win.

Oh, grant thy patience, Lord, to share
    Thy holy purpose, life to bring.
May I the inexperience bear
    Of those who need love's fostering.

Norman E. Richardson

690   *A TEACHER'S PRAYER*

I ask thee for a sure and certain skill,
A patient and a consecrated will.
I ask thee for a white and perfect dream,
A vision of the deep and wide Unseen;
Dear Lord, I need these things so much, so much,
A little child lies plastic to my touch.

I ask thee for a love that understands
When it should reach and when withdraw its hands;
A selflessness that flings the locked door wide,
For youth to enter while I step aside,
Dear Lord, I need these things so much, so much,
A human soul lies plastic to my touch.

Eleanor B. Stock

691   *I CANNOT COUNT THE THINGS*

I cannot count the things you did for me:
You wakened me, and led me forth to find
Immortal company, and made me see
My path in the republic of the mind.

You taught me scorn for methods that are cheap,
For flashy work unworshipfully done,
And gave me, too, the sacred flame to keep
And share with many a spiritual son.

Fitzgerald Flournoy

Topics, Texts and Themes

692   *THE EDUCATION OF JESUS*

And [he] was subject unto them. LU. 2:51

The Gospels record not only the final examination to which he was subjected
at the end of his schooling, but the actual response he made to such a test. It
took place, as you will remember, on an isolated mountain-top at the very
beginning of his ministry and commonly we speak of it as his temptation.
Here he showed unmistakably that, indifferent though his training was from
our point of view, he had acquired from it certain convictions and attitudes

without which the noblest education may well be a futility. He knew his way to an invisible source of strength on which he could draw in any emergency. He had learned to distinguish between ephemeral and lasting values. He was schooled in selflessness. He had acquired a sense of responsibility which gave to his life a clear-cut purpose. He had been rubbed free from petty racial and social prejudice until he could see the world in terms of humanity. All this rings through his words and shines from his face, when we see him there on the mountain-top during his hour of ordeal, robust and vigorous in his young manhood, as he squares himself to face his task in the world.

Carl Hopkins Elmore

693   *CHRIST AS TEACHER*

Until we all attain . . . the knowledge of the Son of God, and reach mature manhood. EP. 4:13 (Goodspeed)

Christ placed no premium on ignorance. Half-truths with him, like the tares, were gathered and burned. The lad of twelve was not content with a "village-mind." The great minds of Israel at the temple knew God and might teach him. "He grew in wisdom."

His disciples called him "Teacher." His followers were his disciples, "learners." How much time he spent in teaching them to think! What were his methods? (1) Parables, demanding thinking, and thinking in a practical way, "blessed is he that hears and does"; (2) questions, "is it lawful to do good or evil on the Sabbath?" "Who do you say I am?" questions not of fact, but calling for earnest, realistic thinking; (3) his life, dedicated to the mission of Truth: through a Cross of love, faith, forgiveness, and fellowship. Have you permitted the Christ to be your Teacher? What would he have you learn and think about today?

Lawrence Warren

694   *THE GOAL OF EDUCATION*

Religion has had, for at least a generation, too little a place in our institutions of learning. Higher education long ago came to be a synonym for mere intellectualism. Then we realized that the student had a body as well as a mind, and we began in a systematic way to lay proper stress on physical development. So far so good: but we have hitherto neglected the soul. We have starved our students spiritually. We have no right to expect anything but the disproportionate and unsymmetrical product that has been developed. . . . I am insisting that true Christlikeness is the goal of education, and I am deploring a system which emphasizes the mind and body to the neglect of the soul. Would that we had not forgotten that "holiness" means "wholeness." Were it not so, I could say without any danger of being misunderstood that the highest education aims to make holy men.

George Wharton Pepper

695   *GOD IN EDUCATION*

Ye shall know the truth, and the truth shall make you free. JN. 8:32

"I want my son to have an education." How many fine, Christian parents have not only made that statement but have sacrificed time and health and even their financial integrity to give their offspring this supreme benefit. I talked to one fine churchman who expressed the nagging doubt that assails the minds of so many parents after their children have attained the coveted college degree and then gone into the world no better and frequently not as good as their parents. Said this father: "My boy has less respect for God, less capacity for hard work, and at times, I believe less ability to think than many of his friends who never had the advantage of a college education. Why?" I would like to ask those who are beginning to question the value of an education two simple questions: "*From* what do you expect a man to be educated?" and "*For* what do you expect a man to be educated?" These are the two forgotten questions of education.

Ensworth Reisner

696   *FAITH FOR THE NEXT GENERATION*

We older people have done damage to the cause of Jesus by presenting him to youth as a theological figure instead of a daring adventurer. We may be interested in him as a source of theological speculation, but he held the interest of his contemporaries because of his bold challenge to the existing order. Remember, the Master died when he was thirty-three years old, a youth of daring spirit risking everything on the reality of the unseen, believing that the impossible was possible. . . . The technique of transmitting religion to the next generation depends upon our ability to remember the impulses that quickened our spirits in the days of our youth, and to forget, for the time being, our own mature interests, so that we may present him to the young in terms of the things that appeal to the young.

The younger generation will be drawn to the Christ not so much by what he gives as by what he asks. They want to have another try at the impossible.

So did he. Let them go with him. They want to adventure in a course that will require all their courage. So did he. Let them go with him. They want to feel that some one is depending upon them for what they can give. So did he. Let them go with him.

Echoing from everything we say in church, young people ought to be able to distinguish the voice Isaiah heard when he entered the temple as a young man—God, musing over the unfinished problems of life, saying, "Whom shall I send and who will go with us?" Young people will feel impelled to make the response of an Isaiah, "Here am I; send me." Give them their chance and they will find the "faith of our fathers living still."

Theodore Cuyler Speers

697 *A TEACHER'S WORD TO TEACHERS*

And Jesus said unto them, Come ye after me, and I will make you to become fishers of men. MK. 1:17

These words were spoken by a great teacher, and in saying them he defined both the aim of the teacher's work and the method by which he must fit himself to do it. The aim is the making of persons. The method is the surrender of the will to the leadership of the greatest of persons.

William Adams Brown

698 *FROM LIFE TO LIFE*

Garfield was pointing in the line of truth when he preferred to have President Hopkins sitting with him on the other end of a log to any college he knew. There would be occasions when he would need laboratories and test-tubes and lecture-rooms and a library, but the best moments would undoubtedly be those when he had his rendezvous with President Hopkins on the traditional log.

John Colet visited Florence in his youth and felt the spell of Savonarola's life and words. He returned to England and passed the kindling torch on to Erasmus. Erasmus found Thomas Bilney in his university days and left him "another man." It was Thomas Bilney who awakened Hugh Latimer and kindled the burning passion in his soul. It was Hugh Latimer who in the street at Oxford lighted a fire in England—a martyr fire—which by the grace of God has never gone out. In such ways, from life to life, the torch passes on, though not often, as in the above chain, can the linkages be traced.

Rufus M. Jones

699   *A SUCCESSFUL TEACHER NEEDS*

The education of a college president,
The executive ability of a financier,
The humility of a deacon,
The adaptability of a chameleon,
The hope of an optimist,
The courage of a hero,
The wisdom of a serpent,
The gentleness of a dove,
The patience of Job,
The grace of God, and
The persistence of the devil.

Author Unknown

F. COMMENCEMENT SUNDAY

Commencement Sunday offers the church an opportunity to honor the parishioners who have completed courses of study in high schools and colleges. Included in this section are materials useful for commencement programs and baccalaureate sermons.

Calls to Worship

(Boldface type indicates responses.)

700   The Lord is the portion of mine inheritance.
The lines are fallen unto me in pleasant places; yea, I have a goodly heritage.
I have set the Lord always before me. . . . Therefore my heart is glad, and my glory rejoiceth.
Thou wilt shew me the path of life: in thy presence is fulness of joy; at thy right hand there are pleasures for evermore.

Ps. 16:5-6, 8-9, 11

701   Cause me to hear thy loving kindness in the morning [O Lord]; for in thee do I trust: cause me to know the way wherein I should walk; for I lift up my soul unto thee.
Teach me to do thy will; for thou art my God: thy spirit is good; lead me into the land of uprightness.

Ps. 143:8, 10

702   My mouth shall shew forth thy righteousness and thy salvation all the day. . . . I will go in the strength of the Lord God: I will make mention of thy righteousness, even of thine only. O God, thou hast taught me from my youth: and hitherto have I declared thy wondrous works.

Ps. 71:15-17

Invocations

703   O God, Inspirer and Teacher of men, who art the truth thou lovest: send out thy light and illumine us. Give us a deep and clear knowledge of ourselves; help us to a growing knowledge of our world; confirm in us the

holiness of true reason; strengthen in us the aspiration towards noble and spacious thinking; and, in thy good time, bring us unto thy holy hill and to thy dwelling; through Jesus Christ our Saviour. Amen.

Henry Sylvester Nash

704 O God who art both the author of peace and the disturber of conscience, save us from irresponsible inertia. Give us not over to any death of the soul, but lift us into newness of life, that we may use this day of opportunity and danger to serve thee, yea, to glorify thee and enjoy thee forever; in the Spirit of thy Son whose voice wakes the dead and whose Word giveth life. Amen.

David A. MacLennan

705 O thou who art the light of the minds that know thee, the life of the souls that love thee, and the strength of the wills that serve thee: help us to know thee that we may truly love thee, so to love thee that we may fully serve thee, whom to serve is perfect freedom; through Jesus Christ our Lord. Amen.

St. Augustine

706 O Eternal Light, shine into our hearts. O Eternal Goodness, deliver us from all evil. Eternal Pity, have mercy upon us. Eternal Power, be thou our support. Eternal Wisdom, scatter the darkness of our ignorance. Grant that with all our heart and mind and strength we may evermore seek thy face; and guide us in thy love and mercy in the way that leadeth to life eternal. So strengthen and bless us that, following in the footsteps of thy dear Son our Saviour, we may inherit the promises, and enter at last into the joy of our Lord; for his name's sake. Amen.*

Alcuin

Litany

(Boldface type indicates responses.)

707 O God, our true life, in whom and by whom all things live, who by thy Spirit dost command us to seek thee, and art ever ready to be found; to know thee is life, to serve thee is freedom, to praise thee is the joy and happiness of the soul:

We praise and bless thee and give thanks for thy great glory.

For seasons of bounty and of beauty, for nights of quiet sleep, for days of health, for the glory of earth, and its ministry to our need:

We bless thy name, O Lord.

For all generations before us who through effort and pain have wrought so that we might be heirs of liberty and truth and peace:

We thank thee, our Father, and pray that we may enter into this heritage.

For opportunities used and unused, for victories over besetting sins, for the gladness and courage abiding with loyalty:

We praise thee, O God.

For the discipline that enriches, for the burden that strengthens, for the failure that is true success, and for the sorrow that enlarges the heart:

For these also we rejoice and give thee thanks.

For the soul and its powers, for the impulse to share, to serve, and to save:

We give thee thanks, O Lord.

Keep us, we pray thee, in thy love; and in and through the quickening of our spirits make us worthy of sonship with thee:

And to thee be the honor and glory, world without end. Amen.

Author Unknown

Prayers

708   Eternal God, our heavenly Father, thou art the all-wise and the infinitely patient teacher. From age to age, thou hast shared with those of open mind something of thy truth.

Grant, we beseech thee, thy continued blessing on this school, and more especially on this day when we leave behind us these loved friends and old familiar places.

In this hour, help us to feel the beauty of these illuminated years. In the pain of breaking treasured ties, may we rediscover the goodness of thy love and the thought for us when thou trusted us with such capacity for abiding friendship and enduring loyalty.

Blend within us all high visions and deep resolves associated with these years. May the sparks kindled here by wise and good teachers set our hearts and wills aflame to do thy will. Help us to carry lighted torches into dark places. Continue to increase our knowledge of truth.

When, in other years, we return to this loved spot, may we who have been given so much of light not come back with darkened lamps.

Speak some good word to each of us, we pray, till all that remains of falseness or of selfishness dies in us. Make us faithful and strong, patient and tender, eager to fulfill thy purposes for our lives. Bless us that we may go forth to bless others for thee. In the name of Jesus Christ, the great teacher. Amen.

S. Ralph Harlow

709   O God, Father, Saviour and Revealer, sanctify all those who in the midst of truth seek more truth. As they question the authority of the past, increase their loyalty to the things which are eternal. May liberty of thought leave unsullied the simplicity of their trust in thee. As the steep ascent of truth reveals the ever-widening horizon of thy thought, lead them in the narrow path of humble and sacrificial service. Enable them to share the joy of their emancipation without weakening other men's faith in the God of their own experience. May pride of learning never chill the warmth of prayer. May opposition and misinterpretation arouse within them no bitterness or plans for retaliation. As by thy grace they are led into deeper sympathy with their Lord, may they give to the world their new assurance of the triumph of his Kingdom, rather than the agony of their struggle with doubt. And ever amid the clash of argument may they find the peace that passeth understanding in Jesus Christ our Lord. Amen.

Shailer Mathews

710   Our heavenly Father, we, thy children, who have received the gifts of thy love and concern, come to thee in the name of our youth. Thou knowest that we love them and covet for them every good gift. So we pray that they may have a great sense of their need of thee, who art the source of life and the fountain of wisdom.

Save them from all wrong turnings and evil choices; redeem them from pride and arrogancy; give them thy patience and steadfastness. Let them dream thy dreams for them and be possessed by the vision of the young man of Galilee. Release them from the weight of our compromises and grant that their great expectations may be uncaptured by the weariness of the past.

Make the church a mighty fortress for a new generation, preparing itself for the heat of the battle. Create within our homes the love and security which builds Christian character. And in all the difficult questions which must be answered and all the crucial choices which must be made, give every young person grace enough to sit at the feet of Jesus Christ, the teacher incomparable of the high art of living. And when defeat and disappointment are experienced, suffer not their spirits to surrender nor allow their hearts to be cast down. Let them ever be certain that in Christ there is power enough to live heroically and nobly.

Hear us, we beseech thee, through Jesus Christ our Lord. Amen.

Gerald Kennedy

711   Almighty and most merciful God, humbly because of our unworthiness but boldly because of thy goodness and the ceaseless patience of thy love, we would bow our heads before thee in silent adoration. Thou hast created us, preserved us, and brought us to this day of commencement. Thou hast held out to us when we were most alone the offer of thy companionship, in weakness ministering strength, for darkness light, remembering us thyself forgotten, Friend to all our unfriendliness.

We thank thee that thou hast revealed thyself to us in the orderliness of the universe which thy hands have fashioned, thy majesty in its vast distance on distance, thy nearness in the Word that comes stealing out of that silence into our hearts. The long past echoes of thy name in our ears, from prophet and saint, apostle and martyr, in the march of the years and the destiny of nations: grant us to hear thee now speaking to us by thy Son, and in him to know thee as thou art, entering into this life of ours to bear thyself the weight of it, forever merciful in thy judgments, and just in all thy compassion.

Bear with us as we confess our sins before thee: the selfishness that changes even our good into evil, the prejudice that blinds us, the indifference that keeps us from the knowledge of thy will, and shuts up from the homeless and the hungry the warmth of human kindness and the very bounty of thy providence. Thou canst not heal the world's hurt if we will not be healed. We ask thee on this day of achievement for thy pardon, and for the grace that will make us whole. Cleanse us of the wrong that distorts the mind, of the willful desire that twists life away from thy purpose, of cherished hatred and thoughtless contempt, of pride of place and of envy. Bring us in every moment of decision to set before thee the choices we would make, submitting our knowledge to thy wisdom, and yielding that we are to the service of what thou wouldst have us be.

Have regard, we beseech thee, to all schools and colleges, that they may be dedicated in thy fear to every pure art, and to useful learning, whereby life may be enriched, the bond of ignorance and superstition broken, dullness sharpened into insight, and wonder into reverence. Rid us together in this uneasy world of all that makes for enmity, of the narrow loyalties that breed war, of the cramped horizons where our spirits grow poor. And rule among the affairs of men everywhere to the establishment of righteousness, and in righteousness of peace: that thy mind may be brought by our hands into the future, not in trembling under thy wrath, but in willing obedience; by thy grace in Christ Jesus, to whom with thee and the Holy Ghost be glory and dominion both now and ever. Amen.

Paul Scherer

Poems

712　　　　　　　　*O GRANT US LIGHT*

O grant us light, that we may know
　　The wisdom thou alone canst give;
That truth may guide whate'er we do,
　　And virtue bless where'er we live.

O grant us light, that we may learn
　　How dead is life from thee apart;
How sure is joy for all who turn
　　To thee an undivided heart.

Lawrence Tuttiett

713　　　　　*THE ROCK THAT IS HIGHER*

There is a trail within your life
　　Where you can climb above the crowd,
Where you can rise above the earth,
　　And look far down on haze and cloud.

There is a trail within your soul
　　Where you can climb right up to God,
And know the source whence blessings flow
　　To quicken life in seed and sod.

There is a trail that calls to you,
　　"Come, climb, and conquer heights unscaled,
That you may see with vision true,
　　And find life's goal where others failed."

There is a trail that you can climb,
　　What though death come on mountain peak!
The vision comes to those who climb!
　　Christ's mantle falls on those who seek!

Fred S. Buschmeyer

714　　　　　*GIVE US GREAT DREAMS*

Give us great dreams, O God, while thou art giving,
　　And keep the end; it is enough if we
Live by the hope, nor falter in the living,
　　That lures us on from dust to dignity.

Give us the courage of the soul's high vision,
  Though its fulfilment here we never see;
The heart to make and keep the brave decision,
  And faith to leave the ultimate with thee.

Marie LeNart

715   *PREPAREDNESS*

  For all your days prepare,
    And meet them ever alike:
  When you are the anvil, bear—
    When you are the hammer, strike.

Edwin Markham

716   *WE BREAK NEW SEAS TODAY*

We break new seas today!
Our eager keels quest unaccustomed waters,
And from the vast, unchartered waste in front
The mystic circles leap
Bringing us—what?
Dread shoals and shifting banks?
Clouds and bitter gales?
Wreck and loss?
Or, maybe, golden days
Full freighted with delight!

Each man is captain of his soul,
And chooses his own crew;
But the Pilot knows the unknown seas,
And he will bring us through.

John Oxenham

717   *THE MASTER'S TOUCH*

In the still air the music lies unheard;
  In the rough marble beauty hides unseen;
To make the music and the beauty, needs
  The master's touch, the sculptor's chisel keen.

Great Master, touch us with thy skillful hand,
  Let not the music that is in us die;
Great Sculptor, hew and polish us; nor let,
  Hidden and lost, thy form within us lie.

Spare not the stroke; do with us as thou wilt;
  Let there be nought unfinished, broken, marr'd;
Complete thy purpose, that we may become
  Thy perfect image, O our God and Lord.

Horatius Bonar

718   *From OUTLOOK*

Not to be conquered by these headlong days,
But to stand free: to keep the mind at brood
On life's deep meaning, nature's altitude
Of loveliness, and time's mysterious ways;
At every thought and deed to clear the haze
Out of our eyes, considering only this,
What man, what life, what love, what beauty is,
This is to live, and win the final praise.

Archibald Lampman

719   *From THE TASK* (Bk. VI)

Knowledge and wisdom, far from being one,
Have ofttimes no connexion. Knowledge dwells
In heads replete with thoughts of other men,
Wisdom in minds attentive to their own.
Knowledge, a rude, unprofitable mass,
The mere materials with which wisdom builds,
Till smoothed and squared and fitted to its place,
Does but encumber whom it seems to enrich.
Knowledge is proud that he has learned so much;
Wisdom is humble that he knows no more.

William Cowper

Topics, Texts and Themes

720   *WHAT SHALL WE DO WITH OUR LIVES?*

Give them away. Make a generous gift of them to mankind. Find the thing that is worth dying for as well as worth living for. Die for it daily, not in a spectacular way, but in a silent way. Keep it, if you will, a secret between you and God. Spread your dying out over the weeks, the months and the years. Let your life be consumed in service. Consume yourself valiantly, cheerfully, creatively, skillfully. Put all your intelligence into your self-consumption; put all your skill into it; put all your courage into it. Waste no thought on asking whether you are as happy as you have a right to be. Ask for no guarantees.

Believe me, it will be a great relief. It will be an immense liberation. You will not be miserable. Not a gleam of radiance the less shall fall on your life, but a hundred times more.

L. P. Jacks

721   *WHAT CAN I DO WITH MY LIFE?*

In his autobiography, Dr. Joseph Fort Newton maintains that there are four things, and only four things, that a person can do with his life. First, he can run away from it, or try to, as Jonah did. Second, he can run along with life, hunt with the pack, think with the herd, in obedience to the phrase, "Everybody's doing it, why shouldn't I?", which may be the very reason why he should not do it, if he has any standards or any character. Third, he can take hold of life with singleness of purpose, and submitting himself to discipline, can run it to some end. Fourth, he can give himself up utterly in self-surrender to a Cause or a Person and let the Cause or the Person run his life. If lines of division were drawn . . . would we not find the majority group consisting of those who are running along with life, adapting themselves chameleon-like to their environment, taking on the complexion of their surroundings, molded by society, not its molders?

Robert J. McCracken

722   *A RENDEZVOUS WITH LIFE*

I am debtor. . . . So, as much as in me is, I am ready. RO. 1:14–15

One of the most stirring poems born out of World War I was that of Alan Seeger, "A Rendezvous with Death." What a haunting melody is in the lines:

> I have a rendezvous with Death
> At some disputed barricade
> When spring comes back with rustling shade,
> And apple blossoms fill the air.

And what poignant memories as well:

> And I to my pledged word am true,
> I shall not fail that Rendezvous.

We do not need to diminish our devotion to the memory of those who kept their rendezvous with death if we remind ourselves of our "Rendezvous with Life."

Countee Cullen, the brilliant young Negro poet, has pictured it for us in *Caroling Dusk*. I quote a few lines only:

> I have a rendezvous with Life . . .
> Though wet nor blow nor space I fear,
> Yet fear I deeply, too,
> Lest Death should meet and claim me ere
> I keep Life's rendezvous.

This rendezvous with life . . . implies a life that seeks creative labor, that recognizes relationships and contributes to the common good, life that finds its source and strength in God, that dares all in high endeavor toward a new heaven and a new earth. Such a rendezvous with life claims a quality of courage and devotion that only youth possesses.

Avery Albert Shaw

723   *THE RACE OF LIFE*

> Know ye not that they which run in a race run all, but one receiveth the prize? So run, that ye may obtain. 1 CO. 9:24

In the race of life three things must be considered—distance, direction, destiny. In the distance, life stretches out before us. We do not fix the distance, but the prize must be won in the time allotted. We do not fix the time limit, but we do determine the use of that time. Wisdom decides, "Life is a game; I will play the same with loftiest aim"—to the end. Next, we must know the direction in which we have to go. It must not be a hit or miss journey. Life may have many interests, but there should be one steady purpose. An honorable, purposeful vocation in life enables the Christian to make progress toward God. At the end of life's race is destiny. Like St. Paul, we can deliberately choose the right direction. A divinely inspired purpose, followed through to the end, obtains life's crown.

William H. Burgwin

724   *IS LIFE WORTH LIVING?*

All the days of Methuselah were nine hundred sixty and nine years: and he died. GE. 5:27

"Count no man happy until he is dead," exclaimed Solon, the philosopher. That is the answer he apparently would give to this ever-recurring question, Is life worth living? What is our reply to it? That will be determined largely by what we mean by life. And it is our aim to prove to some who think life is worth living that it is not; and also to prove to others who think it is not worth living, that it is!

The man who is generally credited with the longest span of life is Methuselah. His age is given as nine hundred and sixty-nine years. But was his life worth while? Look at the records. Although he is mentioned seven times in various parts of the Scriptures, in six cases his name is merely cited in some genealogical table. The remaining passage is quoted here, where to the number of his years is added the interesting fact, "and he died."

One of the shortest lives recorded in the sacred writings was that of him who lived only about thirty-three years. Yet the impression which Christ's life made upon the world is immeasurable. Although it was compassed by an obscure Palestinian province, and its sun went down amid thick clouds of horror and shame, its influence is still potent. None can say what it shall yet accomplish. Limited to such a short span, we marvel at the unparalleled splendor of its achievements, the sublimity of its example, the unwavering loyalty to right which marked it. Between the Master and Methuselah there is really no comparison, and yet, looking at the record of Jesus, we may truly say, what a life! Admitting, however, that there can be no comparison, we immediately manifest our inconsistency by instituting one. And it reveals this fact: the value of life depends not on its extent, but on its intent and content. It is not duration, but the divine quality of it that really matters.

J. W. G. Ward

725   *FROM ONE GENERATION TO ANOTHER*

When a cornerstone of a new building was laid at New York State University [in 1950], President Charles W. Hunt enclosed the following message in it: "Greetings: To those who will come after us.

"This May 12, 1950, we lay this cornerstone of a building . . . dedicated to the higher learning.

"We do so as an act of faith.

"We believe in God. We believe in the ability of man to rise again to new heights from whatever depths.

"We believe that education can protect mankind from its inherent weakness.

"We believe that the men and women who go forth from our colleges will make their full and effective contributions to the betterment of this world.

"In these beliefs, we carry on.

"May your world be happier than ours and may some portion of your happiness be due to us.

"So help us, God."

James Keller

726   *DOORS TO A BETTER WORLD*

In the second epistle to the Corinthians, St. Paul says he sees before him doors leading to fields of high service and many adversaries who are determined that the doors shall be closed to him. Moffatt translates the passage, "I have wide opportunities here for active service—and there are many to thwart me." In the Twentieth Century New Testament the passage reads, "A great opening for active work has presented itself, and there are many opponents." All of these translations agree that the Apostle Paul is saying he sees before him doors to great usefulness and hard by those who would close the doors. Readers of the letters of St. Paul are struck by the fact that he never saw a closed door without resolving to get it open.

Marshall Wingfield

727   *MARKS OF AN EDUCATED MAN*

1. Has your education made you a friend of all good causes?
2. Has your education made you a brother to the weak?
3. Do you see anything to love in a little child?
4. Would a lost dog follow you in the street?
5. Do you enjoy being alone?
6. Do you believe in the dignity of labor?
7. Can you look into a mud puddle and see the blue sky?
8. Can you go out at night, look up in the sky and see beyond the stars?
9. Is your life linked with the Infinite?

Author Unknown

IV. The Christian Nation

A. THANKSGIVING SUNDAY

Thanksgiving Sunday is celebrated on the Sunday preceding Thanksgiving Day. Many of the aspects of the Thanksgiving tradition are distinctly American, for the day recaptures the spirit of the Pilgrims who thanked God for their survival. The day is akin, however, to the Hebrew Feast of Ingathering (De. 16:13–17) and to the latter-day Harvest Home festival. Each acknowledges the gathering in of the crops, although Thanksgiving also expresses gratitude for the fortunes and welfare of all the people. Thanksgiving Day is commonly held on the fourth Thursday of November by presidential proclamation.

Calls to Worship

(Boldface type indicates responses.)

728   Make a joyful noise unto the Lord, all ye lands.
Serve the Lord with gladness, come before his presence with singing.
Enter into his gates with thanksgiving, and into his courts with praise.
Be thankful unto him, and bless his name. For the Lord is good; his mercy is everlasting; and his truth endureth to all generations.

Ps. 100:1, 4–5

729   Let the people praise thee, O God; let all the people praise thee.
Then shall the earth yield her increase; and God, even our own God, will bless us.
God shall bless us; and all the ends of the earth shall fear him.

Ps. 67:5–7

730   O give thanks unto the Lord, for he is good: for his mercy endureth for ever.
Oh that men would praise the Lord for his goodness, and for his wonderful works to the children of men!
For he satisfieth the longing soul, and filleth the hungry soul with goodness.

Ps. 107:1, 8–9

731   O give thanks unto the Lord; call upon his name: make known his deeds among the people.

Sing unto him, sing psalms unto him: talk ye of all his wondrous works.

Glory ye in his holy name: let the heart of them rejoice that seek the Lord.

Ps. 105:1-3

Invocations

732   Almighty and most merciful Father, from whom cometh down every good and perfect gift: we yield thee praise and thanks for all thy mercies. Thy goodness hath created us; thy bounty hath sustained us; thy fatherly discipline hath chastened and corrected us; thy patience hath borne with us; thy love hath redeemed us. Give us a heart to love and serve thee, and enable us to show our thankfulness for all the goodness and mercy thou hast conferred by giving up ourselves to thy service, and cheerfully submitting in all things to thy blessed will. Amen.

Book of Common Order

733   Most gracious God, who hast opened thy hand to give us all good things: thou keepest us beneath the shadow of thy wings; thou providest for us as a father; thou lovest us as a friend and thinkest on us every day. Unto thee, O God, we offer praise for our redemption in Christ. Grant now that what thou hast sown in loving kindness may spring up in service; let thy grace strengthen our purpose to do always what is pleasing in thy sight; living here in the light of thy favor, may we at last enter into thy glory, and give thanks to thee for ever; through Jesus Christ our Lord. Amen.

Book of Worship (ER)

734   Most gracious God, by whose appointment the seasons come and go, and who makest the fruits of the earth to minister to the needs of men: we offer thee our thanksgivings that thou hast brought us through the circuit of another year, and that according to thy promise seedtime and harvest have not failed. We thank thee that thou hast prospered the husbandman in his toil, and hast crowned the year with thy goodness. We praise thee, the giver of all good gifts, for the plentiful harvests to feed the hungry and minister to our comfort. At the remembrance of thy bounty we offer unto thee the sacrifices of our thanksgiving, and pray that thou wilt feed our souls with the bread of life. Amen.

Book of Church Services

Litany

(Boldface type indicates responses.)

735 O Lord, who hast set before us the great hope that thy Kingdom shall come on earth, and hast taught us to pray for its coming: make us ever ready to thank thee for the signs of its dawning, and to pray and work for that perfect day when thy will shall be done on earth as it is in heaven. For the work of thy Spirit within and beyond the bounds of thy visible church:
We thank thee, O Lord.

For the work of thy Spirit in the history of the world, through peaceful advance, and through pain and tumult:
We thank thee, O Lord.

For the work of thy Spirit in the history of our own country, through its heroes and leaders, in statecraft, law and industry:
We thank thee, O Lord.

For the work of thy Spirit in science and commerce, in literature and art:
We thank thee, O Lord.

For the work of thy Spirit in the slow triumph of truth over error:
We thank thee, O Lord.

For the work of thy Spirit in the growing desire for true brotherhood between man and every class and nation:
We thank thee, O Lord.

For the work of thy Spirit in the spread of education, in the development of a fuller life for individuals, with healthier surroundings and better conditions:
We thank thee, O Lord.

For the work of thy Spirit in the deepening sense of human worth in all nations and classes, and in the growing reverence for womanhood and childhood:
We thank thee, O Lord.

For the work of thy Spirit in the church, which will not cease until it join all nations and kindred and tongues and people into one great family, to thy praise and glory:
We thank thee, O Lord.

Author Unknown

Prayers

736 We thank thee, O Lord our Lord, for our being, our life, our gift of reason; for our nurture, our preservation and guidance; for our education, civil rights and religious privileges; for thy gifts of grace, of nature, of this world; for our redemption, regeneration, and instruction in the Christian faith; for our calling, recalling, and our manifold renewed recallings for thy forbearance and long suffering. For thy prolonged forbearance many a time and many a year. For all the benefits we have received, and all the undertakings wherein we have prospered; for any good we may have done; for the use of the blessings of this life; for thy promise, and our hope of the enjoyment of good things to come; for good and honest parents, gentle teachers, benefactors ever to be remembered, congenial companions, intelligent hearers, sincere friends, faithful servants; for all who have profited us by their writings, sermons, conversations, prayers, examples, reproofs, injuries. For all these, and also for all other mercies, known and unknown, open and secret, remembered by us or now forgotten, kindnesses received by us willingly or even against our will. We praise thee, we bless thee, we thank thee, and will praise and bless and thank thee all the days of our life; through Jesus Christ our Lord. Amen.*

Lancelot Andrews

737   We thank thee, our Father, for life and love, for the mystery and majesty of existence, for the world of beauty which surrounds us and for the miracle of our conscious life by which we behold the wonders of the universe.

We thank thee for the glimpses of nobility in human life which redeem it from sordidness and reassure us that thy image is in the heart of man. We are grateful for the ties which bind us to our fellowmen; for the common toil in industry and marts of trade; for our joint inheritance as citizens of this nation; for traditions and customs hallowed by age through which our passions are ordered and channelled; for the love of beauty and truth and goodness by which we transcend the chasms of race and nation; for the faith of our fathers by which we claim kinship with the past and gain strength for the present; for the love of dear ones in our homes and for the enlarging responsibilities and sobering duties of our family life; for the serenity of old people who redeem us of fretfulness and for the faith and courage of youth through which we are saved from sloth.

We are unworthy of the rich inheritances of our common life. We confess that we have profaned the temple of this life by our selfishness and heedlessness. We have sought to gain advantage of our brothers who are bound together with us by many different ties. Have mercy upon us that we may express our gratitude for thy many mercies by contrition for our sins and that we may prove our repentance by lives dedicated more fully to thee and to the common good; through Jesus Christ our Lord. Amen.

Reinhold Niebuhr

738   We are reminded, our Father, by the return of Thanksgiving day, that every good gift comes from thee. Give us today the feeling of dependence which thy children should have, and with it the free, joyous spirit of childhood. Help us to realize that we do not grow a grain of wheat nor breathe a breath of air aside from thee, for thou hast made it all possible. Save us from the hardness of self-sufficiency as we gradually master the world about us, and ever increase in us the capacity for awe and gratitude.

We are grateful for our country, and for those chapters in her history which this day recalls. We are glad it was founded in a passion for freedom and human rights. Save us, O God, from the dangers of our prosperity; from conceit, and hardness, and lust for power. Show us how the ideas of Jesus may be made the measure of our national greatness, and help us in humility and in faith to make our contribution to the coming of thy Kingdom among the people of the earth. Amen.

W. A. Smart

739   O God of all life, we thank thee for our lives, and all they hold of happiness and work and play, of risk and courage and beauty.

We thank thee for the morning and evening skies of a land where liberty still marches on and freedom can still speak its mind without vanity and without fear.

We thank thee for all heroic souls who shame our cowardice, for all generous souls who give us pure delight, for all saintly souls who kindle our desire to be really good.

We thank thee for the friendship and the faces of those who look kindly upon us even when we fail and who help to bring us back to our bravest selves again.

We thank thee for the encouragements of success, for the disciplines of failure, for the spurs of dissatisfaction and the spirit which arises from defeat to fight better.

We thank thee for the exchange of gifts, for the gentle play of wit, for unforced laughter and for rare splendid moments.

We thank thee for prized books, enchanting music and pictures which move the heart, for letters from those we love and for the song remembered for the singer's sake.

We thank thee for the freedom which growing older gives us from the troubles of being very young, so that we have more big things to care about and fewer little things to cry about.

We thank thee for common joys of all kinds—the waking to sunlight through the window, the good smell of the earth on rainy days, beating to windward, the gift of sleep after tiring work or pleasure, and the affection of dogs and all faithful creatures.

O God of all life, we thank thee for this lovely, troublous, undaunted human life of ours; and may we live for the good of our church, our country, and our world, and ever to thy glory. Amen.

Vivian Pomeroy

Poems

740   *From GRATEFULNESSE*

Thou that hast giv'n so much to me,
Give one thing more, a gratefull heart.

❋

Not thankfull, when it pleaseth me;
As if thy blessings had spare dayes:
But such a heart, whose pulse may be
Thy praise.

George Herbert

741   *THANKFUL HEARTS*

He is the only Maker
Of all things near and far,
He paints the wayside flower,
He lights the evening star.
The winds and waves obey him,
By him the birds are fed;
Much more to us, his children,
He gives our daily bread.
No gifts have we to offer
For all thy love imparts,
But that which thou desirest,
Our humble, thankful hearts.

Matthias Claudius

742   *THANKSGIVING*

Give thanks, O heart! for these: A woman's face,
The gift of love, and love's enduring grace;
For man's firm friendship through the marching years,
The comfort of all children; even for tears

Shed in your grief, because these prove that you
Have pity that is beautiful and true.
Give thanks for raiment, and a loaf of bread;
And for a good thatched roof above your head;
But most of all give thanks if you can say,
"Lord, I have courage on my pilgrim's way!"

Charles Hanson Towne

743   *FATHER, WE THANK THEE*

Father, we thank thee:
For peace within our favored land,
For plenty from thy bounteous hand,
For means to give to those in need,
For grace to help in thought and deed,
For faith to walk, our hands in thine,
For truth to know thy law divine,
For strength to work with voice and pen,
For love to serve our fellow men,
For light the goal ahead to see,
For life to use alone for thee,
Father, we thank thee.

Grenville Kleiser

744   *THE PILGRIM FATHERS*

O God, beneath thy guiding hand
    Our exiled fathers crossed the sea;
And when they trod the wintry strand,
    With prayer and psalm they worshipped thee.

Thou heard'st, well pleased, the song, the prayer:
    Thy blessing came; and still its power
Shall onward through all ages bear
    The memory of that holy hour.

Laws, freedom, truth, and faith in God
    Came with those exiles o'er the waves;
And where their pilgrim feet have trod,
    The God they trusted guards their graves.

And here thy name, O God of love,
  Their children's children shall adore,
Till these eternal hills remove,
  And spring adorns the earth no more.

Leonard Bacon

745   *THANKS BE TO GOD*

I do not thank thee, Lord,
That I have bread to eat while others starve;
Nor yet for work to do
While empty hands solicit heaven;
Nor for a body strong
While other bodies flatten beds of pain.
No, not for these do I give thanks!

But I am grateful, Lord,
Because my meager loaf I may divide;
For that my busy hands
May move to meet another's need;
Because my doubled strength
I may expend to steady one who faints.
Yes, for all these do I give thanks!

For heart to share, desire to bear,
And will to lift,
Flamed into one by deathless Love—
Thanks be to God for this!
Unspeakable! His Gift!

Janie Alford

746   *From BECAUSE OF THY GREAT BOUNTY*

Because I have been given much,
I, too, shall give:
Because of thy great bounty, Lord,
Each day I live
I shall divide my gifts from thee
With every brother that I see
Who has the need of help from me.

Grace Noll Crowell

747   *THANKSLIVING*

> Were thanks with every gift expressed,
>   Each day would be Thanksgiving;
> Were gratitude its very best,
>   Each life would be thanksliving.
>
> *Chauncey R. Piety*

Topics, Texts and Themes

748   *ON BEING THANKFUL*

Thanksgiving is based . . . on an inner attitude toward life. Life has a dark side and a bright side, and always has, and we must decide which we are going to emphasize. Two girls gather grapes; one is happy because they have found the grapes and the other is unhappy because the grapes have seeds in them. Two women examine a bush; one is unhappy because it has thorns, the other notices the roses and is overjoyed with their fragrance. We see exactly what we train ourselves to see in this life. Our outlook on life is all-important, and it is something that depends solely on us.

William E. Park

749   *NOW THANK WE ALL OUR GOD*

Thanksgiving is distinctly an American holiday; there is nothing like it elsewhere in the world. It celebrates neither a savage battle nor the fall of a great city. It does not mark the anniversary of a great conqueror or the birthday of a famous statesman. It does not commemorate the writing of a historic public document or the launching of a new constitution. The American Thanksgiving Day is the expression of a deep feeling of gratitude by our people for the rich productivity of the land, a memorial of the dangers and hardships through which we have safely passed, and a fitting recognition of all that God in His goodness has bestowed upon us. . . . In early New England it was the custom at Thanksgiving time to place five grains of corn at every plate as a reminder of those stern days in the first winter when the food of the Pilgrims was so depleted that only five grains of corn were rationed to each individual at a time. The Pilgrim Fathers wanted their children to remember the sacrifice, suffering, and hardship which made possible the settlement of a free people in a free land. They wanted to keep alive the memory of that long sixty-three-day trip taken in the tiny *Mayflower*. They desired to keep alive the thought of that "stern and rock bound coast," its inhospitable welcome, and the first terrible winter which took such a toll of lives. They did not want their descendants to forget that on the day in which their ration was reduced to five grains of corn only seven healthy colonists remained to nurse the sick, and nearly half their numbers lay in the "windswept graveyard" on the hill. They did not want to forget that when the *Mayflower* sailed back to England in the spring only the sailors were aboard.

Bliss Forbush

750   *THE MAYFLOWER COMPACT*

In ye name of God, Amen. We whose names are underwritten, the loyall subjects of our dread soveraigne Lord, King James, by ye grace of God, of Great Britaine, Franc, and Ireland king, defender of ye faith, &., haveing undertaken, for ye glory of God, and advancemente of ye Christian faith, and honor of our king and countrie, a voyage to plant ye first colonie in the Northerne parts of Virginia, doe by these presents solemnly & mutualy in ye presence of God, and one of another, covenant & combine our selves togeather into a civill body politick, for our better ordering & preservation & furtherance of ye ends aforesaid; and by vertue hearof to enacte, constitute, and frame such just & equall lawes, ordinances, acts, constitutions, & offices, from time to time, as shall be thought most meete & convenient for ye generall good of ye Colonie, unto which we promise all due submission and obedience. In witnes wherof we have hereunder subscribed our names at Cap-Codd ye 11. of November, in ye year of ye raigne of our soveraigne lord, King James, of England, France, & Ireland ye eighteenth, and of Scotland ye fiftie-fourth. Ano. Dom. 1620.

751   *THE ROCK WHENCE YE ARE HEWN*

Today marks the beginning of Thanksgiving week. This has always been considered a favorable time at which to reconsider the history and traditions of our nation.

Periodically the prophets of Israel challenged their people to look back to the hardy pioneers of their race from whose loins they had sprung. "Look," they said, "unto the rock whence ye are hewn, and to the hole of the pit whence ye are digged. Look unto Abraham your father and unto Sarah that bare you."

If it was good for the children of Israel to look back to their ancestors and to examine the foundations of their national life, surely this is a useful activity for us in Thanksgiving week.

John Sutherland Bonnell

752 *A LIFE IN THE SOUL*

A generation fond of pleasure, disinclined towards serious thought, and shrinking from hardship, even if it may be swiftly reached, will find it difficult to imagine the temper, courage and manliness of the emigrants who made the first Christian settlement of New England. For a man to give up all things and fare forth into savagery, in order to escape from the responsibilities of life, in order, that is, to serve the devil, "whose feet are bound by civilization," is common. Giving up all things in order to serve God is a sternness for which prosperity has unfitted us.

Some regard the settling of New Plymouth as the sowing of the seed from which the crop of Modern America has grown. . . . For all the *Mayflower's* sailing there is, perhaps, little existing in modern England or America "according to the Primitive Patern in the Word of God." It would be healthful could either country see herself through the eyes of those pioneers, or see the pioneers as they were. The pilgrims leave no impression of personality on the mind. They were not "remarkable." Not one of them had compelling personal genius, or marked talent for the work in hand. They were plain men of moderate abilities, who, giving up all things, went to live in the wilds, at unknown cost to themselves, in order to preserve to their children a life in the soul.

John Masefield

753 *THE MINISTRY OF THANKSGIVING*

Some one has said that the function of art is threefold: Art teaches us to *see*; it teaches us *what* to see; and it teaches us to see *more than we see*. I think the spirit of thanksgiving performs a similar ministry for the soul. Here in the end of the year there is so much to be seen. He must be a braver, finer soul who sits down and quietly endeavors to understand the appeal which natural phenomena make even to the senses. "How good it is to be alive!" he exclaims. Just to be fevered with the sunset, like Richard Hovey, or to revel in the beauty of noonday, or to rejoice in the freshness of morning; to see the opening bud and fading leaf; to hear the neighing of horses and the lowing of cattle; to listen to the crowing of cocks and the singing of birds; to press the soft earth with eager tread and smell the incense of plowed ground or waving flower— to feel, in a word, our kinship to earth and air and sky, is to bestir within us a quickened sense of the overwhelming richness of the world of Nature.

Like art, also, the thanksgiving spirit teaches us *what* to see. Nature is so abundant in her resources that she threatens to confound by her very opulence. We need to be discriminating and selective lest panic and confusion overtake us. Then the result is a blurred impression rather than a distinct outline, merging anon into clear-cut details, of the feast set before us. Especially is it essential for us to be careful what we see in a world such as ours. Good and evil, love and hate, sin and righteousness are all so strangely interfused that nothing short of the selective vision can help us over many hard places.

And herein does the third function of art answer to the high ministry of the grateful heart: *It enables us to see more than we see.* This is the august value of our Saviour's synthetic and comprehensive view of the universe as compared, for example, with the merely scientific, philosophic, or artistic appraisal. It is a truism that many learned minds see only the mechanics of Nature. Dull in the centers of life, they are keen on the externals; they hurrah for the hands on the face of the cosmic clock and ignore the Mainspring that keeps them moving. Now Jesus knew the throbbing heart of God within Nature's overflowing garments and was grateful for the Fatherhood from whom all childhood borrows their meaning. We are yet far behind the Master's appreciation and interpretation of the earth and her processes.

Frederick F. Shannon

754 *ON A MUCH-NEGLECTED VIRTUE*

Gratitude means that money has come to the aid of purpose, and that praise is reinforcing prayer. Gratitude links the past with the future, the debt incurred with the duty to be performed, the service received with the service to be rendered. The question, "What ought we to do for others?" cannot receive a proper answer until pains have been taken to weigh and value all that others have already done for us. Benevolence is largely an affair of memory and of the gratitude that memory inspires. The benevolence that is most beneficent does not begin, as some moralists seem to think, in a desire to do good to other people, but in adequate recognition of the enormous amount of good which other people have already done to ourselves. Nine-tenths of what we have to give is a gift bestowed on us, and only when this is realized does altruism rest upon its proper ground, or feel the full force of the motives which impel the individual to the service of others. Divorced from gratitude, all the social virtues would shrivel. Nor could they sustain themselves for long in that withered and attenuated form.

L. P. Jacks

755 *THE WITNESS OF THE HARVEST*

[God] left not himself without witness, in that he did good, and gave us rain from heaven, and fruitful seasons. AC. 14:17

Does not the harvest, with its unfailing supply, mean that God has some loving interest in our physical lives? There is something in the fact of life which is infinitely precious to him. He is ever seeking to make our life strong and vigorous. We have no difficulty in feeling the pulse of love behind our human gifts. Why should we find it difficult to feel the beat of the heart of God behind the gifts of life, if only we will think? For every harvest is a miracle. It is something which human toil can never produce. The best we can do with all our arrangements and machinery is to take it in. But further, is there not in these gifts a suggestion of something more than mere sustenance? Is there not gladness in it, enjoyment, an enjoyment which God meant us to have in the very materials that keep us alive? There is nothing so interesting as food to a healthy man, nothing that can give more pleasure; and God meant it so. The sensual man may debase it for his mere self-indulgence. But, on the other hand, there is nothing conspicuously Christian about despising these gifts of life or living on crusts and water. Is not this abundance, this variety which is represented by the fruits of the earth, a witness to the almighty Lover who would make life happy for his children?

James Reid

756   *WORKERS TOGETHER WITH GOD*

I have planted, Apollos watered; but God gave the increase . . . For we are laborers together with God; ye are God's husbandry. 1 co. 3:6, 9

We live in a universe not a multiverse, and the greater part of the universe is spiritual. If we only knew it the material is the symbol, the appearance; the spiritual is the reality. The material is the shadow; the spiritual is the substance. The highest use we can make of the natural or material is to make it the medium and vehicle of the spiritual, which is what our text does. "I planted, Apollos watered, God gave the increase." Which means that *God does the vital part.* The increase is the vital thing, the inexplicable, the miraculous. Planting and watering is just arranging the materials which God has provided. God gave the soil, the stream, the rain, the sunshine and the seed. Man made none of them. In fact he makes nothing. He discovers things, their possibilities and uses, he develops and applies.

Charles Brown

B. INDEPENDENCE SUNDAY

Independence Sunday falls on the Sunday preceding July 4 and marks the anniversary of the signing of the Declaration of Independence in 1776. Prayer for the national welfare and sermons concerning civic life are not only appropriate but also highly desirable if the church is to remain a spiritual conscience for the nation.

Calls to Worship

(Boldface type indicates responses.)

757   Thou art an holy people unto the Lord thy God: the Lord thy God hath chosen thee to be a special people unto himself, above all people that are upon the face of the earth.

Know therefore that the Lord thy God, he is God, the faithful God, which keepeth covenant and mercy with them that love him and keep his commandments to a thousand generations.

De. 7:6, 9

758   Blessed is the nation whose God is the Lord.

O let the nations be glad and sing for joy: for thou shalt judge the peoples righteously, and govern the nations upon earth.

God, even our own God, shall bless us. God shall bless us; and all the ends of the earth shall fear him.

Ps. 33:12; 76:4, 6–7

759   Make a joyful noise unto God, all ye lands.

Sing forth the honor of his name: make his praise glorious.

All the earth shall worship thee, and shall sing unto thee; they shall sing to thy name.

Ps. 66:1–2, 4

Invocations

760   God of our fathers, who didst kindle in them the love of liberty and didst grant them such faith in thee and courage, that wide seas and strange

shores were overpassed and eagerly embraced: bestow upon us, their children, in our day, a love of liberty like to theirs; and prevent us by thy hand, that we neither grow faint in faith nor fail in courage. Amen.

Boynton Merrill

761 We thank thee for our inheritance in the nation of which we are members, for the land we love; for the calling and privileges of the Republic, for the enrichment of mutual interest and service, for exchange of thought, for brotherly emulation, for mutual aid. We thank thee for the gifts of the past and the hope of the future; for the noble traditions and high ideals committed to our charge; for civil and religious liberty; for the open Bible, and the inviolable conscience; for the Gospel of thy grace; for the awakening sense of brotherhood and social obligation; and for the hope of the coming of thy Kingdom. Amen.

Richard Roberts

762 O eternal God, through whose mighty power our fathers won their liberties of old: grant, we beseech thee, that we, the people of this land, may have grace to maintain those liberties in righteousness and peace. Through obedience to thy law may we show forth thy praise among the nations of the earth. In the time of prosperity, fill our hearts with thankfulness, and in the day of trouble suffer not our trust in thee to fail; through Christ our Lord. Amen.

James Harry Price

Litany

(Boldface type indicates responses.)

763 O God, before whose face the empires of the past have risen and fallen away, establish this nation in righteousness; and in personal character and public integrity make her foundations sure:

Lord, hear our prayer and mercifully bless this people.

From the ravages of crime, the disgrace of political corruption, and all malicious designs of lawless men:

Good Lord, deliver us.

From prejudice of race and color, making schism in the commonwealth; from all inequity that, causing a few to be rich and many poor, begets ill-will and spoils fraternity; from loss of liberties bequeathed us by our sires and from careless acceptance of our heritage and neglect of its responsibilities:

Good Lord, deliver us.

From the decline of pure religion; from failure of moral fibre in our citizenship; from all accounting of things material above virtues spiritual; from vulgarity of life, loss of social conscience, and collapse of national character:

Good Lord, deliver us.

By the deep faiths on which the foundations of our land were laid and by the sacrifices of its pioneers:

We beseech thee to hear us, O Lord.

By the memory of leaders in the nation, whose wisdom has saved us, whose devotion has chastened us, whose characters have inspired us:

We beseech thee to hear us, O Lord.

By the undeserved wealth of a great continent committed to us and by our trusteeship of power to work weal or woe on the earth:

We beseech thee to hear us, O Lord.

Keep us from pride of mind and from boasting tongues deliver us; save our national loyalty from narrowness and our flag from selfish shame; by our love for our land may we measure the love of others for their lands, honoring their devotion as we honor our own; and acknowledging thee one God, may we see all mankind one family and so govern our national affairs that the whole world may become one brotherhood of peoples:

Lord, hear our prayer and mercifully bless this people. Amen.

Harry Emerson Fosdick

Prayers

764 Almighty God, who on this day didst direct and inspire the hearts of our fathers to set forth the independence of these United States: we give all glory and praise to thee, the Author of our liberty, and the sure Defense of our safety. We pray that by thy grace we may be enabled to build wisely upon these foundations of freedom and of peace; that we may hold our liberties in due subjection to thy law and in all things seek that righteousness which exalteth a nation. Kindle in our hearts the pure flame of sacrifice to our country's needs and grant that the fires of our patriotism may shine as beacon lights upon thy holy hills, O God, and may point the ways of men toward that universal brotherhood, when the nations of the world shall be one in Jesus Christ our Lord. Amen.

Louis F. Benson

765 God of our fathers, who hast kept our nation's life through peril of its youth and trial of its manhood: we remember before thee this day with heartfelt thanksgiving the blessings that have crowned our lengthening history. For the courage and foresight of those who left their homes and friends to cross the sea; for the steadfast endurance of those who fought to win our liberty and the wise counsel of those who shaped our laws; for deliverance in war and growth in years of peace; for our high place of influence and opportunity among the nations of the earth; for memories that are glorious and hopes that rest upon thy favor: we bring thee joyful praise. Grant strength and good understanding to thy servant, the President of the United States, and all who are in authority over us, and make them willing followers of thy commandments and servants of the people's need. Guide our hearts and minds, that we may not be tempted to offend against thee in pride or selfishness, and leave us not to our own thoughts and ways in any hour of triumph or of trial. Amen.

Isaac O. Rankin

766   Almighty God, who hast given us this good land for our heritage: we humbly beseech thee that we may always prove ourselves a people mindful of thy favor and glad to do thy will.

Bless our land with honorable industry, sound learning and pure manners. Save us from violence, discord and confusion; from pride and arrogancy and from every evil way. Defend our liberties, and fashion into one united people the multitudes brought hither out of many kindreds and tongues.

Endue with the spirit of wisdom those to whom, in thy Name, we entrust the authority of government; that there may be justice and peace at home, and that through obedience to thy law we may show forth thy praise among the nations of the earth. In the time of prosperity fill our hearts with thankfulness, and in the day of trouble suffer not our trust in thee to fail; all which we ask through Jesus Christ our Lord. Amen.

George Lyman Locke

767   Grant us, O God, a vision of our land, fair as she might be; a land of justice, where none shall prey on others; a land of plenty, where vice and poverty shall cease to fester; a land of brotherhood, where success shall be founded on service, and honor be given to worth alone; a land of peace, where order need no longer rest on force, but on the love of all for their land, the great mother of the common life and welfare. Hear thou, O Lord, the silent prayer of all our hearts, as in city, town and village we pledge our time and strength and thought to hasten the day of her coming beauty and righteousness; through Jesus Christ our Lord. Amen.

Leslie D. Weatherhead

Poems

768   *From STANZAS ON FREEDOM*

Men! whose boast it is that ye
Come of fathers brave and free,
If there breathe on earth a slave,
Are ye truly free and brave?
If ye do not feel the chain,
When it works a brother's pain,
Are ye not base slaves indeed,
Slaves unworthy to be freed!

James Russell Lowell

769   *LORD, WHILE FOR ALL MANKIND WE PRAY*

Lord, while for all mankind we pray,
Of every clime and coast,
O hear us for our native land,
The land we love the most.

O guard our shores from every foe;
With peace our borders bless;
With prosp'rous times our cities crown,
Our fields with plenteousness.

Unite us in the sacred love
Of knowledge, truth, and thee,
And let our hills and valleys shout
The songs of liberty.

Lord of the nations, thus to thee
Our country we commend;
Be thou her refuge and her trust,
Her everlasting friend.

John R. Wreford

770   *AMERICA'S MAKING*

God built him a continent of glory and filled it with treasures untold;
He studded it with sweet flowing fountains and traced it with long
    winding streams;

He carpeted it with soft rolling prairies and columned it with thunder-
    ing mountains;
He graced it with deep-shadowed forests and filled them with song;
Then he called unto a thousand peoples and summoned the bravest
    among them.
They came from the ends of the earth, each bearing a gift and a hope.
The glow of adventure was in their eyes, and in their hearts the glory
    of hope.
And out of the bounty of earth and the labor of men;
Out of the longing of hearts and the prayer of souls;
Out of the memory of ages and the hopes of the world,
God fashioned a people in love, blessed it with purpose sublime, and
    called it America.

Abba Hillel Silver

771   *From MY AMERICA*

In thoughts, as wise as is her prairie sea;
In deeds, as splendid as her mountain piles;
As noble as her mighty river tides.
Let her be true, a land where right abides;
Let her be clean, as sweet as summer isles;
And let her sound the note of liberty
For all the earth, till every man and child be free!

Thomas Curtis Clark

772   *THE CALL*

In days long gone God spake unto our sires:
"Courage! Launch out! A new world build for me!"
Then to the deep they set their ships, and sailed,
And came to land, and prayed that here might be
A realm from pride and despotism free,
A place of peace, the home of liberty.

Lo, in these days, to all good men and true
God speaks again: "Launch out upon the deep
And win for me a world of righteousness!"
Can we, free men, at such an hour still sleep?
O God of freedom, stir us in our night
That we set forth, for justice, truth and right!

Thomas Curtis Clark

773   *From L'ENVOI*

Our country hath a gospel of her own
To preach and practice before all the world,—
The freedom and divinity of man,
The glorious claims of human brotherhood,—

❋

And the soul's fealty to none but God.

James Russell Lowell

Topics, Texts and Themes

774   *DECLARATION OF DEPENDENCE ON GOD*

He multiplieth nations, and destroyeth them, and restoreth them again
after they were overthrown. JB. 12:23

On June 12, 1775, one year before the Declaration of Independence was
written, the Continental Congress, aware that a choice between war and peace
was imminent, issued what has come to be called a "Declaration of Dependence
on God." In a most specific way, it reflects the religious outlook that prevailed
in early America. The document reads in part: "This Congress . . . do earnestly
recommend that Thursday, the twentieth day of July next, be observed by the
inhabitants of all the English colonies on this Continent as a day of public
humiliation, fasting, and prayer; that we may, with united hearts and voices,
unfeignedly confess and deplore our many sins, and offer up our joint supplications to the all-wise, omnipotent, and merciful Disposer of all events; humbly
beseeching Him to forgive our iniquities, and remove our present calam-
ities. . . ."

Each of us can do his part to bring this spirit of dependence on God increasingly into our government, especially in these critical times when so much
misery has come about because men have abandoned or defied Him.

James Keller

775   *GOD IN A NATION'S LIFE*

If thou wilt walk before me . . . I will establish . . . thy kingdom . . .
for ever. 1 K. 9:4–5

The entrance of the Almighty into a nation's life is always via the long
corridors of human personality and life. During long periods of social struggle
and in moments of social crisis, those individuals who have woven God into

their lives and made him the foundation stone on which they have built have been the ones who have ushered him into the nation's life. There is a close relation between national security and personal integrity. When the individual members of any society choose not to walk before God, soon that fact is inevitably reflected in the diminishing security of that society. When leaders of men in any area of life choose to turn away from God, that area is certain to suffer. It is just as true that when leaders of a nation and the individual citizens of that nation choose to walk together before God, that nation will be established and secure.

Paul E. Ertel

776 CHRISTIANITY AND DEMOCRACY

Stand fast therefore in the liberty wherewith Christ hath made us free, and be not entangled again with the yoke of bondage. GA. 5:1

It is interesting that our word "church" comes from a Greek word, "ecclesia," which was the very word used for the sovereign assembly of the people at Athens in a political democracy. The early church was democratic in organization and Jesus' primary emphasis was on the worth and importance of the individual. The things democracy stands for are the things Jesus stood for: personal liberty, religious freedom, racial tolerance, decency between individuals and groups, the sanctity of the pledged word, and an economic system which has a place for every willing person, and encourages individual responsibility and enthusiasm for life.

Herbert W. Hansen

777 THE AMERICAN FAITH

Faith is the substance of things hoped for, the evidence of things not seen. For by it the fathers obtained a good report. Columbus sailed through unknown seas for many days, mid perils of wind and perils of water, mid perils from faint hearts, mid perils from false brethren, and revealed a new world, and died knowing not what he had seen. By faith Puritanism, beginning even as a grain of mustard seed, brought forth Eliot and Hampden and Cromwell and Milton and Vane and planted New England. By faith the Pilgrim Fathers, when they were called to go out into a place which they should after receive for an inheritance, obeyed; and they went out, not knowing whither they went. By faith they sojourned in the land of promise, as in a strange country, with Winthrop and Cotton Mather and Roger Williams, heirs with them of the same promise.

By faith Samuel Adams refused to admit of bondage, and was not afraid of the king's commandment. By faith Washington drew his sword, and Jefferson saw that which was invisible. By faith independence was declared by a nation that was not yet a nation. By faith the farmers stood at Bunker Hill, by faith they endured at Valley Forge, by faith they conquered at Yorktown.

And what shall I more say? For the time would fail me to speak of Lafayette and the faith that worked mightily for us in other lands; of Franklin and Madison and Hamilton, who by faith brought us out of confusion into order; of Lincoln, also, and the noble army of those who redeemed the land from slavery; of Garrison, who worked mightily with the newspaper, of Phillips on the platform, and Parker in the pulpit, and Whittier with the song, and Mrs. Stowe with the novel, and John Brown on the scaffold; of America in the council of the nations, of faithful soldiers coming up from lowly homes and lying down in unknown graves; of faithful women giving up brothers and sons and husbands. And some had trial of bonds and imprisonment, being destitute, afflicted, tormented. These all, having obtained a good report through faith, labored for our welfare and to safeguard democracy throughout the world; and posterity has entered into the fruits of their labor.

Wherefore, seeing we are compassed about with so great a cloud of witnesses, and that with so great a price freedom has been purchased, let us lay aside every weight of selfishness and sloth, and the sins of partisanship and pride, which so easily beset us, let us walk worthy of our great inheritance, let us be creditors of the future even as we are debtors to the past; and let us know that the spirit of history is the God of nations, whose other name is justice.

Edwin D. Mead

778 *SACRED SOIL*

We need not go to Mecca or to Palestine to find the Holy Land. Sacred are the Mount of Olives and the Garden of Gethsemane; sacred the field of Thermopylae and the Town Common at Lexington; sacred are Plymouth Rock and Bunker Hill. All are sacred because they bear the stamp of man's immortal soul.

James Freeman Clark

779 *AN AMERICAN'S CREED*

I believe in America because in it we are free—free to choose our government, to speak our minds, to observe our different religions;

Because we are generous with our freedom—we share our rights with those who disagree with us;

Because we hate no people and covet no people's land;

Because we are blessed with a natural and varied abundance;

Because we set no limit to a man's achievement: in mine, factory, field, or service in business or the arts, an able man, regardless of class or creed, can realize his ambition;

Because we have great dreams—and because we have the opportunity to make those dreams come true.

Wendell Willkie

780 *THE NATION FOR THE NATIONS*

We . . . that are strong ought to bear the infirmities of the weak, and not to please ourselves, RO. 15:1

No one can hear such words as these without both a sense of shame and a sense of stimulation. For we know that we are strong, and while we are stirred to a proper use of strength we cannot but recall how frequently we have used it amiss. These words are of deep concern to us, for they indicate the right and the wrong way of using stength. Strength is a force, not a luxury—an instrument, not a toy. It is our boast nationally, to whatever Western race we belong, that we are a privileged people. . . . Let us proclaim our strength, Christian, national and individual, as not being a possession wherewith to please ourselves but to help the less favored.

Charles H. Brent

781 *MY COUNTRY'S BIRTHDAY*

It is not for me to glorify . . . the country which I love with all my heart and soul. I may not ask your praise for anything admirable which the United States has been or done. But on my country's birthday I may do something far more solemn and more worthy of the hour. I may ask for your prayers in her behalf: that on the manifold and wondrous chance which God is giving her . . . on her unconstrained religious life; on her passion for education and her eager search for truth; on her zealous care for the poor man's rights and opportunities; on her quiet homes where the future generations of men are growing; on her manufactories and her commerce; on her wide gates open to the east and to the west; on her strange meeting of the races out of which a new race is slowly being born; on her vast enterprise and her illimitable hopefulness— on all these materials and machineries of manhood, on all that the life of my country must mean for humanity, I may ask you to pray that the blessing of God, the Father of man, and Christ, the Son of man, may rest forever.

Phillips Brooks
Westminster Abbey
July 4, 1880

782 *From WHAT IS AN AMERICAN?* (*1782*)

He is an American, who, leaving behind him all his ancient prejudices and manners, receives new ones from the new mode of life he has embraced, the new government he obeys, and the new rank he holds. He becomes an American by being received in the broad lap of our great *Alma Mater*. Here individuals of all nations are melted into a new race of men, whose labors and posterity will one day cause great changes in the world. Americans are the western pilgrims, who are carrying along with them that great mass of arts, sciences, vigor, and industry which began long since in the east; they will finish the great circle. The Americans were once scattered all over Europe; here they are incorporated into one of the finest systems of population which has ever appeared, and which will hereafter become distinct by the power of the different climates they inhabit. The American ought therefore to love this country much better than that wherein either he or his forefathers were born. Here the rewards of his industry follow with equal steps the progress of his labor; his labor is founded on the basis of nature, self-interest; can it want a stronger allurement? Wives and children, who before in vain demanded of him a morsel of bread, now, fat and frolicsome, gladly help their father to clear those fields whence exuberant crops are to arise to feed and to clothe them all; without any part being claimed, either by a despotic prince, a rich abbot, or a mighty lord. Here religion demands but little of him, a small voluntary salary to the minister, and gratitude to God; can he refuse these? The American is a new man, who acts upon new principles; he must therefore entertain new ideas, and form new opinions. From involuntary idleness, servile dependence, penury, and useless labor, he has passed to toils of a very different nature, rewarded by ample subsistence. This is an American.

Michel G. J. de Crèvecœur

783 *AMERICAN SYMBOL*

Our flag symbolizes for us all the beauty and charm and high ideals of our homeland. Its red stands for courage, moral as well as physical. Its white is symbolic of purity, which cannot flourish amidst hate and fear and prejudice. Its blue stands for truth and loyalty. Let us then pledge allegiance to our flag, with a renewed sense of being loyal every day of our lives. Let us see that everyone in this country gets an equal opportunity to enjoy its privileges.

Jesse H. Holmes

784   *ON THE FLAG*

This flag means more than association and reward. It is the symbol of our national unity, our national endeavor, our national aspiration. It tells you of the struggle for independence, of union preserved, of liberty and union one and inseparable, of the sacrifices of brave men and women to whom the ideals and honor of this nation have been dearer than life.

It means America first; it means an undivided allegiance. It means America united, strong and efficient, equal to her tasks. It means that you cannot be saved by the valor and devotion of your ancestors; that to each generation comes its patriotic duty; and that upon your willingness to sacrifice and endure, as those before you have sacrificed and endured, rests the national hope.

It speaks of equal rights; of the inspiration of free institutions exemplified and vindicated; of liberty under law intelligently conceived and impartially administered.

There is not a thread in it but scorns self-indulgence, weakness, and rapacity. It is eloquent of our common interests, outweighing all divergences of opinion, and of our common destiny.

Given as a prize to those who have the highest standing, it happily enforces the lesson that intelligence and zeal must go together, that discipline must accompany emotion, and that we must ultimately rely upon enlightened opinion.

Charles Evans Hughes

C. NEW YEAR SUNDAY

New Year Sunday is commonly observed on the Sunday preceding January 1. The day offers an opportunity for a review of the past accomplishments and the future prospects of the individual, the church, and the nation. It is a time of confession, dedication, and resolution. Watch Night services on New Year's eve mark with reverence and commitment the beginning of another year.

Calls to Worship

(Boldface type indicates responses.)

785   I will extol thee, my God, O king; and I will bless thy name for ever and ever.

Every day will I bless thee; and I will praise thy name for ever and ever.

Great is the Lord, and greatly to be praised; and his greatness is unsearchable.

One generation shall praise thy works to another, and shall declare thy mighty acts.

Ps. 145:1-4

786   Behold, the former things are come to pass, and new things do I declare. . . . Sing unto the Lord a new song, and his praise from the end of the earth.

Is. 42:9-10

787   Glory ye his holy name: let the heart of them rejoice that seek the Lord. **Seek the Lord, and his strength: seek his face evermore.**

Remember his marvellous works that he hath done; his wonders, and the judgments of his mouth.

He hath remembered his covenant for ever, the word which he commanded to a thousand generations.

Ps. 105:3-5, 8

788   Be strong and of a good courage, fear not, nor be afraid . . . for the Lord thy God, he it is that doth go with thee; he will not fail thee, nor forsake thee.

De. 31:6

Invocations

789   O Almighty God, who alone art without variableness or shadow of turning, and hast safely brought us through the changes of time to the beginning of another year: we beseech thee to pardon the sins we have committed in the year which is past, and give us grace that we may spend the remainder of our days to thy honor and glory; through Jesus Christ our Lord. Amen.

The Book of English Collects

790   Eternal God, who makest all things new and abidest forever the same: grant us to begin the year now opening in thy faith, and to continue it in thy favor, that, being guided in all our doings and guarded all our days, we may spend our lives in thy service, and finally by thy grace attain the glory of everlasting life; through Jesus Christ our Lord. Amen.*

Divine Service

791   O Christ, who art Alpha and Omega, the beginning and the end: encompass our lives, we pray thee, with thy completeness; that whether as young men we see visions, or as old men we dream dreams, we may steadfastly look to thee, who livest and reignest with the Father and the Holy Spirit, one God world without end. Amen.

John Wallace Suter

792   Father, as the old year ends and a new year begins, forgive us for the failures of the vanished days, and bless us in whatever we have truly striven for in days that do not die. Keep us from vain regrets, and let us face forward in the light of the best that we have learned. Purge our hearts both of shallow self-confidence and of cowardly fears, so that we may know that without thee we can do nothing but that in thee all things are possible; through Jesus Christ our Lord. Amen.

Walter Russell Bowie

793   Almighty God, have mercy upon us, who, when troubled with the things that are past, lose faith, and courage, and hope. In thy grace uphold us, that we, being sustained by a true faith that thou art merciful and forgiving, may go forward; keep thy commandments; rejoice in thy bounty; trust in thy mercy; and hope for eternal life. Grant that whate'er betide we may always remember that we are in thy keeping, so that, in darkest days, close to thee, we may have courage to go on and faith to endure, even unto the end; through Jesus Christ our Lord. Amen.

George Dawson

Litany

(Boldface type indicates responses.)

794   O Lord our God, the Father of our Lord Jesus Christ, we would render unto thee thanksgiving, by all means, at all times, and in all places, for that thou hast sheltered, assisted, supported, and led us on, through the time past of our life, and brought us to this hour. For thy loving kindness guiding us on life's way, for the gifts thou hast bestowed; for the joys thou hast made to abound to us, and the sorrows and trials thou hast overruled for good:
We give thee thanks, O God.

For the protection of our homes, and the preservation of our friends; for the measure of success thou hast granted to our labors, and the sure leading thou hast given us in every path of duty:
We give thee thanks, O God.

For good hopes and precious memories, for strength and courage given us through thine ever-present Spirit, and for the grace and saving health we have received through Christ our Saviour:
We give thee thanks, O God.

Grant, we beseech thee, that the new beginning of days thou art giving us may deepen our gratitude for the innumerable benefits vouchsafed to us, and confirm our trust in thee for all needed help and blessing in the year to come; through Jesus Christ our Lord. Amen.

Book of Common Worship (P)

Prayers

795   Father everlasting, through whose favor we have come to the beginning of the new year, we assemble before thee in gratitude at the remembrance of thy mercies.

We rejoice in the ways we have traveled. Thy love has led us along sunlit glens of quiet joy; thy Spirit has supported us through shadowed valleys of humiliation; and thy presence has encouraged us in tempestuous seas of peril.

We thank thee for the friends thou hast given us. They have been as a refreshing oasis in the desert, as a shade from the burning heat, and as a shelter in the time of storm.

We praise thee for every satisfying experience. For harvests gathered, victories won, progress made, we lift our hearts in gratitude.

And now thou hast brought us to the dawn of this new year. Let thy Spirit lead us along the unblazed trail. Be our companion as we trudge the dusty lane or hasten over the broad highway. Grant us thy presence as we walk in familiar ways or engage in fresh experience.

Teach us to find satisfaction in life's changing scenes. We would rejoice not alone in days that flow like a song but in times that demand strenuous effort and fierce battle, not alone in the quiet dawn and starry heaven but in days that are overcast and nights that are storm-whipped.

Give us an understanding of life's deeper meaning. Make us sensitive to spiritual overtones. Open our eyes to the beauty that lies in common things. Awaken our minds to the joy to be gained through high endeavor.

Strengthen our hearts to face with courage all that may befall us along the unknown trail. Lead us in faith and hope and love. And grant us unfailing confidence in thy Eternal Goodness. Through Jesus Christ our Lord. Amen.

Carl A. Glover

796 O God, eternal and changeless, who through ever-changing scenes of joy and pain, effort and rest, leadest thy people to a nobler destiny than they ever of themselves conceive: grant that, having our minds steadfastly set upon thy commandments and being continually directed by thy voice speaking to us in the events of the passing hour, we may meet with courage whatever the coming days may bring of evil or of good, being afraid of nothing that man or the world may do or threaten, and fearful only of falling below those things which thou hast prepared for us and set forth in the Gospel of thy Son our Saviour Jesus Christ.

For the coming days cause thy grace, O almighty God, to triumph over our infirmities, and grant us inwardly such increased steadfastness, and in our lives such a larger harvest of good that through sunshine and storm we may trust and not be afraid, work and not be weary, suffer and not complain, overcome all evils with patience, and in humility and peace possess our souls; through Jesus Christ our Lord.

To thee, most gracious Father, we dedicate ourselves and all that we have, beseeching thee to guide our hands, our minds and our whole energies to those things which are worthy of ourselves and pleasing to thee; through Jesus Christ our Lord. Amen.

Hugh Cameron

797 O thou who hast set eternity in the heart of man, and hast made us all seekers after that which we can never find, forbid us to be satisfied with life. Draw us away from base content, and set our eyes on far-off things. Keep us at tasks too hard for us, that we may be driven to thee for strength. Deliver us from fretfulness and self-pity. Make us sure of the goal we cannot see, and of the hidden good in the world. Open our eyes to beauty by the way, and our hearts to the loveliness men hide from us because we do not trust them enough.

Bind us by fast bonds to the brotherhood of those who love thee better than they know, who serve thee in the darkness, and even in their doubts will never give thee up. Shine thou upon us with such light as we can bear. Show us such truth as we can understand and obey. Save us from ourselves, and fill our hearts with the vision of a world made new. Help us to desire no reward but the utter freeing of our souls from the bonds of flesh when the days of our years on the earth are fulfilled. Amen.

John Rothwell Slater

798   O thou who inhabitest eternity, and before whom the centuries pass as a watch in the night; who measurest the waters in the hollow of thy hand, and countest the nations as the small dust of the balance: be graciously pleased to take into thy keeping our labors of the closing year; forgive what was done amiss, pardon our neglect of the good works which thou didst prepare for us, and give us grace to forgive any who may have injured us in body, mind or soul.

Lead us forward into the New Year with our vision made clean from all self-seeking, that we may look upon the stricken and sorrowing world with the eyes of thine eternal truth. Where there is cruelty, inflame our minds with an indignation that will not flag until every impulse of unbrotherliness is removed even from ourselves; where there is fear, let us plant respect and reverence until the desert shall rejoice and blossom as the rose; where the spirit is enslaved by outward force or inner poison, let our dedicated skill deliver all men from the bondage of corruption into the glorious liberty of the sons of God.

Lift thou up our eyes, that we may behold him that sitteth upon the circle of the earth and spreadeth out the heavens; the Holy One, the everlasting God. So wilt thou renew our strength; and in the coming days we shall mount up with wings as eagles, we shall run and not be weary, we shall walk and not faint. Glory be to thee, O Lord, Most High!

John Wallace Suter

Poems

799   *From DOOR AND KEEPER*

We pause beside this door.
Thy year, O God, how shall we enter in?

✳

The footsteps of a Child
Sound close beside us. Listen! He will speak!

His birthday bells have hardly rung a week,
Yet has he trod the world's press undefiled.

*

"Enter through me," he said, "nor wander more;
For lo! I am the Door."

Lucy Larcom

800 *NEW YEAR*

Upon the threshold of another year
   We stand again.
We know not what of gladness and good cheer,
   Of grief or pain
May visit us while journeying to its close.
   In this we rest,
God dealeth out in wisdom what he knows
   For us is best.

Thomas Wearing

801 *From THE GATE OF THE YEAR*

And I said to the man who stood at the gate of the year:
"Give me a light, that I may tread safely into the unknown!"
And he replied:
"Go out into the darkness and put thine hand into the Hand
   of God.
That shall be to thee better than light and safer than a known
   way."
So, I went forth, and finding the Hand of God, trod gladly
   into the night.
And he led me toward the hills and the breaking of the day in
   the lone East.
So, heart, be still!
What need our little life,
Our human life, to know,
If God hath comprehension?
In all the dizzy strife
Of things both high and low
God hideth his intention.

Minnie Louise Haskins

802   *A WAY TO A HAPPY NEW YEAR*

To leave the old with a burst of song,
To recall the right and forgive the wrong,
To forget the thing that binds you fast
To the vain regrets of the year that's past,
To have the strength to let go your hold
Of the not-worth-while of the days grown old;

To dare go forth with a purpose true,
To the unknown task of the year that's new;
To help your brother along the road
To do his work and lift his load;
To add your gift to the world's good cheer
Is to have and to give a glad New Year.

Robert Brewster Beattie

803   *TO THE NEW YEAR*

One song for thee, New Year,
One universal prayer;
Teach us—all other teachings far above—
To hide dark hate beneath the wings of love;
To slay all hatred, strife,
And live the larger life!
To bind the wounds that bleed;
To lift the fallen, lead the blind
As only love can lead—
To live for all mankind!

James Whitcomb Riley

804   *FACING THE NEW YEAR*

We pledge ourselves
To follow through the coming year
The light which God gives us:
The light of Truth, wherever it may lead;
The light of Freedom, revealing new opportunities for individual
     development and social service;
The light of Faith, opening new visions of the better world to be;

The light of Love, daily binding brother to brother and man to
    God in ever closer bonds of friendship and affection.
Guided by this light,
We shall go forward to the work of another year with steadfastness
    and confidence.

Author Unknown

805   *From THE EXPLORER*

"There's no sense in going further—it's the edge of civilization,"
    So they said, and I believed it—broke my land and sowed my crop—
Built my barns and strung my fences in the little border station
Tucked away below the foothills where the trails run out and stop.

Till a voice, as bad as Conscience, rang interminable changes
    On one everlasting Whisper, day and night repeated—so:
"Something hidden. Go and find it. Go and look behind the Ranges—
Something lost behind the Ranges. Lost and waiting for you. Go!"

Rudyard Kipling

Topics, Texts and Themes

806   *THE MEANING OF THE NEW YEAR*

The new year's chief value to us is its spiritual opportunity. A year from
now we may be richer or poorer than we are today; stronger in body or weaker;
more famous or more obscure. Whatever these results may be, they will not
interpret the real significance of the year. That will only be revealed by the
application of finer tests. If the year makes us more patient and courageous,
with a purer zeal for righteousness and a consciousness of deeper fellowship
with the Spirit of Christ, it will have brought us the richest harvest it can
bring. Whatever else the new year may mean to us, it surely means the
opportunity for spiritual attainment. If we go forth into it with the full appreciation of that fact, and the purpose and prayer to redeem the time, we shall
estimate our experiences by a true standard, and be certain not to fail to gather
the choicest fruitage of the days.

George E. Horr

807   *NEW YEAR'S RESOLUTIONS*

We make them every year. Many of them we break. Sometimes we laugh
when we speak of New Year's resolutions, and, of course, some of them are so

ridiculous as to deserve ridicule. However, there is a serious aspect of the whole question of resolutions. It is that the vision of high moment has a tendency to vanish, the ideals dissolve, the screen becomes dark. William James, the great philosopher, once said, "If you have an emotion do something, if you don't you won't have it any more." Ideals, like muscles, atrophy. We must do something about them. We must keep them alive or we shall hear, "In a little while ye shall see me no more."

G. Bromley Oxnam

808   *UNKNOWN POSSIBILITIES*

The New Year's Day divides the past from the present; it draws a sharp line between the has been and the may be. It compels us to think of what is gone forever; it brings us face to face with the unknown possibilities of what is to come.

Every new day does this; each night when we lie down to rest marks something that has slipped away beyond our grasp, and each morning sunrise opens a new unwritten and unknown chapter in our lives. The new year does the same thing, only in a larger and therefore more searching and disturbing manner. It compels us to think, not simply of yesterday, but of a whole year of yesterdays past and gone. Few of us can look back over a year of yesterdays without being reminded of things that have made a difference in our lives.

The new year also compels us to look forward, not simply toward tomorrow, but into the unknown possibilities of three hundred and sixty-five tomorrows. It matters little that no vision of ours can pierce those morrows; the very fact of the new year projects the shadows of these morrows before our faces. We wish each other a happy new year. It is a good, a kindly wish; yet the wishing of it is a confession that the new year contains possibilities beyond our power to reach with anything more than kindly wishes. The new year brings us face to face with the ever present mystery of time. Ordinarily we live in the present, and it is well for us that we must do so. Our duties, our work in life requires our presence in the present. But it is a mistake to depreciate the past, and a greater mistake to be unmindful of the future.

Ira Seymour Dodd

809   *THE LURE OF THE UNKNOWN*

Is it yesterday, or tomorrow, which makes today what it is? Which has the more power, the push of the past or the pull of the future? Both of these forces are operating steadily, but the future seems to have the upper hand. "Your young men shall see visions and your old men shall dream dreams." They will be pulled along by that which their imaginations picture as possible. They go feeling their way after something, if haply they may find it. They find great sections of it—they catch up with their dreams, and then dream of something yet higher. It is the way of wholesome advance. The future is more powerful than the past, as a source of motive.

Charles R. Brown

810   THE THRESHOLD OF LIFE

Carrying forward all that is good of the old year, some things ought to be left behind forever! From time to time, the housewife carries to the garret things she ought to have carried to the ash barrel. Then, from time to time, she cleans out the garret, and to the ash barrel they go, until the city itself, with its snow, carries the sweepings and filth of the streets, and drops them into the abyss of the sea. The old year also holds many things that should be left behind forever. Having made the failures, do not be discouraged. Why should you allow the sense of failure to dampen your ardour or chill your enthusiasm? Next year you will succeed. Have you suffered heavy losses and defeats? Losses are God's challenges to a man to do his best. In this way he puts the youth upon his mettle. Overcome by temptation, have you yielded to folly and to sin? Having fallen in the slough stand again upon your feet, cleanse your garments and go forward into newness of life! If God casts your sins behind his back and forgets them, why should you hug them to your heart, clasped by memory? If the housewife cleanses the garret and makes every room spotless of dust, why do you not gather up every evil thing in your life—yea, if repented of, if restitution has been made, if forgiven, why do you not forget your very sins, and begin the new year as if your feet had for the first time touched the threshold of life? Is it not a time for forethought? Is it not a time for planning and high resolves?

Newell Dwight Hillis

811   THE OLD AND THE NEW

Behold, I make all things new. RE. 21:5

Let this New Year be the beginning of a new life in each of us wherein "old things are passed away." Not the old thoughts, of course, which are still true: but those that remain to nurse and encourage our prejudices. Not the old emotions that are filled with kindness: but all anger and bitter feeling and railing. Not the old reverence for the authority of God: but all fears born of our unworthy service apart from him.

Not the old gracious ministries that blessed mankind: but the harsh words, the suspicious looks, the clenched hands, and unwilling feet. Not the old habits that keep us in the straight way: but the new fashions that make us unmindful of those things which hold life together in the unity of good manners. Not the old friends who grow more beloved each year because their worth is better appreciated: but the new associations made from mercenary motives.

Let all blessed old things stay, but let the clutter of our heads and hearts be removed, that new inspirations and new affections may come in to gladden our lives.

Chester Burge Emerson

812   *THE FORWARD LOOK*

No man, having put his hand to the plough, and looking back, is fit for the kingdom of God. LU. 9:62

There are four looks one may take: the backward look, the inward look, the upward look, and the forward look. The backward look is retrospective. It has its virtues, for the past has much to teach us; but the backward look sometimes saddens or embitters us, and it always arrests us. No one can look backward and go forward at the same time. We cannot live in retrospect. The inward look is introspective; it is valuable but may produce morbidity and spiritual self-consciousness. The upward look releases one from the habiliments of the flesh and elevates him into the spiritual stratosphere.

But the forward look to the earnest Christian is enticing, alluring and challenging. It is prospective and purposive. It was the great quality of Jesus' life. He had respect for the past but never worshipped it. He was a forward-looking man. In the presence of danger and death his face was steadfastly set to go to Jerusalem. Elements of the forward look are faith, optimism, courage, confidence, earnestness and enthusiasm. Jesus had all of these.

Walter Gillan Clippinger

813   *AN UNCHARTED JOURNEY*

Ye have not passed this way heretofore. JOS. 3:4

We cannot remind ourselves too often, when we say "we walk by faith not by sight," that stress should be laid on the verb. Faith is a way of walking, not a way of talking, or as Benjamin Whichcote put it, Christianity is a divine life, not a divine science. If we only talk, we shall very likely come to the conclusion that Christianity is played out. If we try to live in such a way that Christ would approve our life, we shall certainly not think that. "Lord, to whom should we go? Thou hast the words of eternal life." There are some permanent acquisitions of the human spirit, from which it cannot go back, and of these the Christian revelation is the greatest. It is a principle of life, and it can therefore change, as only the permanent can change. But to us, as to past ages, it can be and will be the guiding light which we may follow over the uncharted country through which our path lies. It has not failed us who are old; it will not fail you who are young. But unless you follow the gleam, you will soon see it no longer. Faith begins as an act of will, "the resolution to stand or fall by the noblest hypothesis." "Who chooseth me must give and hazard all he hath." Explain it how we will, that is the condition of spiritual vision.

W. R. Inge

814   THE UNKNOWN JOURNEY

He went out, not knowing whither he went. HE. 11:8

Abraham began his journey without any knowledge of his ultimate destination. He obeyed a noble impulse without any discernment of its consequences. He took "one step," and he did not "ask to see the distant scene." And that is faith, to do God's will here and now, quietly leaving the results to him. Faith is not concerned with the entire chain; its devoted attention is fixed upon the immediate link. Faith is not knowledge of a moral process; it is fidelity in a moral act. Faith leaves something to the Lord; it obeys his immediate commandment and leaves to him direction and destiny.

And so faith is accompanied by serenity. "He that believeth shall not make haste"—or, more literally, "shall not get into a fuss." He shall not get into a panic, neither fetching fears from his yesterdays nor from his tomorrows. Concerning his yesterdays faith says, "Thou hast beset me behind." Concerning his tomorrows faith says, "Thou has beset me before." Concerning his today faith says, "Thou hast laid thine hand upon me." That is enough, just to feel the pressure of the guiding hand.

John Henry Jowett

815   THE GUIDEPOST OF THE CHANGING YEAR

When eight days were accomplished for the circumcising of the child, his name was called Jesus. LU. 2:21

A noted Scottish preacher, in writing concerning the observance of what he calls "that uncomfortable day, the first Sunday of the New Year," is oppressed by the difficulty of treating these occasions in an adequate manner. And he goes on to say, how very wisely: "How much more blessed a thing it is to number our days in the precincts of Bethlehem, rather than upon the denuded summit of a mere point in time."

It is true that the New Year can be the most forbidding of occasions. Another division of human time has gone by with its unfulfilled hopes and its wasted irrevocable opportunities. I am not greatly enamored of the New Year as a national festival, but in the Christian church at least we always try to put it in its proper setting. We remember that we are still "in the precincts of Bethlehem," that the New Year marks the circumcision of the Holy Child, that the New Year bears on its forehead the name they gave him that day. For when eight days were accomplished, his name was called Jesus, which was so named of the angel before he was conceived in the womb. And he was called Jesus because he was to save his people from their sins.

John Wilson Baird

816   *A VERSE FOR THE NEW YEAR*

Be careful for nothing; but in every thing by prayer and supplication with thanksgiving let your requests be made known to God. PH. 4:6

"Careful" means full of unnecessary care—crossing rivers before we reach them, dreading troubles that never come, expecting evil of the Lord instead of good; in a word—worrying.

Do not worry is a hard word, but it is a plain command. The anxious Christian hurts more than himself; he hurts the faith of those who know him and the good name of his Lord who has promised to supply all his needs.

Go deeper into the text: *"But in everything* by prayer and supplication let your requests be made known unto God." That means there is nothing we cannot pray about. Why do we not believe it and act upon it?

What we can take to God we can trust to God. What we put our fidelity into, he will perfect by his faithfulness. While we work for the best, he works the best for us. We may not succeed as we hoped; we may have discipline we little expected, but the Father knows what his child needs.

What God has for us to do we can do, or to bear we can bear. When he says "My grace is sufficient for thee," dare we doubt it? Is there not enough in his ocean to fill our pitcher? With the need of every day will come his promised supply.

And do not forget the words, "with thanksgiving." Be on the lookout for mercies. The more we look for them the more of them will we see. Blessings brighten when we count them. Out of the determination of the heart the eyes see. If you want to be gloomy, there's gloom enough to keep you glum; if you want to be glad, there's gleam enough to keep you glad. Say "Bless the Lord, O my soul, and forget not all his benefits." Better lose count in enumerating your blessings than lose your blessings in telling over your troubles. "Be thankful unto him, and bless his name. For the Lord is good, his mercy is everlasting."

Unbraid the verse into three cords and bind yourself to God with them in trustful, prayerful, thankful bonds—anxious for nothing, prayerful for everything, thankful for anything "and the peace of God which passeth all understanding shall keep your hearts and minds through Christ Jesus."

Maltbie Davenport Babcock

817 MEMORY, HOPE AND EFFORT

That they might set their hope in God, and not forget the works of God, but keep his commandments. ps. 78:7

My text tells us how past, present and future—memory, hope and effort—may be ennobled and blessed. In brief, it is by associating them all with God. It is as the field of his working that our past is best remembered. It is on him that our hopes may most widely be set. It is keeping his commandments which is the consecration of the present. Let us, then, take the three thoughts of our text and cast them into New Year's recommendations.

Alexander Maclaren

818 DREAMS WORTH DREAMING

I must also see Rome. ac. 19:21

Every life has its secret hope, its hidden desire. Our work lies, so to speak, in the provinces of life, but our heart often goes out to the capital. Life is not fully expressed for any of us in the routine of our service. It is not measured by the inch-tape of experience. It is larger than these things. It has room for the unrealized. And if we should be very frank with ourselves and each other, we should confess that one of the inspirations and comforts of life for us, especially as we most feel the limitation and difficulty and irksomeness and prosaism of it, is the whisper to our own heart, "I must also see Rome." And the first thing I want you to let St. Paul teach you is this, that only the religion of Jesus Christ can make your dream of Rome worth dreaming.

Percy C. Ainsworth

819 *AN APPEAL FROM THE PRESENT TO THE FUTURE*

I cannot realistically be a cynic. I cannot believe that this generation is utterly different from every other. I hear the raucous noises which fill the public places of the world, but when I think of what our children's children will say about this age when they look back on it, I am sure we would be utterly astounded could we listen. Always it is what the contemporaries miss that turns out to be important.

So in his time Kepler was content to say that since God had waited thousands of years for an observer of his stars, he, Kepler, could afford to wait a century for a reader. So Spinoza was banished from his home city because he was unorthodox, and after his death it was almost a hundred years before people dared mention his name with respect, much less acknowledge their indebtedness to him. So Milton got a paltry ten pounds for "Paradise Lost," and Mozart, dying in poverty, was buried in a pauper's grave. As for Socrates and Jesus, think what their contemporaries did to them!

Seeing all this, the cynic says, What is the use, then, of believing or endeavoring great things? To which I answer, Friend, these things that the contemporaries missed were going to be the masterpieces of the world. It takes a long time for a masterpiece to win its way into the acceptation of mankind but when it is there it stays. Ten thousand lesser things rise and pass away but the masterpieces stay. Great things come slowly but they last.

Therefore pray for eyes lest we should miss the really momentous affairs of our day. Be sure of this, they are not spectacular and noisy. They are not in the limelight on the public stage. What if the great thing in our time were not violent nationalism but the slowly emerging idea of a world community? What if the great thing in our time were not economic chaos but the slowly growing idea of a new, amazing technology, socially employed to abolish poverty? What if the great thing in our time were not our miserable religious partisanships but the slowly growing possibility of a more united Christendom? What if our children's children looking back, should say, This was the creative movement of that age to which the future was to belong? Should *that* be so, our generation would be running true to history.

Harry Emerson Fosdick

D. MEMORIAL DAY

Memorial Day, often called Decoration Day, is celebrated in most states on May 30. Originating in the South shortly after the Civil War, the day by custom is a time for the honoring of those who have fallen in all wars. The day has become an occasion for the decorating with flowers of the graves of all honored dead. Ministers are frequently invited to participate in Memorial Day services sponsored by the various veterans' organizations. The Sunday before Memorial Day is sometimes used for the commemorating of those of the membership who have died during the previous year. It is also a logical time for churches to invite servicemen and veterans to worship individually or in a body.

Calls to Worship

(Boldface type indicates responses.)

820   God is our refuge and strength, a very present help in trouble.
He maketh wars to cease unto the end of the earth; he breaketh the bow, and cutteth the spear in sunder; he burneth the chariot in the fire.
Be still, and know that I am God: I will be exalted among the heathen, I will be exalted in the earth.

Ps. 46:1, 9–10

821   [The Lord] shall judge among the nations, and shall rebuke many people: and they shall beat their swords into plowshares, and their spears into pruninghooks: nation shall not lift up sword again nation, neither shall they learn war any more.
Come ye, and let us walk in the light of the Lord.

Is. 2:4-5

822   How beautiful upon the mountains are the feet of him that bringeth good tidings, that publisheth peace; that bringeth good tidings of good, that publisheth salvation; that saith unto Zion, Thy God reigneth!

Is. 52:7

Invocations

823   To thee, the everlasting Father, before whom stand the spirits of the living and the dead, we offer hearty thanks for all fair and noble memories;

for all who have witnessed a good confession for the faith; for all who have laid down life for their friends; for all the unknown dead whose forgotten labors have made earth better for their presence; humbly beseeching thee that we may live worthily as becometh those who are bought with a great price; that, being sanctified by their influence through all our earthly days, we may greet them in the land of the living with faces unashamed, and souls triumphant in the God of our salvation; through Jesus Christ our Lord. Amen.

Congregational Worship

824   O God our Father, on this day of remembrance, look upon the unrest of the world and be pleased to complete the work of thy healing hand. Send peace upon the earth, a deeper and more lasting peace than the world has ever known. Draw all men unto thyself, and to one another by the bands of love. Grant understanding to the nations and an increase of sympathy and mutual good will, that they may be united in a sacred brotherhood wherein justice, mercy and faith, truth and freedom may flourish, so that the sacrifice of those who died may not have been made in vain; for the sake of Christ Jesus our Lord. Amen.

A Chain of Prayer

825   O Lord our God, whose name only is excellent and thy praise above heaven and earth: we give thee high praise and hearty thanks for all those who counted not their lives dear unto themselves but laid them down for their friends; beseeching thee to give them a part and a lot in those good things which thou hast prepared for all those whose names are written in the book of life; and grant to us, that having them always in remembrance, we may imitate their faithfulness and with them inherit the new name which thou hast promised to them that overcome; through Jesus Christ our Lord. Amen.

Frank Edward Brightman

826   Lord God of Hosts, in whom our fathers trusted: we give thee thanks for all thy servants who have laid down their lives in the service of our country. Unite all the people of this nation in a holy purpose to defend the freedom and brotherhood for which they lived and died. Grant, we beseech thee, that the liberty they bequeathed unto us may be continued to our children and our children's children, and that the power of the Gospel may here abound, to the blessing of all the nations of the earth, and to thine eternal glory; through Christ thy Son our Lord. Amen.

Book of Common Worship (P)

Litany

(Boldface type indicates responses.)

827   For the land of our birth with all its chartered liberties, for all the wonder of our country's story:

We praise thee, O God.

For leaders in nation and state, and those who in days past and in these present times have labored for the commonwealth:

We praise thee, O God.

For those who in all times and places have been true and brave, and in the world's common ways have lived upright lives and ministered to their fellows:

We praise thee, O God.

For those who served their country in her hour of need, and especially those who gave even their lives:

We praise thee, O God.

O almighty God and merciful Father, whose nature and whose name is love: as we give thee thanks for the courage and the strength vouchsafed to these thy servants, we would remember before thee those who mourn them as their kindred. Look in mercy upon them; and as this day brings them memories of those whom they have lost, may it also bring them consolation from thee, quickening in them the sense of communion with the world unseen, and confirming their assurance of that great day when thou shalt restore to them their own in the very presence of our Lord and Saviour Jesus Christ. Amen.

Author Unknown

Prayers

828   O God and Father of mankind, we gather on this sacred day to bear solemn testimony before thee and our fellow men to our loving gratitude for all those who, at the country's call, have met the rude shock of battle and have surrendered their lives amid the ruthless brutalities of war. We pray thee, Lord, to grant them safe lodging in heavenly mansions and a holy rest. Forbid that their sufferings and death should be in vain; and mercifully vouchsafe that through their devotion the horrors of war may pass away from the earth and thy Kingdom of right and honor, of peace and brotherhood, may be established among men. Comfort, O Lord, we pray thee, all who proudly mourn the loss of those near and dear to them, especially the families of our brothers departed. Support them by thy love. Give them faith to look beyond the troubles of this present time and to know that neither life nor death can separate us from the care of God, which is in Christ Jesus our Lord. Amen.

Charles H. Brent

829 O God, by whose grace thy people gain courage in the way of the heroes of faith: we lift our hearts in gratitude for all who have lived valiantly, and for all who have died bravely for truth, and liberty, and righteousness. Especially do we thank thee for the heroes of the common good, who suffered and made trial of bitter sacrifice in achieving the freedom of religious worship and the measure of social and political and economic liberty we enjoy in this good land.

God of our fathers, help us to prize very highly, and to guard very carefully, the gifts which their loyalty and devotion have passed on to us. Grant unto us the gift of a living and vigorous faith, that we may be like the heroes: that we may be true as they were true, that we may be loyal as they were loyal, and that we may serve our country and the cause of pure religion all the days of our lives; and grant that we with all those who depart hence in the faith of thy holy name, may wear at last the victor's crown; through Jesus Christ our Lord. Amen.

The Hymnal, Army and Navy

830 Eternal and ever-loving God, we thank thee for the privilege of meeting on this hallowed day in this free nation and under these spacious skies to honor our noble dead and to rededicate our lives to thee and to our country.

We thank thee that we are permitted to live through days of challenge, for the hours of testing in our loyalty to our national heritage, and for our devotion to the high ideals for which our fathers, brothers and sons have surrendered their life.

Bless, O God, the thousands of disabled veterans in our hospitals today. Assuage their pain, ease their suffering, and give them cheer and hope. Help us to respond gladly and generously to their needs of body and spirit.

Let thy benediction fall upon our splendid women, the nurses and auxiliary helpers, who suffered with them. We thank thee for consecrated womanhood. Grant especially thy special favor upon the Gold Star mothers. Give them sustaining grace and divine peace.

We remember in prayer our allies. Grant that they may be kept from disruption and dissension. Save us from distrust and discord. Keep us together in peace as we were one in war. May nothing destroy the fellowship and comradeship which we have known. Help us to work together and serve together for the cause of humanity and human brotherhood.

And help us, O Lord, to keep our poise. Save us from enemies without and from fear within. Give unto us power and wisdom to deal justly and firmly with all who spread seeds of discontent, hatred and disloyalty among us. Keep us from breaking faith with thee and with those who have died.

On this day of sacred memory we ask for grace and power to live truer lives, to be better servants of the living God, finer fathers and mothers, nobler sons and daughters, and more loyal citizens of this great country and of thy world.

Lord, grant that we may yet see the day when war and the fear of war shall be no longer, the day when peace shall have become our common possession, the day when thy will shall be done on earth as it is in heaven. O Lord, hear this our prayer for Christ's sake. Amen.

Gordon Palmer

831 Eternal Spirit, revealed to us in all goodness, all truth, all beauty, whose presence we have felt in our seers and saints, in friends whose lives have been our benedictions, and above all in Christ: be real to us that in our own hearts, too, we may hear thee speaking. This universe and our lives within it are full of mystery beyond our understanding, and of tragedy beyond our enduring. Yet light is here, too, light that no darkness has put out. Lift us out of discouragement today once more, as in great hours gone by, to believe in the light. Here is chaos, but here is creative power too, ugliness but beauty too, discord and violence but humaneness and mercy too, satanic evil but God too. Spirit of the Eternal, win a victory in our lives that we may believe in and commit ourselves to the light and not the darkness.

We pray for the peace of the world. Stay the evil forces that withstand good will and already set the trap of misunderstanding and division whereby our children shall be caught again in the steel teeth of war. For wisdom to seek peace and pursue it, for faith and character to use aright the powers man now has laid his unworthy hands upon, we pray. To that end, our intercessions rise for our nation, its President and all who influence its policies, and for us the whole body of the people that the tragic sacrifices of war may not end in the disillusionment of mankind's hopes and the despair of our children after us.

Because there will be no peace for the world save as it springs from the hearts of men, we pray for ourselves. Make us worthy to live in so momentous a time. From self-centered living, from narrowness of vision and all mean prejudice of race and nation, from corrupt and dissipated lives, and all wastage of character in a time when the world's hopes depend on character, deliver us. In humility and penitence, in fresh resolution and loyalty, cleanse our lives and set us to seek first thy Kingdom and thy righteousness. Amen.*

Harry Emerson Fosdick

Poems

832   *From CHAMPAGNE, 1914-15*

That other generations might possess—
   From shame and menace free in years to come—
A richer heritage of happiness,
   He marched to that heroic martyrdom.

Alan Seeger

833   *From CLIFTON CHAPEL*

To count the life of battle good,
   And dear the land that gave you birth,
And dearer yet the brotherhood
   That binds the brave of all the earth.

Henry Newbolt

834   *From LEXINGTON*

Their feet had trodden peaceful ways;
   They loved not strife, they dreaded pain;
   They saw not, what to us is plain,
That God would make man's wrath his praise.

No seers were they, but simple men;
   Its vast results the future hid;
   The meaning of the work they did
Was strange and dark and doubtful then.

Swift as their summons came they left
   The plough mid-furrow standing still,
   The half-ground corn grist in the mill,
The spade in earth, the axe in cleft.

They went where duty seemed to call,
   They scarcely asked the reason why;
   They only knew they could but die,
And death was not the worst of all!

Of man for man the sacrifice,
   All that was theirs to give, they gave.
   The flowers that blossomed from their grave
Have sown themselves beneath the skies.

John Greenleaf Whittier

835   *From MY TRIUMPH*

Others shall sing the song,
Others shall right the wrong,—
Finish what I begin,
And all I fail to win.

What matter, I or they?
Mine or another's day,
So the right word be said,
And life the sweeter made?

*

Ring, bells in unreared steeples,
The joy of unborn peoples!
Sound, trumpets far-off blown,
Your triumph is my own!

John Greenleaf Whittier

836   *From VICTORY*

There's but one gift that all our dead desire,
   One gift that men can give, and that's a dream,
Unless we, too, can burn with that same fire
   Of sacrifice; die to the things that seem;

Die to the little hatreds; die to greed;
   Die to the old ignoble selves we knew;
Die to the base contempts of sect and creed,
   And rise again, like these, with souls as true.

And that's not done by sword, or tongue, or pen,
   There's but one way. God make us better men.

Alfred Noyes

837   *THE DREAM ABIDES*

God of humanity, hear our vow—
    We who dwell in a world of hate:
War we have served, how long! but now
    Our lives to peace we dedicate.

By the graves of our dead we mutely stand,
    In tears renew our consecration:
We will strive and pray till every land
    Becomes a part of a new world nation!

Thomas Curtis Clark

Topics, Texts and Themes

838   *MEMORIALS AND THEIR MEANING*

This day shall be unto you for a memorial. EX. 12:14

The memorial idea has prevailed among all kinds of people from the earliest times. The Old Testament contains the record of many memorials. The greatest of these was the day set apart to commemorate the safety of the people of Israel from the destroying angel and their deliverance from bondage to the oppressor. Year by year, generation by generation, this occasion was ordered set apart as a time of joyous gratitude to God.

We too have a Memorial Day. We as a people are also summoned to remember. Ours is not primarily a religious institution, yet it has for us a profound spiritual significance. While we separate the functions of church and state, we do not separate religion from the total life of the nation. As a people we have reason to be profoundly grateful to the Father of nations because we have been delivered from fear and oppression and been given opportunity for the freest life any citizens have ever known.

William Everett Roberts

839   *LEST WE FORGET*

Other men labored, and ye are entered into their labors. JN. 4:38

No man has ever been independent; every man has leaned upon the past. Every liberty we enjoy has been bought at the cost of martyrs' blood; every achievement of the race has been made at the cost of incredible toil. There is not a privilege nor an opportunity that modern society grants to us that is not the product of other men's labors. We drink every day from wells that we have not dug; we warm by fires we have not kindled; we live by liberties we have not won; we are protected by institutions we have not set up. Our churches are built upon the rocks that have been put in place by martyrs of the ages past. Our governments rest upon the foundations cemented in place by the blood of soldiers who tracked their way, barefoot, through icy battlefields or over burning sands. Our courts are reared upon the bodies of those who died for freedom. No man liveth unto himself; all the past has invested in him.

Roy L. Smith

840   *UNFINISHED LABORS*

Other men labored, and ye are entered into their labors. JN. 4:38

The last word is the one to emphasize. We hear a good deal about reaping where others have sown: about enjoying the results of other people's labors. There is not talk here of reaping, or of results. Others have labored, to be sure: but they have not finished. The task sometimes outlives the toilers. We have entered into their labors—not their results. The results are still a long way off, and the time to inherit them has not yet come. But the labor is as yet unfinished, and calls to us as it called to those others before us, whose memories and examples we cherish today.

It is a perfectly natural mistake to look upon Memorial Day as something final, marking the end of a task. In a measure, this is true. The task has ended for the toilers of former times, and Memorial Day invites us to think of those toilers with becoming pride and gratitude. But just because they have finished their shift, it does not follow that the task is finished. Memorial Day speaks in a sterner mood: the task is yet with us. We have entered into the labor. It is hard for us to see life in its continuity. We measure life in terms of personalities and generations. But life asks to be measured in terms of eras and millenniums. There is victory in the future: it is for us to understand that we are still working for that victory.

Charles E. Park

841   *WHAT HAS WAR TAUGHT US?*

Then Samuel took a stone, and set it between Mizpeh and Shen, and called the name of it Ebenezer, saying, Hitherto hath the Lord helped us. I S. 7:12

The Philistines had surrendered unconditionally to their age-old enemy. The battle had been conclusive and Samuel, who was prophet, priest, and king, in order to commemorate the victory, took a stone and set it up on the battlefield and called it "Ebenezer." The word "Ebenezer" is now a good English word and has found its way into the hymnal and into the dictionary. It means "the stone of help," and its interpretation is to the effect that "Hitherto hath the Lord helped us." It was a memorial stone, a stone of remembrance, a stone of thanksgiving. On this Memorial Day we, too, should think of erecting our Ebenezer, our memorial to the goodness of God and the brave men who have fallen in battle.

Hugh Thomson Kerr

E. BROTHERHOOD SUNDAY

Brotherhood Sunday, observed on the third Sunday in February, introduces Brotherhood Week. Preaching and worship emphases include the Christian witness of human brotherhood.

Calls to Worship

(Boldface type indicates responses.)

842   This is the message that ye heard from the beginning, that we should love one another.
We know that we have passed from death unto life, because we love the brethren.
Hereby perceive we the love of God, because he laid down his life for us: and we ought to lay down our lives for the brethren.
Let us not love in word, neither in tongue; but in deed and in truth.

1 Jn. 3:11, 14, 16, 18

843   Thou shalt love thy neighbour as thyself.
Love worketh no ill to his neighbour: therefore love is the fulfilling of the law.
As we have therefore opportunity, let us do good unto all men, especially unto them who are of the household of faith.

Ro. 13:9–10; Ga. 6:10

844   If we love one another, God dwelleth in us, and his love is perfected in us.
God is love; and he that dwelleth in love dwelleth in God, and God in him.
Herein is our love made perfect, that we may have boldness in the day of judgment: because as he is, so are we in this world.
We love him, because he first loved us.
This commandment we have from him, That he who loveth God love his brother also.

1 Jn. 4:12, 16–17, 19, 21

Invocations

845   O God, who biddest us to dwell with one mind in thine house: of thy mercy put away from us all that causes faction and bitterness, that, through thy bountiful goodness, we may keep the unity of the Spirit in the bond of peace; through Christ, the Prince of peace. Amen.

Rodborough Bede Book

846   O God, our Father, increase in every nation the sense of human brotherhood, true respect for man and for woman, loyalty in service and charity, happiness in work and justice in reward; that our homes may be kept safe and pure, our cities renewed in beauty and order, and all the world may reflect the radiance of thy throne in heaven. Amen.

Book of Worship (ER)

847   O Lord, grant to us so to love thee with all our heart, with all our mind and with all our soul, and our neighbor for thy sake, that the grace of charity and brotherly love may dwell in us and all harshness and ill-will may die in us; and fill our hearts with feelings of love, kindness and compassion, so that, by constantly rejoicing in the happiness and good success of others, by sympathizing with them in their sorrows, and putting away all harsh judgments and envious thoughts, we may follow thee, who art thyself the true and perfect love. Amen.*

Treasury of Devotion

Litany

(Boldface type indicates responses.)

848   Jesus, born in poverty, workman at Nazareth, lover of all children of God:
Teach us to love one another.
Jesus, in whom all the nations of the earth are one, in whom is neither bond nor free, black nor white, brother of all:
Teach us to love one another.
From hatred and malice that crush human life, from contempt of others that destroys personality, from selfishness that brings suffering to others, from oppression and injustice that stifle growth, from reluctance to trace our common kinship with thy children everywhere, from misunderstanding of thy purpose which prevents thy Kingdom:
Turn us aside, O Lord.

Into an appreciation for the gifts of all races and nationalities, into an increasing sense of human worth, into a growing desire for brotherhood, into a deepening consecration to thy Kingdom:

Lead us, O Lord.

We pray, Lord of all, who lovest all men, for a new America, a new Europe, a new Asia, a new world, wherein every race may be free:

Receive our prayer, our Christ. Amen.

Challenge and Power

Prayers

849   O God, our Creator and Preserver, who hast made of one blood all nations to dwell on all the face of the earth, and who didst reveal thy will for men by thy Son, the Prince of peace: give us charity, we pray thee, to regard all men as our brethren, and to share with them the heritage which we have received from thee. Deliver us from ungodly pride, ungenerous judgments, and presumptuous claims. Help us to put away selfishness and malice, suspicion, envy, and anger, and all the unrighteous passions which cause men to be enemies, one to another. Give us a mind to understand the aspirations and needs of those who are not of our race and tongue; and teach us to live in modesty and simplicity, giving no occasion for envy or fear, but, being kindly affectioned one to another, to follow peace with all men, and advance thy Kingdom of good will upon earth.

Grant us grace, we beseech thee, amid the confusions of the world and the disappointments of human hope, ever more to exalt, as the only Saviour of the world, him whom thou hast made to us wisdom and righteousness and redemption, Jesus Christ thy Son, our Lord; to whom, with thee the Father and the Holy Spirit, be glory and honor, dominion and power, world without end. Amen.

Prayers for the Christian Year

850   Heavenly Father, by whom all men were created as one species, and who by accidents of climate, geography, and environment became separated into races, colors, and creeds: help us to perceive the basic oneness we were born to realize. Forgive our tendency to transform prejudice into principle, to condemn those awakening energies in servant peoples which we boast of in ourselves, or to think that sentimental gestures are equivalent to brotherly devotion.

Thou knowest the critical time in which we dwell, when to preserve those institutions and ideals we believe are the genuine fruits of our faith we must manufacture weapons of total destruction and condemn other men and nations as agents of the gross darkness. As we gird with strength to preserve our goodly heritage, save us from losing the perfect good of thy vision for mankind.

Because the vision seems beyond achievement in this generation, inspire us to more zealously apply it where we are free to do so, in our own country, until all artificial distinctions and unjust exploitation shall be abolished, and our people live together as citizens of one union, and children of thy family. Amen.

Ralph Sadler Meadowcroft

851   Eternal God, we remember the numberless souls around the world, of every name and sign and of many diverse faiths that this day are seeking thee. Help us not to think of ourselves as though we uniquely were children of the light and they children of darkness. God forgive us for our pride and our condescension. We, too, are often aliens. We, too, are often children of darkness. Therefore we gather up all thy children in our supplication, and beseech thee for those who on this day shall seek thee in Jewish synagogues, and Buddhist shrines, and Moslem mosques, or on the open hillside. O God, our Father, gather us all in. Thou carest for us every one. Thou art not the God of the Jew only and not of the Gentile; thou art not the God of the Gentile and not of the Jew. All souls are thine. Draw us closer to thyself and even though our prayer be partial, help us. Even though the windows that we offer thee to shine through be soiled, yet come through, O thou Sun of righteousness.

We pray thee for all manner of Christians, of whatever name or sign, who have found in Christ the revelation of God. Make us more worthy of our high calling. Let Jesus rise upon us this day and break through the barricades that we too often have put against him in our lives and in our thoughts. O God, draw all those who call themselves Christians to Christ and make us his better disciples, we beseech thee.

Draw together all classes and societies of men. Forgive us that we so mark the distinctions that separate us here on earth. Lift us to a higher plane this day that race, and nation, and class may be seen as thou seest, O thou who hast made of one blood all men that dwell upon the face of the earth. Make us fit to live upon a planet. Keep us from the provincial mind. Break down our prejudice. Give us generosity, magnanimity, kindliness, comprehensiveness of care. Make us citizens of thy universe.

O God, as thus we pray for thy world-wide Kingdom, so we would remember our own hearts. Help us to begin with ourselves today. Lead us back into our own problems. Give us thy spiritual resources that we may be more than conquerors over our private sins, over our intimate sorrows. May we transcend them, be not conformed to this world but transformed by the renewing of our mind so that today, going forth from this place, we may lay hold upon our divine heritage and live, as never before, as becometh those who have had this high dignity bestowed upon them that they should be called children of God.

We ask it in the name of thy first-born Son, our Elder Brother. Amen.*

Harry Emerson Fosdick

852   Almighty God, eternal Spirit, we for whom thou art the only hope of life acknowledge our need of thee now.

By the skill of head and hand, man has shortened the distance between the homes of his fellows, till all on our globe are now neighbors.

Help us, O God, joyful Spirit of universal love, to make this new closeness a blessing to us all. Help us to believe in our heart's core that none of us can know joy, safety, content, if others do not know hope.

By the skill of head and hand, man has brought forth such wealth of material goods as no other generation has known. Help us to know that none of us is safe in the enjoyment of our man-made wealth if all cannot have a share.

Almighty God, move us to put our whole trust in thee and thy all-powerful spirit of love. May we draw from thee that faith in the human spirit which alone gives meaning to efforts for the common good. Inspire us with that universal faith in the might of goodness, which means wholeness and life for all human souls. Amen.

Dorothy Canfield Fisher

Poems

853   *THE NEW TRINITY*

Three things must a man possess if his soul would live,
    And know life's perfect good—
Three things would the all-supplying Father give—
    Bread, Beauty, and Brotherhood.

Edwin Markham

854   *From JERUSALEM* (Pt. IV)

Jesus said: "Wouldest thou love one who never died
For thee, or ever die for one who had not died for thee?
And if God dieth not for Man & giveth not himself
Eternally for Man, Man could not exist; for Man is Love
As God is Love: every kindness to another is a little Death
In the Divine Image, nor can Man exist but by Brotherhood."

William Blake

855 *From SPEECH TO THOSE WHO SAY COMRADE*

Brotherhood! No word said can make you brothers!
Brotherhood only the brave earn and by danger or
Harm or by bearing hurt and by no other

Brotherhood here in the strange world is the rich and
Rarest giving of life and the most valued:
Not to be had for a word or a week's wishing.

Archibald MacLeish

856 *BUT WHEN YE PRAY*

But when ye pray, say *our*—not *mine* or *thine*;
  Our debts, *our* debtors, and *our* daily bread!
Before the thronged cathedral's gracious shrine,
  Or in thy closet's solitude instead,
Whoe'er thou art, where'er thou liftest prayer,
  However humble or how great thou be,
Say *our,* thy brother man including there,
  And more and more it may be thou shalt see
Upon life's loom how thread to thread is bound;
  None for himself, but man and fellow-man,
Or near or far, meet on one common ground,
  Sons of one Father since the world began.
    So shall God's Kingdom come in might and power
    When all can pray, not mine or thine, but *our.*

Frances Crosby Hamlet

857 *From WORK FOR SMALL MEN*

Despise not any man that lives,
Alien or neighbor, near or far;
Go out beneath the scornful stars,
And see how very small you are.
The world is large, and space is high
That sweeps around our little ken;
But there's no space or time to spare
In which to hate our fellow-men.
And this, my friend, is not the work for you;
Then leave all this for smaller men to do.

Sam Walter Foss

858   *TO THE CHRIST*

Thou hast on earth a Trinity,—
Thyself, my fellow-man, and me:
When one with him, then one with thee:
Nor, save together, thine are we.

John Bannister Tabb

859   *I LOOKED FOR CHRIST*

I looked for Christ on Madison Street
Where men went by with stumbling feet,
Where heads were bowed in the darkness there
Of gray clouds hanging low in the air.

I looked for him, a vision of white—
But gay burlesques with their crimson light
Have led my steps to a darker place
Where smoke of passion hid Christ's face.

I looked for Christ in the hidden skies,
A flaming vision to blind my eyes—
While Christ walked by with stumbling feet,
Along with the men of Madison Street.

Raymond Kresensky

860   *From A DAY'S WALK*

I pray each morning that I be not blind
To the Christ who moves that day among my kind.
I dare not turn a hungry man away,
Lest I be leaving him unfed today.
I dare not slight some tattered, unclothed one
Lest I should fail to warm and clothe God's Son.

Grace Noll Crowell

861   *ORTHODOX*

They questioned my theology,
And talked of modern thought:
Bade me recite a dozen creeds—
I could not as I ought.

"I've but one creed," I answer made,
"And do you want another:
I know I've passed from death to life
Because I love my brother."

Mark Guy Pearse

862   *WHO IS SO LOW*

Who is so low that I am not his brother?
  Who is so high that I've no path to him?
Who is so poor I may not feel his hunger?
  Who is so rich I may not pity him?

Who is so hurt I may not know his heartache?
  Who sings for joy my heart may never share?
Who in God's heaven has passed beyond my vision?
  Who to hell's depths where I may never fare?

May none, then, call on me for understanding,
  May none, then, turn to me for help in pain,
And drain alone his bitter cup of sorrow,
  Or find he knocks upon my heart in vain.

S. Ralph Harlow

863   *IN THEE IN ME*

In thee
In me
In all men
There dwelleth the One God;

In all
He suffers
And he suffers
For all;

In all everywhere,
See thyself.
Abandon this thy ignorant conceit,
Which holds that thou art separate from other men.

From the Sanskrit tr. by Mohandas Gandhi

864 *PRONOUNS*

The Lord said,
"Say, 'We'";
But I shook my head,
Hid my hands tight behind my back, and said,
Stubbornly,
"I."

The Lord said,
"Say, 'We'";
But I looked upon them, grimy and all awry.
Myself in all those twisted shapes? Ah, no!
Distastefully I turned my head away,
Persisting,
"They."

The Lord said,
"Say, 'We'";
And I,
At last,
Richer by a hoard
Of years
And tears,
Looked in their eyes and found the heavy word
That bent my neck and bowed my head:
Like a shamed schoolboy then I mumbled low,
"We,
Lord."

Karle Wilson Baker

865 *GIVE US, O GOD, THE STRENGTH TO BUILD*

Give us, O God, the strength to build
The city that hath stood
Too long a dream, whose laws are love,
Whose ways are brotherhood,
And where the sun that shineth is
God's grace for human good.

Already in the mind of God
That city riseth fair,—
Lo, how its splendour challenges
The souls that greatly dare,
Yea, bid us seize the whole of life
And build its glory there.

Walter Russell Bowie

866   *NO MAN IS AN ILAND*

No man is an Iland intire of it selfe;
Every man is a peece of the Continent,
A part of the maine; if a Clod bee washed away by the Sea,
Europe is the leese, as well as if a Promontorie were,
As well as if a Mannor of thy friends or of thine owne were,
Any man's death diminishes me, because I am involved in Mankinde;
And therefore never send to know for whom the bell tolls;
It tolls for thee.

John Donne

867   *From EACH FOR ALL*

Each with its own heart and mind,
Each of its own distinctive kind,
Yet each a part and none the whole,
But all together form one soul;
That soul our country at its best,
No North, no South, no East, no West,
No yours, no mine, but always ours,
Merged in one power our lesser powers,
For no one's favor, great or small,
But all for each and each for all.

Edmund Vance Cooke

Topics, Texts and Themes

868   *THE COMPULSIONS OF BROTHERHOOD*

Nothing is more significant than the serious way in which the early Christian testimony enforced the compulsions of brotherhood. The word brother
was given a freshness and dignity. In a way never before used, Jesus, whether

formally regarded as Messiah, Redeemer, Saviour or God, came affectionately to be remembered as Elder Brother. And the living sense of kindred that animated the Christian community is plain to any reading of the New Testament. The early co-operative fellowship in Jerusalem in which none regarded what he had as his own—and this utterly free from external coercion; the amazing generosity of the saints in Asia Minor toward the destitute brethren in Jerusalem whom they had never seen and for whom they felt no concern except as they felt them their brothers; the quick rebuke that unbrotherly behavior invited—"Admonish him as a brother," Paul tells the Thessalonians; and the way in which love of the brethren for each other was regarded as the only evidence of the love they felt toward God—"If anyone says 'I love God' and yet hates his brother, he is a liar"; and the peremptory command that all but encompassed every other ethical obligation—"This is the command that we get from him, that whoever loves God must love his brother also": all this is evidence of the pervasiveness of the brotherly necessity in the first century of Christian history.

A transition is definitely marked in the gradual displacement of *frater* by *fidelis* as a Christian greeting. It meant that being a Christian had become more of a response to the constraints of orthodoxy—*fidelis* meaning "faithful one"—than to the compulsions of brotherhood. And that change in casual usage was a symptom of an illness that still mortally affects the body of the world. For to this very hour men *must* be wise; they *may* be brotherly. To be faithful to truth is required; to be faithful to the fact of human kinship is elective. We see society concerned mightily in making the mind rational, and yet not consciously directing its efforts toward making the heart fraternal. And out of the heart are the issues of life.

Edwin McNeill Poteat

869 MEN ARE BROTHERS

Am I my brother's keeper? GE. 4:9

All men are brothers. That truth is written in the facts of life and in the faith of all benign religions. There is only one race upon earth, the human race.

Men are brothers in body. The organs and functions of the body are the same in every race. The blood in the veins of men is everywhere the same; no one can detect any difference.

Men are brothers in mind. Socrates made the discovery—one of the greatest ever made—that when the great men of all races think about the basic issues of life, they come to the same basic truths. From this fact he inferred that at bottom, as in its height, the human mind is one.

Men are brothers in spirit. The high faith of the race is one: God is the father of the human family; every soul is sacred; each personality is an end in itself; justice is the basis of life; love is its saving power; brotherhood is its crown; a beloved community its goal.

"One God and Father of all, who is above all, and through all, and in you all," said Paul. "The universe is a commonwealth of men," said Cicero. "The men of the four seas are kinsmen," said Confucius. "Arise, tune the harp of brotherhood," Iphal added. Thus all great souls join in one symphony of fraternity.

Why, then, is the earth a jungle, ravaged by war, hideous with injustice, cruelty, and horror, saturated with brother-blood? Because man will not admit his brotherhood, will not live and let live, much less live and help live. He must dominate his brother, exploit him, rule him, or ruin him.

Joseph Fort Newton

870   *FELLOWSHIP*

> This then is the message which we have heard of him, and declare unto
> you, that God is light, and in him is no darkness at all. If we say that we
> have fellowship with him, and walk in darkness, we lie, and do not the
> truth: but if we walk in the light, as he is in the light, we have fellowship
> one with another, and the blood of Jesus Christ his Son cleanseth us from
> all sin. 1 JN. 1:5–7

I chose these texts with the idea of emphasizing the essential oneness of our common humanity, that as many drops of water combine to make the ocean, and many grains of sand unite and form the earth, and as the innumerable rays of the heavens blend into the one principal light—so must we live in fellowship with others, if we would make the most of ourselves, and do the most for them.

The drop of water which separates itself from other drops of water is helping to defeat the beneficent purpose of the sea; if all the rest did what this one has done, there would be no sea. If all the grains of sand should repent themselves of their unity, there would be no earth; and if all the rays of light refused to combine, the world would be left in darkness. God's physical universe fulfils the purpose of its creation because in spite of innumerable diversities, it is one at its center. And because all are one at the center, all nature declares the glory of God and renders obedience to the will of God. All the elements of nature obey God's fundamental law of fellowship, and united they achieve his purpose.

John W. Phillips

871   *CHRISTIAN CHARITY*

And there came a traveller unto the rich man, and he spared to take of his
own flock and of his own herd, to dress for the wayfaring man that was
come unto him. 2 s. 12:4

The poor are always with us. The wayfarers come to us continually, and
they do not come by chance. God sends them. And as they come, with their
white faces and their poor scuffling feet, they are our judges. Not merely by
whether we give, but by how we give and by what we give, they judge us.
One man sends them entirely away. Another drops a little easy, careless,
unconscientious money into their hands. Another man washes and clothes them.
Another man teaches them lessons. Thank God there are some men and women
here and there, full of the power of the Gospel, who cannot rest satisfied till
they have opened their very hearts and given the poor wayfaring men the
only thing which really is their own, themselves, their faith, their energy, their
hope in God. Of such true charity-givers may he who gave himself for us
increase the multitude among us every day.

Phillips Brooks

872   *THE GOSPEL OF "WE"*

For none of us liveth to himself, and no one dieth to himself. ro. 14:7

And after he had seen the vision, immediately we endeavoured to go into
Macedonia, assuredly gathering that the Lord had called us for to preach
the gospel unto them. ac. 16:10

The "we" spirit is the very essence of Christianity. It takes at least two people
to practice the teachings of Christ. Jesus said that love to God and love to one's
neighbor was the summing up of all the law and the prophets. He announced
that "where two or three are gathered together in my name there am I in the
midst." Notice that the lowest number is two, that it takes at least yourself and
somebody else and God to form this trinity. When Jesus sent his disciples out
he sent them two by two. Thus we have again exemplified the "we" spirit.

Edgar DeWitt Jones

873   *HUMAN BROTHERHOOD*

I dare not speak of human brotherhood without speaking first of divine
sonship. There is no meaning to the word "fraternal" until we have learned
the meaning of "filial." There is no meaning to brotherhood until we have
been taught the meaning of fatherhood and sonship. If I said nothing else

but this one thing, and were able to say it in terms which would go home to your inmost being, that you are the sons of God, I would have done a great thing, because a man who has once learned that he is the son of God must forthwith accept all of his race as his brethren. Look at the one spotless figure that stands out in the midst of history. Look at the Lord Christ and see how he began his work of public ministry. He identified himself with the human race and its weakness, but he saw that it was only in his divine sonship that he could fulfill a life of service, and at his baptism, before he went among men to preach and to teach about the Kingdom of God, he rose to the supreme consciousness of that sonship. He heard his Father say: "Thou art my beloved son, in whom I am well pleased." . . . God does not expect you to use any more faith than you have got, but he does expect you to use what you have. It may be but a tiny spark, yet that spark must glow heavenward, Godward, in the filial relation. Upon that we base the fraternal.

Charles H. Brent

874　　　ON PRAYING "OUR FATHER"

When he bade us say, "Our Father," Jesus spoke from that consciousness of human solidarity which was a matter of course in all his thinking. He compels us to clasp hands in spirit with all our brothers and thus to approach the Father together. This rules out all selfish isolation in religion. Before God no man stands alone. Before the All-seeing he is surrounded by the spiritual throng of all to whom he stands related near and far, all whom he loves or hates, whom he serves or oppresses, whom he wrongs or saves. We are one with our fellow-men in all our needs. We are one in our sin and our salvation. To recognize that oneness is the first step toward praying the Lord's Prayer aright. That recognition is also the foundation of social Christianity.

Walter Rauschenbusch

875　　　APOSTLES OF BROTHERHOOD

We improve with the improvement of humanity; nor without the improvement of the whole can you hope that your own moral and material conditions will improve. Generally speaking, you cannot, even if you would, separate your life from that of humanity; you live in it, by it, for it. I charge you then, O my brothers, by your duty and by your own interest not to forget that your first duties—duties without fulfilling which you cannot hope to fulfil those owed to family and country—are to humanity. You are all brothers. Ask yourselves whenever you do an action in the sphere of your country, or your family, If what I am doing were done by all and for all, would it advantage or injure humanity? And if your conscience answers, It would injure humanity, desist; desist, even if it seem to you that an immediate advantage for your country or your family would ensue from your action. Be apostles of this faith, apostles of the brotherhood of nations, and of the unity of the human race—a principle admitted today in theory, but denied in practice. Be such apostles wherever and in whatever way you are able. Neither God nor man can demand more of you.

Giuseppe Mazzini

876 *WE ARE ONE*

Each year we should see more and more of ourselves in the lives of others; we should identify ourselves more closely with them. Here, in this crowded city, wherever we walk, wherever we look, in the thick, swarming street, in the busy offices, in the low stifling dens, we should say: "There am I. I see myself in all these tribes: I am one with all these poor sufferers. They work for me; our souls run together; we are one. The whole teeming life of this vast London is my life; I fling myself into all these efforts; its hopes, its labors, its weariness, its pain, its undying hope. I grow with its growth; I feel myself alive in it: and therefore I am utterly committed to it. I am at its disposal. These weary folk shall have my very best; and if the wolf comes to devour them, it is I who ought to die."

H. Scott Holland

877 *THE VOICE OF WORLD FAITH*

Says the Buddhist: "He who is just, speaks the truth, and does what is upright and good. Minister to others by courtesy, generosity, and faithfulness."

Says the Confucian: "These things are good: respect for others, charity, sincerity, kindness. What you do not like when done to yourself, do not do to others."

Says the Hindu: "Righteousness is that which prevents injury to others. Do nothing to others which if done to you would give you pain."

Says the Jew: "What does the Lord require of thee but to deal justly, to love mercy, and to walk humbly with thy God?"

Says the Christian: "Thou shalt love thy neighbor as thyself. Whatsoever ye would that men should do to you, do ye even so to them."

The great religions are alike in teaching us to respect the knowledge, the point of view, and the faith of our neighbor.

Says the Buddhist: "The root of religion is to reverence one's own faith and never revile that of others."

Says the Hindu: "Heaven is a palace with many doors where each man may enter in his own way."

Says the Mohammedan: "Whatever be your religion, associate with men who think differently from you. If you can hear them without anger, you have attained peace."

Says the Zoroastrian: "Broad is the carpet God has spread, and beautiful the colors he has given it. Whatever road I take joins the highway that leads to him."

Says the Jew: "Who gains wisdom? He who receives instruction from all sources. The fear of the Lord is to hate evil, pride, and arrogancy."

Says the Christian: "Judge not that ye be not judged. God is no respector of persons, but in every nation he that feareth him and worketh righteousness is accepted with him."

Eva Taylor

878 *AN AFFIRMATION*

I will always seek to discover the best and strongest points in my brother's behavior.

I will give him credit for sincerity.

I will try to avoid classifying him, and assuming that he has all the characteristics of the class to which he is supposed to belong.

I will emphasize our agreements.

When others criticize, I will try to bring out favorable points.

Where there is misunderstanding, either I of him, or he of me, I will go to him direct.

I will seek opportunities to pray together.

I will try to remember that I may be mistaken and that God's truth is too big for any one mind.

I will pray for those from whom I differ.

Henry Hodgkin

879 *THE CREED OF A GOOD NEIGHBOR*

I believe that good will is the divinest activity of the spirit of man, the wisest method, the secret of co-operative living, the most powerful force in the realm of human affairs.

I believe in the sacred sovereignty of my neighbor over his own life. Therefore, I will not trespass in his domain, or seek domination over his ideas or conduct in any way.

I believe in the good will of my neighbor; I believe that he is trying, according to his lights, as I am trying according to mine, to do what is right and good, even when we do not agree.

I believe that I see some truth which my neighbor may not see, and to which I must be true. I believe equally that my neighbor sees some truth which I may not see, so I must be not only open-minded but sympathetic—because I want to know his truth too.

I believe that I have more defects in manner, speech, disposition and temperament than I can detect or am willing to admit. Therefore, it ill becomes me to be too sharp a critic of my fellows.

I believe that the happiness and success of my neighbor are as important as my own. Therefore, I will seek in behalf of others the same things that I seek and ask for myself.

I believe that humor is one of the major gifts of God. I hope for my sake that my neighbor possesses it; I pray for his sake that I may have enough of it to laugh at myself.

I believe in the Eternal Good Will; that there is a Spirit in this universe which prompts, inspires, and sustains men who make life an adventure in brotherhood; and I trust that Spirit.

Joseph Fort Newton

F. RACE RELATIONS SUNDAY

Race Relations Sunday is the Sunday nearest to Lincoln's Birthday, February 12. The spirit of this day may be featured in worship and preaching, youth discussions, and Sunday school programs. Churches representing different racial groups frequently join in union worship. Pulpit exchange on an interracial basis is common.

Calls to Worship

(Boldface type indicates response.)

880   Now in Christ Jesus ye who sometimes were far off are made nigh by the blood of Christ. For he is our peace, who hath made both one, and hath broken down the middle wall of partition between us. Now therefore ye are no more strangers and foreigners, but fellowcitizens with the saints, and of the household of God.

Ep. 2:13-14, 19

881   The God of patience and consolation grant us to be like-minded one toward another according to Christ Jesus: that ye may with one mind and one mouth glorify God, even the Father of our Lord Jesus Christ.

Wherefore receive ye one another, as Christ also received us to the glory of God.

Ro. 15:5-7

882   We took sweet counsel together, and walked unto the house of God in company. Of a truth I perceive that God is no respecter of persons: but in every nation he that feareth him, and worked righteousness, is accepted with him.

Ps. 55:14; Ac. 10:34-35

883   Have we not all one father? hath not one God created us? why do we deal treacherously every man against his brother, by profaning the covenant of our fathers? There is one body, and one Spirit, even as ye are called in one hope of your calling; one Lord, one faith, one baptism, one God and Father of all, who is above all, and through all, and in you all. But unto every one of us is given grace according to the measure of the gift of Christ.

Mal. 2:10; Ep. 4:4-7

Invocations

884 Almighty God, who by thy Son Jesus Christ hast broken down the walls of partition between Jew and Gentile, slave and free, rich and poor, break down, we beseech thee, all that divides us one from another. Shame our jealousies, frustrate our pride, destroy our prejudices, and forbid that from pride of race or hardness of heart, we should despise any for whom Christ died, or injure any in whom he lives. Amen.

Book of Worship (ER)

885 Blessed Lord, who hast given us a new commandment that we should love one another, and hast taught us that where envy and strife are, there is confusion and every evil work: give grace unto us thy servants, that we may be kindly affectioned one to another. Enable us to put away all bitterness, and wrath, and anger, and evil-speaking, with all malice; and grant that in honor preferring one another, we may walk in love, even as thou, Lord, didst love us and give thyself for us. Amen.

Book of Common Order of the Church of Scotland

886 O God, who art the hope of all the ends of the earth, the God of the spirits of all flesh: we beseech thee to hear our humble intercessions for all races and kindreds of men, that thou wilt turn all hearts unto thyself. Remove from our minds hatred, prejudice and contempt for those who are not of our own race or color, class or creed; that, departing from everything that estranges and divides, we may by thee be brought into unity of spirit, in the bond of peace. Amen.

Book of Common Worship (P)

Litany

(Boldface type indicates responses.)

887 Let us pray for the church in the new age: By this may all men know that we are his disciples:

That we have love one to another.

God, our Shepherd, give to the church a new vision and a new charity, new wisdom and fresh understanding, the revival of her brightness and the renewal of her unity; that the eternal message of thy Son, undefiled by the traditions of men, may be hailed as the good news of the new age; through him who maketh all things new, Jesus Christ our Lord.

Let us pray for the nation in the new age: Thou shalt wipe away all tears from their eyes:

For the former things are passed away.

God, our Ruler, give to every nation the dawning spirit of human brother-hood, a new respect for man and for woman, new loyalty in service, compunction and charity, new happiness in work and justice in reward; that our homes may be restored in thee, our cities rebuilt, and all the world may reflect the radiance of that new Jerusalem whose river is the water of life, and whose light is the Lamb that was slain and now liveth for evermore.

Let us pray for the world in the new age: Unto the Father of our Lord Jesus Christ:

Of whom the whole family in heaven and earth is named.

God, our Father, give to the nations of the world a new heart of comradeship; the old man of ignorance and cruelty being done away, and the new man put on, renewed in knowledge, to strengthen and to serve the brethren; that every people may bring its tribute of excellence to the common treasury, without fear, and without the lust of domination; and that all the world may go forward in the new and living way which he hath consecrated for us; who now liveth and reigneth, with thee and the Spirit of truth, one God, world without end. Amen.

The Kingdom, the Power and the Glory

Prayers

888 O God, we thank thee thou hast made man in thine own image. Help us to see ourselves as thou seest us, all standing in need of thy mercy yet dear unto thee. We confess to the many injustices and prejudices of which we are guilty. Our arrogance and pride make us unworthy to be called thy children.

We rejoice that thou art no respecter of persons. We know thou sendest rain on the just and the unjust. Help us to grasp the truth that thou hast made of one blood all nations of men for to dwell on all the face of the earth. Since we have all sinned and come short of thy glory, may we cling to thy Cross by which thy love is commended to all. May we in honor prefer one another.

In the light of thy redeeming grace help us to strive for reconciliation among all races and kindreds of men. Remove from us all unchristian attitudes. Beget in us the mind of Christ. Lift us above all that alienates and separates in the human family. Through Jesus Christ enable us to strive in this world for that fellowship of kindred spirits to which we look forward in the heavenly King-dom. In his name and by his power who is the Saviour of the world. Amen.

John S. Land

889   If we acknowledge a universal fatherhood or work for a universal brotherhood, save us, O God, from both hypocrisy and sentimentality in our attitude toward the man who is not of our race. May we treat him as a brother, acknowledging his rights, recognizing his differences, and having regard to the welfare of the whole human family. ·

Help us to recognize the value of things that divide men as well as the worth of things that unite men. Let not selfishness, pride or power betray us into unbrotherliness toward any man. Neither let us ignore the great basic fact of diversity in unity which thou hast written all over the universe.

Grant to us, each one, that grace of heart and poise of mind that will enable us to contribute our little share toward a just and happy solution of the great race problems that so vex the world. Amen.

George W. Coleman

890   O Father, who art the Maker and Lover of the myriads of men that populate the world, arouse us to a practical belief in the full breadth of our human relationships, that we may be rid of the shackles of sectionalism, national pride and racial prejudice, and in the spirit of mutual helpfulness combine to establish those conditions of brotherhood and amity which it is our responsibility to promote. Hush the proud boastings of the nations of the Western World, that they may learn to use their strength, their knowledge, their material greatness to support the weak, to enlighten the ignorant, to enrich the poor. Beat the harsh armaments of war into the kindly implements of industry and peace. Bind together the peoples of East and West by the ties of sympathy, respect and service, that in appreciative recognition of one another's virtues and with considerate forbearance in our differences, we may be unified into one family according to thy purpose; through Jesus Christ our Lord. Amen.

Charles H. Brent

Poems

891   *From BYRON*

In men whom men condemn as ill
I find so much of goodness still,
In men whom men pronounce divine
I find so much of sin and blot,
I do not dare to draw a line
Between the two, where God has not.

Joaquin Miller

892   *AFRICA*

I slept. I dreamed. I seemed to climb a hard, ascending track
And just behind me labored one whose face was black.
I pitied him, but hour by hour he gained upon my path.
He stood beside me, stood upright, and then I turned in wrath.
"Go back," I cried, "what right have you to stand beside me here?"
I paused, struck dumb with fear, for lo! the black man was not
      there—
But Christ stood in his place!
And oh! the pain, the pain, the pain that looked from that dear face.
                                           Author Unknown

893   *WE ARE ALL KIN*

We are all kin—oh, make us kin indeed!
Spirit of Christ, we answer to thy call
Our Father makes of us one family
One Infinite Great Love doth claim us all,—
    All one in him!

We are all kin, though wide our various ways.
Spirit of Christ, that lives within all life,
Break down the barriers that time has reared,
Heal every wound and end the fruitless strife!
                                             John Oxenham

894   *OUTWITTED*

He drew a circle that shut me out—
Heretic, rebel, a thing to flout.
But Love and I had the wit to win:
We drew a circle that took him in!
                                          Edwin Markham

895   *From THE HEATHEN*

Yes, you'd know him for a heathen
If you judged him by the hide,
But bless you, he's my brother,
For he's just like me inside.
                                         Robert Freeman

896   *SIMON THE CYRENIAN SPEAKS*

> Look not on me with scorn because
>   My skin's of darker hue—
> Remember once these shoulders bore
>   The cross he bore for you.

Glen Baker

897   *AND WHAT SHALL YOU SAY?*

> Brother, come!
> And let us go unto our God.
> And when we stand before him
> I shall say—
> "Lord, I do not hate,
> I am hated.
> I scourge no one,
> I am scourged.
> I covet no lands,
> My lands are coveted.
> I mock no peoples,
> My people are mocked."
> And, brother, what shall you say?

Joseph S. Cotter

898   *TABLEAU*

> Locked arm in arm they cross the way,
>   The black boy and the white,
> The golden splendor of the day,
>   The sable pride of night.
>
> From lowered blinds the dark folk stare,
>   And here the fair folk talk,
> Indignant that these two should dare
>   In unison to walk.
>
> Oblivious to look and word
>   They pass, and see no wonder
> That lightning brilliant as a sword
>   Should blaze the path of thunder.

Countee Cullen

899 *CAREFULLY TAUGHT*

You've got to be taught to hate and fear,
You've got to be taught from year to year,
It's got to be drummed in your dear little ear—
You've got to be carefully taught!

You've got to be taught to be afraid
Of people whose eyes are oddly made,
And people whose skin is a different shade—
You've got to be carefully taught.

You've got to be taught before it's too late,
Before you are six or seven or eight,
To hate all the people your relatives hate—
You've got to be carefully taught.

Oscar Hammerstein, 2nd

Topics, Texts and Themes

900 *KINSHIP*

One touch of Jesus makes all the world kin. That is true in the common practical give-and-take. One touch of Jesus reveals the fact that all the race is kin. He indirectly makes clear the essential unity of the race.

There is a peculiar separateness between the East and the West. It persists, tenaciously, intangibly, unchangeably, despite contacts of commerce and travel.

Men are always more alike than different. But the differences do stare one in the face, and are apt to rub him the wrong way.

That separateness makes the humanness of Jesus—innate, instinctive, distinctive humanness—stand out sharply. A Westerner, by blood and breeding, in intimate continued touch, feels it keenly as he sojourns in the East.

The exclusive Chinese, the conservative Briton, the dark-eyed, quick-tongued Latin of the south of Europe, the flaxen-haired, rugged-speeched Scandinavian; the intense Gallic, either north or south of the Pyrenees; the phlegmatic Hollander, all alike glow, and glow together, in heart and eye and tongue when in touch with Jesus.

The Alpine mountaineer, the dike-dwelling lowlander, Swiss and Hollander, join together in heart unity, with city dweller, and the tiller of the soil, and with the savage-born kraal dweller, and their hearts burn with a common fire, when touched by the human touch of Jesus.

S. D. Gordon

901   *BRIDGEBUILDING BROTHERS*

Make ye ready the way of the Lord. MAT. 3:3 (ARV)

Jesus entered a world of sharp class distinctions, bitter prejudices, racial animosities, and arrogant nationalism. What did he do about these things? He lived and taught the creed of fellowship without frontiers. Rich and poor, respectable and outcast, man and woman, adult and child, Jew and Gentile—all were enclosed and embraced within the limitless circle of his love and interest. Jesus was always removing barriers. He was always opening new and cluttered roads of understanding and spiritual commerce. And, with the sign and secret of a Cross, he threw bridges over every conceivable kind of peril and prejudice. And that which began as a scandal in the first century of our era has managed to live on and become, in the twentieth century, the most glorious heritage and inspiration of our broken world. For mark you, the church of Christ, with all its human faults and frailties, is the only genuine international and interracial unity on earth today. Only the church continues to make distinction between the things that are Caesar's and the things that are God's. The church is the one and only living bridge uniting men and women of good will and God-centered loyalty wherever they may be found. Only the church, which yesterday was condemned for being "behind the times" when in reality it was only "behind the scenes," possesses the vision and the secret by which tomorrow's pilgrim hosts may move up into the fellowship of today's authentic prophets and pioneers.

Hobart D. McKeehan

902 *THE TRANSFORMATION OF HUMAN RELATIONSHIPS*

The history of human relationships might be summed up as five stages: (a) owner and slave; (b) master and servant; (c) employer and employee; (d) comrades and deviators; (e) brothers.

E. Stanley Jones

903   *RACIAL LABELS*

Our fathers worshipped in this mountain; and ye say, that in Jerusalem is the place where men ought to worship. JN. 4:20

The Samaritan woman, perceiving that Jesus was of the Jewish race, attributed to him the standard Jewish belief that men ought to worship in Jerusalem. It was an utterly superficial judgment. Jesus was a Jew, but not in the sense that he shared all opinions with his compatriots. Naturally as a Jew, and until the authorities of his own people cast him out, his worship centered in Jerusalem. But it was not a narrow nationalistic worship that he observed in the national shrine. He told that worldly woman, "The hour cometh and now is, when the true worshippers shall worship the Father in spirit and truth." Neither the Holy Mountain of Samaria nor the Holy City of Jerusalem was the exclusive place of worship. For God's call is for the spiritual worship of the heart which is subject to no form, time or place.

The Samaritan woman made a serious mistake in attributing an opinion to Jesus on the basis of her observation of certain racial characteristics. Even so, to apply a racial label to any man without considering whether or not he deserves it is a great injustice. And this is true both by way of commendation or blame. For each individual is not only a representative of his race or nation. He may be, first of all, a man.

Henry and Tertius van Dyke

904   *FATHERHOOD, SONSHIP, BROTHERHOOD*

Religious individualism and universalism mean that the Christian life is lived entirely within one context: the Fatherhood-sonship-brotherhood context. The moment we step out of this context in any of our relationships and activities, we have deviated seriously from the Christian position. Let us suppose that we substitute the terms "Negro" and "white" for the terms "son" and "brother" in the Fatherhood-sonship-brotherhood pattern. Immediately the pattern loses its meaning. In the original pattern the son is son because of the Father; and the brother is brother because of the Father. The Father is the basis and determining factor in their relation. But in the pattern in which the terms "Negro" and "white" are substituted, the Negro is Negro because some particular, finite characteristic is singled out and the white man is white for the same reason. This particular, finite, and transitory characteristic becomes the basis and determining factor in their relation. And since it is a particular, finite, and transitory characteristic and is chosen for the purpose of pointing up difference, it is by its very nature a principle of disunion. It is rooted in the Fall of man; it belongs to the divisive element in life. The very term "interracial" is under Christian moral suspicion. It suggests two camps standing over against each other. It suggests the *we-they* relation, a relation in which *I and thou,* two souls under God, can never meet. All Christian activity and relations must submit to the Fatherhood-sonship-brotherhood context.

George D. Kelsey

905   *CROSSING RACIAL BARRIERS*

One of the main duties of the Christian is to foster Christian fellowship across the racial lines. "In Christ there is neither Jew nor Gentile, bond nor free, male nor female." In the area of race relations today, the church is weak. It is so partly because it usually denies Christian fellowship across racial lines. Most of our churches are not churches of God but churches of men, of custom, and of tradition. Until the individual Christian and the clergy are able to set themselves over against the state, against tradition, and against custom and say by words and deeds that when a member of any racial group crosses the threshold of this house, he is no longer in the custody of men but in the custody of God, and that in God's house the state or society has no voice and no jurisdiction, the church will be weak and impotent; it will have no right to speak to the secular order about its behavior. Freedom of worship, if it means anything at all, means freedom to worship God across racial lines and freedom for a man or woman to join the church of his or her choice irrespective of race. Separate churches for the people may not be un-Christian but segregated churches are un-Christian. Denominational churches, for example, are not necessarily un-Christian; but churches organized purely along racial lines can hardly qualify as Christian. If worship and fellowship are denied because of race, it is definitely un-Christian.

Benjamin E. Mays

906   *IF CHRISTIANS WERE CHRISTIANS*

If Christians were Christians, there would be no race prejudice. For the essence of Christianity is brotherhood. Prejudice, of course, is a sin not of Christians alone but of humanity at large. It has grown as a pestilential weed in the soil of every land and in the atmosphere of every heart. Yet the early Christians met the challenge of race prejudice, and overcame it. Jesus met it in his friendly relations with the Samaritans, who were as much despised by the Jews of his day as the Negroes are commonly despised by the white citizens of this country today. Philip, Jesus' disciple, met it when an Ethiopian, black as midnight, asked to be received into the Christian company, and was baptized in honor as one of the brethren. Peter, the first of the disciples, met the test when he received the Roman centurion, Cornelius, with the unforgettable words, "God is no respecter of persons, but in every nation he that feareth him and worketh righteousness is acceptable with him." Paul met the test when he went to Rome, as cosmopolitan a city in its day as New York is in ours, and preached to all the people without distinction that they should accept the gospel of the risen Christ.

John Haynes Holmes

907   *THE PERSON IN A DIFFERENT SKIN*

I am the person who was born to live in a skin with a different color from yours.

I could not choose my parents, nor you yours.

Thus, the color pigments embedded by the unchangeable hands of nature in your skin are perchance white, while mine are black, or brown, or yellow.

But, underneath, I am just like you.

My muscles ripple in the same waves of power and thrill to the same throb of joyous action.

My mind is as good as yours.

I reach out, just as you do, in aspirations of the soul.

I love and hate, hope and despair, rejoice and suffer, along with you.

When my children lose their fair chance at life and become aware of the bitter road of prejudice they must tread, then I know what my color has cost.

I offer my hand in rebuilding an unjust world that you and I can make more Christian than we have found it.

I am the person in a different skin.

Percy R. Hayward

G. LABOR SUNDAY

Labor Sunday precedes Labor Day, the first Monday in September. Observance of Labor Day was begun in 1869 as "a laborer's national holiday." The church on this day re-emphasizes the role which the Christian conscience has played in fashioning more just and humane labor conditions and in exalting and honoring all honest toil. Members of labor unions are often invited to attend services.

Calls to Worship

908 [Jesus saith] Come unto me, all ye that labor and are heavy laden, and I will give you rest. Take my yoke upon you, and learn of me; for I am meek and lowly in heart: and ye shall find rest unto your souls. For my yoke is easy, and my burden is light.

Mat. 11:28–30

909 Except the Lord build the house, they labor in vain that build it: except the Lord keep the city, the watchman waketh but in vain. Blessed is every one that feareth the Lord; that walketh in his ways.

Ps. 127:1; 128:1

910 We are laborers together with God: ye are God's husbandry, ye are God's building. Let every man take heed how he buildeth. . . . For other foundation can no man lay than that is laid, which is Jesus Christ.

1 Co. 3:9–11

911 Let thy work appear unto thy servants, and thy glory unto their children. And let the beauty of the Lord our God be upon us: and establish thou the work of our hands upon us; yea, the work of our hands establish thou it.

Ps. 90:16–17

Invocations

912 O God, who worketh in all things, who hast called us to be fellow workers with thee, and dost assign to every man his separate task: teach us, in

421

our several callings, what thou wouldst have us do, and make us faithful to do it, in thy name and in thy strength; for Jesus Christ's sake. Amen.*

Daily Prayer

913   O God, who didst give over thy Son to the toil and burdens of our human lot: we pray that all who earn their daily bread by the labors of their hands may enter into fellowship with him, who came to do thy will. Strengthen our hands, encourage our hearts, and grant us the reward of our labor in all reasonable comfort for our families. Regard the well-being and prosperity of our farms and foundries, our factories and work-rooms, and all places of honorable industry. Establish there thy Kingdom, we beseech thee, in social righteousness and mutual good will. So govern men's hearts that the love of man may subdue the love of gain; that all occasions of strife may cease, and the counsels of selfishness be turned to seek the common good; for Christ's sake. Amen.

Louis F. Benson

914   Almighty God, who didst ordain that thy Son Jesus Christ should labor with his hands to supply his own needs, and the needs of others: teach us, we pray thee, that no labor is mean, and all labor is divine, to which thou dost call us; to the glory of thy holy name. Amen.

Daily Prayer

915   Almighty God, who, being sovereign Lord of all, dost never rest from the labors of thy hands; husbandman preparing the fruits of the earth, sower and reaper, healer and teacher, helper of them that need: teach us, we pray thee, the divine dignity of labor, of whatsoever sort it be, if only from thee and for thee, to the well-being of thy creatures and the glory of thy holy name. Amen.

Daily Prayer

Litany

(Boldface type indicates responses.)

916   O Lord, who didst create the earth for our habitation, and the increase thereof for our enrichment:

Have mercy upon us.

On the earth and all that is therein; on the harvest of the soil; on the trade and industry of our people; on the toil by which the sons of men obtain thy abundant gifts:

We pray for thy blessing, O Lord.

On those who search for thy treasures hidden in the earth; on those who labor to make them fit for the use of man:

We pray for thy blessing, O Lord.

On those who work in the building and adorning of the churches in which we worship, of the homes in which we live, and the goodly palaces of art, and government, and commerce:

We pray for thy blessing, O Lord.

On manufacturers and craftsmen; on those who devise cunning machines and are skilled in all manner of workmanship:

We pray for thy blessing, O Lord.

On merchants who bring thy gifts from foreign lands; on the men who go down to the sea in ships, and occupy their business in great waters:

We pray for thy blessing, O Lord.

On all who trade with us in the shop, or in the market; on all who serve at the counter, or in the office; on those who bring what we need for life, or comfort, or enjoyment, within reach of our homes:

We pray for thy blessing, O Lord.

O Lord, how manifold are thy works:

In wisdom hast thou made them all.

O Lord, how manifold are thy works:

The earth is full of thy riches.

O God, who orderest all things both in heaven and earth: grant that every man, according to the business which he hath undertaken among the sons of men, may know that he is thy servant therein; that whatsoever his hand findeth to do, he may do it as in thy service and to thy glory, through Jesus Christ our Lord. Amen.

Rodborough Bede Book

Prayers

917 Lord Jesus, bless all who serve us, who have dedicated their lives to the ministry of others—all the teachers of our schools who labor so patiently with so little appreciation; all who wait upon the public, the clerks in the stores who have to accept criticism, complaints, bad manners, selfishness at the hands of a thoughtless public. Bless the mailmen, the drivers of streetcars and buses who must listen to people who lose their tempers.

Bless every humble soul who, in these days of stress and strain, preaches sermons without words. Amen.

Peter Marshall

918   O God, thou mightiest worker of the universe, source of all strength and author of all unity, we pray thee for our brothers, the industrial workers of the nation. As their work binds them together in common toil and danger, may their hearts be knit together in a strong sense of their common interests and destiny. Help them to realize that the injury of one is the concern of all, and that the welfare of all must be the aim of every one. If any of them is tempted to sell the birthright of his class for a mess of pottage for himself, give him a wider outlook and a nobler sympathy with his fellows. Teach them to keep step in a steady onward march, and in their own way to fulfil the law of Christ by bearing the common burdens.

Grant to the organizations of labor quiet patience and prudence in all disputes, and fairness to see the other side. Save them from malice and bitterness. Save them from the headlong folly which ruins a fair cause, and give them wisdom resolutely to put aside the two-edged sword of violence that turns on those who seize it. Raise up for them still more leaders of able mind and large heart, and give them grace to follow the wiser counsel.

When they strive for leisure and health and a better wage, do thou grant their cause success, but teach them not to waste their gain on fleeting passions, but to use it in building fairer homes and a nobler manhood. Grant all classes of our nation a larger comprehension for the aspirations of labor and for the courage and worth of these our brothers, that we may cheer them in their struggles and understand them even in their sins. And may the upward climb of Labor, its defeats and its victories, in the farther reaches bless all classes of our nation, and build up for the republic of the future a great body of workers, strong of limb, clear of mind, fair in temper, glad to labor, conscious of their worth, and striving together for the final brotherhood of all men. Amen.

Walter Rauschenbusch

919   O God, thou art thyself the great Creator, the Master Workman. Hast thou not also revealed thyself to us in Jesus the carpenter, whose roughened hands bear eternal testimony to the dignity of toil?

We sense thy presence in the upward surge of the masses, who with the awakened self-respect of children of God, have through the centuries cast off the shackles of slavery and serfdom, and stand now gazing toward the dawn of a greater freedom.

We praise thee for those brave spirits who have led the way; who have dared to risk even their children's bread in organized endeavor to improve the lot of all; who for their unselfish devotion have been condemned as outcasts of society; endured prison; sacrificed their lives as martyrs to the cause.

Help thou the labor movement of our day to be worthy of its heritage. Unite in high purpose the workers in the factory and on the farm. Preserve them from temptation to selfish complacency in partial gains for any favored craft or race or nation. Guard their leaders from lust for personal power. Guide them in the service of the common good.

Help the workers of all lands to stand shoulder to shoulder for justice and peace among the nations. Save them from the sin of selfish nationalism. Give them a wider vision of world government with justice and liberty for all.

Grant to labor the wisdom to seek a world of peace and plenty by means of organization and the ballot, keeping their movement free from hate and violence, building into the cooperative commonwealth those spiritual values which alone can make it endure.

Bring, at last, all workers by hand or brain into world-wide brotherhood; into closer fellowship with thee, O God, the Father of us all. Amen.*

James Myers

920   Guide, protect and inspire, our heavenly Father, all those who learn and labor truly to get their own living:

For men who face peril,
For women who suffer pain,
For those who till the earth,
For those who tend machinery,
For those who strive on the deep waters,
For those who venture in far countries,
For those who work in offices and warehouses,
For those who labor at furnaces and in factories,
For those who toil in mines,
For those who buy and sell,
For those who keep house,
For those who train children,
For all who live by strength of arm,
For all who live by cunning of hand,
For all who control, direct, or employ,
For all who enrich the common life through art, and science, and learning,
For all who guide the common thought, as writers or as teachers,
For all who may serve the common good as pastors, physicians, lawyers, merchants, for all social workers, leaders, and statesmen, we beseech thee. Amen.

The Kingdom, the Power and the Glory

Poems

921   *WORK*

> Close by the careless worker's side,
>   Still patient stands
> The Carpenter of Nazareth,
>   With pierced hands
> Outstretched to plead unceasingly,
>   His Love's demands.
>
> Longing to pick the hammer up
>   And strike a blow,
> Longing to feel his plane swing out,
>   Steady and slow,
> The fragrant shavings falling down,
>   Silent as snow.
>
> Because this is my work, O Lord,
>   It must be thine,
> Because it is a human task
>   It is divine.
> Take me, and brand me with thy cross,
>   Thy slave's proud sign.

G. A. Studdert-Kennedy

922   *LORD, MIGHT I BE BUT AS A SAW*

> Lord, might I be but as a saw,
> A plane, a chisel in thy hand.
> No, Lord, I take it back in awe;
> Such prayer for me is far too grand.
> I pray thee, rather let me lie
> As on thy bench the favored wood;
> Thy saw, thy plane, thy chisel ply
> And work me into something good.

George Macdonald

923   *THE CARPENTER OF GALILEE*

> The Carpenter of Galilee
> Comes down the street again,
> In every land, in every age,
> He still is building men.
>
> *Hilda W. Smith*

924   *From AURORA LEIGH* (Bk. 8)

> After Christ, work turns to privilege,
> And hence forth, one with our humanity,
> The Six-day Worker, working still in us,
> Has called us freely to work on with him
> In high companionship. So, happiest!
> I count that heaven itself is only work
> To a surer issue.
>
> *Elizabeth Barrett Browning*

925   *EVERY MASON IN THE QUARRY*

Every mason in the quarry, every builder on the shore,
Every woodsman in the forest, every boatman at the oar
Hewing wood or drawing water, splitting stones or cleaving sod,
All the dusty ranks of labor in the regiment of God,
March together toward his triumph, do the task his hands prepare;
Honest toil is holy service, faithful work is praise and prayer

Henry van Dyke

926   *THE COMMON TASKS*

> The common tasks are beautiful if we
> Have eyes to see their shining ministry.
> The plowman with his share deep in the loam,
> The carpenter whose skilled hands build a home,
> The gardener working with reluctant sod,
> Faithful to his partnership with God—
> These are the artisans of life, and oh,
> A woman with her eyes and cheeks aglow,
> Watching a kettle, tending a scarlet flame,
> Guarding a little child—there is no name

For these great ministries, and eyes are dull
That do not see that it is beautiful,
That do not see within the common tasks
The simple answer to the thing God asks
Of any child, a pride within his breast:
That at our given work we do our best.

Grace Noll Crowell

927   *From ANDREW RYKMAN'S PRAYER*

If there be some weaker one,
Give me strength to help him on;
If a blinder soul there be,
Let me guide him nearer thee.
Make my mortal dreams come true
With the work I fain would do;
Clothe with life the weak intent,
Let me be the thing I meant;
Let me find in thy employ
Peace that dearer is than joy;
Out of self to love be led
And to heaven acclimated,
Until all things sweet and good
Seem my natural habitude.

John Greenleaf Whittier

928   *HERE IN MY WORKSHOP*

Here in my workshop, where I toil
  Till head and hands are well-nigh spent;
Out on the road where the dust and soil
  Fall thick on garments worn and rent;
Or in the kitchen where I bake
  The bread the little children eat,
He comes: his hand of strength I take,
  And every lonely task grows sweet.

Author Unknown

929   *WORK*

Let me but do my work from day to day,
  In field or forest, at the desk or loom,
  In the roaring market-place or tranquil room;
Let me but find it in my heart to say,
When vagrant wishes beckon me astray,
  "This is my work; my blessing, not my doom;
  Of all who live, I am the one by whom
This work can best be done in the right way."

Then shall I see it not too great, nor small,
  To suit my spirit and to prove my powers;
  Then shall I cheerful greet the laboring hours,
And cheerful turn, when the long shadows fall
At eventide, to play and love and rest,
Because I know for me my work is best.

Henry van Dyke

Topics, Texts and Themes

930   *I AM WORK*

I am the foundation of all business.
I am the source of all prosperity.
I am the parent of genius.
I am the salt that gives life its savour.
I laid the foundation of every fortune.
I can do more to advance youth than his own parents, be they
  ever so wealthy.
I must be loved before I can bestow my greatest blessings and
  achieve my greatest ends.
Loved, I make life sweet, purposeful and fruitful.
I am represented in the humblest savings, in the largest block
  of investments.
All progress springs from me.
I am work.

Author Unknown

931 *A CALL FOR WORKERS*

The lazy and idle seldom hear the call of God. It is often when intent on some useful work and while pursuing a helpful calling that God's voice is heard. Here are a few examples from the Bible:

Moses was busy with his flock at Horeb.

Gideon was busy threshing wheat by the wine press.

Saul was busy searching for his father's lost beasts.

Elisha was busy plowing with twelve yoke of oxen.

David was busy caring for his father's sheep

Nehemiah was busy bearing the king's wine-cup.

Amos was busy caring for his sheep and sycamore fruit and attending the market.

Peter and Andrew were busy casting their nets into the sea.

Lydia was busy preparing and selling her purple fabrics.

James and John were busy mending their nets.

Matthew was busy collecting customs duties.

Mary and Elizabeth were busy with their homemaking.

Jesus was busy probably in the carpenter shop and about his Father's business.

Author Unknown

932 *THE THRILL OF WORKING WELL*

My heart found pleasure in all my toil, and this was my reward for all my toil. EC. 2:10 (RSV)

The author of Ecclesiastes was a deep-dyed cynic. He had tasted of life from many springs and had found them all bitter. His outlook on life was therefore that of one who expects nothing, so that when he finds nothing, he is satisfied, for he feels that his cynicism has been abundantly justified.

In one significant particular, however, he exhibits a gleam of faith and optimism. He has worked hard and found pleasure in so doing. He asks for no better reward from life than the satisfaction that comes from working well.

Roy L. Smith

933 *CONSECRATED ENDEAVOUR*

The sweeper of the city street who sweeps in the dark corner where no inspector comes, simply because it is his business to have the streets clean, has a touch of consecration in him. The lighthouse-keeper who rows out night after night to the lonely rock, though he knows that for weeks together no ship goes by his coast, and who does it because he is counted on for that, is in the same list.

The shoemaker in the little island town who makes an honest shoe for some unknown customer across the world and who feels the sacredness of his work, is in his humble way consecrated. The scientist who counts nothing too hard in his unwearied struggle to win one more secret from the unknown, that he may add it to the slowly growing total of human knowledge, is to be enrolled among those who are consecrated.

The daughter who smothers all her own personal dreams to care for an invalid mother or a widowed father, the reformer who spends his days study-ing the slums that he may hasten the day when there shall be no slums, the Christian teacher who counts no obstacle too difficult if so by it he may make one more person enter into the real meaning of the love of Christ—all these are examples of consecration.

Rufus M. Jones

934   *THE KITCHEN IS HOLY GROUND*

Work is simply human activity directed to the business of sustaining life; and commerce is at bottom simply an organization of the processes whereby society is provided with food, clothing, shelter, heat and light. . . . The modern trouble is that the economic interest is enthroned over life. . . . But commerce was made for man and not man for commerce. Nor was it made for man in the sense of being an opportunity for self-aggrandizement, for making money. It was ordained to be a cooperation in the service of life. But today it is on the throne.

The man is lost in the merchant or merchandise. Yet the relation of the economic end of life is nothing more than the relation of the kitchen to the rest of the home. It is essential, necessary, yet strictly subordinate. We reach the real business of life when we are through with the business of making and eating bread. This does not imply contempt for the kitchen. Properly understood, the kitchen is holy ground, full . . . of intimations of God. . . . The kitchen, ceases to be holy ground . . . [and] becomes a thieves' kitchen when it sets up to be the whole of life or asserts an ascendancy over the rest of life. Money and merchandise are holy things when they minister to life: they are wholly evil things when they become masters of life.

Richard Roberts

935   *LABOR IS LIFE*

There is a perennial nobleness, and even sacredness, in work. Were he ever so benighted, forgetful of his high calling, there is always hope in a man that actually and earnestly works: in idleness alone is there perpetual despair. . . .

The latest gospel in this world is, *Know thy work and do it.* . . . It has been written, "An endless significance lies in work." A man perfects himself by working. Foul jungles are cleared away, fair seed-fields rise instead, and stately cities. . . .

Blessed is he who has found his work; let him ask no other blessedness. He has a work, a life-purpose; he has found it, and will follow it. . . . *Labor is life.*

Thomas Carlyle

936   *HAPPINESS AND WORK*

Hard physical labor! One actually stops thinking. I often work long without any thought whatever, so far as I know, save that connected with the monotonous repetition of the labor itself—down with the spade, out with it, up with it, over with it—and repeat.

And yet sometimes—mostly in the forenoon when I am not at all tired—I will suddenly have a sense as of the world opening around me—a sense of its beauty and its meanings—giving me a peculiar deep happiness, that is near complete content.

Happiness, I have discovered, is nearly always a rebound from hard work. It is one of the follies of men to imagine that they can enjoy mere thoughts, or emotion, or sentiment! As well try to eat beauty! For happiness must be tricked! She loves to see men at work. She loves sweat, weariness, self-sacrifice. She will be found not in palaces but lurking in cornfields and factories and hovering over littered desks: she crowns the unconscious head of the busy child. If you look up suddenly from hard work you will see her, but if you look too long she fades sorrowfully away.

David Grayson (Ray Stannard Baker)

937   *THE MATURE WORKER*

In defining the mature worker, Sticker and Appel, University of Pennsylvania psychiatrists, have included such qualities as stick-to-itiveness; the readiness to give more than is asked in a given situation; the persistence to carry out a goal in the face of difficulties; the ability to size things up and make one's own decisions; the exercise of a considerable degree of independence, determination, or the will to succeed, and achieve; the capacity to work with others and to work under authority; flexibility and tolerance.

Louis Binstock

938   *THE TOILER BECOMES THE THINKER*

The people that walked in darkness have seen a great light. IS. 9:2

Yesterday! A rude figure, "bowed by the weight of the centuries," leaned upon his hoe. "The emptiness of the ages" was in his face, and on his back were "the burdens of the world." Millet, the painter, and Markham, the poet, called him "The Man with the Hoe."

Today! A self-respecting man stands erect. There is light in his eyes and upon his lips an emancipating cry. He demands that mankind lay hold upon science on the one hand and religion on the other to "control the controllable" in the interests of social well-being. He is "The Man with a Hope," refusing to believe that "swinehood hath no remedy." He has seen the shackles of slavery triumphantly torn from his brother's wrists. He has witnessed the passing of feudalism. He has beheld the coming of liberty in a "government of the people, by the people, and for the people."

He envisions a day in which abundant life will be the lot of all men, in which the major objective of social endeavor will have shifted from profit-making to personality-making, in which the work-life will be "of the people, by the people, and for the people"—in a word, a day in which Christian ethics will be transformed by economist, educator and engineer into the common practice of men.

G. Bromley Oxnam

939   *AN INDUSTRIAL CREED*

I believe that labor and capital are partners, not enemies; that their interests are common, not opposed; and that neither can attain the fullest measure of prosperity at the expense of the other but only in association with the other.

I believe that the community is an essential party to industry, and that it should have adequate representation with the other parties.

I believe that the purpose of industry is quite as much to advance social well-being as material prosperity; that, in the pursuit of that purpose, the interests of the community should be carefully considered, the well-being of employees fully guarded, management adequately recognized and capital justly compensated, and that failure in any of these particulars means loss to all four parties.

I believe that every man is entitled to an opportunity to earn a living, to fair wages, to reasonable hours of work and proper working conditions, to a decent home, to the opportunity to play, to learn, to worship and to love, as well as to toil, and that the responsibility rests as heavily upon industry as upon government or society, to see that these conditions and opportunities prevail.

I believe that diligence, initiative and efficiency, wherever found, should be encouraged and adequately rewarded, and that indolence, indifference and restriction of production should be discountenanced.

I believe that the application of right principles never fails to effect right relations; that the "letter killeth but the spirit giveth life"; that forms are wholly secondary, while attitudes are all important; and that only as the parties in industry are animated by the spirit of fair play, justice to all and brotherhood, will any plan which they may mutually work out succeed.

I believe that the man renders the greatest social service who so cooperates in the organization of industries to afford to the largest number of men the greatest opportunity for self-development and the enjoyment of those benefits which their united efforts add to the wealth of civilization.*

John D. Rockefeller, Jr.

H. RURAL LIFE SUNDAY

Rural Life Sunday is observed on a Sunday in May and recognizes the contributions of religion to rural life and the significance of rural life to the national history and the common welfare. The importance of the day is not limited to rural communities. Urban and rural pastors occasionally exchange pulpits for the day.

Calls to Worship

(Boldface type indicates responses.)

940   The earth is the Lord's and the fulness thereof; the world, and they that dwell therein. O come, let us worship and bow down: let us kneel before the Lord our maker.

For he is our God; and we are the people of his pasture, and the sheep of his hand.

Ps. 24:1; 95:6-7

941   The heavens declare the glory of God; and the firmament sheweth his handywork.

O Lord our Lord, how excellent is thy name in all the earth!

Ps. 19:1; 8:1

942   Come and see the works of God. The works of the Lord are great.

His work is honorable and glorious: and his righteousness endureth forever.

Let us search and try our ways, and return again to the Lord.

We will lift up our heart unto God in the heavens. Unto thee, O Lord, do we lift up our souls.

Ps. 66:5; 111:2-3; La. 3:40; Ps. 86:4

943   I will lift up mine eyes unto the hills, from whence cometh my help.

My help cometh from the Lord, which made heaven and earth.

Ps. 121:1-2

944   Thus saith God the Lord, he that created the heavens, and stretched them out; he that spread forth the earth, and that which cometh out of it; he that

giveth breath unto the people upon it, and spirit to them that walk therein: I the Lord have called thee in righteousness, and will hold thine hand, and will keep thee.

Is. 42:5–6

Invocations

945   Almighty God, who hast promised in thy mercy that seedtime and harvest, cold and heat, summer and winter, day and night, shall not cease, and hath blessed the earth that it should be fruitful and bring forth everything that is necessary for the life of man: bless all farmers in all their labors, and grant such seasonable weather that they may gather the fruits of the earth and ever rejoice in thy goodness, to the praise of thy holy Name; through Jesus Christ our Lord. Amen.

A Chain of Prayer

946   O heavenly Father, who hast filled the world with beauty: open, we beseech thee, our eyes to behold thy gracious hand in all thy works; that rejoicing in thy whole creation, we may learn to serve thee with gladness; for the sake of him by whom all things were made, thy Son, Jesus Christ our Lord. Amen.

Book of Common Prayer

947   God of all beauty, who dost make the sun to rise in splendor, and in glory set, and the stars to march in quiet radiance across the sky: open our eyes until we see thy beauty on the face of the earth, that we may more fully know thee and may love all beauty because it speaks to us of thee; through Jesus Christ our Lord. Amen.

Author Unknown

948   Most glorious Lord God, who hast created the world and upholdest its fabric in a marvellous order and beauty: give us grace so to meditate on thy workmanship and wisdom, thy power and great mercies, that we may thank thee, adore thee and praise thee forever; through Jesus Christ our Lord. Amen.

Daily Prayer

Litany

(Boldface type indicates responses.)

949   Thou visitest the earth and waterest it: thou greatly enrichest it with the river of God, which is full of water: thou preparest their corn, when thou hast provided for it.

Thou waterest the ridges thereof abundantly: thou settlest the furrows thereof: thou makest if soft with showers: thou blessest the springing thereof.

For the rain cometh down and the snow from heaven, and returneth not thither, but watereth the earth, and maketh it bring forth and bud, and giveth seed to the sower and bread to the eater.

So shall my word be that goeth forth out of my mouth; it shall not return unto me void, but it shall accomplish that which I please, and it shall prosper in the thing whereof I send it.

They that sow in tears shall reap in joy.

He that goeth forth and weepeth, bearing seed for sowing shall doubtless come again with joy, bringing his sheaves with him.

But this I say, He that soweth sparingly shall also reap sparingly; and he that soweth bountifully shall reap also bountifully.

But he that soweth righteousness hath a sure reward.

Now he that supplieth seed to the sower and bread for food, shall supply and multiply your seed for sowing, and increase the fruits of your righteousness.*

George T. Kerr

Prayers

950 O, Almighty God, who hast given us the grass of the lawns and of the fields as a great benediction to man, who hast given us the succulence of the mountain sides to feed the cattle upon a thousand hills, who hast given us the verdure of the rough places to be the great forgiveness of nature for the marring and the scarring of the face of the earth by the hands of men, grant that we, like this God-woven coverlet of the land, may be as a covering benediction to the mars and scars, the cares and worries and the sorrows of our fellow men. And, as thy bringing of the springtime grass foretells the bounty of our falltime harvest, so may our bursting love of all life foretell in us the continuing harvest of human happiness throughout the coming years. Through him who said "as a man soweth, so shall he reap, as a man scattereth, so shall he gather." Amen.

George B. Gilbert

951 Almighty God, whose garden was Eden, whose righteousness is like the great mountains, whose glory the heavens declare: we thank thee for calling us to preach thy Gospel in the green places of earth, where the songs of the birds and the music of the winds in the pines are never drowned by the roar of the street. For the beauty of the earth, we thank thee. For the holy quiet of dawn over the waking world, for sunrise and the falling of the rain, we praise thee. For silvery choirs of frogs in the swale, for hermit thrushes in the forest at twilight, we praise thee. For moonrise on the mountains, for lonely blue lakes, for the forests which shine in October with all the colors of thy heavenly city, O God, we glorify thy holy name. Amen.

Arthur W. Hewitt

952 Almighty and most gracious Lord, thou who didst create and dost sustain unto this very hour the earth and all that is in and upon it: we humbly come into thy house that we might seek thy blessing upon our lives and upon the labor of our hands. We rejoice in this opportunity of worship which thou has made possible and beseech thee to help us use it to the fullest measure.

Forgive us, O Lord, our sins, even as in these moments we forgive those who have sinned against us. As we will remember their sins against them no more, so blot out from remembrance our sins against thee. Forgive us that we have selfishly reaped the harvests of the good earth only to build bigger barns and to say, "O my soul thou hast much goods laid up to do thee many years," and so have closed our hearts and ears to the cries of the starving millions of the earth. Create in us a new heart, O God. Create in us hearts of compassion and love for all thy creatures, wherever they may be found.

We thank thee, our Father, for every material blessing thou hast seen fit to bestow upon us. We thank thee for the rich, abundant land upon which we dwell. We thank thee for the great harvests of the past. Now as we face the season of planting we seek again thy blessing upon the seeds and the sowers. Give the sowers strength and wisdom to till their fields so that they may bring forth an abundant harvest and yet remain undepleted for the use of coming generations. Cause, Lord of seedtime and harvest, the sun to shine, the rain to fall, and the wind to blow, each in its own season, for the full development of a great harvest.

And, Lord, as we till the earth, and handle its increase, may we be constantly thinking and praying for wisdom to distribute with equity the coming harvest, that the scourge of hunger might be wiped from the face of this fair earth.

So, grant us thy blessing, and teach us how to use it to thy glory now and forevermore, we pray. Amen.

C. R. McBride

953 O God of the field and forest, who madest the hill and stream: thy world is fashioned more perfectly than we often have the power and wisdom to perceive. Create in us a wonder for sky and brook and stone, for we know that all good and beautiful things were made at thy command.

For bountiful fields, for barns with harvest filled, for our fellow creatures that give us milk and meat and hide, we thank thee. For the glorious inspiration of the brilliant dawn and sunsets fading from blue to gold, for the choir of birds which sing by day and for the friendly chirping of the cricket which breaks the silence of the long night, we thank thee, O God, who madest the countryside. Help us to keep clean and pure the rural fields that they may be places fit for the nourishing of man's body and soul.

We remember that our Lord and Master sought refuge on a hill and that in the stillness of a garden he sought and found thy will.

Bless, O God, the rural churches. May they lift the souls of hardworking men and women and growing children to thee. Instill in their leaders a vision of the divine companionship which men of the soil may know as they share thy good purpose of sowing and reaping in the service of their fellows and thee; in Christ's name. Amen.

Graham R. Hodges

954   O God, the Holy Ghost, Lord and Giver of Life, we beseech thee to hear us, O Lord God:

That it may please thee to bless all those who sow the seed and reap the harvest of the world;

That it may please thee to bless the homes and home life of our country districts that they may be pure and happy abiding places for the children that shall come to them;

That it may please thee to give to all churches serving in villages and country a broad vision of their privilege, and to give them grace to minister to their people with unwavering love and devotion;

That it may please thee to send forth laborers into thy harvest;

That it may please thee to grant to all people living in lonely places the ministration of thy church and the comfort of thy presence;

That it may please thee to bless all national and state governments in their efforts to promote the welfare of those living on farm and ranch, in little village and open country;

That it may please thee to give and preserve to our use the kindly fruits of the earth so that in due time we may enjoy them.

O God, Father of all and lover of all, we beseech thee to bless all those who through thy church seek to serve thee in the rural areas of the world. Help them in their efforts to sow the seed of thy Kingdom and, when the harvest seems meager or far off, confirm thy promise to them and make them believe that in due season they shall reap if they faint not; through Jesus Christ our Lord. Amen.

National Council

Poems

955   *From THE PROUD FARMER*

Into the acres of the newborn state
He poured his strength, and plowed his ancient name,
And, when the traders followed him, he stood
Towering above their furtive souls and tame.

That brow without a stain, that fearless eye
Oft left the passing stranger wondering
To find such knighthood in the sprawling land,
To see a democrat well-nigh a king.

He lived with liberal hand, with guests from far,
With talk and joke and fellowship to spare—
Watching the wide world's life from sun to sun,
Lining his walls with books from everywhere.

He read by night, he built his world by day.
The farm and house of God to him were one.
For forty years he preached and plowed and wrought—
A statesman in the fields, who bent to none.

Vachel Lindsay

956   *COUNTRYMAN'S GOD*

Who reaps the grain and plows the sod
Must feel a kinship with his God:

For there's so much on earth to see
That marks the hand of Deity.

When blossom springs from tiny shoot:
When orchard yields its luscious fruit:

When sap is running from great trees—
On all occasions such as these

The man who breathes fresh country air
Must know full well that God is there.

Roger Winship Stuart

957   *PARTNERS*

Who digs a well, or plants a seed,
A sacred pact he keeps with sun and sod:
With these he helps refresh and feed
The world, and enters partnership with God.

Edwin Markham

958   *From FIFTIETH BIRTHDAY OF AGASSIZ*

And Nature, the old nurse, took
   The child upon her knee,
Saying: "Here is a story-book
   Thy Father has written for thee."

"Come, wander with me," she said,
   "Into the regions yet untrod;
And read what is still unread
   In the manuscripts of God."

Henry Wadsworth Longfellow

959   *THE HIGHER CATECHISM*

Where shall we get religion? Beneath the blooming tree,
Beside the hill-encircled brooks that loiter to the sea;
Beside the twilight waters, beneath the noonday shades.
Beneath the dark cathedraled pines, and through the tangled glades;
Wherever the old urge of life provokes the dumb, dead sod
To tell its thoughts in violets, the soul takes hold on God.

Sam Walter Foss

960   *From SONG OF MYSELF*

I believe a leaf of grass is no less than the journey-work of
   the stars,
And the pismire is equally perfect, and a grain of sand, and
   the egg of the wren,
And the tree-toad is a chef-d'œuvre for the highest,
And the running blackberry would adorn the parlors of heaven,

And the narrowest hinge in my hand puts to scorn all machinery,
And the cow crunching with depress'd head surpasses any statue,
And a mouse is miracle enough to stagger sextillions of infidels.

Walt Whitman

961   *FLOWER IN THE CRANNIED WALL*

Flower in the crannied wall,
I pluck you out of the crannies,
I hold you here, root and all, in my hand,
Little flower—but *if* I could understand
What you are, root and all, and all in all,
I should know what God and man is.

Alfred Tennyson

962   *BLIND*

"Show me your God!" the doubter cries.
I point him out the smiling skies;
I show him all the woodland greens;
I show him peaceful sylvan scenes;
I show him winter snows and frost;
I show him waters tempest-tossed;
I show him hills rock-ribbed and strong;
I bid him hear the thrush's song;
I show him flowers in the close—
The lily, violet and rose;
I show him rivers, babbling streams;
I show him youthful hopes and dreams;
I show him maids with eager hearts;
I show him toilers in the marts;
I show him stars, the moon, the sun;
I show him deeds of kindness done;
I show him joy; I show him care,
And still he holds his doubting air,
And faithless goes his way, for he
Is blind of soul, and cannot see!

John Kendrick Bangs

963 *OVERHEARD IN AN ORCHARD*

Said the Robin to the Sparrow,
"I should really like to know
Why these anxious human beings
Rush about and worry so."

Said the Sparrow to the Robin,
"Friend, I think that it must be
That they have no heavenly Father
Such as cares for you and me."

Elizabeth Cheney

964 *GIVE US THIS DAY OUR DAILY BREAD*

Back of the loaf is the snowy flour,
And back of the flour the mill,
And back of the mill is the wheat and the shower
And the sun and the Father's will.

Maltbie D. Babcock

965 *THE CROSS AND THE TREE*

A tree is such a sacred thing;
I never knew just why
Until I saw my Savior, Christ,
Stretched on a cross to die;
And heard him lift his pleading voice
In one great, tender cry.

And now I know why poets sing
About a common tree
As if it were a sacred thing
Of God-like destiny.
As if each stalwart oak had roots
That reached to Calvary!

William L. Stidger

966   *THE BIBLE, A RURAL BOOK*

The Christian farmer reads his Bible regularly and finds its language and pictures alive with his own experiences and way of life. It is no mere literary figure to him when he reads, "I have swept aside your ill deeds like a mist, and your sins like a cloud" (Is. 44:22, Moffatt), for with anxious eye he has watched the wind dissipate the threatening storm. It is with understanding heart he knows the meaning of "fear not . . . for I pour water on the thirsty land and streams on dry ground, I pour my spirit on your children" (Is. 44:26). Most any day's experience will recall what he has seen as he reads, "He ruins rulers of the world—scarcely planted, scarcely rooted in the earth, when at a puff from Him they wither" (Is. 40:24).

When Paul says that we (the church) are God's field to be planted (1 Co. 3:9) and Christ calls his Father the Farmer (husbandman) (Jn. 15:1) the Christian farmer gives immediate assent and recognizes the spirituality of his own means of livelihood.

Charles K. Hartman

967   *NATURE REVEALS GOD*

To the Hebrew mind, Nature was a medium of revelation. "The heavens declare the glory of God; and the firmament sheweth his handiwork. Day unto day uttereth speech, and night unto night sheweth knowledge." Nature reveals the character of God because Nature is the creation of God. "Who covereth the heaven with clouds, who prepareth rain for the earth, who maketh grass to grow upon the mountains. . . . He giveth snow like wool. He scattereth the hoarfrost like ashes. He casteth forth his ice like morsels. . . . He sendeth out his work, and melteth them: he causeth the winds to blow, and the waters flow." And because God has created the forces of Nature, all these forces are his servants, and they exist solely to do his will. "Praise the Lord from the earth, ye dragons and all deeps; fire and hail, snow and vapours; stormy wind fulfilling his word." Paul was true to the Hebrew conception when he wrote to the Romans that "the invisible things of him since the creation of the world are clearly seen, being understood by the things that are made, even his eternal power and Godhead."

If, then, the physical creation is a revelation of the character and will of the Eternal, why should a Christian minister ignore Nature in his preaching? Why should he deal solely with ideas uttered by holy men of old, and turn his back upon the fresh revelation which God is making daily in the phenomena and processes of the material creation? As Emerson long ago wrote: "The foregoing generations beheld God and Nature face to face, we through their eyes. Why should we not also enjoy an original relation to the universe?" If some one says that the preacher is bound to get his sermon out of the Word of God, the reply is that he does not forsake the Word of God when he goes to Nature. What is the book of Nature but a version of the Word of God? Is not the book of Nature a Bible—an earlier Bible—God's oldest Bible—and why should we allow the recent Bible, the Hebrew and Christian Scriptures, to crowd the ancient Bible completely out? Sir Thomas Browne was a wise man when he wrote: "There are two books from which I collect my divinity: beside the written one of God, another of his servant Nature, that universal and public manuscript that lies expansed unto the eyes of all. Those that never saw him in the one have discovered him in the other."

Charles E. Jefferson

968   *A SERMON OF THE SKY*

The heavens declare the glory of God. PS. 19:1

When the Hebrew came and walked out among the starry constellations, he saw it was God that has brought the glory down and let it be, and let the noon light shine on him with its glorious torch. He could not let the solar luster be unhuman. He could not let the glory fall in his eyes and ask no amazing, passionate question. But, instead, when he saw the glory, he saw through it the heavenly face as through an open window, and saw him—him! And the heavens, to the Hebrew mind, declared the glory of God. That is why the Hebrew vocabulary and the Hebrew understanding and the Hebrew poesy and the Hebrew profundity answer to the human heart. And this race of people, this nation, as it was the nation of thousands of years ago, was never content to let things rest as things. Behind the mathematics they sought the mathematician; behind the door they sought the maker of the door, and behind the stairway they sought the carpenter who built the stair, and behind the constellations they looked for the fingers of fire that flung the stars out into space. Then they called, "The heavens declare the glory of God."

William A. Quayle

969   *THE SUMMONS TO THE HILLS*

I will lift up mine eyes unto the hills. PS. 121:1

The shrines and altars of religion have usually been found on the hilltop, for religion looks at life from a high perspective, and measures it by its farthest horizons. To see God one must lift his eyes. To find God one must rise above the common level of pain and strife, above the vain show of earthly things, to the higher glory of things eternal.

For the Psalmist the hills were a constant reminder of God. They symbolized the timelessness of God. "Before the mountains were brought forth or ever thou hadst formed the earth and the world, even from everlasting to everlasting, thou art God." Their rugged strength suggested the protecting power of God. "As the mountains are round about Jerusalem, so the Lord is round about his people, forever." The soul in distress can "flee as a bird to the mountain." When the heart of man is overwhelmed, from the end of the earth he cries, "Lead me to the rock that is higher than I."

Harold Elliott Nicely

970   *THE BLESSING OF THE DEW*

I will be as the dew unto Israel. HO. 14:5

Palestine lived by its dews almost as much as by its rains. Moisture-laden winds drenched the cool nights with dew and kept the pastures alive, as though each grass blade made its own cloud and welcomed the dawn with jeweled drops. Life, said the sad poet-prophet, is like that. When the greater blessings are withheld we must learn to live by the lesser mercies—and they will not fail us. Indeed the greatest blessings reach us only in intimate ways. Love comes to our hearts from our hearthstones. Duty is the succession of daily tasks, happiness is the well-being of the near and the dear. Like the dew of Palestinian hills, the ocean of God's providence comes to us in such ways as even a grass blade can take and grow by.

Gaius Glenn Atkins

971   *PERPETUAL MIRACLE*

Go out into the garden and examine a seed; examine the same plant in the bud and in the fruit, and you must confess the whole process a miracle, a perpetual miracle. Take it at any period, make yourself as familiar with all the facts as you can at any period, and in each explanation there will be some step or appearance to be referred to the Great Creator; something not the effect of the sower's deposit, nor of the waterer's hope. It is not the loam, nor the gravel, it is not the furrow of the ploughshare, nor the glare of the sun that calls greenness from the dust, it is the present power of him who said, "Seedtime and harvest shall not fail." Needs there, my brethren, any other book than this returning summer that reminds us of the first creation, to suggest the presence of God?

Ralph Waldo Emerson

972 *NATURE SPEAKS OF GOD*

Nature seems to speak of God. Go, stand out on a summer night and look upwards to the sky where the million stars go sailing through that great wide sea of blue, like silent ships that pass in the night. . . . Go, walk in the woods on a day in April and watch the beauty of nature repeating the eternal resurrection, and rising from the grave of winter to the splendor of spring. Go, stand and watch the sunlight die, and all the west grow wonderful with a thousand colors past the power of human artists to express. Look at a mountain towering up to kiss the sun, pluck the tiniest flower that grows upon its side; and if you are a healthy man or a healthy woman there will be something that will call you—call you to the worship of the Maker and Creator of it all, and to the love of the great Artist in whose mind the ever-changing picture that the world presents was born.

G. A. Studdert-Kennedy

973 *GOD—MAN—NATURE*

Life is a unity and is a result of the cooperative activity of the trinity of God, man, and nature. Without the gift of vital life, man and nature would not be able to produce food and complete processes whereby man is sustained. Without man, God would not bring forth from nature that which glorifies himself and brings companionship unto him. Without nature, God and man would not have the structural basis for growth of human personality. This trinity is ever dependent one upon the other, and this dependence is here today realized again and recognized for the humility of man and to the glory of God.

James William Sells

974 *CREDO*

We are the farmers.

We stand on the land—and from it we view and judge the world.

The soil about our feet becomes a part of us.

We were born on it, and almost, it seems to us, from it, for what it is enters into us.

Its steadiness, its dependability, enter into our souls and cause us to expect the same from the world.

Its obedience to the laws of growth, moisture, sun, maturity, harvest—this also becomes a part of us.

Its readiness to receive and to give, to deal fairly with those who till it—this is another gift of the good earth to us.

And these which we have learned from the soil, we expect from the world.

When the world we live in proves undependable; when it follows the laws of chance instead of growth; when it tricks us instead of giving us an honest return for our labor—then we are confused, suspicious, desperate.

We trust our native soil and we tend to distrust all else.

We—and you—will wreck our world in strife, or we will together rebuild it in fairer and more Christian forms.

We are the farmers.

Percy R. Hayward

975 THE CROSS AND THE GARDEN

Now in the place where he was crucified there was a garden. JN. 19:41

And the garden, if they had understood and believed its message, made the resurrection inevitable. For the garden was a collection of choice flowers that Joseph of Arimathaea had been gathering together through the years. It was his dream that some day he would sleep in the midst of his garden when life's fitful fever should be over. He would lie down among the flowers that he had loved so well, not as in our horrid custom, enclosed in a wooden box, buried deep beneath the sod; but he would repose upon a ledge, preserved by the spices of the garden among the flowers that he had loved all his life.

F. W. Norwood

I. LAYMEN'S SUNDAY

Laymen's Sunday, observed nationally on the third Sunday in October, offers Christian laymen an opportunity through their participation in the church services to pledge their loyalty to Christ and his church and to call upon all laymen to support the local church and its pastor through consecrated lay leadership.

Calls to Worship

(Boldface type indicates response.)

976   The Lord is nigh unto all them that call upon him, to all that call upon him in truth.

He will fulfil the desire of them that fear him: he also will hear their cry, and will save them.

My mouth shall speak the praise of the Lord: and let all flesh bless his holy name for ever and ever.

Ps. 145:18–19, 21

977   Lord, thou hast been our dwelling place in all generations. Let thy work appear unto thy servants, and thy glory unto their children. And let the beauty of the Lord our God be upon us: and establish thou the work of our hands upon us; yea, the work of our hands establish thou it.

Ps. 90:1, 16–17

Invocations

978   O Lord Jesus Christ, who didst send forth thy first disciples to proclaim thy Kingdom, and to teach thy commandments: give to us, thy disciples, this day, such an understanding of the word, that we may teach to others what we have been taught of thee; to the glory of thy name, and the spread of thy Kingdom. Amen.

Daily Prayer

979   Give unto us, O God, we beseech thee, an unreprovable faith, a humble hope, and a never failing charity. Grant unto us true humility, a meek and quiet spirit, a loving, friendly and useful conversation, the denying of self, and

the bearing of the burdens of our neighbors. Grant us the blessedness of doing good. May we be strong in purpose, diligent in duty, slow in anger, and ready for every good work; through Jesus Christ our Lord. Amen.

Jeremy Taylor

980 O Master of men, set our hearts on fire with the desire to know thy blessed will, and send us forth amongst thy people to teach and to save. Set us free from vanity and fear, to the end that thine everlasting Gospel may through us reach the world without hurt or hindrance. Give us, O our Teacher, the lowliness and loftiness of mind becoming those who are thinking thy thoughts after thee. Amen.*

Henry Sylvester Nash

Litany

(Boldface type indicates responses.)

981 We are disciples of Christ and called by his name. Let us draw near unto him, who is the Living Way:

Help us, O Master, to walk in thy way.

For our weakness and failures, grant us true repentance; and that we may *turn* from self to thee:

Help us, O Master, to walk in thy way.

Through each day's plans and choices, grant us vision and courage to *follow* thee:

Help us, O Master, to walk in thy way.

Grant us growing minds, that by eager study we may *learn* ever more of thee and of thy truth:

Help us, O Master, to walk in thy way.

In joy and in sorrow, in victory or defeat, in all times and occasions, be thou our confidence and strength as we *pray* in thy name:

Help us, O Master, to walk in thy way.

Stir us to go forth and *serve* thee, thou who art one with all sufferers, the perplexed, and all who need:

Help us, O Master, to walk in thy way.

In thy house and at thine altar, in fellowship with thy people, grant us through *worship* new power to do thy will:

Help us, O Master, to walk in thy way.

By thy gift on the Cross, by thine eternal self-giving, make us ready to *share* with all who will receive:

Help us, O Master, to walk in thy way.

Forward Movement

Prayers

982   God, our Father, who hast commended thy love toward us, in that while we were yet sinners, Christ died for us, the just for the unjust, that we being enemies might be reconciled unto thee by the death of thy Son, and saved by his life: bow down thine ear to us and hear, as thou hast ever done, before all things else the unuttered yearning of our souls as thy presence makes itself felt like the silence; those deep desires that never can put themselves into words but struggle noiselessly to their feet at thy touch and stand before thy face with mute lips and hands outstretched, knowing not what to ask, and so asking only thyself.

Lift us then each of thy mercy to his stature, sons and daughters of thy grace, and heirs of life eternal, none of us forgotten, not one unknown. Deliver us from all the poor bondage of little things, from every petty slavery that narrows us and hedges us about. Rid us of mean resentments and crippling fears, of the memories that are too bitter and the sorrows that are too old; of the disappointments that hold us back from trying because there we failed, and of the barren, futile victories we have won because somewhere else we had our way. Let thy charge be upon us this day, each alone before thee, as upon those whom thou hast chosen for thy peculiar purpose, leaving thine honor in our keeping, and thy truth as a heritage that we may speak it. Blessed be thy holy name forever!

So bind us in thy peace to one another: loveless whom thou hast loved, unfriendly whom thou hast befriended, pitiless whom thou hast pitied. Teach us ourselves to stoop under some corner of weight that doth continually rest upon thy heart, of this world's evil and its pain, lest any life, shoulder to shoulder with our own, should yet feel itself forlorn, or by lack of our compassion desolate, as if stripped of thine. Until bearing each some other's burden our own is lifted, we wait together redeemed in the shadow of that Cross which has lengthened now all over the earth. Blessed be thy holy name forever! Amen.

Paul Scherer

983   May our prayer, O Christ, awaken all thy human reminiscences, that we may feel in our hearts the sympathizing Jesus. Thou hast walked this earthly vale and hast not forgotten what it is to be tired, what it is to know aching muscles, as thou didst work long hours at the carpenter's bench. Thou hast not forgotten what it is to feel the sharp stabs of pain, or hunger, or thirst. Thou knowest what it is to be forgotten, to be lonely. Thou dost remember the feel of hot and scalding tears running down thy cheeks.

O, we thank thee that thou wert willing to come to earth and share with us the weaknesses of the flesh, for now we know that thou dost understand all that we are ever called upon to bear. We know that thou, our God, art still able to do more than we ask or expect. So bless us, each one, not according to our deserving, but according to the riches in glory of Christ Jesus, our Lord. Amen.

Peter Marshall

984   Our eternal Father, hear our prayers and accept our petitions on this day set apart as Laymen's Sunday. We are thankful for the opportunity to worship as thy humble disciples who, without lofty title or authority, come, nevertheless, in spirit and in truth. We thank thee that the first disciples were laymen and that the church offers laymen salvation in Christ.

We are conscious today of our heritage of devotion, courage and sacrifice. As we acknowledge our own lack of devotion, our fears and our desire for compromise, we ask thy forgiveness for not making the church a mighty fortress for thy truth. Forgive us for the ease and indifference with which we worship in our beautiful churches even as the world cries for a dedicated lay discipleship.

Face to face with our Lord and Master, we hear him calling us anew to a sense of mission, to a sense of duty, to positive and creative belief. In today's crisis we hear him call us to be calm, to go forward and conquer in the Cross. He calls us to action, to Christian fellowship and brotherhood, and to world peace.

We realize, our heavenly Father, that as laymen thou hast called us to become the builders of a greater church for today and tomorrow. Help us with vision and courage to build well and strong. Help us to build cooperatively that the church may have a universal foundation. Dedicated to thee, may we move forward as one united body. Amen.

Stanley I. Stuber

985   Our Father, as we bow our heads and humble our hearts, we gratefully acknowledge thy presence. In thee we live and move and have our being. We give thee thanks for the privilege of worship.

When doubts harass us and we are unaware of thy care and concern, help us to know that round our restlessness flows thy rest, that in the midst of our weakness is thy strength. When we think we are free from any thought of things eternal, something within us challenges us to be better and greater than we are. Save us from foolish choices made through our lack of complete knowledge both of ourselves and of thee.

Because we know thou art good and wise, we offer thee both what we are and have. As unworthy as we are of it, give us that blessedness which goes far beyond our understanding, but which happily can be a part of our experience. We know that what we have belongs to thee, having come to us as thy gift.

Teach us, we pray, the fine art of bestowing what is ours, even when it belongs to thee, so that our talents, our possessions and our lives will all be in tune with thy purposes for us and all mankind. In the name of Christ we pray. Amen.

G. Ray Jordan

Poems

986 ## THE LAYMAN

Leave it to the ministers, and soon the church will die;
Leave it to the womenfolk; the young will pass it by;
For the church is all that lifts us from the coarse and selfish mob,
And the church that is to prosper needs the layman on the job.

Now, a layman has his business, and a layman has his joys;
But he also has the training of his little girls and boys;
I wonder how he'd like it if there were no churches here
And he had to raise his children in a godless atmosphere.

It's the church's special function to uphold the finer things,
And to teach the way of living from which all that's noble springs;
But the minister can't do it single-handed and alone,
For the laymen of the country are the church's corner-stone.

When you see a church that's empty, though its doors are open wide,
It's not the church that's dying; it's the laymen who have died;
For it's not by song or sermon that the church's work is done;
But by the laymen of the country who for God must carry on.

Edgar A. Guest

987 ## MAN-MAKING

We are all blind until we see
That in the human plan
Nothing is worth the making if
It does not make the man.

Why build these cities glorious
If man unbuilded goes?
In vain we build the world, unless
The builder also grows.

Edwin Markham

988   *From BY BLUE ONTARIO'S SHORE*

I swear I begin to see the meaning of these things,
It is not the earth, it is not America, who is so great,
It is I who am great or to be great, it is You up there, or any one,
It is to walk rapidly through civilizations, governments, theories,
Through poems, pageants, shows, to form great individuals.

Underneath all, individuals,
I swear nothing is good to me now that ignores individuals,
The American compact is altogether with individuals,
The only government is that which makes minute of individuals,
The whole theory of the universe is directed unerringly to one
     single individual—namely to You.

Walt Whitman

989   *HE DWELLS IN GOD'S OWN COUNTRY*

Who shares his life's pure pleasures
     And walks the honest road,
Who trades with heaping measures,
     And lifts his brother's load,
Who turns the wrong down bluntly,
     And lends the right a hand;
He dwells in God's own country,
     He tills the Holy Land.

Louis F. Benson

Topics, Texts and Themes

990   *CHRISTIAN LAYMEN AT WORK*

Laymen's Sunday now is an annual observance on the third Sunday in
October in each year. It began with perhaps 250 churches in 1941 and each year
the number has increased. From these churches go out every Sunday Christian
men and women who seek by their daily lives, and because of their love of
Christ, to testify to the power of prayer and love in this world of ours. They are
men and women who believe that "more things are wrought by prayer than this
world dreams of," and who, as they go about their daily tasks, pray to their
heavenly Father for guidance, and are conscious that help does come.

The fifteenth chapter of John gives the keynote of the layman's consecration
to God. "Abide in me, and I in you," said Jesus. "As the branch cannot bear

fruit of itself, except it abide in the vine, no more can ye, except ye abide in me."
Surrender of self to Christ and his leadership marks the layman who consecrates
himself to the Kingdom.

Roscoe E. Edlund

991   THE PLACE OF THE LAYMAN

When we speak of the place of the layman in the church we often refer only
to the work of laymen in the leading of worship, in the church government,
and in the carrying-on of the work conducted by the organized church as such.
These things are important, but they are not the most important work of
Christian laymen. The most important work of the Christian layman is the
daily work by which he earns his living in field, factory, office, school, hospital,
law court, or market. It is in these places that he has to bring the power of the
Gospel to bear on the ordinary life of the world. But during the past few centuries the church has given almost no guidance to Christian laymen who ask:
"How can I be a Christian in my daily work? What difference should my
Christianity make to the work I do, the decisions I make, the principles I adopt,
in my work from Monday to Saturday?" This guidance cannot be given by the
professional clergy, who do not know from the inside the problems of the pro-
fessions. It is necessary that Christian laymen themselves, with such help as
professional clergy can give, should seek together in prayerful study, discussion,
and experiment, to find out how God wishes them to behave in their professional duties.

The Guardian (India)

992   THE CALL TO LAYMANSHIP

God calls men to be ministers—yes, but just as truly God calls men and
women to Christian laymanship. Statistics of church membership notoriously
misrepresent the church's real spiritual power. About half the population of the
United States are Christian lay folk, but that is counting noses, not gauging
spiritual strength. Millions of Christian lay folk have only this much relationship with God—they believe that there is a God, and once in a while they turn
to him for help. That is about the sum of it. But turn now to the Bible and
from one end to the other one finds another kind of experience altogether—men
confronting God, running headlong into him, stopped in their tracks with a call,
a commission, a sense of vocation from which in vain they try to flee. From
Moses at the burning bush, taking the shoes from off his feet because the place
whereon he stands is holy ground and receiving a commission he cannot escape,

or Isaiah in the Temple, hearing a voice divine that he cannot refuse: "Whom shall I send, and who will go for us?" and answering, "Here am I, send me"; to Peter, James, and John, summoned by Christ to follow him, or Paul stopped dead on the Damascus Road with a challenge that transforms his life—such experience, the divine-human encounter from which one goes out under orders with a great vocation, is the very heart of the Bible's religion. Each of these typical men I have just named was a layman. None was a priest, an official ecclesiastic.

Harry Emerson Fosdick

993   *CHRISTIANITY OUTSIDE THE CHURCH*

A layman sometimes feels that he is unimportant in a church unless he is an officer or at least a member of a committee. He should remember that a church without laymen would scarcely be a church at all. The work of a church reaches fruition only when the Christian ideals which it teaches are put into practice outside the church by its laymen in everyday life.

I have said "outside the church" because I do not here refer to the work which a layman does within the church itself. Work done for the church as an organization, our contributions both in money and effort, our services on committees, our assistance in special functions—all these are important, but there is something needed beyond. A church cannot long exist just for itself alone.

And I have said "in everyday life" because I do not here refer to those rather special tasks which a Christian layman undertakes outside of the church. Service for a charity or a welfare organization, participation in or contributions to a drive for a community chest, for the Red Cross . . . all of these things are important also, but there is something needed beyond.

What I particularly refer to here are those acts of everyday Christianity, not of an organized sort, not of the kind that attracts attention, not of the kind that even has a name, but those things which form "that best portion of a good man's life, his little, nameless, unremembered acts of kindness and of love."

These often are the hardest. They are not spectacular. We cannot boast of them, even to ourselves. And these tasks are never ended; we must be forever at them, weekdays as well as Sundays, fifty-two weeks a year, throughout a lifetime. And the necessity for this sort of Christian action extends into every nook and cranny of our lives, even into our thoughts.

Frederick C. Shipley

WHAT CAN A LAYMAN DO?

1. Have faith in God, in man, in yourself—faith in the ultimate victory of right over wrong. Have faith in our leaders and in God's ability to use them for his purposes.

2. Be an island of calm confidence in a world of turmoil—not blind wishful thinking, but belief in the power for right of a God who cares.

3. Be friendly to everyone you meet. Throw a pebble of kindness into the pool of human relations to help overcome hatred.

4. Pray repeatedly, realizing that you are using an overwhelming power for good. Use spot prayers more and more frequently during the day to try beneficially to condition destructive situations as they are reported.

5. Practice the exclusion of doubt and fear from the mind. Keep a record of constructive thoughts put into words during the day, and of destructive thoughts not uttered. Be sure the balance at evening is on the positive side.

6. Develop the consciousness that there is a constructive answer—no matter how depressing events may seem.

7. Look upon yourself as a child of God, made in his image—then love your neighbor as yourself.

The Laymen's Movement

995   *THE CHURCH'S APPEAL TO MEN*

Come with us, and we will do thee good. . . . Leave us not, I pray thee; forasmuch as thou knowest how we are to encamp in the wilderness, and thou mayest be to us instead of eyes. NU. 10:29, 31

It says with assurance, Come with us and we will do thee good; for the Lord hath spoken good concerning Israel. It says this with emphasis: it says it pleadingly. It has blessings, promises and powers, of which it is sure. It knows that men are in need of what it possesses. It sees men living to little purpose and for little ends. It sees the sin and the sorrow. It has deep pity for the deep pathos of human life. Its whole work is to do men good, as it declares the Gospel of the Kingdom, calling them to pardon and peace, offering them salvation, presenting to them the manifold riches of Christ, pointing to the way of life and joy. The heart of the true church yearns over men with a great longing, seeing them to be, though they know it not, wretched and miserable and poor and blind and naked. It has a message for you, which it is irreparable loss for you to neglect. It offers you a great and eternal good.

Hugh Black

996   *THE MANLINESS OF CHRIST*

> Handle me, and see; for a spirit hath not flesh and bones, as ye see me have. LU. 24:39

The real truth about the manliness of Christ seems to be this: that he is so like us that he makes us know that we may be like him, and so unlike us that he makes us know that we must be unlike our present selves before we can be like him. His life fits in among our human lives like a jewel which is so adapted to the gold into which it is set that nobody can doubt that they are made for one another, and yet which so far fails of suiting its place perfectly that we can see that the gold has been bent and twisted and must be twisted back again in order to accommodate it perfectly. He is at once our satisfaction and our rebuke. He has our human qualities; he feels our human motives; but in him they take new shapes. It is with him as it is with our best and noblest friends. They all first claim us by their likeness, and then shame and instruct us by their unlikeness. So it is with the manliness of Jesus.

Phillips Brooks

997   *A MANLY RELIGION*

> Watch ye, stand fast in the faith, quit you like men, be strong. 1 co. 16:13

Too often in these recent years we have thought of Christian discipleship as a profession that calls for little of manhood and less of strength. It may be that we regard our religion and religious practices as something quite apart from the world in which we live. It is here that men have made their great mistake, with the result that we have been faced with the greatest attack that has ever been made upon our boasted Christian civilization. We literally had to fight to preserve that which we carelessly or indifferently recognized as indispensable to our way of life.

The lack of manly, strong expression of our Christian faith and the consistent practice of its great principles have brought us to a condition in which our most cherished institutions are imperiled. For a while it looked as if they might go under in a world holocaust. We have held to the slogan, "For God and country," but we have magnified country and its material wealth and rich privileges. The possible loss of these privileges compels us to think deeply about a more demonstrative and practical application of our Christian faith to the common concerns of our daily life. Again the call comes to us: "Quit you like men, be strong." A manly religion and a strong one can save the world.

James E. Freeman

998   *A VISION OF MANHOOD*

I speak to men who have, in their best moments at any rate, a lofty conception of, and a reverence for, manhood and its possibilities. Probably in the case
of most of us, our earliest awakening to a realization of the potential grandeur
of human nature was due to our being brought into contact with developed
greatness and nobility in a historical character or a living national hero. Though
none can be so thrilled with the limitless possibilities of life as he who has come
to understand it as God purposed it, and has revealed it in the Man of men,
the Hero of heroes, Jesus Christ.

Charles H. Brent

999   *EVERY MAN'S RELIGION HIS OWN*

In the New Testament the Christian Gospel is spoken of in two contrasted
ways. On the one side, it is an objective, eternal fact; whether accepted or
rejected, there it stands, a message to mankind through an historic personality.
So the book of Revelation calls it "the everlasting gospel" and Paul refers to it
as "the gospel of God" and "the gospel of Christ." Paul calls it by another
name, however, suggestive of another range of meaning, when in his letter to
the Romans he writes, "according to my gospel." So, when Christianity came
into Paul's mind and, like the ocean flowing into a special bay, took the contour
of his experience, not only did something profoundly important happen to Paul,
as we have always understood, but something profoundly important happened
to the gospel. As Paul looked at the result, he could call it, indeed, "Christ's
gospel," but also "my gospel"—that is to say, Christ's gospel as it has taken
shape in me, as I have been able to apprehend it, seen with my eyes and
applicable to my life—*my* gospel.

Harry Emerson Fosdick

1000   *SEARCHING FOR FAITH*

Christ should be a power, not a problem. Jesus should be a door which
invites us in, not a wall that shuts out. Jesus Christ should be a help, not a
hindrance to faith. Yet is this always the case?

Our times are serious. Life, deep down, always is serious. There is now, at
least, little place for its lighter sides until the more serious sides have been
attended to.

Everywhere men are searching for faith. They have to have some faith. They need a faith that they can live by and die by. They want no sham, no sentimentalities, no pious moonings. Neither do they want stony dogmas, but the bread of the living truth.

Nels F. S. Ferré

INDEX OF AUTHORS AND SOURCES

This index of prose materials lists authors and sources by item numbers. The small letters following numbers identify invocations and opening prayers by i, litanies and responsive prayers by l, prayers by p, and prose quotations by q. In order that readers may locate quoted extracts in complete context, titles of books and periodicals are given.

INDEX OF TEXTS

This index lists by item numbers text which accompany prose materials.

POETRY INDEX

This index lists by item numbers poets, titles, and first lines of poems. Titles are in italics. When titles and first lines are similar, only the first line references have been included.

INDEX OF SPECIAL DAYS AND OCCASIONS

The following is a cross index of appropriate worship and homiletical materials for the special days and occasions which are listed on the church calendars of one or more of the national denominations. References are to item numbers. The small letters in parentheses preceding item numbers identify calls to worship and opening scriptural sentences by c, invocations and opening prayers by i, litanies and responsive prayers by l, prayers by p, poems and verse quotations by v, and prose quotations by q. Bold-face type identifies main entries.

TOPICAL INDEX

This topical index lists references to prose materials according to item numbers.